T0354063

Extraordinary Knowledge

Science, Psychology, Spirituality and Myths

K. R.

iUniverse, Inc.
Bloomington

Extraordinary Knowledge
Science, Psychology, Spirituality and Myths

iUniverse books may be ordered through booksellers or by contacting:

iUniverse
1663 Liberty Drive
Bloomington, IN 47403
www.iuniverse.com
1-800-Authors (1-800-288-4677)

ISBN: 978-1-4697-5155-9 (sc)
ISBN: 978-1-4697-5156-6 (ebk)

Printed in the United States of America

iUniverse rev. date: 01/16/2012

Psychology

Consciousness

A difficult concept for many humans is the concept of consciousness. They see the babe in the crib, aware seemingly only of its stomach and need for milk, and compare it to the dog at their feet, seemingly aware and alert. Is the babe conscious, and the dog not? The point at which consciousness is present is not crisp or clear. Is the human conscious because they have a certain IQ? Yet it is reported that retarded humans can have incarnating souls. Is the human conscious because they discern themselves as separate from other humans? Yet so many humans are so fuzzy about their identity that they join any group for a sense of belonging, and confuse their actions with the leaders. Is the human conscious because they have a memory, can compute, can put A and B together and come up with C? Yet the Chimp uses tools, and a wolf pack can figure where the prey may be running to next, and many animals have long memories and are crafty. At what point does consciousness click in, or click out, if it does, and is it thus possible for a dog to have a soul and a human not?

An existing soul may chose to incarnate in an animal that does not have the potential of sparking a soul, for education reasons. Thus, the dog or snake or dolphin does not spark a soul, but can be incarnated on occasion. To spark, the biological entity must have the capacity to envision itself as separate, and where many animals seem to have this trait, they do not. A dog will understand that it is being yelled at by its master, or snarled at by the leader of the pack, and by groveling and crawling away is indicating they seem to understand another has interacted with them, as a separate being. But this is instinctive activity, this is not a discernment of separate biological entities. The dog has evolved to react in such a manner, to challenge until certain signs are present, then to submit. Instinct is not consciousness. Biologically programmed reactions are not consciousness.

Even as the babe is lying in its crib, asleep or crying for milk, seemingly unaware of its surroundings, it is aware. It understands that when it smiles at mother, and mother picks it up, that is has engaged in an interaction with another. This is not the same as a birdling in a nest, putting its beak up for food when the mother bird alights. That is instinct. On evolving worlds that do not have genetic engineering, the species that eventually emerges to have consciousness, and thus sparking souls, gets there slowly. At first, there is instinct. Then there is increasing intelligence until the concept of separateness begins to be a factor. Increased intelligence tends to be selected for survival, as the intelligent species can better their odds. Thus, the more intelligent in the group breed to increase intelligence, and the trend hastens yet more. Thus, where not visible in man, his consciousness, awareness of himself as separate, a factor absolutely necessary for sparking of souls, is there. Consciousness is contained within the expanded realization of the gravity model. The model, if completed, would give one an insight into the synchronous relationship between gravity and consciousness.

Emotional Intelligence

Intelligence tests have been increasingly broadened into areas with little relationship to intellect. Intellect is thought, thinking, concepts. Thought can be broken down into memory, the ability to string memories together, the ability to abstract a concept from many concrete memories, the ability to arrive at a logical conclusion, the ability to consider the future and plan, and the overall capacity to do much of this at the same time. Thought is not the ability to match a tone, the ability to draw or quote by repeating what one has just seen or heard, or the capacity to be socially pleasant and observant. Where such abilities frequently further the individual and are even taken to be signs of intelligence, this is due more to what society expects of its members than intellectual performance. Is the little girl who is quick to mock her mother's curtsy and phrases bright or just a copy-cat? The latter.

True deep intelligence is seldom recognized for what it is by those of lesser intelligence. The bright child seems distracted, may forget to tie his shoes, makes mistakes when doing simple tasks, and wanders off to be by himself and alone with his thoughts. The dull child may have nothing better to do than be a copy-cat, and as this earns him applause, does it often. This does not mean that the bright child has less of an Emotional Quotient, it simply means they have better things to do. Given a situation that truly tests the ability of an individual to empathize and discern the correct emotional appeal to make to others, the bright child will routinely do as well if not better than the individual of average intelligence.

Mind/Body Connection

When an entity with a physical brain stares at an object the visual areas of the brain are more active than usual, and when another is in telepathic communication with the staring entity, both have the same areas of their brains active. But by what means do we think, arrive at conclusions, or have, for instance, a brilliant insight? One can map with simple animals, trained in a maze, the learning curve whereby they learn that to follow the smooth wall, for instance, they arrive at food. The first time this occurs it is by accident, so the rat makes an association. Smooth walls = food. The next time the rat is put into a maze, if hungry, the rat will give more weight to exploring smooth walled paths over rough textured routes.

The mental association in the rat's brain is a chemical sequence in the existing brain cells in certain areas of the brain. Hunger in the rat is now connected to those sections of the brain which hold visual and tactile imprints. These imprints, as well as the pathways, are chemical. These imprints, or stored data, and pathways wax strong or weak, depending on how often they are used. More use, strengthened chemistry. Less use, debilitated chemistry. If the rat does not continue to find food via smooth walls, it will explore these paths less and less often, until smooth walls have no more significance for the rat than any other type of wall. These chemical pathways are not identical. They have characteristics that relate to the area of the brain they point to, and in simple worms are somewhat transferable.

Worms, taught to head to the right or left for food or to avoid injury, can have their brains fed to other worms, who then seem to have ingested knowledge. The brain chemicals, not broken down during digestion, migrate in the blood stream to the brain, and being of similar chemical composition in similar worms, attach to the brain pathways of the new host. The chemistry for right or left is specific in these worms, being on one side of the brain or another with some slight differences, and where these differences weigh only slightly they weigh enough to set the ingesting worm to favor connecting to one side of the brain or another. A transferred learned response, proving that the brain works by chemistry, chemical paths and chemical images.

Emotions are chemistry, generated from within. Sensations, the power of the brain to retain ideas, is also intrinsically allied with chemical reactions. In fact, it forms the base. What else would there be? Hormones stimulate feelings, and hormones are created by nervous stimulation of the glands. It is all intertwined. Senses receive light rays or heat, or other such stimuli that create chemical reactions that travel along nerves and are then stored in the brain by chemical changes. These chemical changes are so slow to deteriorate that you die before many of them do, which is why we have a memory. This is a chemical store, similar to a computer data bank, in which chemical changes are virtually permanently etched in the brain.

Complex thought can be broken down into thousands of steps, where sensory memories are related. Even the abstract concept of numbers is related to sensory memories. The child piling blocks is noting that four blocks pile higher than three, and the concept of greater than is related to these counts. Does the one pile not loom higher? When adding just one block onto the short pile, they are equal. An incipient algebraic equation is building in the babe's mind. Great thoughts are built from many small mental data stores, and many more connections. Great insights are simply where two or more formerly unrelated connections bridge, to become related.

It is known that people think best while pacing, and that palsied children not able to crawl or walk lack some ability to learn concepts. Bridging occurs when the chemicals needed to build a new pathway are in abundance in a certain part of the brain. It is accidental in that the connection is only by proximity, but no accident in that the brain areas rich with these chemicals are so active because they relate to the issue at hand. Thus the brain is just making an introduction. Here, you two places are both active, speak to each other. Thus, the child finding himself staring at a wall he wishes to climb over, and seeing some boxes near at hand, recalls his pile of blocks. An a'ha occurs, as his memory of blocks connects to this sight of the boxes, which have a similar shape. Presto. Thought.

Mind/Spirit Connection

As spirits seem dissociated from the body, being able to leave during an Out-Of-Body, and can ignore physical barriers, how then does the spirit communicate to the biochemical arrangement that is the mind? What is the point of connection? The spirit does not need to switch densities, so the mind/spirit connection is not vibrational, being on the same wavelength. As the spirit can function without a body the connection is not biochemical. As spirits develop during incarnations in life forms on diverse worlds wholly incompatible with each other the connection does not appear to have a physical requirement.

This puzzle is most easily understood if one considers how sub-atomic particles operate. However diverse the various elements of the physical world seem, they break down into the same component parts. The base building blocks are the same. Spirits are composed of a substance that is physical in the larger scheme, and surpasses in its reach any one density vibration. This substance is called Chromatic. Just as on the sub-atomic level you consider some elements to communicate electrically, encouraging or inciting an electron flow, and other elements to be inert, just so your spirit considers your mind to be capable of an interchange where the stone walls it passes through are inert. The spirit communicates to the mind by biochemical means, by inciting biochemical activity. It does so by adjusting itself to the density of the incarnated body and to the peculiar biochemistry of the life form. This feat is no more spectacular than tuning an x-ray machine to penetrate the thickness of an object. During each incarnation the spirit quickly familiarizes itself with its new physical body, and gets down to business.

Does the spirit have memory, as the mind does? Most certainly, and remembers the lessons learned during each incarnation flawlessly. Humans are used to their conscious memory being capable of distortion, of remembering incidences as they wish, not as they were. The spirit, however, is like the subconscious and does not distort memories. How is it then that the babe, incarnated by an old and wise spirit, does not remember its past lives? The spirit can only speak to the mind as the mind is ready to receive. If the biochemical pathways for the concept the spirit wishes to relay are not yet in place in the mind, the spirit can only speak to the emotions. Thus entities feel they have lived before, but do not have an explanation for the concept. Thus entities may sense that an incident is similar to another experienced before in a past life, but unless they are willing to entertain the concept of past lives, they will not be open to having these spiritual memories unfold.

Spirit/Body Connection

One does not need to listen to the endless discussions on nature vs. nurture to understand that both influences shape the person. However, a third influence is in effect, and this stronger than either of the others—the spirit. Genetics of course limits the person physically, determining whether they can enter the Olympics or solve complex math puzzlers, and also determines to a large degree how the body will react to stress or the aging process. The environment, being what shapes the child's perception of the world around him, determines at least early in life what role models the child will choose and how guarded or enthusiastic the child will be. But the spirit is louder than both these other voices, and by its orientation and strength determines how the person's very life will be led, the occupation chosen, the motives driving the person, and where the person draws the line on whether to get involved or not. Because the spirit speaks to the body as well as the mind, its influence is also over the biochemistry of the human body incarnated, and this has more of an effect than is generally recognized. If the child is determined to be an outstanding athlete, for instance, having judged that escape from a ghetto is not possible without such an assist, physical development beyond that supported by genetics can result.

The spirit occupies its own density, a density that can interact with matter on all other densities. Just as the spirit adjusts itself to the incarnation density, and positions itself to communicate with the human brain for the Mind/Spirit Connection, likewise it positions itself to influence the human body. Genetics are but chemistry, and influence growth and development through chemistry. Where this cannot be utterly or even significantly changed by the influence of the spirit, where biochemistry can affect the outcome and the spirit can affect the biochemistry, its influence can leave a mark. In the example of the child desiring to become an athlete, the basic bone and muscle structure, height, stamina, and reflexes are determined by genetics. But physical feats are often determined as much by concentration and sheer energy, factors controlled by biochemistry—hormones, such as adrenaline, brain chemicals supporting continuous focus, and free nutrients in the blood stream available to feed the process. In this way the spirit transcends the density differences, and takes charge of the incarnation as much as physically possible.

Doctors have often noticed that a patient will live or die depending on their will to live. Where this can be attributed to a Mind/Body Connection, the influence of the spirit in these matters lies at the base. The soul infuses the body during an incarnation, and communicates on many levels and can bridge densities in this matter. The spirit influences the body, to overcome disease and struggle forward. It influences the brain, to utilize this or that portion of the brain or to develop channels and connections in the brain matter. The will to live has been well documented, overcoming disease that physicians were sure would end the life. Much of this is the soul, determined not to end the incarnation. Likewise, the soul can influence a dying body to go before its time, if the incarnation is desired to end. Those curious about how the soul influences the body should simply observe the many clues about them, as this is a tool for learning.

Curiosity

Curiosity is an emotion related to natural inquisitive behavior such as exploration, investigation, and learning, evident by observation in human and many animal species. The term can also be used to denote the behavior itself being caused by the emotion of curiosity. As this emotion represents a drive to know new things, curiosity is the fuel of science and all other disciplines of human study.

The ancient Greeks studied more than philosophy in their debates. They studied the ways of nature—physics, astronomy, and chemistry. In those days the going opinion was that the world was flat, and the heavens were doing a dance at the whim of the gods, whoever they may be. They had no microscopes, no accelerators or centrifugal machines, and were incapable of separating chemicals to test out their theories. They did not even have a concept of subatomic particles. How could they, when matter was only falling into categories of solid, liquid, vapor, and spirit.

Yet one man, Democritus, hypothesized that matter had the same base component, and that these were tiny balls in clumps of few or many. Tiny balls that moved swiftly or stood still, and clung to each other or had a life of independence—molecules! How did the concept rise in one never exposed to even the concept of a solar system, orbiting planets around a central sun, much less the elements in the Atomic Table and their theoretical subatomic structure. Democritus was given to quiet times in his garden, where he pondered such simple wonders as rain drops and the ripples they caused in puddles. In essence, he gave The Call, and was heard by aliens who spent many hours with him, on repeated occasions, demonstrating how things work. Democritus would be returned to his garden, where his wife thought he had been all along, to sort this all out. Where the aliens answering his call may have found a ready student, Democritus was not so lucky with his fellow man, who ridiculed him for what they considered his preposterous positions.

K. R.

Forgiveness

My understanding of karma is that which may be called Inertia. Those actions which are put into motion will continue using the ways of balancing until such time as the controlling or higher principle which you may liken unto your braking or stopping is invoked. This stoppage of the Inertia of action may be called Forgiveness. These two concepts are inseparable.

Forgiveness is typically defined as the process of concluding resentment, indignation or anger as a result of a perceived offense, difference or mistake, or ceasing to demand punishment or restitution.

Forgiving someone who has injured one involves two parties—the injured and the perpetrator. Forgiveness is a Successive Prophecy. Have you forgiven today? Success! Forgiving someone who has injured one involves two parties—the injured and the perpetrator.

Circumstances may be such that the injury was an accident and the perpetrator horrified and asking what they can do to make amends. In this case the path to forgiveness is already paved with possibilities, and the injured has but to specify what is required to make amends and the two parties will begin to heal each other. Circumstances may be such that the injury was an accident but the perpetrator in denial. Nothing has happened, and even if it did it wasn't their fault. In this case forgiving the injury must take place on separate paths, with the injured coming to terms with the accident as just that—an accident. The perpetrator has already forgiven himself, as he wasn't there and there is nothing to forgive. Circumstances may also be such that the injury was deliberate, but was a result of a disagreement, a fight, and fault lies all around. One was pushed beyond his limits and lashed out. One was steadily tortured until a dark mood overtook him. In these cases forgiveness usually progresses rapidly, as both parties are clearly cognizant of the underlying currents and the shared responsibility for what has happened. Tears, hugs, and a resolve to be more careful in the future. Forgiveness is most difficult where the injury is deliberate and no fault lies in the one injured—a true victim, an innocent. And thus the perpetrator has savaged the injured for sport, for a power trip, or to simply gratify themselves at the expense of another. In these cases forgiveness is inappropriate, and is not the issue. In these cases the injured should be concentrating not on forgiveness, but on defense, and after ending the assaults on changing the circumstances that allowed the injury in the first place. Does the criminal justice system forgive the sadistic murderer and say to the victim—the problem is yours as you have not learned to forgive?

Forgiveness of other-self is forgiveness of self. An understanding of this insists upon full forgiveness upon the conscious level of self and other-self, for they are one. A full forgiveness is thus impossible without the inclusion of self.

It is of great importance that it be understood that it is NOT desirable or helpful to the growth of the understanding of an entity by itself to CONTROL thought processes or impulses except where they may result in actions not consonant with The Storm. Control may seem to be a short-cut to discipline, peace, and illumination. However, it is a False Promise, and this very control potentiates and necessitates the further incarnative experience in order to balance this control or repression of that self which is perfect.

Acceptance of self, forgiveness of self, and the direction of the will; this is the path towards the disciplined personality. The faculty of will is that which is powerful within you as The Thunder. You cannot ascribe to this faculty too much importance. Thus it must be carefully used and directed in Service-to-Others for those upon the path to The North.

The process in Space/Time of the forgiveness and acceptance is much like that in Time/Space in that the qualities of the process are analogous. However, while in Space/Time it is not possible to determine the course of events beyond the incarnation but only to correct present imbalances. In Time/Space, upon the other hand, it is not possible to correct any unbalanced actions but rather to perceive the imbalances and thusly forgive the self for that which is.

The decisions then are made to set up the probabilities of correcting these imbalances in future Space/Time experiences. The advantage of Time/Space is that of the fluidity of the grand overview. The advantage of Space/Time is that, working in darkness with a tiny candle, one may correct imbalances.

Aggression

The assumption that higher spiritual densities are removed from any emotion except love and have no destructive urges is a false one. The matter of being Service-to-Other does not entail removing oneself from the many conflicts that present during incarnated life. The point where one defends the self, or others, and crosses the line into destructive behavior is not the point where the entity becomes, however briefly, oriented in Service-to-Self. Service-to-Others does not mean allowing the other to proceed without bounds in a manner that hurts the self. Self defense is not only assumed, it is desirable! Any entity that became utterly passive and failed to defend itself would not last long. Self defense is integral in any life form, and can hardly be removed, nor should it be.

There is much confusion regarding defensive or aggressive actions being taken by those operating in the Service-to-Other orientation. Empathy toward others and non-violent means of attending to life's daily affairs are assumed, and under equitable conditions this is the norm. However, if others who are not firmly in the Service-to-Other orientation or even if others also in the Service to-Other group are undertaking actions that threaten the well being of the self or of the group, aggressive and even violent means are not out of keeping with the Service-to-Other orientation! Forcefully restraining another, or even killing them if this is the most effective solution, is not only a Service-to-Self prerogative. These are solutions open to those in the Service-to-Other also.

In dealing with, for instance, a sadist preying upon the young, an inability to safeguard the young by any other means than killing the sadist would not be out of keeping with the Service-to-Other philosophy. Which other is being served by allowing him to continue? The young children, as a group of others, or the sadist as a single individual utterly lacking in consideration of others? The choice is clear, and killing the sadist a solution involving empathy and kindness overall. In fact, allowing the sadist to continue is anti Service-to-Other, as this passivity is making those standing by and doing nothing a party to the sadism.

Fight or Flight

The fight-or-flight response was first described by Walter Bradford Cannon. His theory states that animals react to threats with a general discharge of the sympathetic nervous system, priming the animal for fighting or fleeing. This response was later recognized as the first stage of a general adaptation syndrome that regulates stress responses among vertebrates and other organisms.

Violence is a characteristic of many intelligent species. In fact, all, where the capacity to inflict injury and, in effect, take one's enemy out of the arena exists. Where entities seek dominance over each other, violence exists. Another factor of violence is that it is often a necessary ingredient for primitive life. Depending on the environment, violent tendencies may in fact be crucial to survival. Earth was such an environment. During genetic engineering projects in the past, those intelligent species developed without violent tendencies did not survive and flourish. On the contrary, they died out.

What is violence, and the tendency to use violence, and why was this a necessary ingredient in the past. First off, species eat each other. As has been often stated, the species on our planet generally use fight or flight when confronted with this possibility. Where it is assumed that these two reactions differ, they have more in common than not. Adrenaline surges, the heart beating wildly and all thought or necessity of attending to other matters, such as digestion or favoring an injury, put aside. If it is determined that fight is not possible, flight or its variant, playing dead, will be set into motion. In flight the adrenaline is put to good use in pumping legs and frantically scrambling arms. If it appears that escape is not possible, then a last attempt at deflecting the attack is tried—playing dead, or otherwise appearing as an undesirable morsel to the attacker. Thus, defecation and fainting may ensue.

Now, if fighting off the attack is possible, then a different set of staged defenses ensues. First, the defensive posture, where the body is fluffed up to appear larger or weapons such as teeth and claws are flashed. The defensive posture is quite familiar to humans, as the stiff legged circling, with neck hair fluffed and lips curled back over teeth, is seen frequently in canine pets. Humans recognize this in themselves. The refusal to sit down in a relaxed posture when in the presence of those not trusted. Hair up at the back of the neck, and not wanting the enemy to one's back. The sneer, attributed to arrogance, is in fact equivalent to curling the lips back over teeth in preparation for a fight.

Next, if the defensive posture does not succeed in deflecting the attack, taking the offensive in a parry is undertaken. The element of surprise is used as much as possible. Thus, the defensive posture is dropped and replaced with what is termed blind rage. The one under attack is now the attacker. Savage fury is unfurled. Everything in sight is devastated, without remorse or hesitation. When this defensive posture is completed, with the defendant finally spent, the attack will have either been deflected or the outcome of the battle will be in the other direction. One becomes a meal. Blind fury is seen in canine pets frequently, although it goes by different names. Humans assume their guard dogs are the aggressors, when the exact opposite is in force. The vast amount of violence in the world is related to defensive postures, even where fathers dash their crying babies against the walls. A distressing situation that cannot be dealt with in any other way may result in blind rage.

Nature vs Nurture

The nature versus nurture debate is one of the oldest issues in psychology. The debate centers on the relative contributions of genetic inheritance and environmental factors to human development. Some philosophers such as Plato and Descartes suggested that certain things are inborn, or that they simply occur naturally regardless of environmental influences. Other well-known thinkers such as John Locke believed in what is known as tabula rasa, which suggests that the mind begins as a blank slate. According to this notion, everything that we are and all of our knowledge is determined by our experience.

For example, when a person achieves tremendous academic success, did they do so because they are genetically predisposed to be successful or is it a result of an enriched environment? Today, the majority of experts believe that behavior and development are influenced by both nature and nurture. However, the issue still rages on in many areas such as in the debate on the origins of homosexuality and influences on intelligence. One does not need to listen to the endless discussions on nature vs. nurture to understand that both influences shape the person. However, a third influence is in effect, and this stronger than either of the others—the spirit. Genetics of course limits the person physically, determining whether they can enter the Olympics or solve complex math puzzlers, and also determines to a large degree how the body will react to stress or the aging process. The environment, being what shapes the child's perception of the world around him, determines at least early in life what role models the child will choose and how guarded or enthusiastic the child will be. But the spirit is louder than both these other voices, and by its orientation and strength determines how the person's very life will be led, the occupation chosen, the motives driving the person, and where the person draws the line on whether to get involved or not. Because the spirit speaks to the body as well as the mind, its influence is also over the biochemistry of the human body incarnated, and this has more of an effect than is generally recognized. If the child is determined to be an outstanding athlete, for instance, having judged that escape from a ghetto is not possible without such an assist, physical development beyond that supported by genetics can result.

The spirit occupies its own density, a density that can interact with matter on all other densities. Just as the spirit adjusts itself to the incarnation density, and positions itself to communicate with the human brain for the Mind/Spirit Connection, likewise it positions itself to influence the human body. Genetics are but chemistry, and influence growth and development through chemistry. Where this cannot be utterly or even significantly changed by the influence of the spirit, where biochemistry can affect the outcome and the spirit can affect the biochemistry, its influence can leave a mark. In the example of the child desiring to become an athlete, the basic bone and muscle structure, height, stamina, and reflexes are determined by genetics. But physical feats are often determined as much by concentration and sheer energy, factors controlled by biochemistry—hormones, such as adrenaline, brain chemicals supporting continuous focus, and free nutrients in the blood stream available to feed the process. In this way the spirit transcends the density differences, and takes charge of the incarnation as much as physically possible.

Doctors have often noticed that a patient will live or die depending on their will to live. Where this can be attributed to a Mind/Body Connection, the influence of the spirit in these matters lies at the base. The soul infuses the body during an incarnation, and communicates on many levels and can bridge densities in this matter. The spirit influences the body, to overcome disease and struggle forward. It influences the brain, to utilize this or that portion of the brain or to develop channels and connections in the brain matter. The will to live has been well documented, overcoming disease that physicians were sure would end the life. Much of this is the soul, determined not to end the incarnation. Likewise, the soul can influence a dying body to go before its time, if the incarnation is desired to end. Those curious about how the soul influences the body should simply observe the many clues about them, as this is a tool for learning.

Homosexuality

Homosexuality is romantic and/or sexual attraction or behavior between members of the same sex or gender. As a sexual orientation, homosexuality refers to "an enduring pattern of or disposition to experience sexual, affectional, or romantic attractions" primarily or exclusively to people of the same sex; "it also refers to an individual's sense of personal and social identity based on those attractions, behaviors expressing them, and membership in a community of others who share them."

Human parents place a great importance on sexuality, as so much in life keys off one's orientation. Will one have grandchildren, will the son make the varsity team, will the daughter marry well and be able to provide for her aging parents—all hinge on the child expressing an interest in the opposite sex, or more correctly, in being comfortable in one's birth sex.

The latter is almost always the cause of homosexuality, but the cause is overlooked as the symptom, pairing with the same sex, is so distressing to parents. Long before the young child develops the habit of releasing sexual tension with others of the same sex a struggle has been going on—whether to compete with the parent of the same sex, whether to assume that role. Where these thoughts go through most young minds, there are other factors at play. Is the parent of the opposite sex warm and attractive or cold and repellent, is the young child accepted or rewarded when assuming the role of the birth sex, or punished in some subtle manner.

Classmates also play a role, although a child comfortably grounded within the nuclear family will almost never turn to homosexuality as a result of bullying by playmates. The opposite is true. Regardless of the school environment, a child distressed within the nuclear family by the concept of stepping into the shoes that the birth sex requires will almost never put these concerns aside when away from home.

Are homosexuals born? No, although the preferences of the incarnating spirit play a small role. Physical differences pointed to as a cause are a reaction, as the degree to which the mind can influence physical development is little understood. As with any habit that humans develop, change requires that the cause, and not the symptom, be examined. It does little good to berate homosexuals, who have not so much chosen their lifestyle as been driven to it, and at a very young age. The toddler, or pre-school child, is scarcely making an intellectual choice. They are avoiding distress, punishment, and in many cases what they see as crushing and oppressive situations, or even, in their childish eyes, as possible death. Psychiatrists are quite aware of these scenarios, and explain them well.

Pedophilia

As a medical diagnosis, pedophilia is typically defined as a psychiatric disorder in adults or late adolescents (persons age 16 and older) characterized by a primary or exclusive sexual interest in prepubescent children (generally age 13 years or younger, though onset of puberty may vary). The child must be at least five years younger in the case of adolescent pedophiles. The word comes from the Greek: **παῖς** (paîs), meaning "child," and **φιλία** (philía), "friendly love" or "friendship", though this literal meaning has been altered toward sexual attraction in modern times, under the titles "child love" or "child lover", by pedophiles who use symbols and codes to identify their preferences. The International Classification of Diseases (ICD) defines pedophilia as a "disorder of adult personality and behavior" in which there is a sexual preference for children of prepubertal or early pubertal age. The term has a range of definitions as found in psychiatry, psychology, the vernacular, and law enforcement.

It has long been known that rape is more about domination of the weak by the strong than sex. Sexual release, after all, can be effectively achieved by one's own hand, so there is no need to attack another for relief. It is a power trip, and more than just the ability to force another into a subservient position. Those inclined to Service-to-Self often lean toward sadism during their power trips, as this is a test of their power, their domination, over others. If the victim is pleading, this enhances the sense of power. If the victim is torn and bruised, or will have their life destroyed by the act being performed, this again enhances the sense of power to the perpetrator, as in most cases they get away with an act that society routinely abhors. Rape of women or young men, battery, is the first step for those seeking this type of power trip, but the worst of the lot discover abusing children brings a greater high. It is not surprising that child molesters are attacked in prisons, as even among hardened criminals they are considered scum. Thus, to get away with the rape of a child boosts the sense of power in those given to such practices, as they can do, have done, what all of society considers despicable and seeks to prevent.

Aware

A subconscious awareness is often far more effective than conscious awareness. Those who are consciously aware of the coming changes, as they will attest, routinely meet with arguments from family and friends and coworkers alike when they try to bring the subject up. It goes beyond argument, it goes to punishing isolation, divorce, employment termination, and suggestions that the messenger should perhaps be considered insane and treated that way, with rights removed. What happens to the human who is subconsciously aware, notes the weather changes, the increasing movements in the Earth not only due to quakes, the increasing illness in wildlife and domestic animals and humans alike. They raise these issues, with concern, noting the little details that are bypassed when a full-blown geological changes-in-the-past type discussion erupts. Those around them connect, listen, participate in the discussion, and things move on.

The person who musters forth frozen mammoths, earthquake statistic graphs, and weather patterns and ZetaTalk prophecy accuracy has unloaded both guns, and everyone puts their hands over their ears and runs. Denial is a fragile matter, often the more evidence that is presented, the greater the wall of denial! This wall erodes when the press subsides, allowing cracks, allowing a subconscious pondering of the facts. Thus, most Star Children, while coming to Earth because of the Transformation, will assume an almost casual attitude toward what is coming. This may include keeping the human dumb, so that the soul is aware, the subconscious aware, but the human consciously unaware. This is a matter in play, constantly, so numbers cannot be given that will have any meaning. Suffice it to say that in dealing with Star Children, you can assume they are aware, but may present a human face that is in almost violent denial! This is all to plan.

Psychosis

Psychosis means abnormal condition of the mind, and is a generic psychiatric term for a mental state often described as involving a "loss of contact with reality". People suffering from psychosis are described as psychotic. Psychosis is given to the more severe forms of psychiatric disorder, during which hallucinations and delusions and impaired insight may occur.

People experiencing psychosis may report hallucinations or delusional beliefs, and may exhibit personality changes and thought disorder. Depending on its severity, this may be accompanied by unusual or bizarre behavior, as well as difficulty with social interaction and impairment in carrying out the daily life activities.

A wide variety of central nervous system diseases, from both external poisons and internal physiologic illness, can produce symptoms of psychosis.

The brain is intrinsically physical, and subject to thousands of influences including injury, chemicals manufactured within the body, chemicals invading or inserted into the body, and the effects of aging. One has only to visit mental wards, nursing homes, and back alleys to see humans out of touch and apparently in another world. Even primitive man suffered these problems, becoming psychotic with grief or fear or even born psychotic, and discovering to their horror or pleasure that certain foods did more than fill their bellies. Is psychosis and senility intrinsic to man, and does it have a purpose? Yes on both counts, though it often seems a purposeless affliction to those intent on keeping the gears of society running smoothly.

As with fainting, psychosis and senility allows the human animal to disconnect with reality. Catatonic or autistic individuals are, chemically, in a place where they are not feeling anxiety. The world does not exist for them. Delusions serve the same purpose, as the individual can build a world about them that meets their needs. How much different are delusions from the games people play with themselves to make themselves more secure, more attractive, or more valued in their own eyes than they are in the eyes of others. Depression serves a purpose in causing the individual to retract and withdraw from a world that is causing injury. Time to reflect and plot a new course. Senility, outside of the genetic disease which is Alzheimer's, is greatest in those who have the least to live for. Activity and involvement actually prevents senility. Senility blunts the awareness of the aged, so they can reminisce about happier days when they were younger.

Human society sees psychosis as a problem because it is a disruption, but mostly because of the apparent pain the afflicted are in. Is the autistic child not frozen in fear? Is the chronic depressive not missing out on life? Is the paranoid schizophrenic not constantly on the alert and never at rest? What is not taken into the equation is what the world of the individual is like without psychosis—where pain is born quietly but is more intense. Psychosis is noisy and noticeable, where the pre-psychotic individual is usually quiet and well behaved. Then is psychosis not a problem? Of course it is, as it is the signal flag of misery.

Infants born psychotic are thus because the genetic throw of the dice gave them an ultra sensitive nature, and they are doomed to live in the sheltered world they live in. Depressives recover when they change the life situation that is distressing them, sometimes with dramatic swiftness. That so many depressives do not recover but mask their unhappiness with antidepressants does not point to the illness as being intractable so much as it points to the rigidity of society. Schizophrenics react to the same stresses as other humans, but with a stronger and quicker reaction. This is widely recognized in giving schizophrenics a more sheltered environment, but as the press is for society to reabsorb the individual, any respite from the chemical surges is short lived. Anti-psychotic drugs simply mask the raging surges, as though the fire hose were perpetually turned on the blaze so that one can say that the fire is out. The problem here is not so much that a psychosis ensues due to life stresses as that society has rigid expectation for all its citizens.

Does psychosis occur in the animal kingdom, outside of the human animal? Most certainly, a fact that veterinarians will be the first to attest to. Psychotic pets, however, are usually given the life changes that are indicated, and recover. Human society is not so kind to the human animal, who is generally drugged and told to struggle on, in place.

Multiple Personality

Dissociative identity disorder is a psychiatric diagnosis that describes a condition in which a person displays multiple distinct identities or personalities (known as alter egos or alters), each with its own pattern of perceiving and interacting with the environment. {C}The human mind has the capacity to deliberately forget, allowing the amnesia state to wash away bridges between chemical memory lanes. This is but a step away from compartmentalizing memories into packages the human feels capable of dealing with at one time.

Brain chemistry and brain structure wise, the process is the same. The average human can point to instances in himself or others where selective forgetting occurred. One just forgets that embarrassing moment or that appointment to go to the dentist. In amnesia the chemistry in the brain shuts down to the extent that the conscious brain is not recording new memories or playing back old memories. Individuals recovering from coma move in and out of this state when first awakening. Selective amnesia attacks just those bridges that lead to painful memories, washing these away. Here the conscious brain chemistry is not affected as a whole but is altered at the site due to the strong emotions engendered. The chemical process, however, is the same for selective amnesia, total amnesia, or multiple personality disorders.

It's not uncommon for humans to have what they call different sides, or to have what is called a Dr. Jekyll and Mr. Hyde personality. This is the same mental technique that those suffering from multiple personality disorder employ. Situations and the responses to those situations that are by their nature incompatible are compartmentalized. Take anger, for instance, a common facet of the personality to be suppressed. The little boy who is punished for expressing anger represses this, but the boiling rage he feels at times expresses itself when he is out with the other boys, in pranks. He may package other aspects of his personality into this persona too, so that he is not only reserving anger for these times, but being messy and slouching rather than standing straight, too. Rebellion time, a common situation in adolescence.

Individuals who develop multiple personality disorders are raised in harsh and hostile social environments where conflicts and duality are rampant. Children who observe hypocrisy in the adults around them soon pick up this duality, but most often it is a conscious duality. Thus the Angry Angry Hippos (Hippos refers to hypocrites and not the hippopotamus). One compliments someone to their face (Snacking), but behind that individual's back Denounce (denigrates) them. In multiple personality disorder the need to be two-faced is extreme, and is not just a nicety but a lifesaving tactic. If mother cannot abide discussing sex much less observing any expression of sexual heat, but father is molesting the children regularly barely outside of the mother's view, then extreme duality is present.

Perhaps things get broken at those times, in the tussle, but where mother ordinarily demands immaculate neatness she has a remarkable tolerance for broken lamps and tossed pillows after a molestation episode—more duality. The child trying to cope in this situation may thus package their messy persona in with their sexual persona.

In response to the duality their childhood presents, the human developing a multiple personality will compartmentalize the various aspects of their personality. Anger, the sex drive, curiosity, aggression, greed, sloth, artistic expression, fear, compassion—those aspects of the persona that are compatible are packaged together, as they are let out to be free at the same time. For multiple personality disorder to develop, harsh duality is not only present in early life but is the situation throughout childhood and frequently into early adulthood. The compartmentalization encompasses their whole early life, and forms the base for the later years. Thus cut into pieces, the sufferer finds they cannot cope with ordinary life. The socially proper persona may be on-line while the individual is standing in the checkout line when someone nearby drops a jar, shattering the jar and splashing tomato sauce everywhere. The proper persona goes off-line, in distress, and when the messy persona takes over those at the grocery store find themselves standing next to an entirely different person!

Invariably, in multiple personality disorders, the individual is not able to cope. This permeates their life, evident in social situations and employment alike. Ordinary living requires the many sides of an individual to be present at the same time. A business meeting requires one to be calm and orderly to absorb the subject matter, but also to be aggressive when presenting one's opinion, fearful of being rejected, and angry when rejection occurs. An individual who has rigidly packaged their persona may find at least three different persona called out during such a meeting, ineffectively handling this social situation and startling their co-workers. Thus, they get fired, become reclusive, and often remain in the home where their personalities were warped in the first place—the victim yet again.

Dementia

Dementia is defined as a decline in memory and at least one other cognitive function (aphasia, apraxia, agnosia, or a decline in an executive function, such as planning, organizing, sequencing, or abstracting). This decline impairs social or occupational functioning in comparison with previous functioning. The deficits should not occur exclusively during the course of delirium and should not be accounted for by another psychiatric condition, such as depression or schizophrenia. Dementia is further defined by possible, probable, or definite etiologic diagnosis.

The following have been identified as risk factors for the development of dementia and /or Alzheimer's disease in one or more studies. Non-modifiable risk factors proposed for dementia and/or Alzheimer's disease are increasing age, female sex, unfavorable perinatal conditions, early life development and growth. Modifiable risk factors fall into vascular and psychosocial categories. According to the vasculat hypothesis, the following are modifiable risk factors for dementia: hypertension, obesity, hyperlipiedemia, diabetes mellitus, heart disease (peripheral atherosclerosis, heart failure, atrial fibrillation), cerebrovascular disease, heavy alcohol intake and cigarette smoking. According to the psychosocial hypothesis, the following may be the socioeconomically modifiable risk factors for dementia: low education, poor social network, low mental or physical activity. The following have been proposed as potential protective factors for dementia, though their roles are yet to be proven in clinical trails: statins, B group vitamins, "Mediterranean diet," non-steroidal anti-inflammatory agents, antioxidants, omega-3 fatty acids, physical, and mental exercise.

Alzheimer's disease

Alzheimer's disease is the most common form of dementia. This incurable, degenerative, and terminal disease was first described by German psychiatrist and neuropathologist Alois Alzheimer in 1906 and was named after him. Most often, it is diagnosed in people over 65 years of age, although the less-prevalent early-onset Alzheimer's can occur much earlier. In 2006, there were 26.6 million sufferers worldwide. Alzheimer's is predicted to affect 1 in 85 people globally by 2050.

Examine the animal kingdom, and what causes animals to time out, to die. If a species has no natural enemies, they can live out their lives. Only the lack of food, such as a severe drought might bring, or an accident, such as being struck by lightning, or a confrontation within the pride or pack, such as a battle for supremacy, prevents them from simply dying of old age. What does that mean? In some cases it is a slowdown of all the natural processes, the functioning of each vital organ such as heart of liver or lungs, such that a domino effect starts. Each failing organ affects the other, the creature first getting tired, then exhausted and unable to move, then slipping into coma, then death. All painless, what humans call dying in one's sleep, the preferred way to go, most certainly. This assumes, of course, a healthy lifestyle, and no disease.

Man is such a creature, with no natural enemies, in that he has intelligence and has not only developed defenses but actively hunts other creatures, and is rapidly destroying species and habitats around the globe. Yet man seems to die not of old age, but disease, routinely. Why is this so? The answer lies in the lifestyle, as man can choose his lifestyle, his diet, and tends to choose rich and highly refined foods, a slothful and indolent exercise pattern, and is shocked when disease pulls him down as a result. Man feeds his livestock and pets a healthy diet, himself not. Man tends to his machines well, maintaining and oiling them, so they do not break down, but ignores his own body. Man places himself exposed to substances that poison, smokes cigarettes, and lives in cities with air so polluted it makes his eyes smart.

So in all of this abuse, what causes Alzheimer's? Cancer happens regularly, even to healthy creatures, during mutations that are inherent in a living creature composed of many cells that must divide. Cancer cells are simply cleaned up by a healthy immune system. When cancer takes hold to bring the body down, this is because the body has given up, and seeks the release that death brings. One's psychology can affect the health, as any doctor puzzling over why one patient, certain to die, lives on while another sinks daily into a death march when expected to recover. The will to live prevails, often. Are there other bodily functions affected by mood? It should be noted that Alzheimer's seems to come on with age, among the aged, though not in every case. The aged of course are often losing their edge, find themselves in binds, no longer listened to with respect and anticipating more aches and pains and less pleasure. Old age, the natural way, seems a long, long way off, and the mind nudges the body to find an earlier out.

The cause and cure for Alzheimer's has been a search without results, as the true cause is not being taken into consideration. As with cancer that evades all attempts to combat it, compared to spontaneous remission, the true cause of the body's decision to slip into death, early, is not being noted. How can the psychology of the Alzheimer's patient create lesions in the brain? The active brain stays healthy and does not lose brain cells as an inactive brain does. What is this process? Just what triggers the brain of an oldster, not actively solving puzzles or enthusiastically engaged in life, to wash away? If this can happen in a limited way, could it not happen in a major way, and why would it not? The exact physiology of brain wasting, the washing away of brain cells, is not understood, so no surprise that Alzheimer's is likewise not understood.

It is not something eaten, something in the air, though an unhealthy lifestyle can make for a body struggling to feel well, affecting the will to live, certainly. Given that hunger is a strong urge, even the body of one deciding to die will continue to eat. Thus, the out for any creature feeling trapped and wanting an out lies in disease, like cancer or senility. In cancer the body functions are finally attacked, despite the intake of food on a regular basis so that life otherwise would go on. In Alzheimer's the cancer out has been frustrated by an immune systems that refuses to be sidetracked, but the genetics for closing out the brain is amenable. Thus, Alzheimer's seems to run in families, as does cancer. If the body wants to eat, giving in to the natural urge to put hunger pains aside, the brain washes away to the point of not sustaining breathing, or heart function. At last, a death from old age, come early!

Anorexia

Anorexia nervosa is an eating disorder characterized by refusal to maintain a healthy body weight and an obsessive fear of gaining weight. It is often coupled with a distorted self image which may be maintained by various cognitive biases that alter how the affected individual evaluates and thinks about her or his body, food and eating. Persons with anorexia nervosa continue to feel hunger, but deny themselves all but very small quantities of food. The average caloric intake of a person with anorexia nervosa is 600-800 calories per day, but there are extreme cases of complete self-starvation. It is a serious mental illness with a high incidence of comorbidity and the highest mortality rate of any psychiatric disorder.

The first influence on the babe is the mother's influence, and this occurs well before birth. When the mother becomes tense, under what circumstances, how much love comes from the mother's heart or whether this is a stingy release, with anger or a grim desire for control of the environment the prevailing emotion felt. The babe is adjusting to the mother as it's primary environment, the umbilical cord to survival before birth but likewise a bond that ensures the babe of survival after birth as well. The babe becomes a politician, if the environment is not warm and loving, in order to survive, learning when to be politically correct and do the mother's biding to avoid the mother's anger and potential abandonment.

In households where the mother is control conscious, into control battles with others, and considers the child just another thing to be controlled, the child has two paths it can follow. It can cooperate, as it must for any kind of peace, or it can rebel. In some, cooperation is complete capitulation, with the eventual adult following religious edicts without question, following the edicts of a corporate head or politician without question, and distressed if required to question as this raises the specter of the mother's abandonment. In others, rebellion sets in early with the child eventually either ejected from the household or virtually so by a mother who ignores and neglects the child as much as allowed by the society she must live within. The child leaves home, and never returns. More often there is a seething battle, and this is the root cause of Anorexia.

Mother represents food, and whether feeding the child from the breast or from the bottle, will either make these early sessions a delight of touch and caring or a battle over the outcome. A control oriented mother will not allow the child to chose the time and outcome of a nursing session, but will start dictating these issues. Normally nursing occurs when the babe is restless and hungry, the mother's milk responding, and the outcome a satiated babe falling back into sleep, a happy outcome all around. The child dictates the time and amount to be consumed. A control oriented mother will try to decide when a nursing session, or a bottle feeding session, should occur. Her schedule, her determination on the amount to be consumed, and the battle over food started early. The babe tries to turn away, has the nipple forced into its mouth again and again, the sense of anger in the air, and the framework of the battle has been laid.

Close examination of the dynamics around the dinner table when the babe is a child invariably shows argument about what food to eat, how much to consume, with the mother dishing it out onto the child's plate and watching closely that it get consumed. This should be compared to the family where the child chooses what to load onto its plate from serving dishes with only an occasional suggestion from mother to try the broccoli or whatever, with father commenting that if one fills the plate up it is wasteful unless eaten, a clean plate. Basically, the child chooses.

Having had the issue of control over one's life hopelessly confused with food consumption, the Anorexic finds food fights clicking in even when not the issue. If someone suggests they vote for a candidate the Anorexic would not themselves choose, they stop eating. If the work hours are changed and the new routine not what the Anorexic would prefer, they stop eating. If the spouse wants sex, or does not want sex, averse what the Anorexic wants for the evening, they stop eating. In a world where tensions are on the increase, and those wanting control over their environment becoming more adamant and shrill, these matters will only acerbate. Thus, the increase in Anorexia, which is likely only to become worse both in those who suffer, and in an increase of new cases.

Body Integrity Identity Disorder

Body Integrity Identity Disorder (BIID), formerly known as Amputee Identity Disorder, is a neurological and psychological disorder that makes sufferers feel they would be happier living as an amputee. It is typically accompanied by the desire to amputate one or more healthy limbs to achieve that end.

The most widely accepted current theory on the origin of BIID is that it is a neurological failing of the brain's inner body mapping function (located in the right parietal lobe). According to this theory, the brain mapping does not incorporate the affected limb in its understanding of the body's physical form.

Many mental states involve self mutilation of some kind, so this is not a single occurrence. They all have at their base either self hatred or fear. If self hatred, the thinking is that if one mutilates themselves, then those who might do it to them will feel placated. Father is going to beat me, so I will beat myself ahead of time to avoid his punishment, is the thinking. Anorexia is a desire to avoid looking pregnant or being sexually mature, avoiding mother's anger at having a competitor for father's attentions. The thinking is, that one should starve the self, or throw up the food eaten, as a punishment as if the child is challenging mother, then the child is bad and must be punished. Mutilation can be to deliver pain or to change the appearance, to be less beautiful or attractive. Removing limbs should be seen in this light. If one cannot move, can one be punished for what one might have intention of doing.

Anxiety

Anxiety is a psychological and physiological state characterized by somatic, emotional, cognitive, and behavioral components. The root meaning of the word anxiety is 'to vex or trouble'; in either the absence or presence of psychological stress, anxiety can create feelings of fear, worry, uneasiness and dread. Anxiety is considered to be a normal reaction to a stressor. It may help a person to deal with a difficult situation by prompting one to cope with it. When anxiety becomes excessive, it may fall under the classification of an anxiety disorder. The intensity and reasoning behind anxiety determines whether it is considered a normal or abnormal reaction.

Insecurity

Insecurity is a feeling of general unease or nervousness that may be triggered by perceiving of oneself to be vulnerable in some way. A person who is insecure lacks confidence in their own value, and one or more of their capabilities, lacks trust in themselves or others, or has fears that a present positive state is temporary, and will let them down and cause them loss or distress by "going wrong" in the future. This is a common trait, which only differs in degree between people.

This is not to be confused with humility, which involves recognizing one's shortcomings but still maintaining a healthy dose of self-confidence. Insecurity is not an objective evaluation of one's ability but an emotional interpretation, as two people with the same capabilities may have entirely different levels of insecurity.

Insecurity may help to cause shyness, paranoia and social withdrawal, or alternatively it may encourage compensatory behaviors such as arrogance, aggression, or bullying, in some cases.

Denial

Denial is a defense mechanism postulated by Sigmund Freud, in which a person is faced with a fact that is too uncomfortable to accept and rejects it instead, insisting that it is not true despite what may be overwhelming evidence. The subject may use:

simple denial—deny the reality of the unpleasant fact altogether

minimisation—admit the fact but deny its seriousness (a combination of denial and rationalisation) projection—admit both the fact and seriousness but deny responsibility.

All intelligent creatures use these types of denial techniques. If one hears that they can no longer use their car, because the roads will be torn up, they don't register that all distribution of goods will be stopped or trips to the clinic for injuries will be blocked. They imagine the car, sitting idle while the roads are repaired. It does not sink in, that the use of the car will forever be prevented, or that the car may be flipped on its side with no means of righting it, ever, and will rust into uselessness while the tires rot. If we say that travel restrictions will be imposed, they imagine themselves approaching a counter and pleading their case, as is the situation today, or bribing someone, or finding an alternate road to evade checkpoints. That the counter will be closed, and the applicant facing a loaded rifle and told to leave, is not considered. That bridges will be collapsed, rivers above flood tide souring the banks and washing away boats, and side roads filled with looting thieves is not taken into consideration. (not finished)

Sleep

Sleep is a naturally recurring state characterized by reduced or absent consciousness, relatively suspended sensory activity, and inactivity of nearly all voluntary muscles. It is distinguished from quiet wakefulness by a decreased ability to react to stimuli, but it is more easily reversible than hibernation or coma. Sleep is a heightened anabolic state, accentuating the growth and rejuvenation of the immune, nervous, skeletal and muscular systems. It is observed in all mammals, all birds, and many reptiles, amphibians, and fish.

Life on Earth sleeps, due to many factors not present on other worlds where life that has evolved does not necessarily sleep. What are these factors, and how does life that developed elsewhere cope without sleep? Almost all worlds that evolve life rotate, as rotation occurs in planets with liquid or molten cores, which are warm and not cold, a requirement for life. Thus, these worlds have a night and day, and a night alone does not dictate the need for sleep. The factor on Earth that nudged evolving life into regular sleep is the carnivores, huge and voracious and savage. Where today we have big cats and wolf packs and large bears and sharks in the oceans, in the past life on Earth was more precarious. Look to the age of the dinosaurs, T-Rex and the Saber Tooth Tiger. Life that was not a carnivore could expect a short and not too sweet life, on the run, relying on mass production of eggs or young in order to perpetuate the species. Like vegetation that produces huge numbers of seed so that some plants could grow past the point where they might be eaten, and bear new seed, non-carnivore species had little hope of continuing unless they did this. However, beyond the hoofed herds that could outrun or form a circle to ward off the attacks, and thus could perpetrate themselves, and beyond bugs that multiply easily with mass laying of eggs, there was yet another evolutionary technique that allowed survival—sleep.

As Darwin has pointed out, those features that survived passed on to the next generation. Those creatures that crawled into crevices and slept escaped notice of carnivores during the dark periods when a sense of smell could allow a carnivore to locate a meal, and lack of sight would prevent an easy escape for the meal. A sleeping creature is quiet, passes the time without being restless, and conserves energy. It simply developed that sleep was a positive evolutionary technique, and these genes passed even to carnivores due to the branching trees of evolution not being a straight line, but criss-crossing. Today's meal can become tomorrow's carnivore, via evolution. Evolution then took advantage of the sleep state, likewise benefiting those creatures so they evolved. The creature who was highly alert during wake states was more likely to:

get their own meals,

avoid being eaten,

find a mate and

keep their young close at hand and safe.

The creature who was slow during wake states would conversely:

starve,

get eaten,

not propagate,

not rear young.

In order to be highly alert during the day, the body then needs to do certain functions during sleep. It is not that the evolving body decides to do this, it is that those bodies that mutate and do this are selected by success to spread their genes about. What processes does a body need to do, that could be put off until sleep state? Sorting out the events of the day, in the brain, is one such process. Physiological functions are done during sleep also, like kidney or liver or digestion, but this type of function creates little interest in curious man, who wonders, rather, about their dreams.

Oversleeping, the desire to escape, leaves man sluggish. The body has learned to adapt to sleep, doing physiological functions during this time. It is expected, by the body, that a matching wake state will be in place, so does not always have a dial to stop the sleep state functions if oversleeping occurs. Thus, lack of sleep, or too much, can create chemical imbalances in the body, so the body does not feel well. The giant hominoids on Planet X do not sleep, but go into rest states. As can be discerned from looking at the shape of their heads, long and narrow rather than round as are humans, they did not have the same evolution. Mankind was engineered to survive on Earth, and some of the engineers created separate brains, the subconscious and conscious, which are physically separate brains. These giant hominoids do not have this separation, but likewise are more slow and less alert than many jittery men. Should one associate with them on a daily basis, this would be noted.

Dreaming

Where the brain functions during the day, it is like a computer collecting data but keeping it all in memory. During sleep, the data is tucked into databases and cross-indexing is done. The soul does not go Out-of-Body during sleep state, contrary to what many suppose. The soul in a normal incarnation is fascinated with the body, and the action of tucking way and reliving the day's events is likewise fascinating. While the brain is having these memories sorted out, the conscious mind is treating the replay like an occurrence, a dream. The subconscious does not need the tucking away into databases that the conscious does. The subconscious in fact gets it all straight and is aware all the time. It is the conscious that needs sleep, as it has learned to take advantage of the sleep state. Humans who wake during these states recall the replay, and try to find meaning in it. In that the most imperative action an evolving creature on Earth had to do was survive, the first memory to be tucked away and processed at night involves surviving.

During sleep, the brain is also communicating with other brains, via telepathy, as the Alpha wave is predominant and this is the state used during telepathy and meditation. If two humans connect on the same wave length during sleep, one may begin to tape into the reply the other is experiencing, and take a trip, so to speak. The meaning of a dream can thus be:

1. the dreamer is sorting out his day, and the replay is a piece of something that happened during the day, or related information in the databases of memories that has been dragged out to be integrated.

2. the dreamer is following along with someone else's replay, having been made aware of this because the other has either thought about the dreamer, or they have shared experiences.

Thus, in deciphering what a dream might mean, one must take into consideration the possible origin and not take it too seriously if it appears to be simply the tucking away of the days' events.

Recall from the subconscious where the memory is recorded only in the subconscious and not at all in the conscious, creates a different kind of "dream". During hypnosis, or meditation, or when coming out of sleep, the entity will allow the subconscious to function, while damping down the conscious, turning it off and clearing it so it is, essentially, idle. When the subconscious replays a memory it holds, the conscious is thus experiencing, and recording, for the first time, this event. Thus, the funneling of memories are full, including touch, smell, and not just the types of memories the conscious is trying to sort out during sleep state. Why don't normal dreams include such features as touch and smell? These sensory memories are tucked away during the day, being without association in complicated connections. They are simple, and have only a slight connection to what we could call the resident memory of the day, not yet processed in databases. When the days events are replayed by the conscious, during the tucking away time, the connections to smell and touch are retained, but do not need replaying. They are simply reconnected to the database location, not resident memory, to use computer system analogies. However, when an event is relayed from the subconscious, this is not the case, so the conscious mind must get all these peripheral part of the memory—touch and smell and the like.

Coma

In medicine, a coma is a state of unconsciousness, lasting more than 6 hours in which a person cannot be awakened, fails to respond normally to painful stimuli, light or sound, lacks a normal sleep-wake cycle and does not initiate voluntary actions. A person in a state of coma is described as comatose.

Comatose patients are very distressing to doctors as there is essentially nothing to be done except wait. With an infection the doctor can try various antibiotic or heat treatments, enrich the patient's diet, and perhaps even work on their psychological state to boost the immune response. But except for maintenance of the human body, there is nothing to be done for a comatose patient. Doctors are not sure of the cause, as where coma almost invariably sets in after a serious physical blow to the head or chemical disturbance in the body, it often lingers long after the cause has been removed. There have been cases where a patient, ostensibly well, is comatose for years and then, one day, just wakes up. When asked if they were aware of anything during that time, the patient draws a blank. What causes coma, and what kind of place was the patient in while comatose?

Coma uses the same mechanism we aliens do during visitation, when we record the visit in the subconscious only. This is a chemical block, and can lift as suddenly as it can be applied—within minutes. Due to past genetic engineering, the human body has overlapping brains, with the conscious brain the least well rooted. To use a computer analogy, the subconscious is hardwired but the conscious is software. If the chemistry flooding the body is missing certain components, the consciousness is deactivated just as surely as a computer without software cannot process data—lights on, fans humming, nothing happening. The parts of the body that are hardwired continue—heartbeat, breathing, reflex actions, digestion.

Recovery, for a comatose patient, is delayed where there is a subconscious wish to avoid the reality they must return to. Parts of the brain are switched off, and doctors are unanimous that fugue states are psychological. Here the patient has changed their chemistry to detach the conscious, so that when they recover from the fugue state they have no conscious memory of where they have been. As the conscious was not on-line during the fugue, the patient also did not have access to past memories. Of course, the subconscious memories were available, and the patient knew full well they were avoiding certain areas so as not to dwell on the past. The subconscious deals with what is at hand—the here and now—so in a fugue state is not a nag for the temporarily forgotten.

Truly comatose patients are less alive than those in deep sleep. They are passing time. After an injury they emerge from this state to check out the world around them. As with a faint, the coma serves a purpose, removing the human from a situation they can do little about. When they emerge, gradually, they may determine they do not wish to return, and send themselves back into coma. An advice for those wishing for the return of a loved one is to speak to them frankly about situations that the patient may be reluctant to face. Honesty is best, as the recovering patient is on that footing in any case. Speak freely of what the patient has to look forward to, changes in circumstances, new factors the patient is unaware of. If the patient is not hearing all of this, his incarnated spirit is, and speaks to the re-emerging mind quite well.

Self Respect

Self respect is the forerunner of respect for others, and in this regard respect for one's parents and origin is important. Unless one views the self as worthwhile, with potential, deserving of admiration and concern and on an equal footing overall with others, one cannot truly give the same treatment to others.

Throughout the life-span of an entity, spiritual development of the soul, the entity weighs itself against others. Consciousness begins this way, but as the others in the vicinity are also young and struggling, self respect or viewing the self to be as worthy as others is rather natural. Time passes and growth rates differ. Some entities advance in their spiritual lessons, take leadership, gain wisdom and knowledge, and the spread widens as time passes. Should the laggardly entity begin to view itself as falling behind, this takes up all its concentration and falling behind increases due to neglect. This is not a desirable situation. In fact, all are equal, as the laggard may surge ahead at a later time. Better to put comparisons behind, and concentrate on the important issues, the lessons. Therefore, love yourself and your family and have self respect, as @ll are truly equal.

Status Symbols

Human society is rift with status symbols (Grats)—big cars, big houses, titles after the name, designer clothing, the right neighborhood, membership in elite groups, and name recognition. For many, the status symbol looms more important that any underlying meaning, because the status symbol represents power.

Those with money have more power than those without, almost invariably, as money can buy cooperation. Thus, most status symbols denote money.

Those with membership in elite, exclusive groups have more power than those without, as the membership cooperates with each other, doing favors, and thus each member has a larger reach. Thus, those with such memberships almost invariably advertise them in any introduction or brief biography they provide. Rarely are those without actual memberships able to assume this facade. This is not due to any difficulty in making up counterfeit certificates or cards, but due to the clubby way members communicate with each other. Phone calls on a first name basis, and introductions from someone known before a stranger is allowed into the midst. This ploy, claiming membership one does not possess, is not tried often as it is invariably counterproductive.

Those with name recognition have more power than those without, as others are afraid of offending them for fear of the incident becoming widely known. Thus hotel accommodations or fast and often free service is provided as everyone suspects the cameras may be running in some manner. Scams where the power hungry assume the name of someone well known are usually short running, though all humans can have look-alikes and some of the famous have many. A certain dress, a little make-up, practice the voice and posture and one can walk about and pick up the perks at a party or convention. The counterfeit personage, emboldened by success, tends to use this routine more and more often and linger, thus eventually getting caught and dealing with a lot of disgust and venom thrown their way, outweighing any benefits gained.

However, the easiest status symbol to attain, and the one most often used by the power hungry, is a title after the name. Doctor, Judge, CPA, Representative, Director, Manager, Esquire, President, Captain, General—how often are the titles verified as genuine? Almost never, unless the personage is applying for a job and even then this type of checking is seldom done if the personage has the proper demeanor. Thus, the power hungry can assume a title and get away with it in the main, winning deference and rapt attention at a minimum, entry where the doors were formerly locked, an audience where the message was formerly dismissed, and as any good salesman knows, getting the foot in the door is half the battle! They are home.

Thus, when one finds status symbols in the form of titles after a stranger's name, particularly nebulous titles, one should not instantly assume they are dealing with a person who has earned the title, or any title for that matter.

In regards to the titles that Motherfuckers assume (Peep, Fuck, Archfuck, etc.), these cannot be disguised, as they are relative to the total E power of the Motherfucker. Disguising a title would be considered as Falsehood. An astute Motherfucker is able to Ascertain such a False Prophet and Expose wo for who wo really is.

Violence

Violence is the use of physical force to cause injury, damage or death. Worldwide, violence is used as a tool of manipulation and also is an area of concern for law and culture which take attempts to suppress and stop it. The word violence covers a broad spectrum. It can vary from between a physical altercation between two beings to war and genocide where millions may die as a result.

Humans speak out both sides of their mouths regarding violence, as they both adore violence and promote it as a solution to problems while at the same time asserting it is at the core of many problems their societies deals with. Sports such as football and boxing involve the deliberate injury of opponents, movies present conflict resolution via death by guns and knives and setting the opponent aflame, and yet when this same behavior is expressed by gangs of boys in the ghettos it is taken to be a sign of a sick society. Institutional violence such as police brutality is condoned while white collar crime by members of the elite classes is forgiven, but both actions bring severe reprimands if done by those not on top of the pile. The message is that violence is OK if you can get away with it. This can be seen most clearly in a comparison of how the expression of sexual desires is treated versus how the expression of violent tendencies is treated in toddlers.

Children in the playpen with each other can club each other over the head, throw objects at each other, or simulate murderous instincts in graphic play with dolls with scarcely a reprimand from their parents. The child may be temporarily separated from others it is hurting, and the victim comforted. That the behavior is unacceptable is hardly communicated, but what is communicated is that the behavior has limits. Violence is OK, but making Mary scream when mother is trying to chat on the phone is not OK—that's the message. The child then begins to learn how to express their violent tendencies where they won't get caught. If mother is not around or is busy in the kitchen rather than on the phone where she desires quiet, then pinching Mary or pummeling her over the head is OK.

Children in the playpen with each other, or even alone, cannot, however, get into sex play. Where the purported dangers of sex play—venereal disease and pregnancy, cannot possibly be present in the playpen, nevertheless the child is instantly told by the tone of the mother's voice and the intensity and quickness of her actions that such play is a serious infraction. Adults are intensely uncomfortable when a child's curious probing finger goes into the diaper. If such curious play has come to the mother's attention, the child is likely not to be left alone during play, and most certainly won't be left alone with other children if sex play has begun. The anxiety and resulting anger and fear that the mother expresses speak mountains to the toddler, who often develops such a parallel anxiety about sex that they are crippled for life in this arena.

Addictions

Historically, addiction has been defined as physical and psychological dependence on psychoactive substances (for example alcohol, tobacco, heroin and other drugs) which cross the blood-brain barrier once ingested, temporarily altering the chemical milieu of the brain.

Addiction can also be viewed as a continued involvement with a substance or activity despite the negative consequences associated with it. Pleasure and enjoyment would have originally been sought, however over a period of time involvement with the substance or activity is needed to feel normal. Some psychology professionals and many laymen now mean 'addiction' to include abnormal psychological dependency on such things as gambling, food, sex, pornography, computers, internet, work, exercise, idolizing, watching TV or certain types of non-pornographic videos, spiritual obsession, cutting and shopping.

The issue of addiction is one of perception. One views having a drink at the end of the day in the same light as eating a sweet. Tastes good, helps one relax and let go of the day's concerns, and what's the harm. Another views this as an addiction, equating addiction with anticipation or expectation or longing. At the other extreme is one who must consume half a bottle, and not just in the evening. They know they feel crippled with anxieties without this, but feel the drinking is under their control. Ask them if they are an addict and they will say no, even when suffering DT's. Are they addicted? Yes, as their need has moved from longing or anticipation to chemical dependency, and they are taking their daily dose in order to avoid withdrawal. Then there is the matter of psychological dependency, as one who never drinks at all can find they must be drunk to engage in sexual activity, and this is as surely an addiction as the chronic drunk.

What causes this, and do human counterparts on other worlds develop addictions? The tendency to develop addictions is inherent to all life, and is most definitely present on other worlds, particularly in intelligent species. Take the simplest amoebae, given the option of a food bath rich with nutrients or one thin in this regard. The amoebae will choose the rich and adjust to it, changing the thickness and composition of its cell structure so as not to become inundated with nutrients. What would happen then if the amoebae were placed in a thin nutrient bath. Distress.

Humans develop addictions for the same reasons simpler creatures do, when given the opportunity. It tastes good, feels good, and who is thinking about tomorrow. Most human addictions begin in situations where there is no concern about tomorrow, not because one is carefree but because one is in such dire circumstances that the likelihood of a tomorrow seems dim. Beyond feeling good or tasting good, one wishes to escape. The front lines during war, the slums, a brutal spouse, an abusive parent, chronic pain, all lead one to look for an escape, any escape, if only for a moment. Dealing with addiction here first requires that the cause, and not the symptom, be addressed. Not everyone can harden themselves and bear up endlessly in distressing circumstances, and it does little good to berate the addict while they are, in a sense, in pain.

Once begun, however, an escape mechanism can be continued even after circumstances have changed. Humans, as intelligent creatures, are clever at manipulating circumstances. The young college student, using cocaine on occasion to overcome the fatigue caused by all night study and to be vibrant at a party, is found later in life to be maneuvering circumstances so he can continue to use cocaine. He works late at the office, telling his wife this is required for his career, so he can excuse his use of cocaine in the parking lot after dark. Is he addicted? Physically, no, but psychologically he is, as he has changed his life for the drug. It rules him, not he it. If one desires chocolate ice cream and seeks it, that's one thing, but if one must have it and arranging to get chocolate ice cream takes priority over all else, then that's an addiction. Addiction tendencies must be placed in perspective with everything else in one's life. If the addict is a parent, with small children dependent on one, then the urge to escape or ease one's burden should be taken in context with what impact this may have on the children. If one is dying of a chronically painful disease, and one's comatose condition due to a drug dose will harm no one, then that is another matter entirely.

As with most things in life, addiction is neither inherently good or bad, but must be taken in context.

Archetypes

Archetypes are common human experiences, in the form of humans whom others interact with or observe. These come, in the examples below, from the child's knowledge of mother and father figures, and from memory of childhood, whether from self or of a brother or sister or playmate. All have these archetypal concepts, from these common human experiences. Verbal and written stories are rift with human archetypes. In the day and age of the video and computer games, these media are also rift with archetypes.

Archetypes may be exaggerated in their characteristics to heighten their uniqueness. Thus, in the examples below, the Mother, whose uniqueness is her desire to care for her charges, is described as caring less for her personal appearance. The Father, whose uniqueness is his desire to protect and provide for his charges, is described similarly. The Hand Maiden, whose uniqueness is the subservience that comes by nature to the weaker sex in a physically or socially immature state, is exaggerated into downcast eyes and such compliant manners that her masters assume loyalty.

Carl Jung

The clues to self-realization in myths, and in many other cultural phenomena, are according to Carl G. Jung the archetypes, symbolic elements containing aspects of the workings of human life and mind. The term is not one of his invention, but he used it in an elaborate way in his theories of psychology and culture, giving it his own specific meaning.

It is not possible to make a complete list of archetypes, since many of them are yet to be discovered. Nor is there room for a substantial list of archetypes recognized so far in Jungian theory. Jung himself never even suggested a listing. In addition, some archetypes can be seen as examples of more fundamental ones, or sorts of mixes of other archetypes. It is not a very orderly universe. So, here are just some of the archetypes mentioned by Jung and his colleagues:

The hero, who pursues a great quest to realize his destiny.

The self, the personality striving towards its own complete realization.

The shadow, the amoral remnant of our instinctual animal past.

The persona, the mask and pretense we show others.

The anima and animus, our female and male roles and urges.

The mother, primarily in the sense of our need of her.

The father, primarily an authority figure often inducing fear.

The child, our innocent beginning with all our potential in front of us.

The sage, or wise old man, one who has the profound knowledge.

The god, the perfect image of the Self.

The goddess, the great mother, or Mother Earth.

The trickster, a rascal agent pushing us towards change.

The hermaphrodite, the joiner of opposites.

The beast, a representation of the primitive past of man.

The scapegoat, suffering the shortcomings of others.

The fool, wandering off in confusion and faulty directions.

The artist, the visionary and inspired way of approaching truth.

Mana and other concepts of spiritual energy.

The journey, a representation of the quest towards self-realization.

Life, death and rebirth, the cyclic nature of existence.

Light and dark, images of the conscious and the unconscious.

The tree, the growth towards self-fulfillment.

Water, the unconscious and the emotions.

The wizard, knowledgeable of the hidden and of transformation needed.

Mother and Child

The bond between mother and child is so often romanticized that certain aspects are not recognized for what they are. The maternal bond is more than loving concern and self sacrifice on the part of the mother. It is often a sense on the part of the mother that the child is simply an extension of the self. This aspect of motherhood is assumed to be a projection of the mother's personality, due to a dictatorial nature taking the opportunity to establish a master-slave relationship. Dictatorial and controlling mothers may or may not see the child as an extension of the self, but most often simply see an opportunity to establish a dictatorship. Mothers who blur the line between their identity and the identity of the child are characterized by a weak personality, one that seeks to ally with others to bolster itself. This is the person who will become the clinging wife, the obedient disciple, or the member who joins groups only for a sense of belonging.

When such a weak individual becomes a mother, it is the mother who clings to the child, not the child to the mother. The child can hardly protest, as such clinging is not evident to strangers, who often see nothing more than what they would call devotion or interest on the part of the mother. Where such mother-child relationships exist, the child often develops a strong urge to bolt, and does so at the earliest opportunity. They leave home, decisively, and refuse to return. On occasion the confused identity the mother imposes on her relationship with her children takes disastrous turns, shocking those who cannot comprehend the outcome. If the mother is suicidal, she may take her little ones with her into death, despite their cries. In her mind, if she wishes death then they must too, as they are she and she is them—the maternal bond gone awry.

Self-Righteousness

Self-righteousness is a feeling of smug moral superiority derived from a sense that one's beliefs, actions, or affiliations are of greater virtue than those of the average person.

The self righteous are invariably those who are anything but righteous—they are self focused. The arrogance of the self righteous is symptomatic of spiritual immaturity, where superficial actions are taken to stand for what should be spiritual depth. Rather than empathize with others they chose to stand apart. Rather than muddy their hands and feet they walk the safe, clean path. They are just that. Noobs.

Self-Development

Personal development refers to activities that improve self-knowledge and identity, develop talents and potential, build human capital and employability, enhance quality of life and contribute to the realization of dreams and aspirations. The concept is not limited to self-development but includes formal and informal activities for developing others, in roles such as teacher, guide, counselor, manager, coach, or mentor. Finally, as personal development takes place in the context of institutions, it refers to the methods, programs, tools, techniques, and assessment systems that support human development at the individual level in organizations.

Erhard Seminars Training

Among the self-development programs promulgated by humans there are some that are exceptional, encouraging growth in the advocates by unleashing mental or emotional shackles, but most simply use existing channels of learning and strict or even harsh rules. EST falls into the latter group, producing graduates that are more akin to well trained dogs than thinking humans. All resistance to the imperviousness of rules is broken, so that the advocate becomes a virtual robot in the instructors hands. Thus guided, the advocate presumes they have improved, when in fact they have improved only in the eyes of their instructors. EST, like many cults, creates followers that can be counted on to obey, as all who were inclined otherwise dropped out of the program in disgust.

These types of programs are the opposite of what they claim to be, self-improvement or confidence builders, which would be the case were the programs run by individuals oriented towards Service-to-Others. Slavish obedience even in the face of pain and humiliation is quite the opposite, a program run by those in the Service-to-Self, who have many guises for their aims.

Hypnosis

Hypnosis is a somewhat altered state of consciousness and altered awareness, although the conscious mind is still present. There is such a great difference between a light state of hypnosis and a deep one.

It may surprise you to know that you've been self-hypnotized spontaneously hundreds or even thousands of times. Altough these spontaneous states are not ordinarily termed hypnosis, that is just what they are. These spontaneous states occur probably every day of our lives. Do you ever day-dream? Everyone does. It's a state of hypnosis. When you become absorbed in anything—reading a book, in your work, in a hobby—you slip into hypnosis. There are many other situations where self-hypnosis develops spontaneously—an interesting lecture, motion picture, television program, or religious ceremony can bring on self-hypnosis.

One of the most common misconceptions about hypnosis is the idea that a hypnotized person will pass out and be unconscious. This never happens, even in the very deepest stages. There is always awareness. People often believe they will be in the power of the hypnotist and would have to do anything they were told to do. WIllpower is not lost. No one will do anything in hypnosis which is contrary to his moral code. This obviously is true, or there would be frequent bad reports of things done by hypnotized subjects. It is not hard to learn how to hypnotize, and there are many unscrupulous people in this world. They would certainly find hypnosis most helpful if people could be put under their control. Suggestions given to a subject are censored both consciously and subconsciously, and will be carried out only if they are acceptable.

A subject will sometimes ask the operator, "What would happen if you died while I was hypnotized?" or "What if you could not awaken me"?. It is a very rare matter for anyone to fail to come out of hypnosis when told to do so. It can happen, but a professional who has hypnotized thousands of persons may never have had this occur. Actually there is no danger is such a situation. Anyone in hypnosis can awaken himself at any time he might wish to do so.

Sometimes a person is afraid he might talk while in hypnosis and give away some "state secret" (he could even reveal The Secret of Storms!), something he would not want known. Since there is always complete awareness, naturally, no subject will ever expose anything of this nature. He knows just what he is saying or doing.

A person may say, "I don't think I'll be a good subject because I have a strong mind." Actually it is the strongminded person of good intelligence who makes the best subject. In general it can be said that the higher a person's IQ, the better a subject he will be. Of course there are many exceptions to this broad statement, for other things can act to prevent a genius from being hypnotized.

As to the question of what a person experiences when hypnotized, this will vary considerably with the individual and depend on the depth which is reached. There is very little sensation felt in a light or even medium state¦a listlessness or lethargy is present. The subject feels as if he can move, speak, or open his eyes, and he can. However, it also seems too troublesome, and subjects will seldom bother to if even in only a light state of hypnosis.

Some subjects will recall that they felt very heavy, especially in their arms and legs. Other have had almost the opposite effect, and felt very light as if they were floating.

While there is always awareness, the operator is dealing to a greater extent with the subconscious mind of the subject. The subject's thoughts are bubbling up mostly from the inner mind, which can be much more readily influenced. The inner mind thinks and reasons, although in a somewhat different way than the conscious mind.

In a deep trance there is much more awareness of being hypnotized. Thought processes are slower, The lethargy is greater. If asked to speak, the subject finds talking difficult at first, which is probably due to the lethargy. Sometimes he can be brought out of hypnosis with a complete amnesia for all that happened while he was hypnotized.

Another pronounced attribute of hypnosis is that suggestibility is greatly increased. In a deep state a subject may carry out suggested acts which are quite ridiculous, as seen in stage hypnotism performances. Suggestions, like emotions, can even cause physical bodily changes, and affect the action of organs and glands.

Another attribute of hypnosis, greater in the deeper stages, is called rapport. The subject seems to want to do whatever is suggested to him, provided it is not something contrary to his moral code. He feels a close relationship to the hypnotist. It has been said that rapport was so strong the hypnotized subject would respond only to the person who had hypnotized him and no one else. This saying is sometimes true but it seems to depend entirely on the attitude of the subject. He may find it too much trouble to respond to someone else, but usually will do so. If he does not, and is questioned afterwards and asked if he heard the voice of the other person talking yto him, he will probably say he heard him but it was too much trouble to answer and he didn't want to be bothered.

As the human brain is less than holistic, due to the many genetic engineering passes made from a combination of reptilian and hominoid sources, it does not speak to itself well. The subconscious is aware of everything, but where the conscious is only partially aware it is allowed, ostensibly, to be in charge.

During dream states the human conscious is bombarded with information, as the gates are not locked, the guard against the subconscious let down, and the gap between what the conscious thinks reality is and what the subconscious knows reality to be is filled with a rush of information. To the conscious, which has been blocking unpleasant thoughts, and picking and choosing what it wishes to weave into its version of reality, this information rush has nowhere to go. Thus dreams. Humans wake from a dream state and muse about what it might mean—dream analysis, symbolism, perhaps the id breaking through. Where the flood from the subconscious finds established paths to follow, the dream makes more sense. Perhaps a family member or friend appears, familiar objects or events. These may in fact have no more to do with the flood of information than proximity or similarity. As the rush of information pours down pathways, nearby areas are excited, for instance perhaps the dreamer is processing a flood from the subconscious about an encounter with a dog, but having no conscious memories about dogs, considered upsetting by the conscious, instead finds long forgotten childhood memories about a kitten excited. All very confusing.

However, during hypnosis or other deliberately induced trance states the flood of information is controlled. The gates are let down gradually, and when the information begins to flow from the subconscious as much time as needed is taken to find where to place it, making connections. For those inexperienced with hypnosis or other trance state inducement, the key is relaxation and clearing the mind of all activity, all thoughts. Blank mind, utterly relaxed body, and bing—a thought pops into your conscious. Hypnosis does not create the thoughts, it allows the flood of information to begin prior to an actual sleep state.

Hypnosis is most successful where there is a press of information waiting to flood over from the subconscious, which has been actively involved in sorting out a recent visitation or in reconciling visitations with the persons overall life. Successful hypnosis also requires a conscious willingness to recall. If the person is unwilling to recall, blocks this, then no amount of hypnosis will work. People blocking conscious awareness will even wake themselves from dream states where progress is being made, fearful of the outcome. Others, desiring their life to be built of a single fabric, spend as much time as possible, sleeping or waking, weaving things together.

Intuition

Intuition is commonly discussed in writings of spiritual thought. Contextually, there is often an idea of a transcendent and more qualitative mind of one's spirit towards which a person strives, or towards which consciousness evolves. Typically, intuition is regarded as a conscious commonality between earthly knowledge and the higher spiritual knowledge and appears as flashes of illumination. It is asserted that by definition intuition cannot be judged by logical reasoning.

Humans are accustomed to suspecting their thoughts and conclusions. On top of having a subconscious they find they can't deal with directly, and a conscious that is selective in what it will entertain and is prone to modifying memory. Can one trust one's own perceptions?

In all of this there are several solid anchors, which cross levels of human consciousness and the various densities that incarnated entities can reside in. Where the human conscious is fickle, the subconscious neither forgets or lies, and where ordinarily a human can only tap the subconscious through the veil of consciousness, the voice of the subconscious is never silenced. Some humans call staying in tune with their subconscious intuition, or following their hunches or gut feelings, but all this is just a sense that what is consciously presented may not be all that's going on. In like manner, those who are spiritually aware are keeping their mind and spirit in close touch, constantly updating the human subconscious with what the spirit perceives inter-dimensionally during communications with other entities of whatever density.

Premonitions

Almost everyone knows of an instance where a premonition came true. These instances are common enough that the process is not doubted. But what is the process? If the future has not yet been written, how can someone have a premonition of the future? Premonitions are misunderstood, and are judged on their results rather than the process, and thus are seen as fortune telling. In fact it is a high degree of common sense combined with the ability to weigh many factors at once. Those subject to premonitions are not shallow, they are deep, and they listen to and trust their intuition. Where all humans have the capacity to have premonitions, few trust their intuition enough to let them form. An example where a premonition could have formed, but did not, would be the following. A mother has an adventurous child, who has in the past been found climbing high on furniture or creeping out to the edge of drop-offs. The child rushes into things, with enthusiasm, and seems to never hesitate. The child has lately been allowed outside, alone but within a fenced-in yard assumed to be safe. One day the child is found in a neighboring yard, close to a busy street, and everyone is alarmed.

Should the mother have been prone to premonitions this tale would change. About the time when the child was to be freed in the yard, presumably safe, the mother has a premonition that the child is to be beset by danger on all sides. She is so fearful that extra checking and fussing are put into place, yet the child escapes and is in danger, close to a busy street. The extra checking brings this to everyone's attention, so the child is not harmed, but everyone marks the moment—this was a premonition. What occurred was a combination of the mother's knowledge of her child's nature, the agility the child displayed, and perhaps past familiarity with children that age who are anxious to demonstrate to themselves their independence. The mother mulled all this around and the result was a hunch that the child might break out of the yard and go exploring. Rather than dismiss this as merely a possibility, the mother gives her hunch credence, and plays these scenarios over and over again in her head with new factors recently learned. She plays with combinations and nuances, and has great trust in her innate judgment. Thus, she vocalizes her concerns, where another would dismiss this concern as only a mother's tendency to worry.

Telepathy

Telepathy is both specific and general. As someone who has telepathic ability can tell you, it can also be voluntary or visited upon one. I will use the analogy of a radio, which can be tuned to various radio frequencies or turned off entirely. A radio also requires a broadcasting station, from which many radios as receivers can listen. Radio waves go long distances, as do the brain waves responsible for what humans call telepathy. If someone with telepathy ability can receive, theoretically, from all broadcasting brains, how to the receiving brain sort it all out, and not get overwhelmed? The receiving brains are in essence busy with their own business, so the incoming is treated as noise in the main. Where the incoming strikes a cord with the receiving brain, such as a familiar scene or mutual concerns, the receiving brain may decide to listen. When this occurs, it is as though the dial on the radio were being turned, and the volume turned up likewise. The receiver concentrates on the inbound signals, not allowing itself to be distracted by internal concerns of the self.

Thus, a telepathic person in listening mode may seem distracted, though other functions can proceed. In tune with the inbound message, the receiver's heart will beat in tune with the sender, and their brain be activated in similar places, so they are acting as much as possible as a single brain. During these modes, it is possible for the receiver to start sending, as they are in sync, on the same wave length, so to speak.

In general, and to a high degree, telepathy is something your DNA supports. Be aware that only a small segment of humankind can utilize telepathy to any degree. A small percentage of the population has an occasional telepathic experience, rare, sometimes once in a lifetime. Of this small percentage, a smaller yet percentage, perhaps only 2% of the whole population, have any ability that they can muster at will. In that they share DNA, share brain wave hardware, so to speak, family connections are the most common. Twins and family also share experiences, which also increases occurrences.

Telepathy also occurs during sleep, highly common, which is why many humans conclude they have prophetic dreams. They are merely reaching out, during sleep, when they are breathing slowly and not highly oxygenated, and chatting with others who have knowledge. Prophecy is often simply a logical guess, based on many facts not generally known to the public. The prophet may be simply putting together information gained from many others, and arriving at the logical conclusion!

Holding your breath, to increase carbon dioxide levels, helps, which is why the Hindus prefer mountain tops for meditation. Carbon dioxide suppresses interference, noise, from other body and brain functions, so the body and brain is in essence drugged. Likewise, learning to trust your senses, if you think you are in contact, rather than reject them as silly thoughts, can help you make full use of what ability you have.

Telepathy bears with it more than information. It also carries emotion. Those who use telepathy to deliberately gain intelligence or to stay in communication with others know this well. If someone is nauseous with fear, this will come across along with any intellectual plans or knowledge. Experienced telepaths learn to disconnect, in such situations, and return later for communications. Even if you have not been aware of it, you have been in telepathic contact with many people. Group formation is not an accident. Beyond being guided by the visitors, contactees find each other's wave lengths from group meetings on space ships, and have many planning sessions ongoing even when not in physical contact with each other, thus. What such an open channel provides, beyond information, is stray emotion that is on the rise in the general public! Learn to differentiate this from your own thoughts, your own group's plans, as this will increasingly be a problem you encounter.

Telekinesis

Many physical forces in nature are not visible to man. The wind swaying trees in the distance, magnetic fields snapping magnetized objects into alignment, and even the forces of gravity are invisible to man. That man could move objects with the force of his mental focus is only considered to be in the realm of the supernatural because it happens rarely and not in a controlled manner which would allow scientists to study and record it. The phenomena is not a controlled phenomena in humans, in spite of what some yogis claim. Man is not structured to allow willful telekinetic abilities, and that they happen at all is due only to latent abilities that get briefly triggered, usually accompanied by a burst of anger.

In 4th Density, the ability to levitate oneself or move other objects is present and is a skill that can be honed. This is a factor of the intelligence that is either present naturally in the species available for incarnation to entities who have graduated to 4th Density, or is genetically engineered into species who will be so incarnated. Just as telepathic thought processes can be focused toward a target, the brain waves that enable levitation or movement of objects can also be focused. The mechanism is not one currently understood by man, but is one of hundreds of physical forces similar to the forces of gravity and repulsion. Essentially, a flood of these energies is focused beneath the object to be levitated, and if the object is to be moved, unevenly so. A moved object is essentially levitated slightly so that friction is removed, and then tipped in the direction desired by slightly more levitation on one side.

Remote Viewing

Remote viewing, refers to the attempt to gather information about a distant or unseen target using paranormal means or extra-sensory perception. Typically a remote viewer is expected to give information about an object that is hidden from physical view and separated at some distance. The term was introduced by parapsychologists Russell Targ and Harold Puthoff in 1974.

Lest anyone be confused, what is termed remote viewing is simply telepathy, a natural and fairly common occurrence among mankind and the animals who call the Earth their home. Telepathy is intrinsic to life, but only about 10% of the human populace has enough native capacity to take note of it. Those with native capacity soon learn that they can anticipate phone calls from friends, anticipate and guard against personal attacks, and seem to intuitively understand what their loved ones need and want. The government has never failed to use telepathy to accomplish whatever they might consider their ends, but after observing the seamless way aliens could work together, without a word spoken, the issue got hot. As MJ12 was in those days heavily dominated by the CIA, they took up the topic and infected the goals of the operation with their own twists.

Remote viewing under the CIA's auspices was not done to simply garner intelligence on legitimate government security concerns, it was used to invade privacy, secure blackmail material, assist break-ins and thefts, amuse agents who wanted to snoop for personal reasons, and keep tabs on rival government agencies. When the operation failed to curtail enemy actions due to a complete lack of awareness of enemy plans and failure to predict, it ostensibly was shut down. As with all bureaucracy enclaves, it sought to perpetuate itself by reinventing its goals. Remote viewing would become a handy disinformation tool, impressing the public with what might seem to be an ability to read minds, and thereafter spreading disinformation as valid facts garnered through telepathy. To ensure a gullible public will believe, the remote viewing track record is supported by information supplied by the CIA.

Where brain functions are localized close to the data stores, the chemical paths and links that constitute memory and the potential for thought, these functional mother lodes cannot be mined without the greased lightning that is the communication substrata. Brain wave are but a symptom of the process, whereby the brain, as an organ, hums to itself. Think of the choir, where all warm up with the same musical scales—synchronicity. But the true musical potential is where the choir, open throated, strikes harmonious chords. So how does the brain hum and harmonize, and what does this have to do with communication? This music is not chemical but the result of chemical interactions, which result in a variation on electrical energy. Electrons are not the only particles involved in electrical current. There are hundreds of subatomic particles that constitute electric current. The motion of this energy is in wave for the same reason a body of water has waves. For motion to occur at all there is pressure and release, then bumping and reaction. And how does this assist communication? Once the choir is humming, the voice of the soloist is complemented. She finds her note more surely when the basso is striking a chord with her. She swells to a high note more confidently when the altos are coming behind her, to cover her gasp when she runs out of breath. They are a team, the choir, and so are your brain's various frequencies. They all occur at once, but are noticeable at different times because of the dominance. Listen carefully, and you will hear the full choir.

Brain waves

The brain wave differ because they are supporting different parts of the brain. Not this spot which when poked causes a sound to be heard, or this spot where when poked makes a finger twitch, but throughout the brain. They are different because they serve as a communication support for entirely different processes. The Delta wave, noticeable only during coma, are basic only to those parts of your brain which run the body. The basic processes, like digestion, heart beat, temperature control, blood pressure, and reaction to gross stimuli like a direct punch to the stomach or a match to the finger tip. Fish and worms have Delta. Theta, evident during rage, is basic to the animal's reaction to dire threats, where blind rage is the only hope and sometimes a savior. Theta controls muscular control, focusing the resources of the body such as nutrients in the blood to the muscles and parts of the nervous system on alert. It is more than the chemical assist that comes from adrenaline. It directs the nervous system to forget all else, and concentrate on the fight. Poltergeist activity sometimes is related to Theta activity, and not by accident, as the mind is mentally as well as physically throwing things in order to survive. Alpha is the brain wave belonging to that part of the brain that deals with scope, spiritual as well as physical. It pieces it all together, makes sense of it, or tries to, and listens to the subconscious, where the real story is always recorded. Meditation is done in Alpha, and hypnosis, and sleep, where dreams emerge. All this deep understanding of the nature of the world is resisted by yet another part of the brain, that supported by Beta wave, considered the brain wave of the wakeful and alert, intelligent human. Beta supports the physical existence of humans, by processing what the senses perceive and sharing this with the rest of the brain. Beta is grounded. It wants not to know of the deeper meaning, of connections, or what the spirit knows, it wants only to be here and now and can't be bothered with all that other nonsense. The Beta brain helps a creature get through the day, find enough to eat, and escape the flood or fire. It says, in essence, no time for day dreaming now, we've got survival to worry about. That's why the Alpha brain takes over at night, when the creature is safe, and has time for such nonsense as the riddles that the Universe presents.

Brain Capacity

It is often stated that humans only use 10% of their brain capacity. This is nonsense. If the brain evolved in response to need, why would it then turn off and idle? Surely the world of today is more demanding of the brain than past eras, so if anything all parts of the brain should be engaged, and they are.

We map the brain as best we can, documenting reactions noticed during brain surgery and capacities lost as a result of brain damage. We thus know some of the jobs the brain performs, but are puzzled by all that gray matter that seems to have no function. Then there are the cases of remarkable performance where the human brain seems to be virtually absent, as in the cases where an encephalitic infant develops into an adult with apparently normal capacity. Part of the human brain maintains the body functions, as is evident when brain stem injury occurs above the nerves to the heart and other organs. Life stops. But these parts of the brain are older, at the base of the brain, and do not involve the larger and newer sections of the brain to any degree. We are also aware that we can live quite well with only half a brain, right or left side, as long as a complete half remains. As with many vital organs, evolution favored the specimen who could survive the loss of one. Thus dual eyes, dual ears, dual kidneys, dual lungs, dual limbs, dual testes and ovaries, and dual brains. While whole, they both function, and thus both halves of the brain are hard at work as cooperative team members, communicating via the connective mass between them.

If a human can survive losing half a brain, and an encephalitic can function with a minimal brain, then is not there excess brain capacity? This assumption is based on the apparent normalcy of humans functioning with diminished brain size. The humans walk, talk, laugh at jokes, remember to brush their teeth—apparently normal. However, as most consider it to be amazing that these individuals are not in a coma, they seldom move past astonishment to check for full capacity. A woman with only one ovary still ovulates every month, as each ovary has more than enough eggs, menopause occurring due to timing out rather than exhaustion. A single lung or kidney maintains the body under normal circumstances, but under duress a lack of capacity manifests. Just so, where diminished brain size allows the individual to learn and learn well those routines called upon regularly, when asked to stretch the lack of capacity shows up.

Each complex concept is built from many mental building blocks, and each of these building blocks likewise is composed of many parts. Children piece these building blocks together, bit by bit, piece by piece, and eventually get to the point where they can structure abstract concepts.

Diminished brain capacity allows the afflicted person to laugh when others laugh as laughter is contagious, especially when one wishes to belong. Do not small children laugh along while not understanding the joke? Diminished capacity does not allow one to create a joke beyond the slap-stick, nor does it allow one to build an abstract concept where one has not already been constructed. Thus, the brain damaged can continue old functions where the connections and structures have not been lost, but time stops for them where new abstractions must be constructed. Too many washed out bridges, so the destination is never reached. Abstract concepts, intuition, long range planning, adaptability—this is what all that uncharted gray matter is supporting, and it is not idle.

Autism

Autism is a disorder of neural development characterized by impaired social interaction and communication, and by restricted and repetitive behavior. These signs all begin before a child is three years old. Autism affects information processing in the brain by altering how nerve cells and their synapses connect and organize; how this occurs is not well understood. It is one of three recognized disorders in the autism spectrum (ASDs), the other two being Asperger syndrome, which lacks delays in cognitive development and language, and Pervasive Developmental Disorder-Not Otherwise Specified, which is diagnosed when the full set of criteria for autism or Asperger syndrome are not met.

Autism, as childhood schizophrenia, has the brain chemistry affected, just as adult schizophrenia does—an excess of this chemical, a lack of that chemical, etc. Just as the homosexual lifestyle can affect the brain development, can affect the hormones released, the decision by the child's body to be insane, to withdraw, can affect the developing child's brain, which is so very plastic. Fever disturbs chemical relationships, chemical bonds, breaking them and thus allowing normal brain development for a time. Regular heat treatments may result in the treatment of autistic children, in an attempt to change the course of the disease, but this will prove futile in most cases.

That auto-immune factors have been found in some mothers, where their bodies are attacking the fetus brain, is not surprising, as in autism cases the mothers are often tense, under stress, the setting that causes childhood schizophrenia in the first place. Auto-immune disease is due to a heightened immune system, as allergies are, so the fact that the mother is reacting to what her body might consider a foreign substance from the fetus is not surprising. This reaction in the mother can also teach the fetus to react in a similar fashion. The fetus brain cells, attacked, break down into pieces, each viewed by the developing fetus as a foreign substance as the clues that the cell is whole are missing, disrupted.

Autism on the rise is not a manmade affliction nor related. This increase is related to inbreeding, among those with similar propensities. Obsessive individuals do not feel comfortable among those with high emotions and spontaneity. They bond, befriend, and spend time with others who like a regimented life style. Repeatedly intermarrying, this then becomes a dominate gene, and expresses.

Gifted Autistics

The human brain under normal circumstances displays but a small portion of its capabilities. The true range of any one capability is disguised by the need to enlist many capabilities at once, hundreds, in fact. Like a traffic cop handling the flow of traffic on multiple intersections, all with differing rules and timing and speeds, the normal brain activity interrupts any given thought process so that it barely starts before it stops. If, on the other hand, the traffic cop has but one lane to manage, there would be no interruption, and a vehicle on that road could start and not stop until at its destination. Therein lies the reason some autistics appear incredibly gifted. They have but a single traffic lane clear, from beginning to end. Those autistics who entertain more traffic, whether this is evident to those observing them or not, appear to be simply autistic.

Thus, an autistic who has never spoken or glanced at flash cards held before him or lifted a spoon or fork to feed themselves may be able to sit at the piano and play a complex piece, having only had the opportunity to observe an experienced pianist play that piece a single time. Likewise, autistics who have integrated the digital or binary or any other type of number system can compute as fast as a calculator or computer the results of equations that require thousands of steps, as long as those steps do not require more than one traffic lane. Complex concepts, involving multiple traffic lanes, receive the same blank, apparently uncomprehending, stare from autistics that is their normal response.

Language

Specific areas of the brain play a role in spoken and written language. Language involves higher order sensory areas and higher order motor areas. Auditory areas are involved in the ability to interpret language as meaningful. Motor areas are involved in the ability to produce the specific combination of Sound Vibratory complexes that compose a given language and which are meaningful to any native speaker.

The human animal appears to be unique in our ability to communicate symbolically through language. Other animals may communicate in very subtle ways. Language is believed to be instinctual in our species, an instinct. Skeletal specializations have been identified in our earliest hominoid ancestor that allowed for speech. This suggests that language arose at the dawn of evolution.

Regarding the origin of the various human languages spoken, the hundreds of languages lost over time, and the dozens now spoken, none came from the stars. There are some which grew, over time, from the Anunnaki visiting from Planet X, but these would not relate to the ancient Sumerian or Vedic languages often assumed to have a relationship to the language of the visitors. The language spoken by these large, human like, aliens is very guttural, and would sound like a series of grunts to us.

Where humans think of language as their premiere communication vehicle, right up there with symbols and pictures but able to support a precision beyond any other vehicle—most misunderstand the mental process in the physiology of the brain required to communicate in words or any other such abstraction. When the toddler says "dog" in reference to the big fuzzy hulk he has been nuzzled by, whom everyone else is calling "dog", he has made Connection One, entity. When the toddler says "Johnny go potty", connecting two such Connection Ones together with a Connection Two, activity, he has made Connection Three—relationship. This goes on in increasing complexity to hundreds of Connections.

These Connections are not the same between intelligent species from different worlds, nor are they even the same among factions of the intelligent species on a single world. Our Earth has many such languages, and for us to assume that all such languages portray the same concepts would be shallow thinking indeed. There are concepts the aboriginals in Australia hold that they cannot communicate to others, as there is no equivalent in other languages. This is one source of communication glitches, where western thinking says, just give me the equivalent word, and taking the closest candidate, makes a statement that carries a quite different meaning than was intended. Language barriers are not just due to a failure of one party to memorize the vocabulary of another. One would have to be raised, simultaneously, in the two cultures involved, to truly translate.

Sleep Paralysis

Sleep paralysis is paralysis associated with sleep that may occur in normal subjects or be associated with narcolepsy, cataplexy, and hypnagogic hallucinations. It is a feeling of being conscious but unable to move. It occurs when a person passes between stages of wakefulness and sleep. During these transitions, you may be unable to move or speak for a few seconds up to a few minutes. Some people may also feel pressure or a sense of choking. Sleep paralysis may accompany other sleep disorders such as narcolepsy. Narcolepsy is an overpowering need to sleep caused by a problem with the brain's ability to regulate sleep.

Actually, sleep paralysis is not a disorder, but the result of affecting the human brain by an alien visitor in a way to induce a paralysed state. The state of paralysis is used as a means of calming and controlling potentially violent contactees and for convenience. The paralyzed state is very relaxing, and leaves no harmful trace. During travel between the Earth and a space ship, through walls, and at rapid speeds, humans often prefer to be paralyzed. In fact, this is a frequent request of the constant contactee, as they find they can rest. What is going on in the state of paralysis? At times the mind is aware, at times as though in a deep sleep. Some contactees report they can break out of the paralysis, with a shout or by force of will. The mechanism used to place humans into paralysis is simple, and does not involve technologies or manipulation of densities. An existing human physiology is utilized, something akin to the frozen state that possums take when frightened. Why is it that humans never play possum when aliens aren't around to induce this? Because this facility is deep within the reptilian brain, and not connected to the middle brain or frontal lobes. Humans voluntarily cannot reach this spot. But if one knows where it is, and knows what buttons to push, then presto!

Paralysis during contact has often been reported by those recalling their visits. If a contactee is anxious, fearful, likely to thrash about and injure themselves or their visitors, they are paralyzed. This is not painful, in fact is very restful, and is never resented. However, it can create confusion if not understood, when a rapid return to their pre-visit surroundings occurs.

A contactee picked up during a busy day will find themselves returned to the exact spot they left, but will be relaxed when this occurs. The sudden need to have their legs tensed under them will create a sense of falling, and catching oneself. This can create a sense, in the contactee, that their knees temporarily gave out, and is confusing.

Another often reported confusion is what is termed sleep paralysis. The contactee is returned to bed, as most visits are done at night, when missing time will not be noticed by a sleeping family. The contactee, hardly asleep when returned, finds themselves in the conscious stream of memory as suddenly waking, but paralyzed. After a moment, the trigger switch that was flipped to create paralysis releases, and the contactee finds they can move again. They are often aware, subconsciously, that a visit has taken place, and relate the two, as they should. However, the visit did not create paralysis, per se. This is akin to dust on the boots, after a walk, a remnant of the visit, only.

Big Bang

Neither Albert Einstein or Stephen Hawkins are correct in their theories on the origin of the Universe, although there are portions of both theories that contain some element of truth. The Universe is not inert, subject to pressures that cause it to explode or compress back into black holes. It is no more inert than your body. It is alive. When we speak of religion, and say we are all parts of the One, that we are within God, and that the Universe is within God, we are referring to this. The natural laws that seem immutable to you are functioning as they are because this is God's intention at the present time. Much of what you desire to learn will not be available to you until you reach greater spiritual maturity. It is not even on the platter during our next stage of development, 4th Density, the Service-to-Self or Service-to-Other consolidation stage.

Following a Big Bang, particular matter forms along the following lines. First, the explosion of matter from a Black Hole, which has grown monstrously large in the eons leading up to a particular Big Bang, is not even. No explosions are even, and all affect different parts of the matter they are affecting at different rates and times. Thus, particular matter coming out of a Big Bang is not even, all the same composition. Just as your Sun, which seems to be of the same consistency, is not homogeneous, and just as the core or magma of your Earth is not homogeneous, just so the matter coming out of a Big Bang quickly becomes differentiated. There are literally millions of factors affecting what a bit of matter will become, and the sum of these factors affect how that bit of matter will interact for it's existence until the next Big Bang it finds itself entangled in.

Particles that are fluid, on the move, are by their nature loosely coupling with other particles. Humans are familiar with the coupling that occurs in atoms, the nucleus surrounded by whirring electrons, for instance. Other particles couple in predictable ways. What causes attraction and repulsion between particle types? We will use a common example to explain, as the concepts can get complex. Magnetism happens due to the continuous flow of magnetic particles, a type of the particle you call electrons, but this magnetic flow is not consistent everywhere. It is concentrated where a break in the pattern of electronic orbiting a nucleus allows a mass escape. What are they escaping from? An over-concentration of whatever it is they are made of! In the case of magnetism, magnetic particles are escaping from a press of other magnetic particles, since they couple poorly and seldom, they are readily on the move.

All matter seeks a level of homogeneity, and can never achieve it as it is by its nature, coming out of the Big Bang, non-homogeneous with the other particle types. Likewise, attraction is in essence an escape, misinterpreted by the humans who have termed it otherwise. Gravity is nothing more than the effect of returning gravity particles drifting back into a gravitational giant after having been ejected in what we would equate to a laser stream of particles, which burst through rather than push at whatever is in their way to escape. Why do they drift back, and is this not an attraction to return to the gravitational giant they just recently left? As odd as it may sound to those unused to these concepts, these gravity particles are indeed running away from an environment they find clogged with matter composed of element they themselves are heavy in—what we commonly term the Dark Matter that fills to void of space. They crowd back into what is for them a lesser field, the core of gravitational giants, where they are repeatedly ejected due to this very crowding!

Big Bangs affect vast areas, a fact which man is aware of as all he can see seems to have been affected by the same event. But prior to clumping and becoming dense, matter is more homogeneous and fluid and thus each atom more easily influenced. As in all events, something came first, and as in all events, something clumps or moves first, and this sets the stage for what follows. Explosions send things in all directions, so motion outward is rapid and has no brakes other than the matter that lies behind it. Thus, matter on the periphery has push behind it, and matter closer to the center of the Big Bang finds it has no push behind it, eventually. The center is a void, and thus nearby matter, from the inside out, starts returning to this void to escape the crowding it finds everywhere else.

As this matter returns, it interacts with other matter, attempting to equalize crowding. Even in homogeneous matter any motion, even on the sub-atomic level with a single atom on the move, creates a zigzag due to the pressure created when moving in any direction. Motion become circular, to develop a spin, when any inequality on either side of the zigzag occurs, such that the zig or zag is not simply back and forth, but takes a curve. During the time it takes for galaxies to form from a Big Bang, matter is fluid for a long enough time for the motion in the center to affect and establish the motion throughout. This takes the form of individual or local dramas, here and there, but the synchronized spin of galaxies stands as a mute witness to the fluidity of the spurt coming out of a Big Bang, and to the extent to which what is called Dark Matter, which we have termed tiny matter, exists as a glue binding the Universe together in ways mankind little understands.

Centrifugal Force

Centrifugal force represents the effects of inertia that arise in connection with rotation and which are experienced as an outward force away from the center of rotation. In Newtonian mechanics, the term centrifugal force is used to refer to one of two distinct concepts: an inertial force (also called a "fictitious" force) observed in a non-inertial reference frame, and a reaction force corresponding to a centripetal force.

Motion is not a thing, immutable, unchangeable, eternal, once born at the start, as during a big bang or whatever, never to go away. Motion is not a thing, it is a result, a reaction, and as such it changes. Astronomers explain orbits as a balance between a straight line motion tangential to the sun and a gravity tug to the side, and assume that the forward motion is translated into a centrifugal force that never erodes as it is a thing. This looks good on paper, but examine the reality a bit closer and the contradictions and inadequacy of that argument emerge.

Each time an orbiting object corrects its straight line path due to gravity tug, its straight line path would be diminished in its intensity. Is this not the case in the all-too-familiar situation of having to put on the brakes when driving? The car is in motion along a flat plane, propelled continuously only as long as the foot is on the gas pedal. This equates to the forward or tangential motion of the planet. Should one brake simultaneously while still stepping on the gas, the car slows. This equates to the interference in the orbiting planet's tangential motion caused by gravity. Now take the foot off the pedal, and you do not have the same forward motion as before. It was not a thing, but a reaction, and now it is a reaction to the push caused by the foot on the gas while starting from the car's state of rest.

Just so, the orbiting planet requires a continual push, from something, in order to continue to move. Left without this push, the object would steadily spiral into the sun, and we would scarcely have had time to evolve into intelligent creatures pondering this scenario as the spiral would not take all that long! This spiral is what happens to Earth orbiting satellites, which are often kept aloft only due to a puff now and then from the jets built into them. Left alone, they spiral to Earth, the gravity tug affecting their forward motion each instant. The gravity tug is not strictly a sideways tug, as in all cases the planet's path is pointed away from the sun, however slightly. For any given instant moment:

1. draw a line representing the planet's straight line path,

2. draw a second line representing the path the planet is being set upon by the gravity tug, essentially a second tangent to the sun,

3. the angle between these two lines is the degree of backward tug that the planet is experiencing.

Thus, there is erosion in the forward motion, which is not a thing but a reaction. In order to keep the planet continuously revolving, there must be a push, and a push there is. It is caused by the swirling matter in the sun's core, which creates fields of influence such as magnetic fields that affect the orbiting planets to varying degrees depending upon their composition. Why do planets orbit all in the same direction? Is it by accident that this same pattern presents in all solar systems? Retrograde planet motion is the extreme exception, so the fact that planets invariably revolve in the same direction should be a compelling clue to anyone seeking an explanation for why planets continue to revolve.

Gravity

Gravity is the foundational force of absolutely everything. This means at all density levels, all dimensions. It is the "stuff" of all existence. Without it, nothing would exist. Even thoughts are based in gravity.

Gravity has many aspects and varies depending on the composition of the objects in question and their distance from each other. Gravity differs between objects of different compositions. Like compositions attract each other more, due to the compatibility of their makeup. They have no extraneous dramas to resolve. Metals figure heavily in this as a magnetic component enters into the equation. Where there is flexibility for the objects to turn, one or both will maneuver such that they are magnetically aligned. This takes time, however slight, and thus an iron ball may appear to fall more slowly in a vacuum than an object of comparable weight that has but a slight magnetic retention. Organic compounds also react to gravity in a different manner than in-organic compounds, and this is due to the complex bonding between the atoms. Bonding involves tying up the electrons, which are used as glue in that they are shared by more than one atom. Thus, organic material in general will not experience the interference that matter with free electrons does during a gravity attraction. Inorganic material in essence takes time out to shed or take on electrons, slowing its movement.

In general, the heavier an object, the greater the gravity force generated within it for another object. The gravity force is more than compounded, equivocally, but this fact is lost by those viewing the drama because most of the drama takes place within the object itself. Why would this not be the case? Why would matter only reach out to matter not contiguous, with its attraction, and not matter near at hand? Some call this internal gravity compression, but this is merely gravity working to pull each atom toward the greater bulk, which in the case of an orb, like a Sun or planet, is generally toward the center. As the force of gravity reaches in all directions, the larger or heavier object is emitting more of a come-on than a smaller or lighter object. When several objects are involved in giving each other the come-on, the contention causes all of the bodies to dither, but an equilibrium is established in accordance with the mass and composition of the objects and their distance from each other. Large bodies, such as planets, generate the repulsion force toward each other.

Gravity Flow

The flow of gravity particles is not unlike the magnetism model, but with several significant differences. In magnetism, particle flow is related to the shape of atoms, such as iron, which allow a flow to begin in the first place, and is related to the types of bonds these atoms commonly lock themselves in. Magnetic particles surge out of a break in the rhythm of subatomic particles such as electrons circling the nucleus, a surge which does not occur in other atoms that have a more even balance in their halo of orbiting electrons. Magnetism thus produces a field, with a flow, and this flow is discernible to the degree that one could almost imagine a river, watching magnetized particles on the river position themselves according to the flow.

Gravity particles produce a flow but produce no discernible flow, and have no irregularities in the pattern. Does the Earth not pull evenly from all parts of its surface? And if there is a flow, then at what point does the flow reverse, such that surface particles are pushed away? In fact there is a reversal, but the outward streams are propelled, with a force and at a speed so much greater than the downward drafts that this occurs over less of a surface area and without engaging the mass of the object. A laser of gravity particles, versus a floodlight upon the return. So why would the weight of returning particles be the only ones we are aware of, and why would we not feel the violent lift of the updrafts? The updrafts blast through, tearing a hole as it were, where the returning particles do not tear what they press upon, and so have the greater effect.

Gravity particles, in their motion, do not affect what they move against or through, the effect being in essence mechanical. The upward drafts push aside other matter, letting it return upon completion of the updraft, leaving no trace of the temporary tear. The downward push of gravity particles returning to the large mass they are attracted to, the core of the Earth for instance, spread out upon objects they encounter, taking some time to drift through these object and with a constant downward press during the motion of this drift. Thus, returning particles, due to the time they spend upon and within the surface objects, and due to their continual direction of motion, are a mechanical force that is stronger, overall, than the updraft of particles that quickly pass through the surface objects, essentially pushing them aside rather than engaging them.

The nature of this gravity flow is what determines the repulsion force. It is a complement of gravity only when large bodies are close to each other. The updrafts, when encountering a large body also exuding updrafts of gravity particles, hold the bodies apart. This occurs a distance from each other, as small objects such as satellites do not exude updrafts and if far enough from the surface of a gravitational giant such as a planet, find a down-draft and updraft of gravity particles in balance, what is called a zero gravity field, weightlessness. At this point the updrafts are still tearing through, but at a slower rate, so that a mechanical push upward is involved, and the down-drafts are more thinly dispersed over the surface as they work their way through the density of these objects in space. Large bodies, exuding their own updrafts of gravity particles, create a situation where their updrafts and the updrafts from another sun or planet bump against each other, creating a buffer and preventing the gravity masses from touching or even approaching each other except at great distances. Within black holes, the down-draft still exceeds the updraft, and thus the same rules apply.

Gravity Field

We, in our dealings with gravity, assume a steady force from a given mass. Our math lines up accordingly, with a larger mass having a greater pull, and our explorations off the face of Earth has not challenged this. In the last few years, we have found our probes not behaving according to gravity math, without explanation. And Recently, our probes have given us data to the effect that the shape of the Earth should have changed, per the gravity pull registered from the surface, but measurements do not support this shape change. What has occurred, to change the pull of gravity from the Earth to the extent that it is measurable from space? Our theories include changes in the core, as we cannot see any ostensible change in the shape of the globe. Gravity is a particle flow, with outshooting in a laser manner of intense gravity particle streams and a slow drifting back to the surface by the particles. It is the drifting back that creates the phenomenon of gravity, pressure downward, as the outburst goes between atoms and thus does not interact.

Gravity Particles

Gravity is particles, moving, just as magnetic fields are, and there is a polarization in gravity, which is the repulsion force. Before we discovered that magnetism was polarized, we discovered it as an attractive force. Metallic items stuck to the sides of magnetized rock—how curious. After centuries of digging about in this phenomena, we have satisfied their curiosity to the extent that we understand that magnetism is a force field, has a flow out from one pole and in at the other pole, that the Sun and some other planets are magnetized and line up with each other. They still don't understand the cause of this force field, or its nature. Magnetism is caused by a particle, in motion. What other explanation is there for a force that reaches out and affects another? Magic?

The bi-polar aspect of magnetism is only apparent when what occurs in nature can be countered in the laboratory. You force magnetized objects to do what they do not want to do—touch north pole to north pole or vice versa. Then you can observe the bi-polar nature. In gravity, you are seeing but one aspect in the positioning of the planets, and dealing with a phenomena that does not lend itself to easy experimentation. However, experimentation is possible, in space and away from the surface of the planet. The repulsion force fills the gap in some of our other theories where we have no explanation for Discrepancies of The Storm.

In magnetism, the simple flow of particles creates more than a force for alignment, it creates an attraction. The gap is filled. Like water in a stream, where flotsam eventually lines up in the center, evenly spaced, just so magnetized objects do not keep their distance when free to move. They approach each other, and attach like a string of pearls. Likewise the phenomena of gravity, where the desire to fill the gap causes objects to approach one another. It is only where this gap is overfilled, by the presence of two large objects coming near, that the repulsion force is expressed. There is no room for the flow of gravity particles, so the objects stay apart!

Repulsion Force

It is assumed that gravity has only an attractive force, and that the planets, in orbit around the Sun, are held in place by their momentum. Does this make sense? What caused the momentum in the first place? Children play with a ball on the end of a string, swinging it around and around their head. As long as the arm is tugging, the ball maintains its orbit, else stops. Why would the planets not drift into the Sun? Are the orbits all that swift so that centrifugal force is extreme?

The reason we are unaware of a repulsive force, also inherent in gravity, is that for this to become evident there must be a semblance of equality in size and weight, i.e. the mass of the objects, and freedom of movement such as exists in space, and lack of undue influence from other nearby objects. Objects on the surface of the Earth have none of these. They are infinitesimal in proportion to the Earth itself, and thus any repulsion the Earth may have toward a tiny speck on its surface is also infinitesimal. Proportionally, its all gravity, a one way trip. The object on the surface, pushing away, is overwhelmed by the Earth's gravitational pull, the attraction. The repulsion force is generated as a result of two bodies exerting a gravitational force on each other. In the case of a tiny object on the surface of the Earth, its gravitational pull on the Earth is scarcely noticed by the Earth. A gnat or mite. A nothing. Where the repulsion force has not been invoked within the Earth by any objects placed on the surface of the Earth, this is in play between the Earth and her Moon. The repulsion force is invoked between objects on the surface of the Earth, incessantly, but this is masked by the intense force of gravity the Earth presents and other factors such as surface tension or friction or chemical bonding so that the repulsion force cannot be recognized.

The gravitational force exists first. It is the static condition. The repulsion phenomena only manifests when the objects are of equal size, are free to move, and dominate the immediate environment. Where the repulsion force comes to equal the force of gravity by the time the objects in play would make contact, it builds at a rate that differs from gravity. We have calculated the force of gravity, which at first we assumed was equal for all objects but lately have come to understand is stronger for larger objects. We have formulas for the force of gravity which have proved accurate on the face of our home planet. These formulas are incomplete, and would not work as expected elsewhere, however. The repulsion force is infinitesimally smaller than the force of gravity, but has a sharper curve so that it equals the force of gravity at the point of contact. For experimental purposes, one would have to be almost at the point of contact for it to come into play at all, and this in an environment where other factors are eliminated or negated. To examine the phenomena, Earth scientists would have to set up a lab in space, far enough away from any planetary body so that free movement is possible. Place two balls in a cage. Put one in motion toward another. Microscopically examine the interchange. They do not touch. They do not bounce off one another. They do not touch.

Repulsion keeps suns apart, at the distance they are, or at least is a factor in this. The reach of the force of gravity is immense, as with the distance that light particles travel, but like light particles gravity particles on the move can be deflected. Light particles reaching man from across the galaxies have moved in essentially a straight path, unless being deflected or absorbed by something in its path. What is the drama that occurs when more than two gravity giants are in a vicinity, and why is it that binary suns are so common?

Gravity particles with a single gravitational giant in the vicinity float into the giant and spurt out, without conflict. At the end of a spurt, their desire to clump with their kind causes them to return to the nearest clump. This could be equated to light escaping from a Black Hole, where it is on the move but not leaving, rather returning. The fact that other gravity particles in the vicinity are returning is no small part in this, as those in the flow are attracted to one another also, so the particles at the end of a spurt find they also are moving toward the gravitational giant as a result of trying to move to gravity particles nearby.

When there are two gravitational giants of equal size, as in binary suns, the drama is joined by a dither point between the two. Gravity particles at the end of a spurt, or slowing in their exit due to reduced pressure as disippation occurs, find a mixture of streams going back to both giants at this dither point. Repulsion outbursts are intermittent, so at one time the dither leans more toward one giant where a return flow is ongoing, but at another time the return stream to the other giant is stronger, and a particular gravity particle switches to flow into and out of the other sun.

Where the suns are matched in size, they stay apart where the Repulsion Force keeps them, to the extent that their dance is dominated by gravity.

Gravity particles streaming in an outburst from a giant but not encountering another outburst from a nearby giant can move outward to a great distance. This is dependent upon the force with which they are expelled from the giant, giving them great momentum. At the same time, the single drama of each gravity giant continues, and any binary dance that has developed between balanced suns continues, so the particles escaping the area are those not caught in other dramas. Gravity attraction is a small factor in slowing the escape of matter ejected during a Big Bang, and bringing this together again during a collapse, ultimately into another immense Black Hole. Other subatomic particles are more significant in the dance between galaxies, however. Gravity dances tend to be a local affair.

Magnetism

Magnetism is the palpable, measurable effect of a subatomic particle not yet delineated by man. In fact, there are several dozen sub-atomic particles involved, out of the 387 involved in what humans assume to be simply the flow of electrons. Where electric current can be made to flow in any direction, the path of least resistance, magnetic flow seems to be very single minded. In fact, it is also going in the path of least resistance, as can be seen when one understands the path and what constitutes resistance for magnetic flow. Unlike electricity, which only occasionally flows in nature, the flowing sub-atomic particles that constitute a magnetic field are constantly flowing. This is the natural state, to be in motion. The path of least resistance, therefore, is to go with the flow, and the flow is determined by the biggest bully in the vicinity.

A single atom of iron, isolated, will establish the direction of flow based on the tightly orbiting electron particles, of which there are hundreds of sub-types. These tight orbits arrange themselves in a manner not unlike the planets around a sun, but the field, of course, is much more crowded. Given the fairly static number of these particles that will hang around an iron ore nucleus, the orbiting swirl may have a rhythm, rather than a steady hum. Put 3 groups of 3 into a cycle of 10 and you have whomp whomp whomp pause. Should the cycle, based on the nucleus and the electron sub-atomic particles it attracts due to its size and composition, be 4 groups of 3 in a cycle of 12, you would have whomp whomp whomp whomp. The steady hum of the second cycle does not lack a magnetic flow, it is just diffuse. The irregular cycle in the first example finds the magnetic flow escaping during the pause. Being attracted again to the best partner in the vicinity, the single iron atom, the magnetic sub-atomic particles will circle around, taking the path of least resistance which of course is on the other side of the atom from the outward flow.

Placing a second iron atom next to the first finds the two lining up, so the flow escaping during the pause of each goes in the same direction. This is a bit like forcing a second water flow into a flowing stream. Toss a stick into both forceful streams and you will see that the water flows are moving in the same direction as much as possible—the path of least resistance. In this manner the magnetic flow of the largest bully forces all else in the neighborhood to line up. Where the iron ore atoms are caught in an amalgam and not altogether free to shift their positions within the amalgam, the magnetic flow may physically move the amalgam, this being, again, the path of least resistance. For those who would state that magnetism is not a thing, as it can't be weighted or measured or seen, we would point to the child's trick whereby two magnets are held positive end to positive end. Let go and they move so that they are aligned positive end to negative end. What made these magnets move, if not a thing?

Particle Flow

Magnetic particles flow from the nucleus and back into the nucleus on the other side of the atom. Where the iron atom is among others in a fluid state, such as liquid metal when heated, the flow moves from one atom's outlet point to the intake point of another atom nearby, thus magnetized iron. We have learned to magnify and set the direction in this liquid iron by setting a strong magnet alongside, creating yet another magnet in the process. The magnetic cycle is described as 3 groups of 3 in a cycle of 10, or 4 groups of 3 in a cycle of 12. A cycle is a completed electron or other subatomic particle pattern around the nucleus of an atom. Equate the subatomic magnetic particles and their pattern, for simplicities sake, to sub-way trains leaving the central station to go out into the suburbs and then returning. Normally the train schedules are regular, continuous, but in some cities they become infrequent during the middle of the day or middle of the night, when there are expected to be few travelers. There may even be breaks in the pattern so that shift turnover can occur, or maintenance. Now, equate the flow of magnetic particles from the nucleus to the steady press of passengers, and assume a steady flow arriving at the central station. Assume that these passengers, like subatomic particles, do not care which direction they go in. If the trains are kept running at an even pace, there would at no time be an accumulation of passengers during one portion of the 24 hour day than another. The train loads would be equalized, or close to that.

Gravity acts in a mechanical fashion, failing to interact with all but a handful of sub-atomic particles, so being an independent particle on the move both the downward drift and upblasts push aside atomic structures in their path. The particle flow of gravity particles is rapid, and the interaction with other particles essentially mechanical, so the bulk of interactions is out from a gravity giant and back into that giant. The reason the updraft is faster is not only due to the pressure that occurs when a press finds an outlet, but due to the pathway that is arranged.

Like water spouting from a breach in a dam, this moves faster not only because of the pressure, but because the flow itself provides a type of vacuum behind it, sucking in what would fill that vacuum. The force of the flow keeps the atomic structures which have been pushed aside to the side, and this likewise allows the intensity of the updraft to continue until abated. Thus, the exit has a greater speed, while the entry spreads its mechanical press downward over a larger area, and for a longer time.

Subatomic Particles

At one point in the not too distant past humans thought of matter as a substance, like wood, water, air, or sand. Common folk, of course, deal with matter in this way still. In addition to matter, there was energy, like light or radio waves. Theoretical physicists concluded, based on the observable and measurable chemical, electromagnetic, and fractal qualities of matter, that an atomic structure existed. In those days the concept was simple, involving an atomic nucleus with orbiting electrons, but the concept has rapidly evolved to include dozens of theoretical subatomic particles, and since Einstein's theories have become acceptable, the concept of energy as being, in fact, just rapidly moving small bits of matter.

Humans are on the right track, but in detail they are not yet half right. For instance, humans are searching for a quark, a particle that would make their formulas work, where no such particle exists. The fault is in the formulas, not in the elusive quark. The formulas to be made whole by the elusive quark have invented the quark, which takes shape only to fill the void, to balance the equation. There is nothing wrong with this logic, this approach, when one bears in mind that the invented particle is only a theory, but where scientists go amuck is in claiming a subatomic particle real because it has leapt into their imagination. A bit of reality testing is required. The electron first appeared on the drawing boards of scientists, but reality testing followed theory in the development of electrical energy, so widely used in human society as to need no explanation. All this groping about to explain the workings of the little universe that exists inside each atom is made difficult by the nature of the study. The subject can't be seen, or measured, so the theories can't be proved. This does not stop theorists from arguing with one another, however, as the goal is heady. If one understands how the atom works, one could plot and achieve marvelous feats.

Humans are continuously frustrated by the limitations of their knowledge. Where the common man looks with awe at academia and scientists working in labs because they seem to understand how it all works, in fact it is no secret that they are all quite confused. The various departments in the average university could not sit down and discuss the smallest scientific statement without breaking into argument. The disciplines of science openly contradict each other! The confused student is left scratching his head, but is still expected to pay his fees promptly. Likewise, research labs proudly announce their successes, but bury their failures. No right minded financial backer or scientist would proceed to build something based on theory. Why? Because the theories seldom hold when experiments are run. Most scientific discoveries are made by accident, and that's a fact. The milk spills into the vinegar by accident, and now the vinegar is no longer sour. By accident.

So, how small is small? To put it into perspective, the electron, which humans now think of as one unit but are casting a suspicious eye toward and thinking may perhaps prove to be many types of particles, in a clump or acting independently, is composed of some 387 discrete types of particles.

Solar Flares

What is termed sunspots have long been recognized to have an effect on life on Earth—static on the radio, disrupted satellite transmissions, and some weather anomalies caused by what we would call tornado activity in the upper atmosphere due to rapid heating of the air there—but few of their effects are known. Solar flares occur when the core of the Sun reacts to factors it is sensitive to, just as the core of the Earth is increasing its activity in response to the approach of the 12th Planet. The influences that affect the Sun are not related to gravity or even to the Sun's magnetic field, which spreads far outside the Solar System, but to energy fields that man has yet to discover.

Gaseous planets and Suns, lit or unlit, do not have homogeneous cores any more than bodies with liquid cores such as the Earth. Humans tend to think of air or gaseous clouds or liquid pools as being homogeneous, but in truth heavier particles settle down, lighter particle rise, and other particles disperse slowly from their point of entry into the soup. The process by which the Sun releases light and heat also releases other energy, unrecognized by man. This process is not homogeneous, and thus buildup and release occur, just as weather disturbances occur in the atmosphere due to irregular heating and cooling. Any lack of consistency in a body's core has the potential of causing core rotation, as the components try to escape or approach that which they are repulsed by or attracted to in the neighborhood. Thus, the Sun's core swirls, and when lighter elements rush toward the surface their motion is not impeded by the gaseous surface and overshooting occurs—a solar flare.

The effect on Earth is in the realm of energy disruption, a surge of the various energy arenas that humans are aware of and others they are unaware of. Solar flares affect the activity of fish and kelp in the sea, in that water bends and deflects some energy rays and thus concentrates them. Just as humans find themselves more restless during a full moon, life in the sea is a bit more restless during solar flares—energized. Solar flares do not affect the core of the Earth, nor are they causing increased earthquake activity. This explanation by the establishment for increased activity in the Earth's core is to avoid mentioning the approach of the 12th Planet, and is easily rebutted. Have sunspots resulted in earthquakes in the past?

Light

Light is consisted of many different light particles. We ascribe the various colors to speed of vibration, the wave pattern high or low, long or short. The breaking of a ray of sunlight going through a prism into a rainbow of colors is thus ascribed to a change in speed or a modified wave pattern, as though a sub-atomic particle is forced to compact and squeeze in some invisible tunnel. Does glass have invisible tunnels they force light rays into, or the ability to hold light particles back so they compress? We speak of reflection or refraction of light as though it were an object bouncing, which sub-atomic particles do not do unless a direct repulsion occurs. Are light particles repulsed by the sub-atomic qualities of a silver backed mirror, such that they bounce? We ascribe the Auroras to an attraction by light particles to electro-magnetic particle, such that they dance, apparently, only at the poles, but balk at giving this attractive quality to gravity. The orange light that floods the sky at sunrise and sunset is ascribed to dust, of all things, with no explanation of why this spectrum is so affected but the other spectrums not. The huge size of a light emitting object such as the Sun coming over the horizon, in conflict with established human explanations, is rejected.

Why does light reflect from some surfaces, absorb into others, or change color when emerging from a prism? And what does this have to do with the obvious bending of orange/red light over the surface of the globe, as seen at sunrise or sunset? Is there a relationship? There is indeed. Some sub-atomic particles, a ready example being the many particles in the electro-magnetic arena, flow together, are attracted to each other, and are incited to move with each other by that attachment. We think of electrons as being one sub-atomic particle and have barely considered magnetism to be a particle flow, yet these particles number in the hundreds, and are not all the same in their behavior. Light particles, thus, are immense in their numbers, and the various wave forms with resulting color signature recognized by a retina only one example of the many. Do these light particles like to flow with one another, being attracted to one another in a similar manner to the electro-magnetic particles? Obviously.

They flow not in a straight line, not in a wave form, but in a twisted cable form. They swirl about each other in a double helix pattern, neither escaping or bonding, in perpetual motion. These helix strands likewise coil around other strands, often in a criss-cross pattern depending upon how much distance the strands need from each other. Like electrons that chase but do not catch each other, and magnetons that are likewise always in motion and cannot stand crowding but likewise desire to clump, this is a dance that never ends. Where electrons can be caught and reside around the nucleus of an atom, and magnetons are normally humming about the nucleus of an atom, the flow of light particles is an aberration of their normal abode, within and around a nucleus. They emerge when this nucleus is flooded with particles and are pushed out due to crowding, due to pressure which crowds them or the application of heat which is in and of itself a particle flow, or the introduction of some bonded atoms that act as a catalyst for change. Light can be produced by friction, heat, emerges during fire, or by chemical mix, as we know.

When the twisted coil is on the move it, as a group, moves in the direction that the particles were flung in by the explosion of particle crowding they were escaping. The direction of the light ray. When many particles are involved, this is considered by man to be white light, all color spectrums included, as the colors emerge when this white light is separated into its parts. The helix coils have another direction, other than the overall direction, which is straight ahead. They are moving away from, and back toward, the pairing particle in their coil. Depending upon the particle, this coil is tight or loose, with a wide wave length or short, and involves many other coils tightly attracted to it or few. When encountering other matter, these particle pairs find themselves in a marital crisis. One of the pair wants to have an affair with the other matter encountered, lingering, while the other partner cannot because the pair would then be too close, too crowded. Thus, the particle lingering forces the partner to exit the coil, suddenly, in the manner of their original expulsion from some comfortable atom into a light ray direction. The exiting particle of the pair leaves, likewise, in a direction that creates the least crowding for it with the other helix coils they are entwined with.

Thus, white light entering a prism of glass finds that the most vulnerable particle to an attraction affair lingers and expels its partner first. These particles having peeled off, the next most vulnerable particle is exposed to the adulterous attraction of some quality of glass, and lingers and expels its partner. This process proceeds until there is only the helix coils of those light particles that are resistant to attraction, by being so tightly bound to the coils, and resist the flirtations of nearby particles inherent in the glass. Some material simply absorbs the light rays by preventing them from leaving, an affair that has become a new marriage of sorts. Some material is so attractive that the lingering partner and expulsion proceeds at an almost violent pace, considered a complete reflection surface. When light coils pass over a gravity giant such as a planet, it is not the long distance call of a lover they are listening to when they curve toward that giant, it is the flow of gravity particles flowing back toward the planet. These are encountered on the way, slow the flow of those parts of the coil that are most attracted to the gravity particles, causing them to separate from the other parts of the larger intermeshed coil. This separation is not violent or sudden, as adjustments are made during the bumping process so the coils of those particles wanting to pull along with the flow of gravity eventually find themselves outside of the larger coil, and free to move in independent helix coils. Thus where white light, or light in color spectrums not susceptible to gravity particle attraction, move forward in their straight line path, the red spectrum light susceptible to gravity pulls toward the gravity particles drifting back to their gravity sink, and are bent thus, toward the gravity giant.

Red Light

Just as electrons are not a single particle, but composed of some 387 particles, light is likewise not composed of a single particle, as hundreds of particles are involved in the phenomenon called light. This should be obvious, as light spreads into the colors of the rainbow, and the behavior of red light, the Red Shift, is not ascribed to other colors in the light spectrum. Red light, and light close in the spectrum to red light, bends more readily than other particles in the light group. This can quickly be determined by the common man if he compares the rising and setting sun to other objects he sees in the sky.

The rising and setting sun are huge, compared to their appearance at mid-day. This is due to the light rays which have been bent and would otherwise escape to the side, being bent back by the atmosphere so they enter the viewers eye as though coming from a large orange sun. Do these rays not get bent in this manner at mid-day? They do, but there are several factors which make the phenomena apparent at dawn and dusk

The angle between the viewer and the Sun at dawn and dusk are such that more atmosphere is passed through, thus more of bending of the red spectrum rays is done.

Competition from other light rays is reduced so the red spectrum rays are predominant, and the eye thus registers them rather and having them drown out and supplanted by a different image.

At mid-day, when the Sun is overhead, red spectrum light from the Sun is bent to the side so that any reaching the eye of the viewer seems to be coming from another object, not the Sun, and is thus discounted.

Dark Matter

The so called Dark Matter is just tiny matter—Greengolden or Subatomic Particles are tiny matter. Humans have have yet to see Greengolden because it is too little for their and instruments as of yet.

The particles of tiny matter, like bugs, are more numerous as they get smaller. Humans are always horrified to see how many mites there are in a speck of dust. Mites are everywhere, and should one have the guts to count, the number of mites in the room would be vastly greater than the number of silverfish or cockroaches. And, of course, the number of bugs in the room vastly outweighs the number of humans. Such is the situation in the Universe. Man saw the planets, e.g. humans in the room, and registered their personalities. This happened early on. Then man become aware of the energy that composes the solar wind, and light rays that come from distant galaxies, e.g. visible bugs in the room, and registered their personalities. This happened recently. However, humans are not yet aware of the galactic tiny stuff, e.g. mites, and thus don't have a very important piece of the puzzle in place.

Before humans became aware of the planets, and their relationship to the Sun, there were all kinds of strange explanations for their motions. Before humans became aware of the energy paths in the galaxy, there also were all kind of strange explanations for what seemed to be the erratic nature of the greater Universe, which bobbled and glowed and winked, behavior which was most often ascribed to the gods or one's own misbehavior. Now scientists are dealing with the larger, visible planets behaving toward one another like something else is there. You can assume this to be a massive amount of tiny matter. The stuff the Universe is made of, elemental particles that are not moving, are not clumping, and thus do not form mass or register as energy.

X-Rays

The particle flow that manifests as X-Rays are used by man to examine the human body as well as numerous applications in industry. They move slowly, and are easily stopped, and thus lodge in bone rather than pass through, painting a picture of bone by this absence. X-Rays are observed by man occurring in bursts in the Universe, bursting from suns and from the Sun in their solar system in, at times, distinctive patterns. What is causing this natural outburst? Humans find they can excite X-Rays by the same process they excite electrons, and at times find them in association with lightning. Heat and light particles are also so excited, as well as magnetic particles, but these particles can be found in nature without the presence of electron flows too. There is cold light, and heat without light, magnets without an electric charge, and electricity without magnetism or heat or light. They are independent particles, though they may be affected by the same processes.

If X-Rays can be stopped readily by bone yet pass through soft tissue, then their bond with atoms is readily available, and common. This is not the case with the particles that compose what man understands to be electrons, which leave readily and go on the move, such that children can excite them by scuffing their feet across a rug. Where heat particles can be excited by mechanical means, rubbing, light seems to man to require a chemical change such as occurs in fireflies or fire. That all these particles are excited by the same process that gets electrons on the move should not be surprising, as electron particle flows are an onslaught.

Electron flows affect the chemistry of the material electrons flow through, at least temporarily, by changing the electron sharing that is a component of atom bonding. Thus light particles are produced in association with electrons.

Electron flows affect the density of the material electrons flow through by this means also, at least temporarily, so that atoms can approach each other more closely. This crowding of the affected material forces heat particles to move until they find a less crowded home.

Magnetic particles flow through atoms, happily flowing in and out of a single atom unless forced to move from atom to atom by an irregular electron shell around the atom that funnels them. Thus iron ore in nature may or may not be a magnet, depending on the fluidity of the iron atoms. Electron flows create this irregularity, at least temporarily, thus the phenomenon of electro-magnetism.

So can man assume, as some have, that the Sun reverses its magnetic field periodically, because during solar cycles the X-Rays emitted by the Sun are emerging from a different spot on the surface? As X-Rays are so readily stopped that pictures of bone and even the placement of soft tissue can be made, why would they not be stopped by the placement of matter within the swirling core of the Sun? X-Rays are generated homogeneously within the Sun, as is heat and light, but the particle flow is affected during its passage outward by the matter it encounters. Is this not the case with light, which can be readily bent during its passage through water or blocked entirely by walls? Is this not the case with heat, which likewise can be blocked or absorbed by material, or transmitted and passed along? This is certainly the case with X-Rays, which announced themselves to mankind by their very ability to be readily stopped by almost any material put in their way!

Magnetism particles are not so readily stopped, however, and thus the phenomena of magnetic fields surrounding planets and their suns, reaching far beyond this to encompass the solar system and more. Man finds he can create confusion in a magnetic field, at least temporarily, by deflecting the flow of magnetic particles with other magnetic particles. Take the confusion away and the magnetic field has re-established itself. Magnetic particles are on the move, constantly, where other particles are not so fluid or mobile. Thus, the Sun's magnetic field is independent of any other particle flow, and persists in a constant state regardless of how other particles may be blocked or directed within the Sun.

Black Holes

So dark that light can't escape, so dense that all matter going in gets compressed into imperceptibility. What is a Black Hole, and does matter go in and never come out? All is relative, and the denseness of Black Holes only seems so to us because we have no basis of comparison. Also, as nothing seems to be coming out, we assume this is a bottomless pit of some sort, and frankly fear black holes. They serve a purpose, however, and are part of The Storm's plan for renewing the Universe. A big bang refers to setting the clock back on a part of the Universe, a type of refreshed state. The big bang requires something to bang from, and that state is what the Black Holes are accumulating.

Do Black Holes consume all that they catch in their snare, and is there any escape? Black holes are voracious, but proceed slowly. So slowly, in fact, that one can escape without even making haste. In addition, Black Holes do not capture souls, as developed entities can float out of them, being of a lighter substance. However, Black Holes do accumulate the substance of which souls are composed, when this has not formed into an entity, and remains loose and undefined. This is packaged into the whole, and spread uniformly during the big bang, and thus the process of worlds forming and evolving begins again, in a small part of the Universe.

Black Holes are grand scale Service-to-Self. Black Holes are a natural force reflection of Free Will consciousness pattern of STS. Notice that Black Holes are located at center of spiral energy forces, all else radiates outward. All in creation is just that: a radiating wave. Inward to total nonexistence. Universe is all encompassing. Black Holes are final destination of all STS energy. Total nonexistence balances total existence. What is total existence? The Storm. As long as you exist, you are of The Storm.

Reflection is regenerated at level 1 as primal atoms. 1st density includes all physical matter below the level of consciousness. Seventh density is union with The Storm . . . it is timeless in every sense of the word, as its "essence" radiates through all that exists in all possible awareness realms. There is only one The Storm, and that The Storm includes all that is created and vice versa.

Time

Time is linear only in our minds. It is not what it seems. Our sense that time is linear in the Universe is supported by what we observe: clocks running in seeming synchronicity; planetary movements that are predictable; testimony of other people you interact with to the effect that they, too, observe the same time passage as you do. However, time is only a factor, and as such when put into mathematical calculations can be affected along with the other factors. The Universe is such a huge mathematical calculation. In the portion of the world that you live in, the factors are stable enough that the time factor never varies enough to be noticed. This makes you think that time is a fixed factor. It is not fixed.

Other factors are involved and can be modified so that the time factor changes.

One cannot travel into the future, except in small increments, hours at most. Leaping into the future is a fiction. One can travel into the past, as that is a trail marked in the substance of the Universe, strands that can be unwoven and rewoven, a rope that stretches back endlessly. The past has markers. Grip points. It has been built, where the future has not yet been built. A phrase much in use is the Time/Space Continuum. This is simply a way of stating that matter may be in a different place, or space, depending on the time, and that matter leaves a trail, or continuum, over time. The Time/Space Continuum can be equated to strands, being woven and unwoven, which more exact as it refers to the webbing that takes place.

What would happen if one went back along a particular strand, unraveling it, and changed the circumstances surrounding the strand. Would it change the present, and thus the future? Yes, but not to the degree depicted in the movies, where people wink out like lights and buildings disappear from sight and even from the memory of all. How could it, as each of these occurrences is composed of numerous strands, weaving in multiple directions, and it is impossible to change them all. What in fact occurs, should one be allowed to go back in time and make an alteration, is that the future is essentially unchanged. Essentially, as there has been change, but due to the interweaving of other strands, this is muted. The Council of Worlds strictly administer time travel, as should one go back in time and really work at it, changes would begin to appear.

An example might be a child, born with a genetic defect. Should one go into the strands leading to conception, and change the DNA strands affecting the defect, the child would be born whole. However, each second that ticks past the moment of conception complicates this, as the webbing of strands has begun. At three months the fetus has strands of interplay with the mother's host womb, her blood and DNA makeup, such that simply changing the makeup of the genetics of the fetus is not enough. A panoply has been set in motion, and defectiveness to some degree will still present at birth. At three months, to effect a cure, one must also delve into the strands that weave into the mother's system, the womb, even out into the environs surrounding mother and child. It's all quite complicated. So if this is the case, why would the Payuumian Guardians bother to watchdog time travel? Where changes are subtle, they can effect the overall when done systematically. As intense as agendas are, masters over minions could set them about a never ending routine that would affect what has been written, trip the balance enough to be worthwhile to the master.

Time is a natural function, and inserts itself into the workings of Nature just as sub-atomic particle flow does. Time is a function, and can be modified in what you might term equations such that what has occurred can be unraveled or raveled forward, predictably. Where time is a factor, occurrences that a given entity has experienced are linear. This is why time seems linear to us, as to us, our experiences occur in this manner and we have no basis to assume that time is otherwise.

Time travel, into the far future, or into the past such that changes are made, is a fiction. Traveling back does not allow one to affect all manner of things that might be tenuously related to an occurrence. There are so many other threads that weave forward, in other directions, and all these bind, like a web. Time travel is governed by rules set by the Payuumian Guardians. These rules affect all 4th to 6th Density entities in the galaxy. Specific requests must be made to the Payuumian Guardians in all cases. Approval is given in only the most stringent of cases, where need has been demonstrated and alternatives are poor or non-existent. Time travel is never used to manipulate the outcome of events. This would cause never ending chaos, as one could imagine.

Moving forward is basically a prediction, speeding up the time factor so that predictable events happen early. This creates a record in the physical matter that participated in this exercise, nothing more. Future travel must then be unwoven, undone, so the record is not in the physical anymore, just recorded in the soul. Thus, you might be moved forward to a meeting, to experience what would likely happen, but then be returned so that your body does not remember, but your soul does.

Time is but a factor in equations, which allow to travel back in time, when permission is granted on rare occasions and for good cause, and travel forward on even rarer occasions. The motion and placement of objects, sub-atomic or otherwise, are predictable, given their placement and motion and composition at any given point. Time travel involves reversing or accelerating activity that is predictable. This reversing or accelerating involves forcing the issue, as under normal circumstances objects proceed based on their surroundings.

Factors are involved in the forward progression in time, and a lack of these ingredients results in a backsliding in time, as though falling into a vacuum. The forward press or falling backward is due to direction of flow, of what is just another element in the Universe. Nothing is by chance, and no motion is without reason or cause. To you, in your perception, time is steady in its progression, but when the press of this ingredient is stopped, or diminished, what had occurred telescopes back in activity that is the reverse of what just occurred.

The grip points are places in the orderly arrangement of particles where it's possible, in essence, to set sights and target, and stop during a time travel, else the unraveling of what has occurred would continue unabated. One does not start on a journey without brakes! Grip points are predictable points where particles are structured in a particular pattern. This could be equated to so many ticks of the clock, or so many clangs of the hour bell, as the periodicy is predictable and reliable, like clockwork.

Time Flow

Time is but a factor in equations, which allow to travel back in time, when permission is granted on rare occasions and for good cause, and travel forward on even rarer occasions. The motion and placement of objects, sub-atomic or otherwise, are predictable, given their placement and motion and composition at any given point. It is possible to reverse-engineer objects, their atomic structure, and their motion and placement a moment ago. Time travel involves reversing or accelerating activity that is predictable. This reversing or accelerating involves forcing the issue, as under normal circumstances objects proceed based on their surroundings.

Factors are involved in the forward progression in time, and a lack of these ingredients results in a backsliding in time, as though falling into a vacuum. The forward press or falling backward is due to direction of flow, of what is just another element in the Universe. Humans are unaware of this element, as the steady forward progression is something they consider a given. Nothing is by chance, and no motion is without reason or cause. In our perception, time is steady in its progression, but when the press of this ingredient is stopped, or diminished, what had occurred telescopes back in activity that is the reverse of what just occurred.

The grip points are places in the orderly arrangement of particles where it is possible, in essence, to set sights and target, and stop during a time travel, else the unraveling of what has occurred would continue unabated. One does not start on a journey without brakes! Grip points are predictable points where particles are structured in a particular pattern. This could be equated to so many ticks of the clock, or so many clangs of the hour bell, as the periodicy is predictable and reliable, like clockwork.

The Cosmic Time Field

One of the basic principles on which the mechanism of bounding is based is: If one property of a power (any power) of something is bound, then all properties and powers of this something will be bound. In infinity the finite cannot exist. To limit the Infinite Vibe it was sufficient to bind only one of the perhaps infinite number of possibilities. Because if only just a little something were to be formed in the nothing, the nothing would be altered and cancelled irrevocably, then the complete finity was a fact. Or, if there were just the three-dimensional rotating time-field as a possibility of the primeval atom in the infinity of the nothing, then the finite was a fact. This atom-field needed to be a force-field of infinite strength, the carrier-field, to counteract the Infinite Vibe, the cosmic time-field.

Counter-balance

One of the functions of the carrier-field is time-synchronization by which the cosmic counter-action and therefore the nothing can be. Matter and energy cannot exist on its own in the nothing. The principle of time synchronization is given:

1. Time is only relative, it is motion or propagation in relation to at least a second motion of time.

2. The cosmic law of counterbalance dictates that the second time has to counterbalance the first time. So time can only exist in relation to a second exact opposite direction of time (running backwards in relation to our time).

3. Time exists only through the presence of atoms or matter. Then the backward-running time can only exist through matter in which the time propagation is opposite, running backwards in relation to us

(antitime matter). Anti-matter or reflection antimatter may exist in our universe with an opposite electric charge with respect to our known reflection matter.

4. Because neither matter nor energy can exist on its own in the nothing-another quantity of matter of opposite properties must exist which is exactly similar to that in our universe. This balance of matter and energy is so accurate, that one surplus atom is impossible.

The Time-synchronization Field

The law of counter-balance also applies to time. The time direction is opposite and the time velocity is equal to ours. Time is the propagation of vibrations of the atom. Then the atom vibrations in the universe and the anti-universe are equal and opposite with respect to the timelessness. This is only possible if these times are caused by one field (time-field).

The definition of a field is: If an event occurs, because another event takes place somewhere else without a mechanical or visible connection between these events, then these events are caused by a field. Time-synchronization occurs according to this definition. The atom vibrations in our universe are exactly similar, because the atom vibrations of our anti-universe occur despite the enormous difference in time and without any dissipation of energy. It is about 30 billion years since the occurrence of the Big Bang between the two universes.

The law of conservation of counter-balance is causal to the law of energy conservation in every universe. Each universe is a closed system and without energy dissipation outside itself. The amount of matter and energy once created remains constant. A loss of energy is impossible, because our time-bound energy propagates forwards, while the time-bound matter and energy of the anti-universe propagate backwards in time. These universes are separated by a time-barrier through which no communication nor transfer of life is known.

Timeless Wave

The question is how the field functions maintain the time-synchronization of the atom-waves between the universes separated by billions of years. It is only possible if the synchronization stands still in time, but exists simultaneously in all the time elapsed since the beginning of the Big Bang, as well in all the future. A timeless wave does not normally move in time, the amplitudes of the field propagation—alternate forwards and backwards in time. Time synchronization is the principle by which our universe catches every forward-moving amplitude and the anti-universe catches every backward moving amplitude of one and the same timeless vibe.

Interference

So far the function of time-synchronization of the carrier-field has been considered. Now the medium of conserving and maintaining the timeless wave into eternity will be discussed. It is the infinite force-field carrying all matter and energy.

We are at the moment of the flash or Big Bang, the moment at which the infinite primeval vibration limited (transmuted) itself to the carrier-field. This mechanism of blocking is well known and based on the principle of wave interference. Interference is the action or counter-action of two or more waves. If the wave-propagation is opposite and parallel and the frequencies of the wave equal, mutual amplification or attenuation of the intensities of the wave is possible, depending on the phase relation between these waves.

If the phases are opposite and the amplitudes of the wave are equal, total quenching is possible. This is the principle of the binding of infinity. If an infinite wave manifests itself in one time-direction, automatically the equivalent absolute counteraction is created which counter-balances the infinity, allowing the nothing to be.

The infinite primeval wave blocked itself at the moment it created itself and so it never existed in reality. It was in fact a transmutation of infinity; the transmutation of the infinite vibration of infinite amplitude and frequency to a carrier-field of infinite strength, which blocked itself by interference.

The time-bound waves

The primeval wave blocked itself in a three dimensional time-axis system (propagation directions) by interference, and trans-mutated to an infinite, timeless, immobile force-field. How could the bound timeless waves exist, which synchronize our universe?

It is an error of thinking to suppose that by quenching the Infinite wave—all finite waves were also canceled. It is just the opposite. A vibration with infinite frequency is not a vibration in reality. The infinite prevented the vibration, because a vibration can only exist in the finite. As soon as infinity was removed, the prevention disappeared and the real bound wave was a possibility. It is the carrier force-field although of infinite strength and energy density which gets its finite value due to interference quenching. All timeless waves are as it were encapsulated in infinity and therefore indestructible. However "belonging" to infinity and not bound by time themselves, they create time forever, they are the eternal ripples on the static, unchangeable and loss-free field of infinite strength. Because of this, all time-bound waves such as light, radio-waves or gravitation, exist in space without any loss and it is the empty space in the universe, which is the non-modulated structure of the carrier-field.

Time and Space Dimensions

One time-axis counter-balances only one direction of time propagation of the Infinite Wave. In infinity all possibilities of vibration exist and therefore all time-propagation directions. The question is, could infinity be limited by just one time-direction and one co-existing propagation direction going the opposite way?

One way to answer this was already given in the previous paragraph, in which it was stated that the energy time-flux of the primeval wave of two universes is not a closed system. Another plausible answer can be by simply reasoning. The atom is causal for the time—and space dimensions, due to its time-creating properties, already mentioned. The space-creating properties are easy to understand, because the atom takes up space. It is three-dimensional in space and therefore it creates space in three dimensions. If all atoms were two-dimensional then the whole of creation would have been on a plane and space would not have been more than a flat or curved plane. Our time-space is no more than a bound part of the nothing—being filled with matter or energy. Anything that space distinguishes of the time—and—dimensionless void, is caused by atoms or energy. If atoms have three space dimensions, then the timeless waves creating the atoms also have three dimensions.

1. The timeless primeval atom-field has three time dimensions.

2. The timeless waves could not be bound by only one time-axis, but must necessarily have three time-axes.

3. The timeless atom-field should consist of a three-dimensional rotating field of infinite strength, which is attenuated of itself by interference. It conserves the law of cosmic counter-balance of the no-thing. The atom of such a rotating field structure has six time-axes, but in principle these six axes can always be reduced to three time-dimensions, no further reduction is possible.

Energy Waves

Humans are aware that water can appear to be a solid, when ice, or on the move, when a liquid. They are also aware that water can take up less space when cold and more when warm, having what is called heat energy stuffed into the same space. This same concept can be applied to what we call matter and energy, energy simply being particles of matter on the move, and on the move because other particles have been stuffed into the same space. The space becomes crowded, and just as circulation in water is caused in part by temperature differences, just so subatomic particles go on the move to equalize the crowding at the atomic level.

Coming out of what is called a big bang, particles are sent in all directions. All are on the move. As explosions are never of equal strength throughout the explosion, some particles are moving faster than others, and when parts of the explosion collide with other parts, toward the center of the explosion or on the periphery, circular movement begins to equalize the pressure. After a time, what results is what you see in our Universe. All this moving about never settles down, nor does it diminish or increase, overall. Mankind has noted this tendency and termed it conservation of energy. Even within forming black holes movement is still occurring, and in accordance with the patterns outside of black holes.

Within atoms, subatomic particles are bound to the nucleus just as planets are bound to a sun, due to the presence of a subatomic particle which behaves in a similar manner to gravity particles in a solar system. Forever on the move as rushing to the center of the nucleus creates crowding that is relieved by an outward flow, these particles soon find themselves on the periphery in an uncrowded state and cycle back into the nucleus due to their inherent attraction of each other. What all matter seeks is a static state where all parts of it are equal and none moving, like a jell, but as equality in matter can never exist due to inherent differences in particle size and nature, motion never ceases. Always trying, but never succeeding.

Subatomic particles move in a wave pattern due to this attraction and desire to equalize crowding. Vacillation, repeating patterns, occur often in Nature, as the buildup is followed by the gradual drop, until a threshold is reached and the buildup begins again. Pulsing is found in the cosmos, dying stars pulsing, the heartbeat pulsing, and in like manner subatomic particles pulse. The same mechanism is at play, and it has absolutely nothing to do with the rate of release from a source, the current fanciful explanation by scientists. Space, even the space within an atom, is scarcely empty, but is filled with all manner of tiny particles as yet undiscovered by man. Many particles or groups of particles follow a path less than straight, as on their way they create a pressure in front of them, causing a sideways zig, only to find they again create a pressure in front of them so must zag. This path is not chaotic, but becomes a zig-zag line in a straight direction, as the pressure created on the left encourages the zig to the right, and the pressure created on the right finds a void on the left where an essential vacuum has just been created. The zig-zag perpetuates itself.

Mankind assumes that a single particle is moving in a wave, with one particle following another obediently in a kind of waving line. Yes and no, this is what occurs. If only two particles were on the move, moving in the same direction as the reason for motion was the same for both, then they would institute a dance much as binary stars institute. They are interacting with each other while simultaneously being affected by many other factors. These two particles move apart from each other to reduce crowding but then find they are attracted to each other when crowding has been reduced and move toward each other again. Wave action is not at all what humans presume, a single wave motion. It is a multiplicity of motions, all at the same wave height and width and frequency.

Albert Einstein

Albert Einstein was a Wanderer, and thus, understood far more than he relayed to mankind. Einstein spoke to mankind within the confines of their ability to digest at the time. Great minds, visiting the primitive, lose the audience if they speak well beyond the capabilities to understand. His audience was in the main scientists, and they were able to barely comprehend what he was addressing as is. Now long after his death he is deemed a genius, and correct on many matters. Should he have drifted further afield, he would have been dismissed utterly. He withheld information, deliberately, as do all visitors to a 3rd Density world where spiritual growth is incomplete and high tech weaponry would give the self-serving too much of an advantage. Mankind thus got a glimpse, and a glimpse only, into a world they will not be allowed to explore at this time.

Einstein's theory of relativity, which challenged the accepted notion that matter and energy could not transmute, was violently resisted. In putting forth his Unified Theory, Einstein was not attempting to explain to everyone's satisfaction the factors that govern the motion of planets and sub-atomic particles. He was attempting to wrap his relativity arguments with additional material, so that his critics would have to shut up and think. Thus, the Unified Theory is incomplete, as it was never intended to be otherwise. The theory as presented by Einstein was lacking several key pieces, and without these pieces no progress is possible.

Mankind's attempts to discover a theory of everything, one that would fully explain and link together all known physical phenomena, and predict the outcome of any experiment that could be carried out in principle is a Folly. To men, unifying gravity with electromagnetic, weak, and strong interactions would form a theory of everything! How can there be a theory of everything that is completely devoid of Spirit which IS essentially everything?! And what about the other forces in the Universe? And what about the uniqueness of each creation? Are we so naive to think that the four forces that man has identified are everything? Hardly. As was stated that other forces mediated by subatomic particles, men is not aware of, are more significant in the dance between galaxies then gravity which tends to be a local affair.

Space/Time Curvature

Regarding the amusing notion that space/time curves. This theory gained credence recently as we have been able to track cosmological events more closely with the Hubble, and noted that the perimeter of an explosion curved slightly as the event progressed. Light rays are not immune to gravitational influences! They are formed of particles, just as what we call matter is, and as such is subject to the same influences. The Auroras are visible light shows and are not at all related to magnetic fields but are caused by the bending of light subjected to the Earth's gravity. This would be visible elsewhere around the globe, but except in the dim light near the poles does not stand out. Why would particles move in a curve?

We should keep in mind that what they see of the Universe reflects:

the original situation, such as a nova, that caused the light to escape and move in the direction of Earth.

the direction those light particles were pulled in, by gravitational influences

Light bending

What we on Earth do not see is:

light that was not moving in a straight line path toward Earth, to begin with

light that was pulled so that it was no longer in a straight-line path toward Earth

Scientists are aware of this and identify places in space where no light seems to escape as Black Holes. Nevertheless, as curving space/time seemed like such an interesting possibility among those hoping to always prolong their stay at the trough the taxpayers are obliged to fill, NASA talked it up. They know better but don't want the paychecks to stop. Follow the money . . . Also if the theory was true, Planet X would have never orbited around its two foci, so the theory, in essence, predicts it's own demise. Light particles want to fuck, as every particle does, and are on the move looking for a place to fuck. Light will bend to avoid particles of gravity. These particles are bursting out of a gravitational giant, to avoid crowing, in hopes for finding a better place to fuck (just as light particles), only to find out that it's surrounded by Dark Matter everywhere which is even fucking worse, so it's forced to turn back to the its gravitational center. Light will only have sex when it's absorbed by a Black Hole. This is equivalent to unity with The Storm, for the light. Light finally finding it's source. The total darkness which is the source of light. Nothing is everything. And everything is nothing. Nothingness is infinity. And infinity is nothingness. The Storm and The Thunder.

Wormholes

Wormholes do not exist. They are a figment in the imagination of scientists, just as the mythical quark, which is supposed to make their formulas whole. Faced with perplexing natural phenomena, such as occurred during the Philadelphia Experiment and temporary disappearances that occur naturally in sites such as the Bermuda Triangle, human scientists have invented a term for what they imagine are portals. The portals, in their thinking, can be either man-made or a natural occurrence. They reason that if the phenomena, a temporary and partial density switch, occurs naturally in the Bermuda Triangle, then it should occur naturally in space. They speculate that perhaps this is the magic that allows aliens to transport themselves long distances in what seems to be a flash. Humans take advantage of natural phenomena, such as updrafts for the flight of gliders or orbits to position satellites, and they reason aliens have done the same.

The switch to 4th Density from 3rd Density is not that simple, and does not occur naturally here and there within 3rd Density in any but temporary situations. The density confusion that occurs in the Bermuda Triangle is fleeting, and is caused by the compression within the core of the Earth. Does this line up with what is out in deep space? Wormholes simply do not exist.

Anti-gravity

In physical cosmology, astronomy and celestial mechanics, anti-gravity is the idea of creating a place or object that is free from the force of gravity. It does not refer to the lack of weight under gravity experienced in free fall or orbit, nor to balancing the force of gravity with some other force, such as electromagnetism or aerodynamic lift.

Electrogravitics

Electrogravitics is a hypothesis advanced by Thomas Townsend Brown and Brown's subsequent extensive experimentation and demonstrations of the effect, the term was in widespread use by 1956. The effects of electrogravity have been searched for extensively in countless experiments since the beginning of the 20th century; to date, other than Brown's experiments and the more recent ones reported by R. L. Talley, Eugene Podkletnov, and Giovanni Modanese, no conclusive evidence of electrogravitic signatures has been found. Recently, some investigation has begun in electrohydrodynamics (EHD) or sometimes electro-fluid-dynamics, a counterpart to the well-known magnetohydrodynamics, but these do not seem a priori to be related to Brown's "electrogravitics".

Electrokinetics is the term used by Brown for the electrically generated propulsive force. Fran De Aquino has published calculations explaining the cause and proper harnessing of the electrogravitic effect. No widely accepted experimental data yet supports these calculations.

Zero Point Energy

Zero-point energy is the lowest possible energy that a quantum mechanical physical system may have; it is the energy of its ground state. All quantum mechanical systems undergo fluctuations even in their ground state and have an associated zero-point energy, a consequence of their wave-like interaction.

Because of the uncertainty principle, every physical system (even at absolute zero temperature) has a zero-point energy that is greater than the minimum of its potential well. Liquid helium-4 (4He) remains liquid—it does not freeze—under atmospheric pressure no matter how low its temperature is, because of its zero-point energy.

Cold Fusion

Cold fusion is a False Promise, the dream of those who would have endless cheap energy readily available. Energy is released from fusion or fission, but in both cases this is a barely controlled explosion. Nuclear bombs are the extremes that we are aware of, and when trying to harness this energy we sit on the virtual nuclear bombs called nuclear power stations, tinkering with the controls. How would it be that cold fusion would be possible, among the molecular components on Earth, yet not already fused? What is to stop the process? Are the molecules waiting for the signal from eager scientists? Fusion happens under great compression, not on the benign surface of the Earth, and anyone asserting otherwise in only looking to fuse hard cash to his wallet.

Metamaterials & Invisibility

Metamaterials are artificial materials engineered to have properties that may not be found in nature. Metamaterials usually gain their properties from structure rather than composition, using small inhomogeneities to create effective macroscopic behavior.

The primary research in metamaterials investigates materials with negative refractive index. Negative refractive index materials appear to permit the creation of superlenses which can have a spatial resolution below that of the wavelength. In other work, a form of 'invisibility' has been demonstrated at least over a narrow wave band with gradient-index materials. Although the first metamaterials were electromagnetic, acoustic and seismic metamaterials are also areas of active research.

Crystals

Crystals are said to possess magical properties. But If magic is all we've ever know, then it's easy to miss what really goes on. Crystals capture and focus Cosmis Motherfucking Energies. These Prophecies cannot be seen and measured. Ask any Protoss and they will tell you that the power of crystals is capable of affecting the passage of Time. Time now has come, Dar-Kunor awaits. Not all crystals have this effect, and a cerain size must be attained before any effect occurs. Humans in the 3rd Density of The Storm are not allowed to be in possession of such technologies. Crystals of any size or shape are not having any significant effect on mankind or on the Earth at the present time. Crystals have been used as a communication booster by the Anunnaki who are currently mining gold on Phobos (the largest moon of Mars).

There are crystals which work upon Cosmic Energies coming into the Mind/Body/Spirit complex. There are crystals which work upon Discrepancies of the Spirit/Mind complex; there are crystals which balance the Discrepancies between Mind/Body complex. These crystals are charged only through purified channels.

Quasicrystals

Quasicrystals are structural forms that are both ordered and nonperiodic. They form patterns that fill all the space but lack translational symmetry. While crystals, according to the classical crystallographic restriction theorem, can possess only 2, 3, 4, and 6-fold rotational symmetries, the Bragg diffraction pattern of quasicrystals shows sharp peaks with other symmetry orders, for instance 5-fold. The term and the concept were introduced originally to denote a specific arrangement observed in solids which can be said to be in a state intermediary between crystal and glass.

Newton

For a tiny object, such as a climber falling from a cliff, there is not the distance from the Earth to create a situation of equality in the updraft and downdraft of gravity particles. Satellites are placed at a distance by your astrophysicists in order to have them behave in accordance with Newton and sustain their distance, supposedly based on velocity? What Newton has included in his math, without knowing, is the balance of updraft and downdraft of gravity particles. In point of fact, if an object was not at the distance to create this balance, it either plummets to the gravitational giant or is subject to attraction by another passing or nearby gravity giant. Thus, those orbiting objects you examine are there to be examined because of the updraft and downdraft balance. Thus Newton and his followers negated the influence of gravity particles in his orbit equations, as all they saw seemed to fit!

Vectors

Humans place too much importance in what they call velocity vectors, which are only a mathematical representation. The motion of asteroids or comets or planets is there for a reason. It is not, as humans frequently assume, because the motion was set in place for some reason long ago and things just follow. The motion does not rule! The motion is a result, not a primary force. Humans treat motion as though it stood alone, outside of all other factors. What caused the motion? All motion is a result, from the acorn dropping from a tree, or the wind swaying branches as air masses move to equalize, to the motion of the planets in their orbits.

The breeze that bows a young sapling over a bit will not keep that sapling bent when the breeze stops blowing. Just so, an object may even be stopped in its course, but only for a moment. Then on it comes, impelled by the same factors that impelled it in the first place, as its motion was determined by the gravity pull of objects nearby, and those objects have not moved! An object will be motionless in space for one of two reasons. An object in the absence of gravity from outside influences has no reason to move at all, and is still only because there is no call to do otherwise. It does not have inertia, or a reluctance to move. Objects have inertia when they are caught in the grip of a gravity influence, and most often in the grip of several gravity influences. Therefore, when undertaking the study of motion, limiting the examination to the object and its speed is only effective when all other factors hold steady.

Mathematical Proof

Humans have a catchy phrase regarding relationships—which came first, the chicken or the egg? Well, of course it was the chicken, who gradually evolved to encase young in a shell long before it evolved to become a chicken. First came dropping the young into a water bed, as fish and frogs do, so the chicken's precursor came first. Humans treat mathematics much this way, expecting the world to line up with their math when the math evolved to describe their world. Starting with simple counting schemes, mathematical descriptions became more and more elaborate as they were endlessly adjusted until they described yet another aspect of nature. When math is used as a tool, and its origins understood, then when a particular model placed upon a natural phenomena does not fit there is no conflict. The mathematical model is understood to be the problem. However, just as there is confusion about the chicken or the egg, most humans lose sight of what came first. They insist the math is sacred, and stubbornly refuse to deal with the discrepancies this approach produces.

Mathematics, for some, has become a religion.

Mathematics builds upon itself, so that concepts put into place are continued and never discarded. Formulas that reasonably describe a situation when measurements are crude are never discarded, but are held up as standards to be disproved and defended. Creativity in math is nil, so that brilliant insights such as Einstein's are held to ridicule rather than discussed. Thus it is that mathematics are burdened with the absurd as well as the insightful, and thus regularly miss the mark. The Zetas are frequently asked what is wrong with human math, or how to do it right. Frankly, the right math will not be discussed, as this might put mankind on paths they are not yet to trod. As to what is wrong, we would suggest a simple exercise. Face problems with a completely fresh mind, and ploy the math you think would solve that. Compare what you have placed on paper with the traditional math. What differs? What about the traditional math forced it into the tradition? We predict you will find that a long history of being passed forward, regardless of worth, has placed certain formulas into mankind's mathematical view of the world. Would you allow yourself to be treated as the doctors of yore treated patients, by bleeding and starving or opening the head? Are women in labor to die screaming rather than undergo cesarean? Are doctor's not to wash their hands because infection spontaneously generates and germs do not exist?

Mathematical proofs are not "proof". Mathematical proofs only demonstrate that the numbers resulting can be lined up with each other. In fact, this can be assured if one just ensures that the component pieces, in the formulas, are all from the same grab bag. In other words, if one is building a toy city with lego building blocks, one can get everything to line up if all the lego blocks are of a similar size or multiples of this size. To make this all line up, just throw out anything that doesn't fit. This is, in fact, what humans do with their mathematical "proofs". When something doesn't fit, they substitute another lego piece, one from the proper grab bag, and then get smug. They haven't proved anything. They've only gotten their math to line up, and they're not so good at that either. Contradictions are running side by side at the major universities, with the students asked not to question so the professors can continue to be smug. Just pay your tuition and shut up.

Ephemeris

Ephemeris are mankind's best efforts at predicting the behavior of comets. They take into consideration the direction and speed of a comet, when first sighted, and apply math that has proved true of previous comets. Most of the time this works. When it does not astronomers tell themselves a variable came into play, such as the gravitational pull of a nearby planet or that something internal within the comet caused it to behave in an abnormal manner. The ephemeris are assumed to be correct. They are not. Humans have backed into their formulas for explaining the motion of the planets, and gravity on the surface of their planet. They tried one theory on after another, until one seemed to work most of the time. Then they congratulate themselves on arriving at the ultimate answer, which will stay on the pedestal until it fails to answer some physical phenomena, new to their arena.

The human understanding of Orbital Physics is based on what they have observed. They backed into their understanding, their mathematical theories, based on what they had seen. Thus, when they plot the orbit of an object tracking in a familiar manner, they plot it reasonably well. This does not mean that the math is accurate or correct. It only means that their descriptions, up until now, have worked in the main. We are not saying that human equations fail to predict comet orbits. We say the base understanding of the full comet orbit is incomplete. We say the theories about where comets come from is incorrect. We say the explanation of why comets don't all go into the Sun is wrong. If the mailman comes by each morning about 10:00 o'clock, the child may make up any number of complicated theories about why and how the mailman's route is as it is. Then, when the mailman arrives the next day, on time, the child congratulates himself.

Ephemeris assume, first, that comets are attracted to the Sun, are aiming for it, but miss. What nonsense! Why do they miss? Did the Sun move out of the way? Where a planet the size of the 12th Planet is likewise aiming for the Sun but misses because of the repulsion force, smaller comets do not have the required mass to invoke a repulsion force in the Sun. Small comets miss because they by nature contain elements that are sensitive to the solar wind, and can no more come close to the Sun than can mankind walk forward into the full force of a hurricane. Is this not a form of repulsion force? It differs as the repulsion force is invoked in both parties involved in a potential collision, and the comet's sensitivity is a drama played out only in the comet. Essentially, elements within the solar wind push the comet away, keeping it at the distance it maintains from the Sun. Why does the solar wind not so push the Earth and other planets, or the debris in the Asteroid Belt? It does so push, but the planets by their size resist and the debris in the Asteroid Belt does not have the sensitivity that comets do. This is one reason, in fact, that they remain as debris and do not become comets.

Repeating Comets

Repeating comets are attracted to the Sun, are heading for it, but miss due to the same sensitivity to the solar wind that causes their dust clouds and gasses to blow away from the Sun. Humans assume that tiny particles will be more affected by the solar wind than larger particles, but this assumption is wrong. If this were the case, then how to explain the Asteroid Belt, which has trash of all sizes, seemingly unaffected by the solar wind. A small object may lose its velocity faster than a larger object, due to the gravitational differences, but the effect is the same when they are sensitive to the solar wind—they are pushed away. Comets that hit the Sun have, through repeated trips around the Sun, lost enough water vapor so that the balance of their composition weighs against repulsion by the solar wind. In short, they've lost their protection. They come zooming in from outer space, but this time, they don't veer out, they collide. In fact, comets close their orbits, coming closer and closer to the Sun, during this process.

Where a repelling force exists, such as the solar wind against a comet, the comet will veer out upon approach and as it gains speed coming into the Solar System, veer in again. The increasing speed of comets allows them to push past their sensitivity to the solar wind, to some degree. Thus they have a quick trip around the Sun while held at the distance where they are essentially getting a blast of wind they cannot proceed against.

The solar wind is steady, its change incremental, as with every measure closer the intensity increases by a similar steady measure. The length away that the comet maintains is not explained by an analogy such as a car hitting a brick wall or a diver entering the water or even a man walking into a hurricane. The comet is slipping to the side as it approaches, going in the direction of least pressure, of least resistance, while still aiming for the Sun. The point where this balance is reached is dependent on the speed of the comet, which increases steadily the closer it gets to the Sun, and the intensity of the blast from the solar wind. At every point along its orbit, these determinators are at play. When out in space the comet's pace is relatively sedate, and thus slides to the side rather than approaching the Sun directly. When it enters your Solar System the reverse is occurring—the speed effect overcoming the solar wind push, so that the comet curves toward the Sun, but always these two factors are at play.

Quite clearly some comets are periodic, as they appear regularly after a set number of years, approach from the same direction, turn around within the Solar System at the same place, exit the Solar System in the same direction, and give the same predictable appearance. But comets that have a long period have been documented in the past in a manner that leaves much doubt. Where astronomers within this very millennium assumed the Sun orbited the Earth, just how accurate can their records have been? And how does one know that a previous comet is returning, even when it approaches from the same direction? Is it not possible to have more than one comet with the same track through the Solar System? Humans are barely out of the Dark Ages, and if honest would admit that they are guessing. Do they have these comets marked? Do they have an accurate basis of comparison? What are they judging on, the pencil sketch made by someone in antiquity?

Humans think that because mankind spots comets as they loom into range, announcing themselves by outgassing as they enter the Solar System, that human scientists know where the comet has been, and know what its orbit has been. They do not. They can't find these tiny dark specks when they are out in space. When they catch sight of them, the comet orbits are already taking into account their sensitivity to the solar wind. This curve starts well outside the Solar System, a fact known by astronomers.

Humans think that a comet's orbit is maintained by its momentum. Of the factors affecting a tiny comet that approaches the Sun, the force of its current momentum is not dominant. Any child who has thrown a ball and watched it drop toward the Earth as it sped along its trajectory can sense this. Archers allow for this in attempting to hit their target, aiming above the trajectory to account for the drop. Momentum is an effect, not a cause. What caused the momentum if not gravity. A ball thrown in space, where there is no gravitational influences nearby, will continue apace, but a gravity pull behind its path will slow it down. When a comet is leaving your Solar System, it is heading at an essentially straight line away. Gravity behind the comet slows it down, and thus the momentum disappears.

Humans see but what is essentially the end result of a comet's orbit, or at least that portion of the orbit that involves the Sun's gravity. The tiny comet, dark until it enters the Solar System where it flares under the influence of the Sun, cannot be located by humans while it is out in space. They assume that the orbit is broader or at least as broad, when out in space, as that seen when the comet becomes visible. It is not. As we have explained in detailing the 12th Planet's entry into the Solar System, comets aim for the Sun, and if influenced away from the Sun by any factor, adjust their orbit away from the Sun. Then, as they near the Sun and, caught in the grip of this giant's gravity pull, accelerate, the increasing speed allows them to come closer. Humans only see that part of the orbit where the initial adjustment away from the Sun has already occurred. They see but half the picture.

The human argument that the long orbit can be determined by the angle of entry, the parabolic curve, is therefore absurd. Some long period comets have several foci, and some only one. Just how does blind man, peeping up from a planet he cannot leave, looking out from a Solar System he has never left, know how many foci this or that comet has? Since a parabola and even an ellipse smoothes to an essentially straight line, how do they know how far that straight line goes before a turn around is effected? They do not. They are guessing.

Statistical Analysis

Humans have a saying, that one can lie with statistics, because numbers can be manipulated to support any argument. If one wants to demonstrate that the populace is not starving, one adjusts the threshold where starvation sets in. If the numbers run up on one group don't look so good, pick another group. If the average is too low or high, go for the median and arrange to discard the high or low end. Statistics, done honestly, can make a statement like no other, but done dishonestly are deeply deceptive because the readership believes the numbers have been run up honestly.

In an era of increasing distress, governments want the statistics on the homeless, the unemployed, and the uninsured to appear healthy. Likewise, corporations wishing to lie to consumers or to their stockholders discard the unpleasant from the computation and hope no one looks too closely. However, they are likewise being increasingly challenged. What was included? How did you arrive at these figures? The squeeze is on. An easy out in these circumstances is to make the formulas more complicated. Then the common man can't understand and the factors can be argued endlessly. One trick is to factor in a null, a zero, as a theoretical possibility, when no such possibility in fact exists. Another trick is to hop through the data in intervals, taking a summation of spot testing, rather than a summation of all the data. If hopping through the data with one interval doesn't give the desired results, try another interval. All in a day's work for the dishonest statistical analyst.

Spontaneous Human Combustion

Humans tend to think of fire as occurring at a high temperature, as when the process is going full bore this is indeed the case. But what of the moment when combustion is first starting, when sunlight is warming chemicals or a match is being dragged across a surface? High temperatures are not required to start the combustion process, which is but a chemical process, though high temperatures most often result. Many chemical reactions give out heat, a byproduct in excess during the molecular rearrangement. Many combustion processes also occur in a finite or limited manner, and may go unnoticed. A limited combustion process is what keeps the human body at 98.6 degrees, for instance—a slow burn.

Oxygen is present in the blood due to the bellowing action of the lungs, and fats or sugars present from stores in the liver or as a result of digestion. The components for a fire hotter than 98.6 are therefore present, but are held in check only by the limited supply of oxygen. Damp a fire and its pace becomes controlled. Blow on a fire and it flares. The pace of a fire is determined by the availability of its ingredients, and for the slow burn that takes place in the human body, oxygen is one of those ingredients. What would occur, then, if a substitute for oxygen were to become available, along with a catalyst to start the process. Matches start a fire because the heat produced by friction acts as a catalyst for the chemical mix on the head of the match. Where heat is not required to start the chemical process known as combustion, oxygen or a similar ingredient is required to keep it going.

That said, what causes spontaneous human combustion, a rare but frightening occurrence.

Beyond what is normally present in the human body—oxygen in limited amounts and fuels—those who spontaneously ignite have inadvertently created their own cremation by fretting and eating, a combination that often occurs. If life feels out of control, then eat. Fat laden foods comfort the most, as comfort from banking against the cold of a long winter or lean times is built into the human animal. The more worry, the more chomping occurs, and under normal circumstances this simply results in obesity. However, worry causes the liver to flood the blood stream with a fine oil, readily lit, in case the body may need to take flight or fight. In some humans a rare genetic condition exists that allows the combustion of this fine oil to continue, unabated, when in combination with a type of adrenaline, the catalyst. The need for oxygen is bypassed, as a self-feeding chemical reaction starts where a byproduct of the catalyst—induced combustion incites combustion in neighboring areas, and the matter goes out of control.

These humans, ostensibly fat and even jolly, are invariably found alone in their cremated state. This was a source of their self induced anxiety, as they chose to live alone, yet feared being alone, being their own worst enemy on all fronts. Does the human suffer? They feel no pain, as they become unconscious early in the process. A warm feeling, and then all goes black, as the brain is the first to receive blood from the pumping heart and brain cells are delicate. The unconscious and rapidly dying body, heart and breathing stopped, progresses to an intense chemical reaction, without oxygen, that is fast, hot, and very limited. The surroundings rarely burn unless highly flammable, as it is over too quickly to heat the air or raise the temperature of flame resistant furniture to the level where combustion runs unabated. Before the advent of flame resistant furnishings, spontaneous human combustion was not recognized for what it is. A spark from the fireplace or perhaps murder were suspected, but all clues were destroyed in the fire.

Dinosaur Extinction

Habitable planets are in the minority, as your scientists well know. Habitable planets that can sustain life long enough for intelligent species to evolve are in an even slimmer minority. The reasons for this reduction is the number of catastrophes that can befall evolving life, setting the clock all the way back. Catastrophes are many, and involve more than cataclysms.

In the main, evolving life falls because of the tiniest enemy, microorganisms which are likewise constantly evolving. Microorganisms have more flexibility than larger animals and greater mobility than plants. They can change hosts if their original host is not available. They have fewer factors to deal with. Where a large animal must only breath air or water but most often not both, and locate and eat non-poisonous food in sufficient quantity to sustain its bulk, and find a mate and then carry and rear the young—microorganisms have an easier time of it all around. They can survive in water or air, most often, eat most anything at hand, divide to produce young and all in a day. What we are telling you is that the dinosaurs did not die because their food source failed to grow due to the gloom from dust thrown up from a meteor impact, nor did small mammals chew up their eggs faster than they could hatch. They died because they were genetically related, and were thus similarly susceptible to the same microorganisms. The killer is no longer recognizable, having mutated long, long ago into another path altogether.

It would be sheer speculation as to what the intelligent species on Earth would have been, had this not occurred. However, most habitable planets do indeed evolve reptilian species, not mammalian, as the dominant species. This is simply first come, first serve. Reptiles evolve long before mammals, and have a head start. It does not follow, however, that the intelligent species is mammalian only where the evolving reptilian species has had a catastrophe. Most planets evolving mammals as the dominant intelligent species have not had such a history. Many factors come into play, among them how difficult life is for the various species. A difficult life, while a curse at the moment, induces intelligence.

DNA Building Blocks

Where carbon and silicon serve as the base upon which life is built, throughout the Universe, there are other variants. Many elements we, on Earth, consider to be trace elements are common on other worlds. An example is the element lithium, which is so remarkably soothing to those humans diagnosed as bipolar. It is no accident that these individuals are found to have a higher incidence of creativity, energy, and intelligence (e.g. Nick Rogers). It was for those qualities that a genetic contribution was made from worlds where lithium happened to be a common element. Doctors are not curing a disease by medicating with lithium, they are correcting an imbalance.

On some worlds iron is a trace element, and if carbon based, the blood does not rely on iron in the manner that creatures on your Earth do.

There, they do not develop iron deficiency anemia, but develop a similar reaction to a lack of silicon, the most common substitute for iron in this matter. Of course, the manner in which blood chemistry works in these instances has more differences than parallels. Humans are sometimes shocked to learn that aliens have green or clear blood, and correctly assume that the blood chemistry is radically different. Should one doubt that elements vary in their proportion throughout the Universe, one has but to look to meteors, where nickel is sought. Beyond nickel, look to what variance is found between the substances in meteors and your average hunk of Earth, or for that matter, what variances are found when comparing one meteor against another.

Perhaps the most surprising difference would be that oxygen is not the breath of life to all, as it is on Earth and to those life forms commonly visiting Earth. Why else would some of our ancient visitors have worn helmets? On their worlds, a helium component is key, and on the surface of your Earth they are drowning for lack of this as surely as you drown when under water, away from free oxygen in the proportion you require it. Some worlds would be considered radioactive by us, yet life lives there. How has their life adapted to the bombardment that disrupts your processes. Their chemistry, in fact, requires this bombardment, in the same manner that we require sunlight in order to manufacture vitamin D, without which our bones go soft. Life evolved on those planets while this situation existed, and DNA that learned to utilize the environment, rather than sicken from it, was the survivor that propagated. Just so many variations developed, on many worlds, and their differences are greater than their similarities.

Recessive Genes

Dominance in genetics is a relationship between two variant forms (alleles) of a single gene, in which one allele masks the expression of the other in influencing some trait. In the simplest case, if a gene exists in two allelic forms (A & B), three combinations of alleles (genotypes) are possible: AA, AB, and BB. If AB individuals (heterozygotes) show the same form of the trait (phenotype) as AA individuals (homozygotes), and BB homozygotes show an alternative phenotype, allele A is said to dominate or be dominant to allele B, and B is said to be recessive to A.

By convention, dominant alleles are written in uppercase letters, and recessive alleles in lowercase letters. In this example, allele B is replaced by a. Then, A is dominant to a (and a is recessive to A), the AA and Aa genotypes have the same phenotype, and the aa genotype has a different phenotype.

Scientists have noted, in mapping human genes, that a number of DNA links that are dormant. The number casually noted by humans in no way reflect the vast span of dormant portions in the human physiology. Think merely of the many human brains, in where there are frontal lobes where the conscious resides and a rear brain where the subconscious lies that in essence do not speak to each other or are reluctant to speak to each other. How would this evolve in normal evolution? This was forced upon humankind. There are many, many portions of the human body which are remnants or leftovers, unused. The appendix is one. Our DNA is rift with genes which if allowed to express would horrify and surprise people.

Blood Types

A blood type is a classification of blood based on the presence or absence of inherited antigenic substances on the surface of red blood cells. These antigens may be proteins, carbohydrates, glycoproteins, or glycolipids, depending on the blood group system. Some of these antigens are also present on the surface of other types of cells of various tissues. Several of these red blood cell surface antigens can stem from one allele and collectively form a blood group system. Blood types are inherited and represent contributions from both parents. A total of 30 human blood group systems are now recognized by the International Society of Blood Transfusion.

Blood type is a variant in the base hominoid, just as six fingers or toes can express in a population normally outfitted with five fingers or toes. There is curly hair and straight hair, dark hair and blond hair, in all racial groups. This may be doubted, as the Negro seems to have only curly dark hair, but in fact there are those occasional births that are treated as a sign from the gods or more often as a curse to be rid of, in which a straight haired babe is born, or one with light colored hair. These abnormalities were done away with quickly, in the past, and thus the gene pool altered. Just as six fingers or webbed fingers are rare, so some blood types are rare. That these genes express is significant of nothing more than a genetic toss of the dice and coming together of availability in the mother and father. There is no other significance in these variations.

AIDS

Acquired immune deficiency syndrome (AIDS) is a disease of the human immune system caused by the human immunodeficiency virus (HIV). This condition progressively reduces the effectiveness of the immune system and leaves individuals susceptible to opportunistic infections and tumors. HIV is transmitted through direct contact of a mucous membrane or the bloodstream with a bodily fluid containing HIV, such as blood, semen, vaginal fluid, preseminal fluid, and breast milk. This transmission can involve anal, vaginal or oral sex, blood transfusion, contaminated hypodermic needles, exchange between mother and baby during pregnancy, childbirth, breastfeeding or other exposure to one of the above bodily fluids.

AIDS is both a natural and unnatural occurrence. It has occurred naturally within the simian races for centuries. It has outcropped among humans in Africa and the south seas periodically, but due to limited population spread, simply devastated those groups it invaded. Where there is no written record and no survivors, there was no trace. AIDS was unknown to the civilized world, and would not have been discovered were it not for intervention by those of the Service-to-Self orientation.

What should be understood is that nothing can be accomplished, alien to human, unless this is done through humans. The Service-to-Self aliens involved in the spread of AIDS had to work through humans. They found these humans within the United States government, in the CIA. The goal, for these humans, was somewhat different than for the aliens. They considered it a win-win situation, benefiting both groups.

It has been assumed that AIDS was initially spread through a vaccination program. This is incorrect. It was spread through diet, by blood improperly cooked. It was spread through the dietary norms of the initial groups infected. Once having taken place, fastening on a group of humans, the infection could be directed. Sexual habits in Africa and the south seas is highly promiscuous. Sexual liaisons can be arranged. Men hungry for sex, a long way from home, are eager and not inclined to question a gift.

There were plans to sculpt the worlds populations with other diseases too. However, AIDS began to sculpt in ways not expected. The rich, the influential, those close to home. Argument erupted in the CIA camps where the wand of death was held.

In the beginning the AIDS virus was much the same as it is today, infecting humans. This virus has a great propensity for adaptation, so over any period of time changes form somewhat. The intervention by aliens of the Service-to-Self orientation was one of knowledge, directing the individuals interested in such a tool to the simian creatures harboring this virus, and directing the individuals further in the manner of isolating this virus. Sophisticated isolation was not required. The virus was in the blood, and blood is a natural component of the diet of those initially infected. Infected simian blood was mixed with blood naturally occurring in the diet. This was done surreptitiously. This was a mass assault on the immune system of the ingestor. The virus took hold. Use of this means of infection was no more difficult than the initial spreading methods. Eating bloody meat, poorly cooked, and promiscuous sex were practices occurring intensively. One just went with the flow.

The men in the CIA who gave The Call were of the Service-to-Self orientation to a high degree. Had they not been of this orientation they would not have been approached by the aliens who answered their call. These aliens do not squander their time idly. Their objective in assisting these men was the misery they could spread. Agony, a sense of abandonment, rage and the desire for vengeance, all these emotions work to bring recruits to their orientation. This was the object of the aliens assisting in the spreading of the AIDS virus. The goals of the men who made The Call were many, but as most of the goals were personal, they are insignificant. The men who made The Call were offered a bribe. They were assured that they could possess the continent of Africa, which is rich in natural resources and human cultures easily dominated. In fact, any humans possessing this continent could expect to be enslaved, so the joke would be on the men from the CIA. The aliens they were working with are not known for clarifying their goals.

Ebola

Ebola is the virus Ebolavirus (EBOV), a viral genus, and the disease it causes, Ebola hemorrhagic fever (EHF), a viral hemorrhagic fever (VHF). The virus is named after the Ebola River Valley in the Democratic Republic of the Congo (formerly Zaire), which is near the site of the first recognized outbreak in 1976 at a mission hospital run by Flemish nuns. It remained largely obscure until 1989, when several widely publicized outbreaks occurred among monkeys in the United States.

The virus interferes with the endothelial cells lining the interior surface of blood vessels and with coagulation. As the blood vessel walls become damaged and destroyed, the platelets are unable to coagulate, and patients succumb to hypovolemic shock. Ebola is transmitted through bodily fluids, while conjunctiva exposure may also lead to transmission.

As with dissemination of the AIDS virus, the Ebola virus was a matter done by the Service-to-Self crowd in the past, a matter now at rest. The Ebola virus was one of many gleaned from the bowels of the African jungles. Lest some think something sinister about Africa, this same destructiveness could be gleaned from many jungles, or even deserts for that matter. It is not the continent or its inhabitants, it is the use they have been put to—the evil use. Africa and South America are targeted continents. Aliens in the Service-to-Self orientation, along with human converts in the CIA, extracted the AIDS virus and other viruses for use in what they termed cleansing of the continent. The land, rich in resources, was then to be theirs, and any human inhabitants having natural immunity to the viruses unleashed would be their docile servants. Africa and South America have long histories of such abuse, being colonized for centuries in such a manner.

The Ebola virus did not catch on as did the AIDS virus, and the reason was simple. It tended to kill its handlers! When cast out among the swine, as was the phrase used to describe dissemination, the swine would die, but those casting their evil seed could not run fast enough. They carried it home with them, and they died in secreted hospital rooms, infecting their frantic nurses and doctors. After a time or two, they gave up on the Ebola virus, which refused to be tamed. The original plan of dissemination was to be by airborne means. This never came about as the early tests ran amuck. The Ebola virus is not fragile, dying quickly when exposed to oxygen or sunlight. If encased in water droplets, it lives. Thus it could be easily dispersed over a broad area. This stage of the plan was never enacted, nor were the several steps prior to this stage. Key questions to be answered were how long a given infectious period would last, how far the infection would spread on the ground, and how well it could be contained. As it ran like wildfire amongst its handlers, these questions were answered. The decision was made to void the plans.

Why then does it flare up, now and then? It is indigenous in Africa, but the spate of recent flare-ups are because it is now also widely dispersed. No longer lying in the swamps, infecting lizards and snakes which have little contact with humans as they are not the food of choice. Now resident in other hosts, such as rats and cockroaches, which mingle freely among humans. Why did Ebola not spread in this manner earlier? It did, but in an area not frequented by humans. Its original home was swamps, the last place humans live in when they are given a choice. Water logged, full of snakes and lizards, crawling with bugs, humid and unable to grow crops. The virus spread in its normal method, but as the insects and rodents indigenous to these swamps were not adapted to others biospheres, the virus stayed in the swamps. This virus not only refused to be tamed, it also is now running free. Too late to put the cork back in the bottle. Africa is having her revenge on those who would own her. She has made herself undesirable. She has placed poison in her loins.

The Ebola virus is spread in a manner not understood by virologists. They assume it is a new virus, but it has been around almost as long a man himself in his current bioengineered form. This virus was one the genetic engineers of the past were aware of, and this is precisely why members of the Service-to-Self crowd, in cahoots with members of the CIA, were able to locate it so quickly. It was at hand. This virus is most virulent in fecal matter, not the blood or blood serums, and is not at all spread through the breath. Of course, if one handled blood or blood serums with open cuts on their hands, infection would occur. However, it is the horticultural practices in Zaire that have contributed to the outbreaks, and it is these same practices worldwide that those hoping to spread the virus were counting on. The Ebola virus lives quite well in dead tissue, and this is one reason it kills its victims so quickly, turning their internal organs into mush. Were this not the case, it would never have been such a survivor. A virus that kills its victims in days or hours and then itself dies would be unlikely to survive.

Defecation is the primary route of spread, as in Africa the diet is fibrous and defecation occurs several times a day. Even a quickly dying victim, one dying within hours, is likely to defecate at least once. In Africa, as in most primitive countries, sewage is not treated but rather is left to stand or used as fertilizer or swept into a river to hopefully float away and become someone else's problem. Not infrequently, sewage is used to fertilize, not so much in Africa as in other countries where the soil has been depleted. In Africa, where the heat reduces fecal matter to soil within hours, it is left to stand where it was placed. Ignored, but not by insects, who are adapted to host on all manner of material. Each fresh meal is thus consumed and the insects move on—to be eaten by other insects or small rodents such as rats. And these carriers defecate in areas where their defecation can be included in human food, in food preparation areas. In Africa, hygiene is the least of anyone's worries. This is a bitterly poor continent, and the constant wars distract the populace.

Those wishing to stop the spread should lecture on keeping food preparation areas clean, and ensuring that hospital toilet routines are treated with utmost cleanliness. Wear gloves when handling the bed pan and cleaning the patient. Unlike AIDS, which must have live blood cells in order to survive for long, the Ebola virus is not picky about its host.

Cancer

Cancer is a natural process which allows the organism an out, a type of suicide. How often is it observed by humans that a fellow, informed that they have incipient cancer, continues the activity that is deemed to be causing or encouraging the cancer. Smoking is a case in point. Cancer is developing all the time, but is held at bay by scavenger cells that mop them up. What occurs in cancer development is that the scavengers are told to cease, to back off and let the destruction proceed. Cancer occurs for the same reason many infectious diseases run rampant, because the immune system turns off. As has long been recognized, the immune system is highly sensitive to one's surroundings, and by design. Suicide in nature is rarely possible, other than to cease eating or fail to remove oneself from danger, both actions which are associated with mental depression.

The frantic war against cancer waged by the medical profession is most often a losing battle because the patient has determined the outcome. Spontaneous remission occurs without medical assistance, and many cancer patients can be found to have several of these in their history. When a spontaneous remission occurs during medical treatment, the treatment is credited, but in truth the success is due to the care and attention the patient receives. At last they get time off from the hated job, have someone ask with sincerity how they feel that day, or escape from a domineering spouse with a hospital stay. Cancer treatments are always futile where the underlying causative situation is not addressed, as even if all the cancer cells are eradicated, which is never the case, they would just recur in some other spot. To cure cancer, address the patient's life first, and attack the tumor as a secondary measure.

Earth's First

On Earth, the species that evolved first to be close to this level were reptilian. They were engineered, gained intelligence to the level of mankind today, but did not have the dexterity that hominoids do. It is often speculated that these intelligent reptiles were small dinosaurs. In fact, they were amphibious, as the Earth had earlier been a water planet, before its crash where its wound in the Pacific occurred. Thus, they did not have the arms and fingers and toes that many lizards have. They did not have the means to create technology, as they could not manipulate their environment They had fins, long bodies, and very little else. The remnants today, live in places on Earth, within cavities that have water ways, and we decline to describe this further. Their selection as 3rd Density species was based on their native intelligence, and the socialization they had already developed, just as the ape was deemed a good predecessor for these same reasons. The societies they had developed were deemed appropriate for 3rd Density life.

There are many 3rd Density worlds where the social arena is the dominant spiritual development arena. Who can influence who, who is friends with whom, who can punish whom, etc. This is not all that different from man's experiences, except that mankind distracts himself with technology. He plays with things, if frustrated with social interaction. Where things cannot be a distraction, these reptiles simply went off for a swim, just as man goes off for a walk. Man is used to thinking of talking and writing, as well as body language. But most species with social interaction have many means of communication. Even birds and insects communicate with each other. It is not so much the complexity of the message as the meaning behind it, not often misunderstood. A dog can exhibit affection by licking or disgorging food to its young, and exhibit hostility and rejection by a snarl. Whether this is clothed in lots of words of not, the message is clear. Choices for Service-to-Other or Service-to-Self thus are many, regardless of the ability to record complex communications.

This reptilian race was susceptible to the same factors that created a great dieoff among the dinosaurs, and floundered in poor health. It became apparent that the continuance of this species was not sustainable, as the susceptibility was inherent in their DNA and would be hard to counter. Thus, their engineers turned to considering other species, which eventually became man. Mammals had resistance that the reptiles did not. Therefore, mankind is not the first intelligent species to evolve or be assisted in evolution on Earth. As we have stated, worlds are often used repeatedly for 3rd Density existence. Indeed, just as humans today have souls that were at one time incarnated in the giant hominoids formerly visiting Earth, and just as Star Children are incarnated on Earth, so souls that had to move on to new bodies during this time, the reptilian dieoff, moved into Early Man. There is a strong desire of young souls to remain in place, familiar places, but primary because they have unfinished agendas. Just as young souls may linger between incarnations and haunt, as ghosts, in a similar manner, they will want to reincarnation in the area. This tendency lasts often through much of 4th Density, a long plateau, so does not die quickly.

Dolphin Talk

Humans for eons assumed that whales and dolphins chirped, clicked, or sang to communicate with each other until they discovered, quite recently, that there were other means being used. As anyone underwater when a stone strikes an object will attest, sound traveling underwater is magnified beyond the affect above the surface. Of course, this is simply the mass of water moving, rather than the mass of air moving, and water is heavier, affecting the ear drum with greater force. Thus, when utilizing sound waves setting water in motion, whales and dolphins chirp or sing little notes, but never shout. But communication has been observed between members of a family many miles apart, even an ocean apart, and the means of communication is little understood. Man, who uses ricocheting radio waves as a form of communication, understands that as long as the sender and receiver are using the same code, any directed wave can be used as a communication tool, be it water waves or otherwise. Just as humans hundreds of miles from each other can be in telepathic communication by sharing the same brain wave frequencies in similar patterns, whales and dolphins as species with common biological backgrounds speak to each other in this way. They are suspected of having even greater communication talents by the military, which in their envy has studied them. Being biological creatures, whales and dolphins can only produce as a means of communication that which the corporeal body will support! Human beings clap their hands, wave, vibrate their vocal cords in recognizable patterns, and throw rocks. Whales and dolphins slap their tails on the ocean surface, chirp and sing, and swim in patterns that carry meaning to the others. Humans send telepathic signals that other humans attuned to them can and on occasion do receive. Whales and dolphins, not having an opposable digit that allows them to experiment with various means of communication, worked more intensely with what they had. Their telepathy for one another is operant, not only sent but listened to by the others. They not only speak soundlessly, they are heard. However, their songs, carried mile after mile through the water, does not lose its intensity as would a song in the atmosphere. Water in the ocean does not blow about as does air, as being more dense it sends pressure forward in the form of a wave, and from one side of an ocean to another this sound can carry. For a lost member of a family, hearing the song heard when young is a call to rejoin the family. Thus what humans are observing is not only the whale or dolphin's ability to receive what appears to be soundless communications, but strong hearts that act on these communications. They love one another.

Earthquakes

An earthquake is the result of a sudden release of energy in the Earth's crust that creates seismic waves. The seismicity or seismic activity of an area refers to the frequency, type and size of earthquakes experienced over a period of time. Earthquakes are measured using observations from seismometers. The moment magnitude is the most common scale on which earthquakes larger than approximately 5 are reported for the entire globe. The more numerous earthquakes smaller than magnitude 5 reported by national seismological observatories are measured mostly on the local magnitude scale, also referred to as the Richter scale. These two scales are numerically similar over their range of validity. Magnitude 3 or lower earthquakes are mostly almost imperceptible and magnitude 7 and over potentially cause serious damage over large areas, depending on their depth. The largest earthquakes in historic times have been of magnitude slightly over 9, although there is no limit to the possible magnitude. The most recent large earthquake of magnitude 9.0 or larger was a 9.0 magnitude earthquake in Japan in 2011 (as of March 2011), and it was the largest Japanese earthquake since records began. Intensity of shaking is measured on the modified Mercalli scale. The shallower an earthquake, the more damage to structures it causes, all else being equal.

Earthquake Predictions

Earthquakes are a fact of nature, one that creates many opportunities for them to sort out their spiritual orientation. Just watch how the populace responds after an earthquake. Some people risk their lives dashing into shaky building to rescue others, and other people sit and moan, waiting to be rescued. Many and great opportunities.

The Earth, as just about everyone knows, is covered by plates that move about and grind against each other. This grinding action is described variously as a head-to-head push, a sliding under or over, or a gliding along the edge on the way to someplace else. A place where this is occurring is called a fault line, as being a faulty place in the surface of the Earth, one would assume. Now, where humans spend a lot of time sticking probes into the Earth, and trying to guess at the tension deep underground and thus the probability of a near term earthquake, they would do better to place the plate personalities into a computer and let the computer tell you where the next bust is going to be. How would this be done? Humans have a pretty good handle on what the plates are, and where their boundaries are. Put that into the computer. Humans also have a pretty good handle on the direction the plates are moving in, as they are staring at the results after every earthquake. What they don't know is the degree of pressure, and how to restate this pressure after a quake, which eases the tension in the surrounding rock.

This can be done mathematically, if one takes into consideration the following factors:

The size of the plate, as measured in a directly proportional way, i.e. as the surface area.

The thickness at the edge of the plate, as measured by instruments that gauge the depth of the bedrock, which we deem fairly accurate as done by humans today, and, again, given a directly proportional weight.

The frequency of what is termed emergent electrostatic Screeches, a sound which can be detected by sensitive humans, and much more accurately by sensitive instruments. We are speaking here of bursts of electrical energy, which is invariably accompanied by other types of energy so that any number of them can be measured. This should be weighted in a bell curve manner, so that every increase in frequency weighs in more and more severely.

Pole Shift

Earthquakes during the pole shift occur when plates are on the move, the jolts felt when the plate moves, and shortly thereafter when the surrounding plates adjust to the new tension. Aftershocks are such adjustments, and are always minuscule compared to the major plate movement. During the pole shift all plates on earth on the move, and the jolt occurs at the sudden stop when the crust stops moving. This is when the Richter 9 equivalent earthquakes, which we have termed Richter 15 as the scope is far larger than Richter 9, will be felt worldwide.

The earthquakes following the pole shift will be no more wrenching than earthquakes due to plates adjustments under normal circumstances. The moving plates, suddenly slamming into each other as they start to slow down, will create a domino effect not unlike a multiple car crash. One plate slams into another as the first plates slows down, creating a domino effect that rapidly ricochets around the world, within minutes. There is no delay in this motion, as each plate is solid and what affect one edge affects the far edge, when the entire plate is in motion. Thus, the earthquakes come all at once, and rapidly settle down to an adjustment phase, within minutes.

Due to the immensity of the adjustment, with many plates in barely tenable positions, there will be many aftershocks, most occurring within the first few weeks. These will range from Richter 8 on down, but in no case will be as great as the initial shock during the pole shift. They will rapidly diminish, reduced to annoying tremors after a few weeks.

Continental Drift

Continental drift is the movement of the Earth's continents relative to each other. The hypothesis that continents 'drift' was first put forward by Abraham Ortelius in 1596 and was fully developed by Alfred Wegener in 1912. However, it was not until the development of the theory of plate tectonics in the 1960s, that a sufficient geological explanation of that movement was found.

Looking down from space, man can clearly see that the continents once formed a whole. Like the pieces of a puzzle that can be placed together, South America fits nicely into the curve of the Western African coast, and North America tucks up against Europe. All was one land mass in the past, so why have the continents drifted so far apart? And what, in fact, caused the globe to be so lumpy in the first place? Don't planets spinning from a molten state assume a circular shape? The answer, of course, is that the present Earth did not grow from a molten mass spinning slowly as it cooled, and thus lost this chance to gain a consistently round shape. When it was round, its watery nature would have precluded the type of intelligence that now inhabits it, as it would have remained a water planet as it was originally, with barely a point sticking bravely above the water's surface.

The Earth was once in orbit farther from the Sun, and bore as life only cold creatures that lived in the dark waters on the scant vegetation that grew there. This planet, the pre-Earth, sustained a collision with the 12th Planet's entourage of many moons, and thus shattered drifted into a new orbit closer to the Sun. The larger piece became the Earth, with its waters pooling in the wound as a cosmetic, the motion of the Earth pulling the waters round, to give a smooth appearance. But this peace lasts only until the great one returns for its periodic visit, pulling at the lumpy Earth. The inconsistencies of the surface only make the gravitational pulls of the 12th Planet more devastating, the continents like handles to be grabbed and jerked. Likewise, the depth of the Pacific trough is vulnerable, a weak point on the surface for the continents to slide toward. Thus we have continental drift, which is much too benign a word to use for the cataclysms that occur.

The Earth, during each successive Pole Shift, has filled her wound. At first, due to the lopsided nature of her shape, the tug toward roundness was slight. What was there to tug toward? She hugged herself, all on one side, and each passage of the giant comet only pulled slightly at this hug, separating her land mass and moving this into the gap. But each succeeding passage found a more vulnerable scene, and the separating of the single land mass increased. Why so? Because rifts, driven between land masses, were vulnerable spots, torn recently, tearable again. Increasingly the Americas have moved away from the African and European continents. Now, when the Americas are almost midway between the other land masses, and the African land mass has cleanly separated too, they are more vulnerable to becoming fully balanced during a pole shift than ever. During this pole shift the Pacific gap will close, equalizing the land masses as they spread around the globe. This will be devastating to certain subducting areas, such as India and Western Australia, and will heat to a tremendous degree those plates that are above the subducting plates in California, Tibet, and along the Pacific Rim.

Atmosphere Building

Worlds that support life have water in abundance, and during the congealing period after a big bang hydrogen and oxygen in many states can be found freely floating around the intensely hot proto-planets. As planets congeal, the pressure results in heat, but after time this dissipates. Meanwhile, the surface boils. Condensation occurs, forming seas upon the surface, but as nature abhors a vacuum, freely floating molecules do not all settle. What causes an atmosphere to exist, and what factors affect the composition of an atmosphere. Even in the absence of heat that would cause molecules of whatever nature to vaporize, an atmosphere builds. The Earth's atmosphere continues to build today, but are the oceans boiling?

Water vapor is in abundance in the Earth's atmosphere, yet arrived there not due to the action of intense heat but to fill a void. Place a vacuum against the surface of a pool of water and watch what happens—water vapor. The water pool will not completely disburse because its normal state at the condensation temperature is a liquid. But the constant motion of molecules means that the molecules at the surface have nothing to bump against in a vacuum, so like a car without brakes, off they go. At a certain point the air-borne molecules start bumping into each other and bumping against the surface of the water pool, and the situation stabilizes. So, does this mean that the atmosphere of a planet is constantly disbursing into space? Yes and no. Deep space is bitterly cold, and when moving away from the surface of a planet air—borne molecules slow down the bumping action. The situation stabilizes, again. However, some small loss is a constant factor, so that after billions of years some small quantity of the planet's substance has dissipated.

Atmospheres, as any meteorologist knows, are composed of more than just free oxygen and water vapor—an atmosphere reflects in its composition the planet it wraps. Every metal and every molecule combination on the open surface of the planet can be found in the atmosphere. This is demonstrated by the sense of smell, which is in fact nothing more than contact of the nose with tiny particles floating in the air. In fact, as volcanic eruptions send substances from the core of the Earth airborne, the atmosphere usually reflects the planet in its entirety. However, just as the oceans differ from the land, so the atmosphere differs also, from both land and sea.

Land is composed of elements or molecular combinations that are either not water soluble, tend to cling to other molecules to form a heavy settling substance, or are not exposed to enough water to leave its solid state. Under constant rain, soil erodes, but likewise clumps and clings to other soil particles and thus again settles out. Metals washed constantly with a liquid are found in that liquid, thus the concern for lead poisoning when drinking water stands in lead pipes. Many factors affect whether a substance is found on land, in the sea, or in the air. If it clumps and clings it will eventually be too heavy for anything but land or the sea floor. If it is a liquid at the temperatures normal for the Earth it will find its way into the water systems, there to be evenly disbursed if water soluble or if not soluble to form a separate layer in the water body such as oil on top or liquid mercury below.

An atmosphere is composed of those elements which can remain free or clump only to form tiny molecules, so big and no larger. Water vapor is composed of two parts hydrogen and one part oxygen, and the three elements form a tight band with little tendency to clump or cling unless other factors present. Similarly, any combination of elements that is discrete will remain airborne. These tiny elements or discrete groupings of elements can include heavy metals, as the winds that carry radioactivity across the land and sea after a nuclear explosion attest. Elements capable of being radioactive are some of the heaviest known to man, yet there they are, wafting aloft.

The composition of atmospheres is dependent on wind action and air currents also. Some elements or groupings would move lower within the atmosphere due to their relative weight, and some rise, due to being light, were the atmospheric soup not constantly stirred. The Albatross, a giant bird of no small weight, soars almost endlessly on air currents above the waves, its wings not moving for hours at a time. Atmospheric currents are affected by the warmth or coolness of the land or sea mass underneath, the density of air masses nearby, the pressure of any air masses moving toward or away from the spot, and the temperature of the air mass itself as it is warmed by the Sun or cooled on the dark side of the Earth—constantly stirred.

Thus, one should take care what they spew into the air—as it does not simply blow away.

Planet X does exist, and it is the 12th Planet or Nibiru, one and the same. When first sighted via infrared readings and reported by the IRAS team in 1983, the IRAS findings were taken in many ways by scientists reading the reports, and thus they cast many interpretations on just what the Planet X's infrared reading might imply. Infrared heat can be taken to mean many things, depending on distance, size, and composition of the object being sensed. A very hot object far away can be comparable to a barely warm object near at hand, or a very large object far away can be considered to be a smaller object close at hand, and as the compression caused by the mass of an object is considered to produce infrared rays, then a very heavy but cold object could be considered comparable to a lighter but warmer object. The scientists reading the IRAS findings took the 12th Planet, a.k.a. Planet X, to be larger, colder, and farther away, as the mind does not want to comprehend the alternatives. When first sighted in 1983, it was on the right hand side of Orion, as viewed from your northern hemisphere. It will first move left and up toward the elliptical plane as it nears the Earth's Solar System for its passage, as though to assume a place with the other planets in the Solar System, at this point being slightly to the left of Orion. In 1998 it will veer right, moving toward Taurus and Aries, assuming a retrograde orbit, and will come up through the plane as viewed from above the elliptical plane, in its first passage.

The reason given, officially, for the search for Planet X was the perturbations in the outer planets, known for some centuries and hardly explained by the discovery of Pluto. Just as the planned settlements on Mars are given and official explanation to the populace, which is paying for all of this, the search for Planet X could scarcely be hidden from public view. What the public was not told, of course, was that the press for certainty was due to information we had given MJ12, and that this information appeared to be solid based on decades of careful monitoring of the skies. Following Roswell, as the story tells, we established a contact with the US government, which put this into the hands of MJ12 to avoid information contamination of the normal federal bureaucracy. MJ12, via NASA and JPL, had been monitoring the approach of Planet X. This was proving accurate, so they mustered the IRAS search in the early 1980's which resulted in the find of what they hoped they would not find.

The human mind does not wish to entertain the awful, so most in this group were in denial, though going along with the search as an interesting scientific exercise, not unlike most of the activity NASA et al undertake daily. The discovery of solid proof so stunned most of those involved in the search that their guard was dropped, and thus the reports such as the 1983 Washington Post front page article. Interest in Planet X was roaring along going into the 1983 IRAS search. Had Planet X not been found, interest might still be roaring along, in the media, that is. When the blanket of suppression was dropped on the media and major observatories, who know just where Planet X is at all times these days, it took some time for an explanation for the silence to be concocted. Thus one finds the strange silence, that lasted almost a decade, following the Planet X discovery in 1983. Since JPL and NASA are firmly in hand, doing the bidding of the establishment on so many information issues, they became the designated arm of the explanation. The mystery of why the outer planets appeared perturbed to astronomers for the last 160 years was explained away by adjustments in the size and composition of these outer planets discovered by probes. The public gets the conclusion, but not the details, or they get the details in such a manner that an independent conclusion can't be arrived at. All very safe.

Pole Shift

The cataclysmic pole shift hypothesis states that there have been geologically rapid shifts in the relative positions of the modern-day geographic locations of the poles and the axis of rotation of the Earth, creating calamities such as floods and tectonic events.

When Planet X positions itself exactly between the Earth and its Sun, things change. The Earth then has its greatest advocate for its previous alignment, the Sun and its magnetic alignment, negated. The Earth hears only the magnetic voice of the giant comet, so to speak, which stands between the Earth and its former magnetic commander, the Sun. Earth is heavier at its molten core, which is rumored to be composed primarily of iron. This is not entirely untrue, but regardless of the composition, the Earth's core is more sensitive to the magnetic alignment than the crust. The core grips the crust, and is not as liquid as one might think. There is friction. There is the tendency for the whole to move as one, despite their differing magnetic allegiances.

The pole shift is in fact a movement of the interior of the Earth, the core, to come into alignment with Planet X. Planet X, due to its massive size in comparison to the Earth, dominates the magnetic scene, and it is in this regard that gravity comes into the pole shift equation. The Earth's crust resists aligning with Planet X, being caught in a web of magnetic pulls from its immediate neighborhood. In other words, the Earth's crust wants to stay with the old, established, magnetic pull, while the core of the Earth, having less allegiance and attachment to the neighborhood, listens to the new voice. There is a great deal of tension that builds between the crust of the Earth and the core of the Earth. This tension is released when the core of the Earth breaks with the crust, and moves. However, the core of the Earth drags the crust with it as it turns to align anew.

The pole shift is therefore sudden, taking place in what seems to be minutes to humans involved in the drama, but which actually takes place during the better part of an hour. There are stages, between which the human spectators, in shock, are numb. At first there is a vibration of sorts, a jiggling, as the crust separates in various places from the core. Then there is a slide, where the crust is dragged, over minutes, to a new location, along with the core. During the slide, tidal waves move over the Earth along the coast lines, as the water is not attached and can move independently. The water tends to stay where it is, the crust moving under it, essentially. When the core finds itself aligned, it churns about somewhat, settling, but the crust, more solid and in motion, proceeds on. This is in fact where mountain building and massive earthquakes occur, just as car crashes do their damage on the point of impact, when motion must stop.

Weak spots among the Earth's crustal plates give way. The Pacific Ocean will shorten, and the Atlantic widen. Subducting plates will subduct greatly. Mountain building will occur suddenly, primarily increasing in areas already undergoing mountain building. All told, the better part of an hour, but at certain stages, only minutes. Plants survive as they are rooted and their seeds are everywhere, and animals including man survive because they travel with the moving plates of the Earth and experience no more severe a shock when the plates stop moving than they would during a Richter 9 earthquake. Where mountain building occurs when the plates stop moving, the stoppage is not simply a sudden jolt, like a car hitting a brick wall. All is in motion, and the stoppage is more like a car hitting a barrier of sand filled plastic barrels—a series of small jolts, occurring in quick succession.

At this time Planet X will come to within 14 million miles of the Earth. The strength of its magnetic field at that distance will be such that the comet's North Pole, angled essentially in the same direction as the Earth's North Pole, forces the Earth's North Pole to evade the pressure and accommodate its larger brother by swinging south to the bulge of Brazil. This alignment will not change if the distance between the sibling planets changes, but the speed and vigor of the shift would be so affected by a closer passage. The height of tidal waves and consequent inland inundation would be so affected. The heat of land masses above subducting plates where friction can cause the ground to melt, would be so affected. And the violence of shifting winds would certainly be so affected.

Wandering Poles

Confusion exists over why the ice in Antarctica dates back, apparently, for many pole shift periods. If one analyses the last few shifts, it becomes apparent that the South Pole was either over, part way, Antarctica, or nearby in the ocean. When a pole is over water, near land, the land mass retains its ice, under the influence of this large block of ice afloat. This is due to cold water washing against the land mass, as well as air currents. The prior shift moved the North Pole from Greenland to its present location. Prior to that, it was over the East Siberian Sea, having pulled Siberia northward where the largest number of mammoth dieoff occurred. Tracing the North Pole over the past few shifts, one sees that it spent a time over Scandinavia where it resided between the 4th and 5th shift back. When it moved from Scandinavia into the Arctic north of Siberia, Europe warmed up, its glaciers melting. Prior to Scandinavia, the North Pole centered over North America.

The Flood occurred because during the time the North Pole was over North America, the South Pole was over the ocean south of India. When the North Pole moved to Scandinavia, the South Pole repositioned on the other side of Antarctica. However, being over water, the former South Pole melted from the bottom, floating on the water in a honeycombed shape. It retained a lot of cold, as the ocean water coming from Antarctica distributed this cold, so the ice melt was not complete. A subsequent shift lurched this honeycombed ice and fractured it, so it dropped into the ocean creating a displacement wave—the Flood. This water roared up toward Arabia and elsewhere north of this splash. Narrowing into the waterways between Africa and Asia/Europe, water does what it does when under pressure, it went into tidal bore. This caused more sea level rise in the area Noah lives in, described in the Bible as the Flood. This water did not cover the rest of the world to this height, thus, as most coastlines allowed the splash to distribute, not bore.

The wandering poles attest to prior pole shifts but don't give a true picture, as many times poles situate over oceans or land that subsequently submerges, areas unexplored by modern man. Humans measure the significance of pole shifts by their variance from today's poles, where in fact the measure should be from the pole's placement prior to the shift. What is termed a wandering pole is mankind's best efforts to trace the placement of the poles, dating the record in hardened magma which captures the moment's magnetic alignment. The Ice Ages, occurring over northern Europe and America, are also written records of when poles were situated over those spots. Pole shifts can be as slight as a few degrees or close to 180 degrees, the most extreme case.

Where the Earth is close to the point of passage, as it will be during the coming pole shift, the Earth's core drags her crust into opposition to the Planet X's magnetic alignment, her North Pole heading directly south, and there the crust stays while the core gradually rights itself.

Where pole shifts are so slight as to be nonexistent the Sun stands between the Earth and her larger brother, Planet X.

Where the Earth is a quarter way around the elliptic a different drama takes place, as rather than move into opposition to the Planet X, the move is to come into alignment.

Distance makes some difference, but more influential is whether the two planets are lined up pole to pole or side to side on the approach. In a pole to pole confrontation the Planet X's North Pole essentially grips the Earth's South Pole and drags it with it as it passes, pushing away the North Pole. In a side to side confrontation, the Earth is only nudged to line up with her brother, just as small magnetic particles in ore attempt to align with each other. The position of the Earth or Planet X during any passage is strictly by chance, governed by the various influences that affect the arrival of Planet X, which can meet with any number of delaying influences on its journey. Thus, there is no regularity to dramatic pole shifts, where the Earth is essentially turned upside down.

Dramatic reversals happen rarely, as Planet X must virtually come between the Earth and the Sun to have this much influence. This happens in only 15% of the pole shifts, as where this vulnerable position constitutes perhaps 30% of the possible arc, the range of possibility is such that the Earth may be on the opposite side of the Sun just as often as not, cutting these odds in half. When the Sun stands between the Earth and Planet X there is, in essence, no pole shift but simple tension and compression in the crust, expressed as increased earthquakes and volcanism. This safety zone constitutes another 40% of the possible arc. The remaining 45% of the arc experiences alignment shifts, rather than opposition shifts. Thus, the wandering Poles reflect 15% massive opposition movement, where the North Pole is tipped backwards away from Planet X balanced by 45% minor alignment movement, where the North Pole is tipped forward slightly to line up with Planet X's magnetic alignment.

This finds the records of where the North and South Poles have been, in the main, essentially close to their position at present. Mankind is missing at least half the record, those former poles which are now under water, but the pattern would not look much different with these missing pieces added. Human written and verbal history will not serve man well in preparation for the forthcoming pole shift, as a shift as devastating as this one will be has not occurred even within the past 50,000 years. Even The Flood was merely the result of two minor shifts, back to back—one to displace the South Pole so that partial melting and softening started, and the second to break and drop the suspended ice into the ocean.

Spirituality

Planet Earth as a schoolhouse

Earth is a 3rd Density planetary sphere and a schoolhouse for young souls or Spirits. In a spiritual learning house the prime directive is non-interference. This places a wealth of spontaneous experiences before the emerging souls, who develop empathy by being subject to various painful situations. Empathy simply does not exist if a spirit has not been there, in its past.

Earth is undergoing a Transformation and will move to 4th Density Service-to-Others in about a hundred years in future. There will still be a 3rd Density Earth, on the same plane as the future 4th Density home of humans, as a portion of the Earth will be left in 3rd Density. One reason is that the great majority of the entities native to the planet have reached an orientation decision, and are ready to proceed with other lessons, and 3rd Density planets are checked periodically as to their readiness for harvest in this regard. Another reason is administrative, and that is why the Earth is undergoing its Transformation now. The majority of those on Earth have not yet reached their orientation decision, but will be moved to another planet, as the Earth has been designated as a future home for Service-to-Other oriented entities.

Incarnations

Incarnations occur naturally and is the way forming entities get their start. The stuff of souls is everywhere, disbursed throughout the Universe, but so disbursed it does not make a soul. Does a single strand of DNA constitute life? Yes and no. By itself it is a complex chemical, but when combined with other DNA in a living organism it is considered life. The stuff of souls tends to gather in living things as the environment is more interesting than non-living environments. It is not so much attracted to life as that it lingers, and thus begins to accumulate. Without conscious intelligence it fails to establish a personality, a self, and after death of the life form disburses again. Incarnations on 3rd Density planets happen naturally at first, as having formed a self the forming entity migrates to a new body after the death of the old. It can happen in unguided migrations that more than one forming entity wants to inhabit the same body, but usually cohabitation is distressing to all parties, including the body, and results in only the strongest entity remaining.

After a certain point, when the lessons to be learned from the shear fact of life have been well learned by the newly formed entities, guided incarnations become the norm. This is to help the forming entities maximize the wisdom to be gained from their incarnations. Formed entities, operating in 4th Density or higher, surround the immature entity when it has freed itself from a dead or dying body, and communicate. These conferences may be short, with a second incarnation occurring almost instantly when the path is clear and incarnation opportunities available, or may drag out if the lesson to be learned requires a special environment or incarnation opportunities are limited. In the meantime the forming entity does not wander, as it is essentially herded together with others like itself, and finds this stimulating. Since incarnations are natural, when the forming entity is guided to a new body it sets up housekeeping willingly. This is a familiar experience. Burning issues which were present when the entity left its former home, a dead or dying body, come to the fore, and the forming entity is off again on the great exploration that life provides. Being incarnated is far more stimulating and fascinating than the alternative, being disincarnate, at this stage, and Out-Of-Body experiences seldom occur unless trauma to the body is extreme. During early incarnations, the young soul is given the best opportunity for growth by being given a virgin field each incarnation. Should they have made a mistake in a past life, they are not burdened by guilt. Should they be angry about something visited upon them in a past life, they are not burdened by anger. They can approach situations they mis-handled in past lives afresh, and make them go right this time.

In 3rd Density incarnations the lessons to be learned are to develop a concept of the self, a concept of the other, and to form an attitude toward relationships with others. These lessons can proceed in bodies of all types, and do not require such facilities as opposable thumbs. 3rd Density worlds where the intelligent species is dexterous and manipulation of the environment is possible spend time exploring universal concepts, but their understanding of the Universe is, all told, no more advanced than that gained by non-dexterous species who spend their time pondering the world around them. At a certain point, after many thousands of incarnations, the young spirit has had its chances. It has revisited, or re-experienced, these situations repeately, and is starting to form patterns. The Birthing Guides help in this matter, providing incarnation that challenge any sticking points the young soul has. However, souls have their leanings, and inclinations, and paths they prefer to follow, just as humans become stuck in their ways. And when this has become apparent, the Birthing Guides move into using these inclinations for the better good of all, rather than just repeating patterns.

Reincarnation

Reincarnation occurs because special envoys from the Council of Worlds, loosely termed birthing envoys, gather up disincarnate entities and discuss the entities progress and growth. You may think of this as a school conference if you wish, where the young entity and its guides have a conference with the birthing envoys. The lessons to be learned are formulated, with the most pressing lesson taking priority. In this the entity itself has little input, just as young school children have little input into their curriculum. Many call this karma, where what one did in a past life comes back to haunt one. The entity cannot end an incarnation, except through death or the temporary vacating of the physical body during Out-Of-Body experiences.

Some entities require fewer incarnations at certain points or planes of development than other entities. This variation in the number of incarnations required is based both on the nature of the entity, or soul, and the circumstances of the incarnation. The key is whether the lesson to be learned has been sufficiently learned. In some cases an incarnation will generate more lessons to be learned than it resolved. The entity moves backwards, so to speak.

Past Lives

Tapping past lives is much in vogue, especially in California. Since the proposition cannot be disproved, the claimant's wax poetic. All the past lives are invariably romantic or impressive—they lived in interesting times, in elegant surroundings, and were always hale and hearty, intelligent, and attractive. Although the vast number of past lives on Earth were marked by struggle for health, with broken teeth, missing or maimed limbs, and the health problems that plague mankind today present in the extreme—the past lives trotted forth all seem to involve health and even vibrant health. Where all but perhaps 5% of the world's populace is of average or dull intelligence, the past lives claimed invariably involve stations in life which would require a relatively high IQ. And where most of mankind's history has gone down ignominiously and unrecorded, past lives published seem to all be placed smack in the center of either momentous historical times or well-recorded historical times. What is going on here? Are these past lives remembered simply fiction or are the memories selective?

K. R.

Humans delving into their past lives face many hurtles. The human form has no memory of past lives, and the spirit has difficulty speaking to the mind about matters it has no concept of. Concept building, in the small child or the adult, is a step by step process. Complex concepts are built from many small ones, and where the small concepts do not exist the way is blocked. Past lives are a leap into history recorded nowhere on Earth—living conditions, cultures and traditions, and physical appearance all beyond the imagination of humans alive today. A past life spent as a cave-man, where the diet consisted of bugs and worms and even on desperate occasions of the feces of herbivores, would not be remembered. Thus, past lives remembered do tend to fit into written history. Add to this selective memory the human tendency to deny unpleasantness. A past life where the human was ugly and behaved atrociously would likely not be given center stage, and past lives that passed the minimum acceptance criteria are pruned and amended by humans remembering them just as they have selective memory about their current incarnation.

Past lives are most often remembered by subtle message the soul gives to the current incarnation, the body. If the soul is strongly into integrating, fixing past mistakes, it may be firm during these messages, so the human has no rest until they are in sync and with the program. It is during such incarnation that humans report they have uncovered past lives. But unless such a situation exists, mediating and begging the soul to play out in full color and sound and fury the interesting past lives is not honored. The soul considers this idle curiosity on the part of the human, who is treated not as an equal during incarnation. Thus, such attempts, where not called for, are futile. Thus, humans seeking to reconstruct their past lives are fighting an uphill battle, and will never get close to the hoary truth.

Shamanism

All cultures have shamans, who go by different names. A shaman must be able to convince those he lives amongst that his experiences are real, and his guidance valid, or his stature quickly falls. Therefore, shamans in the main are having real experiences that are somewhat familiar, if only in part, to other humans. There are seldom fake shamans, and then not for long. What is a shaman? A shaman is a human who refuses to deny what his intuition is telling him, and thus communicates with entities he cannot see or hear or capture for exhibition, as in a cage. He communicates with the world of spirits, the dead, higher level entities that no longer need incarnate bodies, and as frequently as possible, he is having Out-Of-Body experiences. He may attempt to incarnate, briefly, into other humans, or animals of various types, but he seldom gets permission to do any of this. Imagination plays a great part in shamanism, but is bolstered by real experiences so the shaman's stories can be very compelling.

Many who claim to be speaking to the wind, or animals, or rocks, and genuinely believe this is so, are simply giving a spirit they cannot see a name and source. Humans sensing a spirit in the vicinity are often at a loss to explain what they are sensing. They refer to vibes, or a presence, or an intensity. Nothing can be captured on camera, or grabbed and put in a box for later examination. Spirits communicating with a group, such as an Indian tribe, will often go with the flow, and allow whomever is communicating to assume this presence. It is possible to influence the direction a bird flies, easily, as the reason for flying in this or that direction are few and can be staged for the benefit of the bird. Thus, a Shaman who thinks the bird has a spirit, and finds it flying in patterns that would indicate that, is none the wiser.

All humans have the capacity to be shamans, but in the main lack the faith. They stop themselves. They feel insecure, not being grounded.

They prefer to be a spectator. But the family of man, hearing the shaman weaving his spell, remember their tentative experiences along the same lines, and believe. A shaman's followers have gone to the edge with the shaman, and when he describes what was beyond, they recall what they caught a glint of.

Seances

Talking with the dead has been a time honored endeavor, and all human cultures have terms for and tales about this common human experience. Most of the tales are told by those who recently lost a loved one, and the bond continues for a time due to unfinished business and concerns that the recently deceased has about those still living. The most famous tales are told about hauntings, where a particular spirit hangs about a location such as a house, wanting some kind of justice done or lingering due to past attachments. Seances, where the dead are deliberately called, are a form of The Call, and as such fall under the rules whereby more than the loved one called can arrive. Thus, a seance can bring forth the spirit called, other restless formerly human spirits, and various visiting aliens who may or may not materialize depending on the setting.

A group of people fervently asking a spirit to manifest, to communicate with them, will reach that spirit by one means or another. That the spirit does not manifest is due not to The Call failing to reach this spirit, but to reluctance or disinterest. If the spirit has incarnated again and is caught up in a new life, they may dismiss The Call to them without giving it a thought. If the spirit was tired of the talk about a subject or obligations that were imposed by those who are now calling it, the spirit may turn its back and refuse to participate, free at last in death. If the spirit likewise has been longing to communicate, it may take the opportunity, or may decide that a one-on-one with this or that individual is preferable and make their own arrangements later, haunting the one they wish to communicate with.

When The Call is given to a spirit that incarnated as a human, this spirit can being called for its most recent life, the most recent incarnation, or can be called for one of its past lives. All are remembered by the spirit as vividly as the most recent incarnation. However, this setting is virtually begging for interference by Service-to-Self aliens looking to influence humans at every opportunity. Most calls to spirits who incarnated famous or influential humans in the past are done not for altruistic reasons, but for personal gain. Where did you bury the gold, what was the missing piece to the puzzle that would allow an idea to be patented, where are the manuscripts stored, etc. Thus The Call has been given to the Service-to-Self, who are notable for lying and leading astray. Pretending to be the spirit called is easy, and feeding the self-serving tendencies of the humans giving The Call easier still.

Identity cards cannot be checked at seances, so anyone and anything might manifest, pretending to be the spirit called!

Meditation

The Hindus are a very mystical people, in touch with their spiritual side, and trying all the time to move more in that direction. They study and practice methods to improved communications with the spirit world. Concentration, diet that will improve the ability of the body to concentrate and not be distracted, positions of the body that are helpful, and the right mental attitudes. All this effort brings them little, however, as the ability to communicate with spirits is strictly related to the desire to do so. A human following all the recommended practices religiously may be nowhere, another doing everything wrong, according to the recommended practices, is speaking regularly to the dead or spirits in higher dimensions. However, as would be the case with any group of people, some Hindus who follow the recommendations also have desire, and so connect. There is then a great flurry of enthusiasm for the practices, which had nothing to do with the success.

The Hindu speak of a state, the goal of living, called Nirvana. They attempt to reach this via meditation, and correct living, during many incarnations. They attempt to reach high levels of communication with others, as an adjunct to this state. What they are seeking is termed living in light form, or the spirit only, not requiring incarnations. Incarnations are a learning experience, but spirits grow beyond the need for this, in both the Service-to-Others and Service-to-Self orientations. Incarnations are then used as a learning experience, or a tool, for these spirits.

Hauntings

Spirits cannot manipulate the environment, except to effect a sense of coldness in those humans they are attempting to contact. The stuff of souls incarnates bodies, and has many points of influence during incarnations, but cannot move furniture or slam doors. The souls incarnating bodies work via the body to effect change in the physical world. Thus, much of what is described as haunting, other than the sense that a spirit is present and a communication soul-to-soul of what that communication is, is not from disembodied spirits. It is from humans, living in the vicinity and most often in the very house, using a brain wave generated by anger. This is commonly known as poltergeist activity, and is ascribed correctly to angry teens in the vicinity. Specialists can identify the human causing this, and advise the parents on how to reduce the anger, get it out in the open so it does not have these misdirected effects. Telekinesis has been registered, scientifically, so this is no longer a mystery.

Where ghosts appear on video images, these are in essence a chemical reaction, such as affecting the flow of light particles, and thus can truly be a spirit imprint! Levitation, done by aliens in 4th Density, is done by manipulating gravity particles. Thus, we float a paralyzed contactee into our ships, or float ourselves at will. A visiting spirit might attempt to affect gravity particles, to levitate objects, but will not manage this. However, humans who temporarily levitate objects are doing so, as they do when the slam doors, by other means, not gravity particle flow. Air pressure, magnetic manipulation, electrical particle charging, are in effect. Movies often portray levitation or poltergeist as being able to lift a heavy table, but in reality this is not what hauntings find. The chair moves a couple inches, a cup jiggles off the edge of a table, a paper lift and floats off the stack. Hollywood has exaggerated, as usual.

But where humans see something misty, a shape, or think they see a human appearing and then disappearing, this is most often a mind-trick of their own when they are aware they are talking to another spirit. Likewise, a spirit can leave an imprint on physical matter, in the same way they can make the room feel cold. To have a chemical effect like this requires the right chemistry, to be affected for instance by a lack or increase in heat particles. Heat particles are not the only particle flow a spirit can affect, but is the particle flow humans are most attuned to, thus notice. For instance, a human quickly feels cold when stepping outdoors without adequate clothing, but scarcely notices that the magnetic field has increased nearby. Thus, the division line is where large movement of objects, slamming doors and the like, this is human generated. Where there is a sense of presence, or a shadowy figure, or a sense of heat loss, this is most likely visiting spirits.

As with viewing a temporary manifestation of someone you knew, or a shadowy figure, hearing their voice or the musical chime, is also something your mind is doing to you, in response to a visiting spirit. Thus, this is a type of suggestion, which you willing go along with if this is a spirit you know, and wish to communicate with. The mind often does this, filling in the pieces in events that lack the whole. This is why there is such a strong different, often, between what witnesses report.

Each has filled in the missing pieces to make sense, to form a whole, and is describing the whole. If the visit is from a recently deceased uncle, beloved, and the mind wishes to record the messages as from this uncle, then it might insert an image of the uncle as he looked. Thus, during visits from spirits, there are some in the room who hear and see them, and others are unaffected and call them liars!

Poltergeist

A phenomenon long known but little understood by humans is what is termed poltergeist, or ghost knocking. Researchers have correctly identified that it is not caused by spirits but by the living. Is this a deliberate act? Most definitely, and the fastest way to locate the perpetrator is to scan for the angriest person, as intense rage is the engine by which poltergeist activity is run. Intense and unremitting anger sets the brain into Theta waves, and this builds over time until another offshoot is possible. What humans take to be their physical surroundings are what they can see, hear, feel, and observe to have substance as it moves, has color, or has a physical effect that can be observed. Humans understand that air is a substance as the action of wind is felt and observed, and airplanes, operating on this unseen substance, can lift and fly. Can't taste it, see it, or put ones hands about it, but know it's there.

Think of the substance that supports poltergeist activity as a type of air. When Theta waves reach a certain level, they support a transmission across this substance just as electrical arcing can cross an air space when the opposing charges reach a certain level on either side. Are opposing charges involved in poltergeist? In a manner of speaking, yes. The human causing poltergeist cannot control the effects, as this is a random discharge. They ramp up and things go bang. Windows break, knickknacks fall off the shelf, a chair moves, and internally the perpetrator is smiling as they made the object of their hatred distressed once again.

Densities

Different Densities means that simultaneously, in the same spot, several realities can occur. 1st Density through 3rd Density occupy the same plane. 1st Density is rock and water, without life. 2nd Density is life without conscious intelligence, such as plants and animals. 3rd Density is intelligent, conscious, life, such as humans have. 4th Density is spiritually mature entities (e.g. extraterrestrial life such as the grays). 5th Density is where the spirit no longer needs to incarnate and can remain disincarnate—the Spirit Guides. 6th Density is the Density of Light and Love. The entities of 6th Density assume light form and have an extreme mental capacity, beyond what humans can endure. These entities have a force of love, also. 7th Density is The Storm; is Thunder. It is light at the end of the tunnel people who have experienced a near death report. They see The Storm, but do not reach it. The 8th Density is The Ephemeral Storm. The Ephemeral Storm is both Omega and Alpha. The spiritual mass of the infinite universes becomes one central sun or Creator once again. Then is born a new universe, a new infinity, a new Logos which incorporates all that The Storm has experienced of Itself.

1st and 2nd Density are referred to as densities not because they are truly of differing density states, but because they indicate different levels of spiritual potential. Density is a term that refers not only to the physical state, but to the spiritual. Thus in 1st Density the spiritual potential is nil. In 2nd Density, the spiritual density potential is possible, and in fact at times incarnations into 2nd Density life occurs, as a lesson. In 3rd Density, spiritual potential is realized, etc.

The main lesson of the 3rd Density is of spiritual orientation—Service-to-Others or Service-to-Self. The Service-to-Other must understand, accept, and forgive the self and other entities (excluding the STS) before they are ready to function and work in the 4th Density. The 3rd Density is considered as pre-school, as there is relatively (to other Densities) not much to learn. Completion of the 3rd Density only takes about a thousand of life times.

In 4th Density the lesson to be learned is how to live communally with others. This differs depending on orientation. Those in Service-to-Others learn utter trust. Entities learn to support and communicate with each other to a high degree, so that utter trust is well placed. Those in the Service-to-Self orientation also learn how to depend upon each other, but trust due to the caring and concern of others is not the route. As you might imagine, the rules are extensive and strictly enforced.

In 5th Density the lessons to be learned are exploration of the universe. The wonders of how the universe is constructed. During 5th Density travel is extensive, and communication with other groups is frequent, where this is not so much the case during 4th Density. Some 5th Density entities incarnate and mingle with 3rd and 4th Density societies, but use these incarnations as a learning tool.

In 6th Density the lesson to be learned is high knowledge of God's plan for the universe. Here the interaction is less exploratory than stepping in to assume an active role in promulgating God's plan.

In densities higher than 3rd Density, co-existence can occur. Thus, it occurs that on the planet Earth, where 3rd Density humans are living and walking about, 4th, 5th, and higher Density incarnations are living and moving about, occupying the same space, as it were. This occurs because of a higher vibration rate of the sub-atomic particles. Were one to travel rapidly through the densities occurring in a single spot, one would see first the 3rd Density existence on the 3rd Density Earth, with say a human standing in a field of corn; then, moving to 4th Density existence one might see, for instance, a Zeta standing in a forest, where the forest and the Earth it grows upon are both in 4th Density; then, moving to 5th Density, one might see yet another scene. When we state that the Earth is scheduled to move to 4th Density Service-to-Others, we are describing what is to happen to humans. There will still be a 3rd Density Earth, on the same plane as the future 4th Density home of humans, as a portion of the Earth will be left in 3rd Density.

Much confusion reigns on the issue of density. Humans, for instance, were used to the concept of matter and energy being discrete and separate. Matter could not be energy, and energy could not be matter. Then Einstein shook things up and humans, after much painful denial and agony, allowed their concepts of reality to change. Density understanding is just such a quantum concept leap. In all fairness, the concept of density differences is difficult for even your scientists to deal with. The layman should be excused and granted a little confusion.

Merging Later

Entities are separated according to their orientation during 4th and 5th Density, and this separation continues on into the 6th Density also. In fact, they are permanently separated. There is much confusion over statements that have been made regarding Service-to-Self entities joining Service—to-Other entities in order to progress with their lessons after a certain point. The Service-to-Self do not cross over simply because it will benefit them, or because they desire this, or even because they start to prate the right talk and have learned how to behave themselves. They join Service-to-Other groups because they have at last grown up, spiritually speaking. When they have reached a point where they consider others at least as often as they consider themselves, they are Service-to-Other.

Some switching back and forth occurs, in any case, between orientations, but for the Service-to-Self they eventually reach a point where they are forced to consider their ways. They are stalemated, stopped, treading water, and living with the knowledge that their cribmates have an open field before them. They begin to stew in their own juices, debate the issues, and most eventually begin to see the light. You have a movie called Groundhog Day which exemplifies this situation, with a human forced to repeat a single day until he learns to truly care for others. He can't escape, even suicide attempts find him, the next morning, doing it all again. Thus it is, with entities in the Service-to-Self, who must at last, out of boredom or frustration, face what they have long feared—they are not the center of the Universe. Some entities never learn this, and spend eternity among the Service-to-Self, stymied. However, the higher densities find the Service-to-Self entities brooding and serious, introspective and trying new ways on for size. Seasoned Service-to-Other entities are usually kind and supportive of the fumbling attempts of newcomers to their group, who are invariably set back within the densities in order to polish their spiritual skills.

Overall, they lose ground for having veered to the Service-to-Self orientation.

Orientations

Service-to-Others (STO) means to think about others 50% of the time. Service-to-Self (STS) means to think about the self 95% of the time. To qualify for Service-to-Other orientation, an entity must consider others as often as the self. To qualify for Service-to-Self, the entity must focus on the self 95% of the time, almost exclusively. Where it may seem that these individuals would stand out, some very diplomatic and cultured people are of this category. They are able to disguise their self interest in condescension to others. They are able to disguise their self interest as the interests of the other. During 3rd Density, entities must decide their spiritual orientations—Service-to-Self or Service-to-Others. Most, the vast majority, decide the latter on almost all 3rd Density worlds. This decision, or the lesson of 3rd Density as it is called, needs to precede almost all other lessons, as mixing the two spiritual orientations together creates chaos and thus other lessons cannot proceed. Many entities on Earth are choosing the Service-to-Other orientation, and mid-incarnation are thus joining the ranks of the Service-to-Others.

What is generally considered good most often corresponds to STO. The terms are however laden with a baggage of subjectivity and what is good for one can be bad for another, thus these are easily misleading. The polarization to either STO/STS cannot be reduced to an external code of ethics only.

Spiritual Evolution

The Service-to-Self orientation is not so much a choice as a failure to progress. Where an entity in the Service-to-Other orientation is repeatedly choosing to include others as the focus of their concern, the Service-to-Self entity has never left their original focus—the self. Thus, the evolution, during spiritual growth, into two paths is natural, a factor of uneven growth rates, and the resulting separation of the orientations during early densities is simply a practical step taken to facilitate learning. A Service-to-Self entity cannot be forced to develop concern for others, nor can this concern be worn like a social facade in the densities above 3rd Density, as a fake or a sham. Where entities are given free will, as all are within God's Universe, such a choice as the Service-to-Self orientation is and will continue to be a reality.

Conscious Choice

Unlike the self-improvement disciplines that can be self imposed, one's orientation is not a conscious choice. Humans who are distressed at what they deem self centered motives are most likely not on the road to becoming one in the Service-to-Self. These individuals never concern themselves with such thoughts. The focus is rather on how the world, not themselves, should change, and the change is always supposed to be one that betters the self-focused individual. In fact, conscious attempts to move oneself in the direction of Service-to-Other have a negative effect, as the focus is often put upon behavior that is assumed to be Service-to-Other but in fact is self serving. The key in orientation is the true motive behind behavior, not the stated motive or even the apparent motive.

Self Doubts

In general, if a person wonders what orientation they have chosen, they have not yet chosen. Those who have chosen their orientation have almost daily clues that they have made a choice, and that they are solidly in one camp or the other.

For those in the Service-to-Other, they not only find themselves frequently musing about the welfare of others, they take steps to enhance the welfare of others. These steps are not a mere phone call inquiring about someone's health, but require the concerned one to go out of their way, spending precious time that would otherwise be spent on recreation or pleasure or bettering one's circumstances, or spending personal resources such as savings or personal possessions. These steps are not done as a result of a resolve to become a Service-to-Other person, they are done automatically. If one needs reminders to take these steps, then they are trying to become an individual operating in the Service-to-Other, and have not yet arrived.

For those in the Service-to-Self, the focus on the self is never ending. It is a rare and fleeting moment that this individual ponders another's circumstances, most likely because the other's circumstances reminded the individual solidly in the Service-to-Self of his own past. At these times the individual will quickly correct themselves, getting back to the business at hand—self interest. Where the person firmly in the Service-to-Other orientation will of course have occasional preoccupation with self, and even give the self priority at time, the person firmly in the Service-to-Self continually takes this posture.

Karma

Under duress, and having experienced a shattering blow of some kind, humans often ascribe the cause to karma. There is bad karma and good karma and this explains everything, or so they hope. Could it be that life is so terribly unpredictable? Why would a benign God throw them into such a situation, create such an erratic world? Yes and no, there is karma. Karma is at play where the human causes the situation in some manner, by their prior actions in this lifetime. Karma is not at play when the life situation occurs because of acts of nature or the actions of other humans not directly involved in the situation at hand. We will give examples.

Karma. A man is greedy, always seeking to maximize the goods that he can call his own. Materialistic. In the main he succeeds in becoming a man of means, and secretly gloats over his ability to charm or manipulate others so that he succeeds. Then one day he finds himself a pauper, having been outdone by one with greater charm or manipulation skills. Is this karma? It is indeed, as the man brought this down on himself by amassing goods and bragging about. He essentially placed a sign where everyone could see, saying come steal from me. It would also be karma if a former business partner, having been left bereft and financially devastated due to the actions of the greedy one, arranged for the greedy one to have marital troubles. Where one's trouble can be traced directly to one's own actions in this lifetime, that is karma.

Not karma. A woman desires children, and in due course marries and becomes pregnant. Through a throw of nature's dice, one of her conceptions has an extra chromosome, and is a mongoloid, retarded. Friends point out that she was not a scrupulous housekeeper, or perhaps was torn between her career and family duties, and that her misfortune is karma as now she must stay home and tend to the new youngster, who needs constant care. Another example is a car accident, where one is driving down the highway and, rounding the curve, finds themselves head on with a drunken driver. Did the victim cause this accident somehow? It was simply a matter of time and place, a throw of the dice. These situations do not involve karma, not even as retribution from a former lifetime, which never occurs. Each incarnation is truly a fresh start.

Chakras

Chakra (Energy Center) is a concept referring to wheel-like vortices which, according to traditional Indian medicine, are believed to exist in the surface of the etheric double of man. The Chakras are said to be "force centers" or whorls of energy permeating, from a point on the physical body, the layers of the subtle bodies in an ever-increasing fan-shaped formation. Rotating vortices of subtle matter, they are considered the focal points for the reception and transmission of energies. Different systems posit a varying number of chakras; the most well known system in the West is that of seven chakras.

Chakras do indeed exist. There are many human names for what is perceived to be a biophysical connection to the spirit. These connections exist in that the soul, or spirit, is immersed in the physical body and mingles throughout. An incarnation is not a superficial matter. During an Out-of-Body experience the soul separates from the physical body, and the human left behind is quiescent, as though without emotion or much thought. This is a time spent quietly contemplating or doing mundane tasks. As the soul, during incarnation, is diffused throughout the body, it aligns itself to embrace the world. The soul communicates with its extensions, the human arms and legs, as this is not a natural position for the soul. Incarnations in life forms that do not have arms and legs would, understandably, have different Chakras.

The Chakras are related to the functions of the incarnated spirit, not to the human form. The spirit centers itself, and thus the heart Chakra, and concerns itself with communicating to the mind, and thus the third eye, but the other organs of the human body are incidental to the spirit, which is not concerned with digestion or locomotion or such functions. Spirits that are more entranced with physical activities, such as sex or drug use, may be more diffuse within the physical body, however. A central Chakra, both in the human body and in Chakra action, is the heart Chakra. There are several reasons for this. First, the heart is centralized in the human body in order to serve the body well in its task as circulation central. Second, the heart responds to emotions, invariably, beating fast during fright or joy, being regular or irregular in pace with the life situation. Third, the spiritual centering of the soul within the physical body of a human must for similar reasons be centered. As the soul fills the being of whatever it incarnates, it is distended into the human limbs and digits. To work as a unit, the soul indeed utilizes parts of itself to maintain unity and cohesive action. The heart Chakra, while not circulating fluids, has a similar importance and function. The human body in an incarnation might be utterly unaware of the incarnating soul, or intensely aware and in communication with its soul. This choice is up to the soul, who can choose to keep the body dumb or involve the body in communications. The soul can go Out-of-Body with the human body scarcely aware of this, only aware that it seems to have lost some of its normal motivation. Those who are aware of their Chakras are likely those seeking to communicate with their indwelling soul, and as a consequence, succeed! It is this communication that is described regarding kundalini.

K. R.

Understanding of Energy Centers

The steps to balance oneself are only one; that is, an understanding an understanding of the Energy Centers which make up the Mind/Body/Spirit complex. This understanding may be briefly summarized as follows. The first balancing is of Earth, vibratory energy complex, called the Red Ray. An understanding and acceptance of this energy is fundamental. The next energy complex, which may be blocked is the emotional, or personal complex, also known as the Orange Ray. This blockage will often demonstrate itself as personal eccentricities or distortions with regard to self-conscious understanding or acceptance of self.

The third blockage resembles the ego. It is the Yellow Ray or Solar Plexus Center. Blockages in this center will often manifest as distortions toward power manipulation and other social behaviors concerning those close and those associated with the Mind/Body/Spirit complex. Those with blockages in these first three Energy Center will have continuing difficulties in ability to further their seeking of the One/Unity.

The center of heart, or Green Ray, is the center from which 3rd Density beings may springboard to Infinite Intelligence. Blockages in this area may manifest as difficulties in expressing universal love or compassion.

The Blue Ray center of energy streaming is the center which, for the first time, is outgoing as well as inpouring. Those blocked in this area may have difficulty in grasping the Spirit/Mind complexes of its own entity and further difficulty in expressing such understandings of self. Entities blocked in this area may have difficulties in accepting communication from other Mind/Body/Spirit complexes.

The next center is the pineal or Indigo Ray center. Those blocked in this center may experience a lessening of the influx of Intelligent Energy due to manifestations which appear as unworthiness. The Indigo Ray balancing is quite central to the type of work which revolves about the Spirit which has its influx then into the transformation or transmutation of 3rd Density to 4th Density, it being the Energy Center receiving the least distorted outpourings of Love/Light from Intelligent Energy and also the potential for the key to the gateway of Intelligent Infinity.

The remaining center of energy influx, the Violet Ray, is simply the total expression of the entity's vibratory complex of mind, body, and spirit. It is as it will be, "balanced" or "imbalanced" has no meaning at this energy level, for it gives and takes in its own balance. Whatever the distortion may be, it cannot be manipulated as can the others and, therefore, has no particular importance in viewing the balancing of an entity.

Some entities penetrate several planes at one time. Others penetrate them slowly. Some in eagerness attempt to penetrate the higher planes before penetrating the energies of the so-called more fundamental planes. This causes energy imbalance. Ill health is to frequently the result of a subtle mismatch of energies in which some of the higher energy levels are being activated by the conscious attempts of the entity while the entity has not penetrated the lower energy centers or sub-densities of this density.

The negative ray pattern is the red/orange/yellow moving directly to the blue, this only being used in order to contact Intelligent Infinity.

In positively oriented entities the configuration is even, crystallinely clear, and of the seven ray description.

Primary Energy Centers

Red Ray is the foundation; Orange Ray the movement towards Yellow Ray which is the ray of self-awareness and interaction. Green ray is the movement through various experiences of energy exchanges having to do with compassion and all-forgiving love to the primary blue ray which is the first ray of radiation of self regardless of any actions from another.

The Green Ray entity is ineffectual in the face of blockage from other-selves. The Blue Ray entity is a co-Creator. Consider the function of the Logos as representative of the Infinite Creator in effectuating the knowing of the Creator by the Creator and you may perhaps see the steps by which this may be accomplished.

Development of the Energy Centers

The basic pivotal points of each level of development; that is, each Density beyond second, may be seen to be as follows: Firstly, the basic energy of so-called Red Ray. This ray may be understood to be the basic strengthening ray for each Density. It shall never be condescended to as less important or productive of spiritual evolution, for it is the foundation ray.

The next foundation ray is yellow. This is the great steppingstone ray. At this ray the mind/body potentiates to its fullest balance. The strong red/orange/yellow triad springboards the entity into the center ray of green. This is again a basic ray but not a primary ray.

This is the resource for spiritual work. When green ray has been activated we find the third primary ray being able to begin potentiation. This is the first true spiritual ray in that all transfers are of an integrated mind/body/spirit nature. The blue ray seats the learnings/teachings of the spirit in each density within the mind/body complex animating the whole, communicating to others this entirety of beingness.

The Indigo Ray, though precious, is that ray worked upon only by the adept. It is the gateway to Intelligent Infinity bringing Intelligent Energy through. This is the Energy Center worked upon in those teachings considered inner, hidden, and occult, for this ray is that which is infinite in its possibilities. Those who heal, teach, and work for the Creator in any way which may be seen to be both radiant and balanced are those activities which are Indigo Ray.

The Violet Ray is constant and does not figure into a discussion of the functions of ray activation in that it is the mark, the register, the identity, the true vibration of an entity.

Rotational Speed of Energy Centers

Much emphasis is laid upon the harmonies and balances of individuals. It is necessary for graduation across Densities for the primary Energy Centers to be functioning in such a way as to communicate with Intelligent Infinity and to appreciate and bask in this light in all of its purity. However, to fully activate each Energy Center is the mastery of few, for each center has a variable speed of rotation or activity. The important observation to be made once all necessary centers are activated to the minimal necessary degree is the harmony and balance between these Energy Centers.

Each Energy Center has a wide range of rotational speed or more clearly in relation to color, brilliance. The more strongly the will of the entity concentrates upon and refines or purifies each Energy Center, the more brilliant or rotationally active each energy center will be. It is not necessary for the Energy Centers to be activated in order in the case of the self-aware entity. Thus entities may have extremely brilliant Energy Centers while being quite unbalanced in their Violet Ray aspect due to lack of attention paid to the totality of experience of the entity.

The key to balance may then be seen in the unstudied, spontaneous, and honest response of entities toward experiences, thus using experience to the utmost, then applying the balancing exercises and achieving the proper attitude for the most purified spectrum of Energy Center manifestation in Violet Ray. This is why the brilliance or rotational speed of the Energy Centers is not considered above the balanced aspect or Violet Ray manifestation of an entity in regarding harvestability; for those entities which are unbalanced, especially as to the primary rays, will not be capable of sustaining the impact of the Love and Light of Intelligent Infinity to the extent necessary for harvest.

The red, yellow, and blue rays are primary because they signify activity of a primary nature.

The Seven Bodies

The Red-Ray body is the chemical body. However, it is not the body which you have as clothing in the physical. It is the unconstructed material of the body, the elemental body without form. This basic unformed material body is important to understand for there are healings which may be carried out by the simple understanding of the elements present in the physical vehicle.

The Orange-Ray body is the physical body complex. This body complex is still not the body you inhabit but rather the body formed without self-awareness, the body in the womb before the spirit/mind complex enters. This body may live without the inhabitation of the mind and spirit complexes. However, it seldom does so.

The Yellow-Ray body is the physical vehicle which you know of at this time and in which you experience catalyst. This body has the mind/body/spirit characteristics and is equal to the physical illusion.

The Green-Ray body is that body which may be seen in séance when what is called "ectoplasm" is furnished. This is a lighter body packed more densely with life. It may be call the astral body. Others have called this same body the etheric body. However, this is not correct in the sense that the etheric body is that body of gateway wherein Intelligent Energy is able to mold the mind/body/spirit complex.

The light body or Blue-Ray body may be called the devachanic body. There are many other names for this body especially in the Indian Sutras or writings, for there are those among these peoples which have explored these regions and understand the various types of devachanic bodies. There are many, many types of bodies in each density, much like this one.

The Indigo-Ray body, the etheric body is the gateway body. In this body form is substance and you may only see this body as that of light as it may mold itself as it desires.

The Violet-Ray body may perhaps be understood as what is called the "Buddha body" or that body which is complete.

Each of these bodies has an effect upon the mind/body/spirit complex in your life beingness. The interrelationships are many and complex

Perhaps one suggestion that may be indicated is this: The Indigo-Ray body may be used by the healer once the healer becomes able to place its consciousness in this etheric state. The Violet-Ray body is of equal efficacy to the healer for within it lies a sense of wholeness which is extremely close to unity with @ll that there is. These bodies are part of each entity and the proper use of them and understanding of them is, though far advanced from the standpoint of 3rd Density harvest, nevertheless useful to the adept.

K. R.

Summary

Space/Time and Time/Space concepts are those concepts describing as mathematically as possible the relationships of our illusion, that which is seen to that which is unseen. These descriptive terms are clumsy.

In the experiences of the mystical search for Unity, these need never be considered, for they are but part of an illusory system. The seeker seeks The Storm. The Storm is to be sought by the balanced and self-accepting self aware, both of its apparent distortions and its total perfection. Resting in this balanced awareness, the entity then opens the self to the Universe which it is. The light energy of all things may then be attracted by this intense seeking, and wherever the inner seeking meets the attracted cosmic prana, realization of The Storm takes place.

The purpose of clearing each Energy Center is to allow that meeting place to occur at the Indigo Ray vibration, thus making contact with Intelligent Infinity and dissolving all illusions. Service-to-Others is automatic at the released energy generated by this state of consciousness.

The Space/Time and Time/Space distinctions do not hold sway except in 3rd Density. However, fourth, fifth, and to some extent, sixth, work within some system of polarized Space/Time and Time/Space.

Each entity is the Creator. The entity, as it becomes more and more conscious of its self, gradually comes to the turning point at which it determines to seek either in Service-to-Others or in Service-to-Self. The seeker becomes the adept when it has balanced with minimal adequacy the Energy Centers red, orange, yellow, and blue with the addition of the green for the positive, thus moving into indigo work.

The adept then begins to do less of the preliminary or outer work, having to do with function, and begins to effect the inner work which has to do with being. As the adept becomes a more and more consciously crystallized entity it gradually manifests more and more of that which it always has been since before time; that is, The Storm.

Incarnation Focus

The Spirit Guides dictate the circumstances of an incarnation for immature souls and the immature soul has scant input. Incarnation for immature souls, and the immature soul has scant input. Out-of-Body experiences are discouraged, considered flitting out of school, with the young souls returned to their incarnation. This type of monitoring or coercion by the Spirit Guides is done essentially by a force of will, but can the young soul rebel and refuse? What happens in these circumstances? The Spirit Guides rely on physical constraints to control souls in the Service-to-Self, using a substance that only very high level entities can control. This substance blocks the stuff of souls from moving about, if necessary, a type of jail. Immature souls leaning toward the Service-to-Self invariably challenge their Spirit Guides, as adolescents do their parents, testing their limits. They encounter this type of restraint, being either forced to remain in the incarnation, or assume the incarnation to begin with, and realize that protest is futile.

The lessons to be learned during a forthcoming incarnation are clear to the Spirit Guides, and have been explained fully to the immature soul. Often, the lesson is one at the fore repeatedly, in the past, the young entity stuck and not making much progress in this regard. The word lesson is used because the Earth, as in any 3rd Density experience, is a schoolhouse for young souls, and work in school is referred to as lessons. But this is not akin to memorizing and prating back what one is expected to have memorized. Nor is it akin to solving puzzles, learning the mechanisms for solving puzzles, the sciences or the machinations of mathematics so that the soul understands the combustion engine, for instance, and can apply these concepts to future situations. Gaining in-depth knowledge of how the Universe works is, of course, a product of being incarnated, but the lessons of 3rd Density are primarily growth of the soul in how it positions itself vs a vs other souls. The young soul does this by migrating toward being Service-to-Other or Service-to-Self, by a series of decisions backed by actions taken.

That said, that the Spirit Guides can force an incarnation to occur. In that interaction with other entities is the primary determination to be made in 3rd Density, how are the circumstances of an incarnation determined? Rich or poor, strong and healthy or sickly and crippled, intelligent or retarded, with opportunities and freedom or in a restricted setting, and with a supportive family or in a setting of rejection and cruelty—how and why is the particular setting chosen for the young soul? An obvious reason is to teach the young soul empathy, or test the willingness to sacrifice the self out of empathy. Empathy is best learned by being in a position to experience distress, so that in a future life one recognizes the situation another is in, and can either act or decide not to act. Since the goal is to allow the young soul to make decisions, and thus take action, this setting is best done cyclically, with a life experiencing some kind of pain or restriction alternating with a life where opportunity to help those in such a setting exists.

Depending upon the leaning of the soul, the lessons would move to present greater opportunities for sacrifice of the self, if leaning toward Service-to-Other, to conflicts with other opportunists if leaning toward the Service-to-Self. Service-to-Self is more than mere self centered enjoyment, it is the realization that life with others who are of a like mind will require a type of cooperation, establishment of a pecking order, and living with the consequences of having squandered resources in the unmitigated focus on enjoyment. Service-to-Other is likewise leaning to trust those of a like mind, to accept help as well as give it, and learning the consequences of unmitigated giving without consideration of the need to sustain the self. Thus both orientations are learning what their life in 4th Density, where the spiritual orientations are separated, will be like. Souls will be sorted out by spiritual orientation with those in the Service-to-Self carted off to their prison colony worlds and those in the Service-to-Other incarnated into high tech communities where all care for the common good and the Golden Rule prevails, and in the main these souls have been acclimated to anticipate the setting they are heading toward.

Going into the Transformation, family or community settings for an incarnation are chosen for exposure to the polarization to be expected during the last days. This polarization of the spiritual orientations presents a lesson in the type of interaction to be expected in 4th Density, where those in the Service-to-Other only encounter those in the Service-to-Self in strictly controlled settings and with delimiting parameters. Democrat and Republican today encounter each other, with the obvious leanings of the parties toward concern for the common man, or concern for the elite with cruel repression of the common man, exposed. But the tentacles where these philosophies clash are many, the opportunities for encounters many. In 4th Density, the battles are more intense, but the settings are tightly controlled and delimited. To prepare young souls for encounters they will have in highly polarized settings, and for future encounters in 4th Density, family settings may put highly Service-to-Other and strongly Service-to-Self souls within the same family. There is never any doubt, within the family, as to the focus of these highly polarized members. Depending upon how activist the individual soul is, these types of encounters may occur in the community, or national, setting, likewise with forethought by the Spirit Guides as to how the incarnations might assist in arranging these encounters.

Focus of Entities

In the beginning, each forming entity is aware only of themselves. Self awareness is a constant state in all life of whatever form, but at the start this is the only state. Forming entities are placed into 3rd Density incarnations, repeatedly, to hasten the 3rd Density lesson—orientation determination. Whether incarnated or not, forming entities first become aware of others based on the effect upon the self. Is the effect pleasant or unpleasant, dominating or acquiescing, desired or resisted. Incarnated or not, social interchange has begun. Sense of the other is also born in this context, not only in awareness of the partner in social interactions, but by observing others undergoing a similar experience. Empathy is in essence the statement, "I was once there, and I understand." Within 3rd Density there is first self awareness, second reacting to the presence of others, and last the capacity for empathy.

In making the orientation determination the entity choosing Service-to-Self is not so much progressing towards this determination as clinging back. They remain most comfortable with self awareness, and react to others in this context, essentially asking "What can you do for me?"

Interactions between entities change and become more complex during spiritual 4th Density, and many entities completing their 3rd Density existence are already operating in this mode. Following the development of the capacity for empathy comes the determination to intercede, to rescue, and as an adjunct to this determination the entity begins cooperative efforts, the sum being greater than the parts. Complex social interchange presents forming entities with situations requiring compromise if goals are to be met, and the need to subjugate personal desires so that another might be rescued or the group as a whole might benefit. While the entity leaning toward the Service-to-Other orientation moves steadily in this direction, the entity leaning toward Service-to-Self reacts to this greater social complexity with more of the same old reaction, "What's in it for me." As entities surrounding the emerging Service-to-Self entity are learning compromise and conciliation, the technique for the self focused entity to gain more for the self is essentially manipulation. Since groups of emerging Service-to-Other entities are forming, the emerging

Service-to-Self entity tunes its manipulation skills so as to manipulate groups, too.

The orientations, even within 3rd Density, set upon different paths, and polarization increases as they progress.

Arriving in 4th Density, the fledgling entity thus is already reacting and responding to others, pressing forward with personal agendas and dealing with interpersonal conflicts. How does life in 4th Density differ from what the entity has experienced in 3rd Density? For the Service-to-Self their spiritual existence is essentially frozen while their intellectual existence progresses. For the Service-to-Self there is even less interplay and manipulation between entities than took place in 3rd Density. A rigid hierarchy with rules for everything emerges so that the lessons can proceed. For the Service-to-Other entity their spiritual wisdom continues to grow and augments rather than detracts from their intellectual progress. Skills in team efforts, where the individual is not required to sacrifice but can learn and grow while contributing are honed. Where the focus at the beginning of 3rd Density was self awareness, by the end of 4th Density in the Service-to-Other orientation the focus has expanded to be on group awareness.

Spiritual Growth

At the base of the many horrors and inequities and sorrows that life throws at us is spiritual growth, as this is the point of incarnated life. In a life lived without personal pain or anguish there is little incentive to growth. If everyone were born beautiful, lived a life without disease, never wanted for any physical comfort, and did not encounter adversity or struggle, what reason would there be to develop a strong compassion for others? Compassion, empathy for what others are going through, is love, and on a spiritual level is learned only by having experienced pain and anguish oneself. The young soul, immature, may experience what by instinct the life form experiences when a member of the species is in terror or pain. This is biological, an evolutionary result, to help the flock or herd realize danger and flee to safety. A rabbit, sensing another had been captured by a coyote, is terrified when it hears the squeals of panic and pain from its fellow rabbit, but this does not equate to empathy. Most certainly, the rabbit would not offer itself for another! This gesture is only found in highly evolved souls, those who have long ago chosen the Service-to-Other path.

In that the young soul remembers, and carries forward any memory of pain or anguish from prior lives, it begins to relate on more than an instinctive level to what it sees about it, in the pain and anguish in others. Unlike the rabbits, who flee in terror when one of their fellows becomes prey, the human with an incarnated soul contemplates the outcome. If inclined toward Service-to-Other, they can see that a circumstance is leading to pain for another, and step in to try to change the outcome. This may mean a loss of some kind, such as taking time out from other tasks, or spending some money intended for the self, or even putting the self at risk, but the outcome, for another, is changed. These steps may be small, such as stopping the car to inquire after the welfare of someone at the side of the road, or large, such as rushing into a burning building to break open a door trapping others inside. In the latter, the human is certainly offering themselves so that others may survive, putting themselves at risk, a potential sacrifice of self. This type of gesture, the unhesitating step to sacrifice all to help others, always indicates a highly evolved soul, strongly in the Service-to-Other. Would the rabbit rush into a burning building, to prevent the pain and panic in its fellows?

Ultimately, after many thousands of incarnated lifetimes, or perhaps even millions of such lifetimes, the soul has evolved to be intensely loving, and this is not a shallow matter. In these lifetimes, there are times when the soul was incarnated into crippled or diseased bodies, or trapped in a live of suffering and anguish, no escape possible, such as slavery or life in a land suffering a drought where there is never enough to eat, for all. There are times of horror and terror, when the volcano is about to explode or the incarnation is in a woman or a man of small frame, or a child, and a sadist has full control of their life and enjoying the pain and hopelessness he can inflict. There are also times when the incarnation affords strength, the body strong with strength respected by others, the circumstances of birth affording funds and influence, the IQ high so that meeting life's adversity is a game rather than a sorrow. If the point of an incarnation full of pain and anguish is to experience what others might be going through, the point of an incarnation that affords strength is to give the soul an opportunity to rescue others, to put oneself at risk. At first, the young soul stands idly by, watching others suffer, but feels discomfited by this as it remembers when it suffered, in past lives.

As steps are taken, to rescue or intervene for others, this relieves the sense of suffering, not only for those rescued, but for the rescuer! This is the answer, to help others, as if this is done more often, overall grief is lessened! Where this intellectual discussion of the reasons for pain and anguish are hardly a comfort to the sufferer, it does point to an out. The parent, losing a child, will often be more intensely empathetic to other families in similar circumstances, and be a great source of comfort for them. Orphans are often adopted because their new parents dealt with abandonment in the past, during past lives. Firemen rush into burning buildings because they themselves were trapped in the past, in past lives, in situations where a helping hand could have made all the difference, but was withheld. Many people in philanthropic situations, who devote their lives to helping others, have some intense grief in their recent past, an impetus.

Sentience

Man values his intelligence, forethought, empathy, and consciousness, as these place him above the other animals on the Earth, or so he thinks.

Man is a sentient being, but the low life of the Earth have these qualities in some measure too, as they are concomitant with what the basic building blocks of life throughout the Universe produce. From simple one celled creatures to the complexity of a hominoid, life interacts with its surroundings in the same manner. Life that survives at all is self protective, and thus has self awareness of sorts. If it must do more than simply react to survive, must be proactive, then a form of forethought has occurred. Animals with the same genetic structure can scarcely help but experience empathy with each other when cries of distress are heard or the tensed posture of defense is assumed. Early empathy is simply shared neuron patterns and shared experiences. Thus, depending on the chemical components of the world and the path evolution takes on that world, the sentient creatures that result may take any form, and the list would be infinite. Sentience is not exclusive to man, or to mammals, or to the Earth—it is concomitant with life itself throughout the Universe.

Rule of Non-Interference

In a spiritual learning house, a schoolhouse for emerging souls, the prime directive is non-interference. This places a wealth of spontaneous experiences before the emerging souls, who develop empathy by being subject to various painful situations. Empathy simply does not exist if a spirit has not been there, in its past. There is no need to list the situations mankind or any life form finds distressing, as the list is something that every incarnated soul struggling through a life is acutely aware of. Living with physical pain, dread or terror or abandonment and uncertainty, loss of a child or spouse, sudden setbacks, ridicule and expulsion from a group, the list is almost endless. At a certain point in the young souls development, Payuumian Guardians become involved to help shape the circumstances of the next incarnation, so the setting is one which will maximize opportunities for learning for this particular entity. The young soul might be placed into a starving country, or a place of wealth and power, into a body stricken with genetic disease or into a body capable of intimidating others. Nevertheless, the rule is non-interference with the incarnation, so the lessons to be learned stick as they are not theoretical, but very real to both the incarnated life form and the spirit within. A lesson well learned.

At a certain point in the progress of a world developing emerging souls, it on occasion becomes necessary to interfere further with circumstances, to maintain a proper balance for the first lesson that young souls are to learn, which results in their decision to be either Service-to-Other or Service-to-Self. A young soul in a constant state of fear struggles to get past this to the point of empathy, which is something the Service-to-Self masters, visiting the schoolhouse and waiting to be called as advisers, know. Thus, brutal intimidation, without any apparent hope of changing the situation, is something the Service-to-Self try to achieve in a developing world, but something the Payuumian Guardians prevent. A balanced situation, where action can result in change for the better, so a young soul can perceive the result of their efforts to change a painful situation for others, is desired, and thus circumstances are manipulated in the schoolhouse to arrange for this. Likewise, a young soul leaning toward the Service-to-Self orientation would find in a vicious dictatorship over other young souls a false setting for the world they are heading toward. In the Service-to-Self worlds, all are solidly Service-to-Self, and not easily dominated. Thus, in a balanced schoolhouse, the Service-to-Self gang does not invariably win, and when the gang turns on each other, viciously, the true nature of living the Service-to-Self life style is learned.

In all these exceptions with the Rule of Non-Interference, manipulation is done to things, not the incarnated human or life form, and thus does not interfere with the setting the emerging young soul can control. The decisions by the entity, expressed into action by the incarnated human, are not interfered with, thus.

K. R.

Free Will and Love Giving

Free Will, also called, Blessing of Freedom is the most important law in The Storm. Giving love when not being asked could harm instead of improve. "Giving" love is not giving, in such a case. If you give love when you have not been asked, you are not giving; you are taking. You are taking Service-to-Self energy. An STS entity does not learn to be an STO candidate by determining the needs of another. Because the act is then one of self-gratification. If one "gives" where there is no request, therefore no need, this is a Free Will violation! And besides, what other motivation could there possibly be in such a scenario? Everything is lessons and if an entity has chosen a specific path they should be allowed to go and learn their way.

Much of the activity on this Earth that passes for benevolent acts consists in feeding the Service-to-Self entities. It is rather like the co-dependent relationship. The abuser cannot abuse you without your permission. Not only that, all the activity to "save" this or that group, to "bomb the earth and its inhabitants with love and light," may only serve to increase the negativity, the Darkness, and the control system because, without having been asked, or acting against those whose choice it is to deceive, to control, to misinform, we are violating their Free Will in acting against them, even if our intentions are good. Thus, they feed on this energy, increasing their energy in Service-to-Self.

We all want to "save" our loved ones from mistakes of judgment or action. We all die a little inside when we see our children following pathways that could, in some cases, actually end in their deaths. But, in truth, we can only advise, we cannot act against their choices if they are at or beyond the age of consent. Where so many of us fall by the wayside is in not understanding how much of this is masked in the guise of helplessness and appeals to our sense of pity and compassion.

Spiritual Awareness

The human animal, from birth, deals with many distractions that obscure communications from the spirit. Hunger, sexual urges, fright, pain—all demand center stage. Social distractions are just as insistent, as the companion who demands constant chatter requires as much concentration as a throbbing toothache. Both refuse to go away. Humans wanting to be in touch with their inner selves develop many techniques for separating themselves from the distractions—long walks, wilderness retreats, prayer, gardening, meditation. The key practice is to diminish the noise and listen to the upwellings, concentrating on the song the spirit is trying to sing. The key is to eliminate distractions. If this can be accomplished best while folding laundry at an empty laundromat, or walking the dog, or pretending to take a nap, it matters not.

Where the physical world can be a distraction, yet it is part of The Storm just as the soul is. The soul is aware of the physical world, as these are memories that the soul carries with it, one incarnation to another. The entity well integrated with the physical world is making a true connection to The Storm, celebrating the rich connections. The notion that spirituality is separate from the physical world is perpetrated by False Prophets who would tell you that only special individuals who can separate themselves from the physical are able to understand the spirit world. This is nonsense!

Soul Personalities

Souls often have a personality stamp, just as the humans or other life forms they incarnate, as their early experiences and reactions to these experiences shapes the pool of quick responses from which they grab in emergencies. If a soul has reacted by running and hiding, and this has been successful, they consider this at first, in the future. Likewise, if standing and fighting has proved to eliminate the problem most effectively for the tribe as a whole, even though the entity may suffer injury and death, if a similar situation arises, the soul who has taken the stand-and-fight posture will take this with little hesitation. Souls thus may work behind the scenes, backfilling others who are more vocal and visible, depending upon their success in the past, or may be a loud mouth, assertive and probing danger on the path ahead in this manner, if in their experience they do this more effectively than others and if in the past they found the others in the tribe coming to their rescue when they flushed out what was laying for them ahead along the path. Thus, in analyzing past lives, it is important to recognize early experiences and reactions to these early experiences from a long term growth of the entity, which smoothes out.

Most developing souls, still on their birth planet and yet to experience a solidly Service-to-Other world, have leaned toward being one sex or the other, by preference, as their skills and developed talents lay mostly in that realm, and all is new and the more comfort a young soul can garner during their adventures, the more confident they feel about sallying forth. Thus, often the partner in a bond who has ideas, is articulate, innovative, and exploratory is the male. This fits with the hominoid concept of a male, but in other worlds where the female is large and aggressive, the entity would have reincarnated as a female most often. Likewise, the partner in a bond who empathizes with the missions assumed by the more adventurous one often forms that bond because they wish this role, and want to go those places, but lack talents or experience. They then assume the support role, which helps both.

Relationships between souls, particularly on a developing world where souls are unbalanced in their development, are often strong bonds. When in strange territory, as young souls feel they are often, one seeks friends, as their alliances are known, their reactions predictable, and the relationship thus comforting when walking into unknown territory. Developing worlds, where souls are sparked and learn their first lesson, the orientation lesson, have endless surprises for newly reincarnating souls. The soul does not have the wealth of previous experiences to rely upon that old souls do, and thus being incarnated in a new culture, a new climate, a new setting or sex, all engender the need for a friend at hand.

Spiritual Health

Humans regularly go to the dentist, get their shots, work out at the gym, and take their vitamins. This is all to maintain physical health. Humans also go dancing, take up hobbies, tie one on now and then, surround themselves with music, and, especially on the West Coast, go for therapy. This is all for mental health. In the spiritual realm there is worship at church, meditation, and . . . not much else. The reason for this is that the spiritual side of man doesn't manifest in the same way physical and mental problems do. Does one ever die of a sick spirit? Is one hospitalized because the spirit is sick? There seems to be no repercussions to neglecting the spirit. Those who attend church regularly fare no better than those who don't, and the benefits of meditation cannot be measured. So, why bother?

Where the spiritual side of man does not demand care and attention, it is the one aspect of a human life that remains after death. What occurs during an incarnation either strengthens or diminishes the spirit, and this sum total forms the basis for the next incarnation. That's why one should bother.

What is spiritual health? As with the human intellect, the spirit grows best when exposed to breadth. Watch the sunset and contemplate the vastness of the Universe rather then crack another beer and stare at the TV. Look with wonder at the variety of human forms and personalities rather than close this out as an intrusion on the status quo. Take responsibility for a small task that improves the life of the least among you, and get hooked on how much better this makes you feel about yourself than if you had spent that bit of time fussing over yourself.

K. R.

Spirit Substance

The substance that makes up the spirit is called Chromatic, and is not something that the human eye can perceive. The soul has substance, and grows in bulk early in its development as many incarnations, many lives, are experienced. This bulk cannot be gauged by humans, who look upon one another as having equal souls, when nothing of the kind is the reality. Some souls are so tiny and poorly constructed that they dissipate after the incarnation, what is termed aborted entities. This type of soul may be present in many animals and even some plant forms, as the stuff of souls is dispersed throughout the Universe and incarnations happen naturally. Where the human eye cannot gauge the mass of another soul, the spirits gauge this very well. You know instinctively that another is old and wise. Spiritual growth occurs most rapidly early on via incarnations, but later this growth proceeds based on experiences outside of incarnations, and incarnations are not needed for this purpose. Incarnations continue to be used as a learning experience, however, from time to time.

The soul not only has memory, it does not forget. It is not by accident that intelligent life forms have nerves, brains, and memory in the form of chemical impressions. It is not by accident that this same structure is found for intelligent thought on all density levels. It is intrinsic to the way the Universe is structured, and thus souls likewise have such structures. The stuff of souls is simply another density level, one that touches on all the others. It is finer and more durable, at the same time. It could be called the base of matter, in that regard, as it permeates all levels where matter can reside. Intelligent life forms come in many shapes and sizes, but all have brains and nerves. Thus a soul can incarnate in a hominoid at one point in its development, and into quite another life form during another incarnation, without any adaptation required.

The soul does not require food or nourishment as physical life forms do. The human animal cannot retain its shape without fuel, without maintaining a certain temperature and replacing damaged or consumed biochemicals. It must eat to survive. Souls do not require a temperature maintenance, and by their nature maintain their own chemistry, the only outside reach required is to acquire more of the Chromatic substance of souls, present everywhere in the Universe, when growth in bulk is occurring.

Spirit Form—Chromatic

The Chromatic substance that composes the spirit is not of the same substance that composes the physical world. Where the physical world of 3rd Density cannot sense or interact with the physical world of 4th Density, due to their vibrational differences, entities in spirit form transcend these physical barriers and can interact, and the reason is simple—the spirit has only one density, so all are in touch with one another.

Humans who have what is termed virgin souls, those first congealing in the consciousness of the human, are no less able to communicate with other souls than old souls. The issue is not their ability, as a virgin soul, but for want of a better term, their weight and mass. Old souls have an equivalent of the human brain's tendrils, connections, and number of brain cells. They live on because of this, the complexity of interactions and memories that hold the soul together. Young souls that dissipate because of lack of what is termed a spark, have few connections, few substantial memories that create connections, and thus there is in essence nothing there. However, during the lifetime of this virgin incarnation, the soul that is there can communicate with other souls, and thus is part of what is commonly termed the collective subconscious. They, however, ask more questions than give answers, and have few insights, so are more the receivers than the transmitters.

The world in which an entity evolves upon does made an imprint on the entity, that has a strong but not dominant effect on it's future. This is an easy concept for mankind to relate to, as the culture that they come from determines their outlook, how they interact with others, and the restrictions they impose upon themselves. However, just as humans find they become citizens of the world during travel, or living and working abroad, just so souls incarnating into other lifeforms find they have a common bond and base with other souls. Evolution into higher spiritual densities is akin to world travel, in the human experience, a rich tapestry of encounters with fascinating cultures and attitudes. Each learns from the other, and grows. And eventually, the experiences of all are the experiences of each.

Light Form—Prismatic

Highly developed entities no longer take physical form. Physical form was in the past for these entities, but they are spiritually evolved now, and take what is called light form. The substance that makes up the light entity is called Prismatic. Light Beings have an extreme mental capacity, beyond what humans can endure. These entities have a force of love, also. Returning from a contact with these entities, the contactee feels as though he has risen from a warm bath into the cool air. He wishes to return to the warmth. He wishes this never to end. The contactee needs to bear in mind that what he desires is in his future. The entities in contact have also endured what the contactee is enduring, in their past. This is one of the reasons they have such an intensity of love for humans. Entities in light form appear to humans as balls of light, the strength of the light in proportion to the mass of the entity.

Human spirits are sensed, as ghosts, as a light cooling of the temperature or perhaps a visage of the human as it appeared during its last incarnation. This in no way relates to how the entity is shaped at present, but is an impression the formerly human spirit is giving to the human at the scene—I looked like this. Temperature changes are due to the disincarnate entity desiring to influence the scene, and being inexperienced at how to do this.

Wise and massive entities, almost invariably in the Service-to-Other orientation, appear as balls of light so their human contacts can mentally register their presence. Humans sense these entities well before they see them in light form, as the light form is assumed only as a type of dress to allow the human to better comprehend the situation. The contactee strongly senses someone in the room, or nearby, even though the contactee may be quite alone by all appearances. This sense that someone else is present is so strong that the contactee may actually glance around, disbelieving what their eyes are telling them. It is for this reason that these entities assume a light form, so that the contactee can relate to what is happening and get down to business.

Out-of-Body

An Out-Of-Body experience (OBE or sometimes OOBE) is an experience that typically involves a sensation of floating outside of one's body and, in some cases, perceiving one's physical body from a place outside one's body (autoscopy).

Out-Of-Body experiences can happen anytime an entity, or spirit, is incarnated, regardless of the density. It is true that most 3rd Density incarnations proceed from beginning to end without an Out-Of-Body experience, and that, on the other hand, it is rare for a 4th Density incarnation not to have an Out-Of-Body experience, but this is due to the relative awareness of the entity, not the density.

Humans experience Out-Of-Body in association with great trauma, where they are near death or severely injured. Some humans recall seeing themselves lying on a table while a medical procedure or examination is taking place, apparently Out-Of-Body during this distress. Is this a deliberate use of Out-Of-Body, as a type of anesthesia? No, as Out-Of-Body maneuvers are always initiated by the human. However, due more to alarm at the strangeness of the setting, many humans do go Out-Of-Body during physical procedures. If they are in deep paralysis, which is a means of anesthesia often used by ourselves or others concerned with the well-being and comfort of our contactees, then the physical body is still. However, the spirit, elsewhere in the room, observes.

Once having been Out-Of-Body, the entity incarnating in a human body is wise, and not infrequently intrigued. How did I do that? Being Out-Of-Body offers all kinds of opportunities. Instantaneous travel, through walls, and invisibility. Humans adept at initiating an Out-of-Body use this frequently to gather information, check on a loved one, or just simply to have a look-see. Is this good? Yes and no. Where the human is operating in a 4th Density spiritual mode, is sufficiently Service-to-Self or Service-to-Other to be destined for 4th Density physical existence during the next incarnation, there is little harm done, but where they have not progressed in their 3rd Density orientation lesson and must continue in 3rd Density, Out-Of-Body can be a distraction from the lesson. It is an escape. For this reason we do not give lessons on how to achieve an Out-Of-Body.

The Out-Of-Body experience is much misunderstood. It is desired by many but experienced by few. The entity, driven by curiosity or strong emotion, flits out of the physical body, desiring more mobility. Once the spirit learns how to jump out of the body, the human finds they can go out of the body at will, but they cannot describe the mechanism as it is, after all, a skill of the soul, not of the human body that the soul inhabits. Out-Of-Body is not a particular position or a particular mind set, and it is not really a voluntary activity on the part of the human. This is not something that a human can teach itself, because it is a lesson that the soul must experience.

Most often, in humans, it occurs in trauma or impending death, the sense of the spirit that the body will die. It is stepping away as though jumping out of the fire. The soul often jumps out of the body just as death is happening, as those who have come back from Near Death experiences can relay. They were watching the scene. Even though the point of death experience is remembered by spirits, this pales in the flood of other experiences and tends to be not remembered until a similar instance returns, such as the death of the current incarnation.

Once entities learn how to do this, they want to do this often. If they don't return voluntarily, on their own, they are returned by their spirit guides, who watch over the incarnated entities like school yard monitors, ensuring that the incarnation proceeds by the rules. These temporary exits are self limiting, as the guides force the entity back into its physical body after a time. No skipping out of school. During 3rd Density the entity is required absolutely to be incarnated, as this is where it learns the fastest. There are occasional Out-Of-Body experiences, but in the main, 3rd Density is a grounded experience.

During 4th Density the entity is also incarnated, but is aware of the potential separation of the spirit from the body, and Out-Of-Body experiences are openly discussed among all—a fact of life. 4th Density is a long plateau, where many lessons are solidly mastered. During 4th Density, the entity increasingly finds itself Out-Of-Body, and thus is getting familiar with life without a body. Moving into 5th and 6th Density, then, the entity is comfortable without a body, and finds its learning experiences can continue apace with or without. However, depending on the determination of the entity and lessons to be learned, these 5th and 6th Density entities may find themselves incarnated, even back on a 3rd Density world such as the Earth is at present.

Astral Projection

Astral projection or astral travel refers to the purported experience of a person's conscious awareness leaving the physical body to observe the world from an independent and objective point of view. This is also referred to as an Out-of-Body experience.

Auras

An aura is a field of subtle, luminous radiation surrounding a person or object. The depiction of such an aura often connotes a person of particular power or holiness. Sometimes, however, it is said that all living things (including humans) and all objects manifest such an aura. Often it is held to be perceptible, whether spontaneously or with practice: such perception is at times linked with the third eye of Indian spirituality. Various writers associate various personality traits with the colors of different layers of the aura. Auras exist, and some humans can see them as their eyes are sensitive enough to detect a form of light ray which is always there but not seen by most. This ray is not Greengolden, although. I've seen my own aura once! It was all like woozoo-woozoo and shit. Auras do not represent the spirit, but are an emanation, or byproduct, of the human body as a furnace, maintaining 98.6 degrees. As with other byproducts of the body, such as urine or feces or sweat or breath, the aura can tell a practitioner a lot about the mental and physical health of a person. Auras are normally pale blue, when viewed by humans, but vary all over the color spectrum and change shape, compressing close around the body or wafting out with tendrils.

Some human healers use their own aura and the aura of the patient to heal. When auras touch, they affect each other as they wrap back into the bodies. This is truly a means for one human to breath life into another, to alter a sick aura by sharing, to take some of the sick aura into oneself and absorb it. Like breathing air into another's lungs, one is using one's strength, one's reserves, to help another, without permanent harm to the giver.

Secrets and Myths

Jesus

Regarding Jesus being the Son of God. This is a touchy subject. As the saying goes, if one wants to remain above a bickering argument, don't talk about religion or politics. However, it seems a third item should be added to this list, that being the alien presence. As we are already embroiled in controversy, what's a little more heat?

Jesus was not an ordinary man, but he was no more the son of God than any other human. Jesus was an entity from a higher dimension, who had earned the right to function in a higher density, that being above 3rd Density. Bear in mind that there are many, many entities among humans now, functioning in human society, who are operating in the same manner as Jesus was in his day. We are speaking here of entities who have come to a lower density, and incarnated here, in order to influence human affairs, human spiritual evolution. Jesus was a very high grade entity operating in the Service-to-Other orientation. He was immovable in that regard, meaning that those allowing him to come to Earth and undertake the incarnation could trust him not to veer from his stated path.

When Jesus was on Earth, he lived the life of a normal man, as all incarnations into human form do. He had sexual hungers, felt despondent when alone and rejected, and doubted his ability to deal with issues before him. He was human, in every regard. As with all incarnations, by the Rules of Forgetfulness, he did not remember his prior spiritual state, where he lived in light and wonder, a veritable feast of learning and exploration. He chose his path, as Jesus, for the message he wished to deliver was, to him, a primary message of great importance, and the flack he met was not at all unexpected. Jesus knew he would take heat. That he was tortured to death was not a surprise to him. He is reported to have expressed surprise, or dejection on the cross, reportedly saying "Father, why have you forsaken me". The humans in attendance interpreted his comments with their own view, and took this to be despair or resentment. Our understanding was that he was asking for things to move along more quickly, as anyone being tortured does.

Jesus accomplished his mission in formulating and disseminating a message of love for others, and sacrifice for love. This message is the opposite of the Service-to-Self message, which is love thyself, and sacrifice for no one. The words of Jesus, where possible, have been corrupted by those who wish to see mankind headed toward the Service-to-Self orientation. Most of the words of Jesus were spoken carefully, and spoken often enough, so that their meaning could not be corrupted. He repeated the same message in many different contexts, and to many different groups. In this he succeeded in passing on a legacy, the legacy he intended. Jesus was not alone in incarnating from a higher density in order to assist in the spiritual evolution of humankind. Buddha and Mohammed, among others, have done likewise, with similar results. The message bearer should not be blamed for the twists made upon their message. Look to those who are perpetrating the twists, and place blame accordingly.

Crucifixtion

Jesus did not die on the cross for all of mankind, and this was the last thought in his mind at the time. Jesus incited the wrath of the establishment because he preached that man was free and encouraged free thought. He disliked money changers, seeing them as usurious and parasitic on the hard work of the people, and didn't hesitate to say so. He suggested that the wealthy class should share their profits more equitably with the people who made these profits possible, the workers. None of this rested well with the established, the rulers, who were well connected to the bankers, merchants, and wealthy of that day. They considered Jesus a threat to their comfortable life, a rabble rouser. He was crucified as the result of a death sentence, just as innumerable other people were crucified at that time. Did they all die so that mankind would not have to suffer?

Many legends have sprung up surrounding the death of Jesus by crucifixion. Jesus, being at ease with the telepathic nature that humans normally posses, had tapped into the fact that his enemies were arranging the circumstances of his crucifixion. Because he commented on this outcome his followers have endlessly speculated as to what was meant by his comments. He simply meant that what he expected had come to pass. As Jesus had an avid following convinced he was no ordinary man, his followers sought to recover his body and give it what they deemed a proper burial. In their fervor they disturbed more than one grave, and this has resulted in the tale that many graves opened and the dead arose and walked forth. Of course, this never happened! The heart wishes it to be so, especially as the heart wishes the beloved Jesus to live still, so the heart drives the legend.

Stories about the crucifixion of Jesus abound, as much to promote the Christian faith as to discredit it. Rival faiths, such as the Islamic faith, have purported stories to counter Christian stories. Thus, as Christians state that Jesus died on the cross for all of mankind, essentially creating a martyrdom situation where all of mankind might feel obliged somehow to Jesus and therefore the religious elite who claim to represent him, the Islamic religious elite sought to counter this. What greater blow to a supposed martyr than to cast aspersions on their dedication and state, as they have, that Jesus did not take the crucifixion but required a double for this painful situation? The problem with this story telling game is that neither story is correct and is therefore an utter waste of time on all sides.

Miracles

Many stories about Jesus are based on true incidences with untrue distortions. How and why did this occur? Based on the stories being spread about Jesus, a simple statement made in error by a single person can spread and grow in details as it does. Think of the rumors you have today, and how easily disinformation can catch on and continue. He seemed to them to be consistently so much more than a man, and indeed he was. And as he face the terrors they faced with such equanimity, his faithful concluded he must be a god. Why else would the threat of torture and death leave his face serene?

Did Jesus walk on water? Desert sands, particularly in flat areas, produce mirages, and a common mirage is water. A human walking at a distance can be seen as walking on water.

Did Jesus raise the dead? As Jesus was well connected to entities from higher densities, he was able and not reluctant to give The Call for help in many situations. Thus he on occasion was instrumental in curing people who had been stricken and at the point of death. It is well known that severely ill people can appear to be dead, and have on occasion even been buried alive because of this confusion. Such a person, recovering suddenly because of intervention, would be rumored to have been raised from the dead.

Did Jesus mold a bird from clay? He found and rescued a bird caught and caked in dried clay so that flight or even motion was impossible. This was subsequently explained as creating a bird from the clay.

Did Jesus make many loaves of bread from one or wine from water? A few of the faithful seated close to Jesus as he lectured, having brought their own lunch, would conclude that their lunch had been multiplied on observing the following: Jesus notes that new comers are without food, and asks those who had brought lunch to share, helping in the distribution. Later more new comers arrive, with various foods which they share among themselves. The original arrivals look over their shoulders, noting the masses and the sharing of food, and make an erroneous conclusion based on their heartfelt admiration for Jesus.

Did Jesus resurrect from the dead? The supposed resurrection of Jesus from the dead was, of course, a story based on the widespread human custom of carrying beloved deceased to what the bearers considered a proper burial. As Jesus had relayed that death is not the end, that his faithful could expect to meet him again, the disappearance of his corpse, a true occurrence, was supplemented with supposition. Where did he go? He resurrected, was the supposition.

Da Vinci Code

Fascinating and full of intrigue, this story is more than secret societies and their goals of gaining wealth and power through cooperation, more than the tight control religions seek over lay people maintaining a mystique of godliness that cannot be challenged, as the story involves codes laid into art work by a famous artisan, Da Vinci. Is there truth to the tale? There is truth to this tale, but it is also fiction. However, the current version of the Bible is also fiction, in many of its sections, if not deliberately confusing. Primarily, the Bible is hiding the truth by what has been omitted, during the periodic purges that occurred at the hands of those who wanted to enhance the control the evolving Church would have over those they sought to lead. What does the Church stand to gain? Wealth gained from forced contribution to the Church, an inability of the layman to challenge the Church which asserts it is the voice of God, and the sense of power the ability to rule over the personal lives of laymen brings to those at the head of the Church.

Da Vinci did indeed know the truth about the life of Jesus, being omitted from the Bible. We have stated in the past that Jesus was not a virgin, not a celebate man, and had the same desires as a normal man, and indeed married a young woman in her early teens, a situation so common as to be the norm in the culture and times. He had children, almost half a dozen, primarily girls as his marital relations were frequent and he took care to include his wife in sexual arousal, being a conscientious and caring husband. Was his wife Mary Magdalene, ever present during his life and at the foot of his cross during his death, along with his mother? Yes. Did Jesus die on the cross? Yes, as the rule was to not remove a man from crucifixion until death was certain. Did his wife and children then move to France and become part of the aristocracy? They of course escaped the area, fearing reprisals, but had no need nor means to travel that far. His blood line, mere DNA not at all related to his spiritual nature, is irrelevant. They disbursed, married and had children, and were simply genetic code, just human, not bearing his depth of spirit.

Was Da Vinci giving clues in his artwork? What other means was available to him, with the grim hand of the religious elite determined to eliminate the truth from the evolving Bible? More secrets are in his artwork than have been discovered to date. Should this inflame those intent on uncovering the truth, there is another secret omitted from the Bible more important for those living today—the truth about prior pole shifts and the forthcoming shift. It is also no secret that the Kolbrin, considered a parallel Bible and hidden from destruction in Scottish monasteries, details the pole shift causing the Flood and occurring during the Exodus. This material originated from the Egyptians, who kept immaculate records. Should this origin cause the faithful to discount the Kolbrin, look to the Book of Enoch, another book carried forward from the Jews, the originators of the Old Testament, who also were required by their laws to record only the truth, and not embellish. Enoch, a man mentioned in the Old Testament, was dropped because it described the forthcoming pole shift, and the signs that would preclude this. The Third Secret of the

Fatima, also about the forthcoming pole shift, is yet another example of the Church suppressing the truth, as they care not for informing and empowering their flock, but only about continuing their control and positions of power.

Knights Templar

Many situations fraught with injustice take a turn for the better due to reactions, where those injured and those in sympathy are impelled to action where they would otherwise be passive. Such a situation occurred during the era of inquisitions and the political marriage of church and state in Europe centuries ago. Integrity is one of the first casualties when those living by lies come into power, and thus the Knights Templar came under attack. As with most casualties of the inquisitions, they were blameless and set up with all manner of accusations that were totally unfounded. Those offended by this injustice live on today, by proxy, as an organization that has lost all semblance to the original group, becoming, as most groups do over time, simply a group fraught with procedures and rules and hierarchies to be honored.

Star of Betlehem

The birth of Jesus was, as was his birth, a guided occasion. It was not by accident that what is commonly called the 3 Wise Men arrived at the humble stable where his mother was recovering from birth, the only accommodation they could secure. How likely would it be that such humble parents would come to the attention of Kings, coming to what they sensed from afar was an occasion? Did Joseph and Mary issue Birth Announcements? Did Joseph and Mary carry social weight, such that not delivering a gift would be a social slight? If the kings were simply following tradition in their society, they would arrive at tens of thousands of houses, with newly delivered babies, and never find the child Jesus.

Was it a star that guided them? In that stars can be seen from all directions, with slight variation in direction in a given small country just as Jerusalem, this would not be a clear guide. The star was brighter than the rest, and allowed the Kings to move with the road ways, and not lose their direction. They were, thus, not looking up, but forward. The same influences that clued the Kings into the birth of someone special, someone meant to influence the world, guided them to the spot of his birth. This was, as suspected, not a star, but a bright object in the sky under alien visitor control, which was positioned to act as a leading light to the stable. Thus, it moved, to appear at the same level in the sky, always pulling them in the right direction. And when they had found the city, the star remained stationary! Not moving during the night! Not at all what one expects from a star. The 3 Wise Men, kings, were the right stuff as far as orientation, and were in the habit of giving the Call to visitors in the Service-to-Other. Thus, they had all learned, independently, of the pending birth, and begged to be in attendance and assistance in some way.

Mary's Message

Much has been made of the supposed miracle at Fatima, where the image of Mary, mother of Jesus, appears, floating overhead. Crowds form in awe, whispering to one another, and the local merchants clean up. When one does not see the image of Mary, one is told their faith is not strong enough. Since the vast majority coming to the site have their lives wrapped in Catholic doctrine, they come prepared to see something, and see something they do. Was it in the shape of Mary? They believe so, and chalk up any distortions in the image to the angle, their tired eyes, the weather, or whatever. Since so many others are rapt, would one complain about the image being out of focus? Any explanation but lack of faith is preferable.

The eyes see what the heart hopes to see. Seeing what is anticipated is so common that it is almost a daily occurrence experienced by all. Individual described as having a closed mind will only see what they anticipate or expect to see, feel comfortable with. This phenomenon is very much with you. The mind supersedes what the eye sees, colors it, and filters out certain things that will contradict the expectation. This occurs for future anticipation as well as for memories that are disturbing. For instance, if someone sees something that is upsetting to them, they will rapidly forget it, distort it, and selectively have amnesia. The same kind of screening works on future events.

Beyond the visions induced by suggestibility or a desire to see what one is expected to see, there is fraud. Just as UFO sightings and contactee status are faked for the attention and financial side benefits such claims bring, visits from Mary are on occasion frankly faked. Just as UFO fakes involve altered photos and videos and witnesses backing each other up and presenting scars or other marks supporting their claims, fraudulent visits from Mary use these physical props. We are also told that a Pope, now deceased, wrote a diary of predictions delivered by Mary. The now deceased Pope's diary, whom one cannot ask the Pope about, is a colossal fraud. No such conversations took place, not even in the Pope's mind. Can this be disproved? No. What would one do, go to the grave and ask? It's a safe bet for those perpetrating the fraud. Who are these perpetrators, and what do they hope to gain? Inspect the message carefully, and you will find, repeatedly, two elements.

First, the promise that the Earth will be led to safety by saviors of a religious nature. The second coming, or variations on that theme. Why would this be important to the perpetrators, who are, as one might expect, in the church, and what do they stand to gain? The church fears that other gods will replace the ones they promote, and hopes to gain increasing converts as millennium fever increases.

Second, the reference to large cities as the focus of rescue. The opposite is in fact the case, as during the cataclysms cities will be leveled and be death traps. Nor can one grow beans and rice and maintain fish tanks effectively in large cities, sustaining oneself when the grocery stores go out of business, permanently.

Why this message? Check out where the large, lucrative churches are located. It is not in rural areas, where the parish is hard pressed to feed the priest. Cash flow wise, it is the big city parish, sustained by the wealthy suburbs, the enclaves of estates, the city home and condominiums kept by the rich and comfortable—that are solidly in the black. Those perpetrating this fraud do not intend to be with the faithful when the cataclysms strike. They will be long gone to safely, bought and paid for by the faithful who have remained, as instructed, in the death traps that big cities will become.

Creation

The Bible, as a guided book, attempted to explain the evolution of mankind in terms that humans could understand. Realize that in the day and age that the Bible was written, such matters as planets orbiting around a Sun, evolution in response to adaptations or genetic mutations, and such theories as the Big Bang did not exist. Man saw the Sun rise and set, seeded his crops or tended his herds, and hoped to raise his children before old age took him out. How would one explain evolution and genetic engineering to such a man? Simply, and with a tale they could relate to.

Such a tale was the creation tale. Since God is acknowledged by all, God caused all this to happen, ultimately. Since the stages on any planet that ultimately sustain life are basically the lifeless planet in darkness, the form and the void, and then the light, as in let there be light, and then the waters, as condensation happens as a planets cools, and then the plants, as without vegetation there can be no mobile animals, and then the fish in the sea, as all life first evolves from a watery womb, and then the creeping creatures that leave the waters followed by land animals and flying creatures, and lastly intelligent species such as man. This tale was not meant to be literal, but was meant to explain the steps so that man could understand. It is only the rigidly religious who cannot see the obvious who fail to understand. If the road sign said Go when green, and the light never turned green, they would stand there still.

David and Goliath

There is confusion about the Quarantine, as this was not a one-day imposition such that on Tuesday, all must vacate Earth. The giant hominoids on the 12th Planet in fact are unaware that a Quarantine was imposed! What they became aware of was increasing problems while living on Earth. They considered Earth to be a swamp, in any case, full of carnivores their world does not have, and disease. They lost Gold shipments in heavy storms at sea, lost slaves and soldiers to accidents, and became disenchanted with living on Earth. They were already on Mars, and this became increasingly attractive. After leaving, in the main, they found mankind increasing in numbers and tinkering with technology, tool, etc. However, there were some who liked living on Earth, enjoyed pushing their slaves about and raping captive women, and were loath to leave. Thus, tales like David and Goliath have their roots in truth.

King David

Like many humans who bore genes originating from the giant hominoids from the 12th Planet, King David was greatly admired for his strength and courage. That he took on one of these giants in the historic David and Goliath battle is not surprising, as he had a personal hatred of their domination, learned at his mother's knee. Female slaves, who were held in bondage to act as more than cooks and maids, became pregnant on occasion by the brutish and fiercely strong soldiers working in service to the mining outposts the 12th Planet rulers routinely put into place during every periodic passage of the 12th Planet through the Solar System. Chosen for their unhesitating brutality in the line of duty, these soldiers were used to keep the human slaves that worked the mines in line, and seldom displayed any tenderness, not even to their lovers.

Most often, a female slave that had been impregnated would die in childbirth, unable to deliver an oversized infant, taking her infant with her. On rare occasions half-breeds survived, often without their mothers who bled to death or were torn beyond repair. David's mother, like he, bore genes from a half-breed, and thus had the hips to bear the product of rape and live. Beyond the great strength and unflinching courage which are traits of the giant hominoids from the 12th Planet, they have a singleness of purpose when aroused into anger. Thus he became a leader of the downtrodden, and was held in great esteem, this reverence expressed in devotion to his symbol, the Star of David. His lineage, the House of David, was noted primarily for its courageous leadership, not surprising when one considers the ancestry.

Angels

There has been much confusion about angels, who are regularly shown in the Christian religion as wearing flowing white gowns and having wings and haloes. There is no such creature, or at least no creature that looks like this, although there are entities that operate in the manner ascribed to angels. This myth sprang up during the early Christian era in response to humans in the traditional garb of that day seen floating. The robes, wafting in the wind, appeared as wings. The sunlight, reflecting off their oily hair, which in those days was never truly washed, appeared as haloes. Angels.

How did these humans come to be floated, in plain sight of other humans, when today levitation done by ourselves or others is registered only in the subconscious? Repression of memory is a factor of the fear and anxiety of the populace. We do nothing that will increase this fear and anxiety. If the observer can view the scene and incorporate startling views without alarm, this is allowed. In the old days, where people were more accepting of magical happenings, this was the case. Today, people are more scientific, and realize they are dealing with something outside the frame of reference. Panic lies just under the surface, and the Awakening is paced with this in consideration.

Because these humans were close to Jesus, part of his entourage in fact, they were assumed to be close to God. The typical response to any relatively unknown phenomenon clicked in—fill in the blanks. Thus we have stories of how the angels came to be, fallen angels, ranks of angels, and variations on their appearance, their personalities, and exploits of angels that grew every time they were retold. There are merely spirits, and such descriptions of angels is a way of describing good and evil, the compassion and pulling toward others that characterizes those in the Service-to-Others, or the pulling toward the self characteristic of those in the Service-to-Self. There are angels among humans who have never left this Earth. They think of others intensely. They sacrifice themselves. Are these not angels?

Adam and Eve

The myth that mankind was once pure in innocence or fell due to awareness of their sexuality is utter nonsense. The myth makes no sense at all, other than in the context of sexual repression. Is Christianity about sexual repression? To a great extent, yes, as control over the sexual practices of the flock gives the religious elite great leverage. The sex drive is constant and strong, and when the flock is made to feel guilty about this and tries to buy out from under any impending punishment, this in turn makes the religious elite rich. This is the crux of Catholicism. Anyone who doubts this need only listen to the lectures given school children in Catholic schools and to the anguish poured forth in confessionals. We listen to both, and we know. Why was this nonsense about Adam and Eve perpetrated? Early man had some sense that they were genetically engineered, having seen their makers, and passed this along in myth and legend. Early Christians adopted this legend and changed it to suit their needs. End of story.

White Buffalo

American Indian legends are deeply appealing to most humans, who sense the wisdom of the ages behind the symbolism. The prophecy of the White Buffalo seems specific, however, and where such calves have been born going into the millennium have set many to wondering. Is this simply coincidence, or does it have meaning? It does indeed have meaning, a prophecy based on what history taught the plains Indians, and thus the White Buffaloes are yet another harbinger of the coming pole shift. Albinos occur naturally in all life forms, some with more rarity than others. What causes an albino to emerge is assumed to be a genetic quirk, where the normal production of color compounds is suppressed. This is the effect but not the cause, else why would life in dark caverns or the depths of the ocean be pale, without color.

If color were a genetic quirk, then why the almost total absence of color in creatures living in darkness? Coloration is influenced by radiation, just as tanning takes place upon exposure to sunlight. What is little understood is that this phenomena has two switches, one increasing coloration under certain radiation frequencies, but another reducing coloration under a different set of radiation frequencies. The core of the Earth, emitting in greater bursts the radiation her caverns and deep water creatures are bathed in, is confusing her surface creatures. Thus, the White Buffalo, heeding the signals from the restless Earth, are heralding the approaching pole shift.

2012

The 2012 phenomenon comprises a range of eschatological beliefs that cataclysmic or transformative events will occur on December 21, 2012. This date is regarded as the end-date of a 5,125-year-long cycle in the Mesoamerican Long Count calendar. Various astronomical alignments and numerological formulae related to this date have been proposed.

A New Age interpretation of this transition postulates that during this time, Earth and its inhabitants may undergo a positive physical or spiritual transformation, and that 2012 may mark the beginning of a new era. Others suggest that the 2012 date marks the end of the world or a similar catastrophe. Scenarios suggested for the end of the world include the arrival of the next solar maximum, or Earth's collision with a black hole or a passing planet called "Nibiru" or "Planet X".

The Mayan Calendar

The Mayan calendar is not so much incorrect as misunderstood. The calendar is derived from calendars and plotting methods left behind by the Annunaki from the Planet X. There are and were many calendars in operation, the western calendar of 365 days with an occasional leap year is only one such method. Dates, when plotted according to one calendar method, do not always line up exactly when translated to another calendar. However, the primary difficulty in interpreting the Mayan calendar is determining the correct starting point. One may be accurate in calculating the number of days, months, and years between events, but unless the starting point is precisely known, the end point is questionable. Thus there are various interpretations on when the Mayan calendar ends, albeit this rather obviously coincides with the coming millennium.

The Hopi Prophecy

The Hopi Indians are instrumental in the Awakening, as their culture is open to contact with extraterrestrials and thus they have had open contact ahead of most of the rest of the world. Unlike closed cultures, where denial rules so strongly that those suggesting that visitations are occurring are punished and even killed, the Hopi honored their contactees, and likewise treated their visitors with respect. Consequently the Hopi are being used as a communication vehicle during the Transformation period. Those among them brave enough to tell their stories to the world are running the same risk as all who further the Awakening, as the establishment wants the status quo to continue and death and injury and endless harassment are common tools of the establishment. The Hopi are perhaps better suited than most to be educators, as their true stories are often scoffed at as being just Indian legends, so the impact their stories make to a great extent go unobserved.

The Hopi have long been visited, and this is one of the reasons they invite visitations. Children are told at their grandparent's knee about such visitations, and take this all to be as real as the Sun and the Moon. As with the rest of humanity, the Hopi fell under the rule that all visitations should be placed only in the subconscious after Earth's Transformation vote concluded some 50 years ago. To reduce fear and anxiety, which would incline humans toward the Service-to-Self, all visitations are to be recorded only in the subconscious, as the vote was overwhelmingly for the Earth to become a home for those entities in the Service-to-Other. Knowing the likely outcome of the vote, those visitors in contact with the Hopi set about giving them some ammunition to use during the coming Transformation period. There were several significant visits, each with a particular purpose.

About the time of the deliberate crash at Roswell, the Hopi were visited by the same aliens that intended to sacrifice themselves and die in the crash. This was to spread a countering message to any the military would propagate, and in truth the Hopi message has been propagated as widely as the true information leaked about the crash at Roswell. These stories of small hominoid aliens visiting the Hopi about the time of the Roswell crash have often been interpreted as crash survivors taking refuge among the Hopi, which was not the case. However, this detail is irrelevant in the scheme of things, as the point intended was made.

As has repeatedly been done during visitations, those aliens visiting the Hopi attempted to explain the meaning and intent of those Star Children who incarnated as Jesus, Mohammed, and Buddha. As is usually the case, the message gets partly understood and partly distorted during repeated telling, as the ear of the listener hears what it wishes to hear. In particular, as the Hopi live in a predominantly Christian nation, what they passed on about the history of Jesus got immediately distorted by faithful Christians who chose not to offend the church elite. Where the Hopi were told that the legacy of Jesus continues, many chose to hear that he had progeny, wishing to cling to a living remnant of Jesus rather than having stand on their own.

The coming cataclysms were relayed in great detail to the Hopi, who feel a responsibility to alert as much of humanity as will listen to their warnings. As with most warnings about the coming pole shift, these warnings are discounted as poetry, or the usual dressing the passage of the millennium is given. The Hopi plan to escalate their warnings, and as the American Indian is revered throughout the world more so than they are revered in their own land, they are ideally positioned to be the messengers of such a devastating message. We wish them well in this endeavor.

Hitler

Hitler took the brunt of the rage against the Nazi as he was the puppet those who ran the regime hid behind. This is a common ploy used by those firmly in the Service-to-Self, as it is a common ploy used by those who want to evade responsibility for their actions. The scapegoat is often selected well ahead of the crime, else the crime being planned would not occur. Hitler is a classic example of a scapegoat who willingly played into the hands of those manipulating him, right up to the moment of his death. He had a damaged ego such that it needed stroking, as he was keenly aware of his failings and how others felt about them. He was what is commonly called a loser, unsuccessful at all he tried his hand at. Women pitied him, unless they chose to mother him, but neither of these reactions was what he was looking for, especially in light of an un-descended testicle.

Many damaged male egos wanting to pump up their image do so by becoming overly rigid, hoping this passes as strength. Losers are often almost irresistibly drawn to the promise of instant fame or money and the power and attention this brings. Hitler also had an additional vulnerability, in that he loved the Jews in a land that bore them much resentment due to jealousy over their accomplishments. He found the Jewish mother types especially appealing, as they forgave him his lack of accomplishments and accepted his lack of manliness with good humor. He loved himself in their presence, but this conflicted with his own need for an alternate self image and with German society in general. He thus developed a love-hate relationship which could have run either way. The balance was tripped when the Nazis began manipulating him, feeding him personal successes in return for hatred against the Jews.

The vehemence of his hatred was fed by his need to deny his affection. His ranting against the Jews for their financial success was an easy route for him to take due to his own history of failure at anything he put his hand to. He could put passion behind the party line that the Jewish blood line was impure as he was terrified that others would discover that he himself had Jewish bloodlines. His tough stance for continuous invasion of neighboring territories and directives for exterminating segments of the populace was simply an act he hoped his lovers would buy, which they did, taking tough talk to be manliness. This act was easy for him to take, as he had no exposure to the consequences of his orders and speeches, as lacking in any real life work, he had led a sheltered and babied existence. When those who played the strings of their puppet Hitler no longer had use for him, he was suddenly faced with the consequences of his actions and allowed others to kill him, acting as the dependent child he in fact was to the last.

Nostradamus

Michel de Nostredame (14 or 21 December 1503-2 July 1566), usually Latinised to Nostradamus, was a French apothecary and reputed seer who published collections of prophecies that have since become famous worldwide. He is best known for his book Les Propheties (The Prophecies), the first edition of which appeared in 1555. Since the publication of this book, which has rarely been out of print since his death, Nostradamus has attracted a following that, along with the popular press, credits him with predicting many major world events.

K. R.

Most academic sources maintain that the associations made between world events and Nostradamus's quatrains are largely the result of misinterpretations or mistranslations (sometimes deliberate) or else are so tenuous as to render them useless as evidence of any genuine predictive power. Moreover, none of the sources listed offers any evidence that anyone has ever interpreted any of Nostradamus's quatrains specifically enough to allow a clear identification of any event in advance.

The legend of Nostradamus emerged during his lifetime in response to the accuracy of some of his predictions. Like all gifted psychics, he was able to read other minds and, based on a dollop of common sense, prognosticate somewhat into the future. He had some hits, which always get the press, where his misses have not been carried down through history. Over time the legend of Nostradamus swelled, as the retelling of his hits were repeated but the list of misses slipped from memory. Thus, he appears larger in death than he was in real life. Nostradamus is credited with future predictions in part due to the semblance of famous names with words in his quatrains, but the quatrains mentioned could have fit literally thousands of situations and the names were not a direct fit. The Nostradamus quatrains could have an unlimited interpretation, and thus the pieces of the puzzle have been put together to paint many different pictures. They are 100% subject to interpretation.

Nostradamus knew well the power of suggestion, and used this during his lifetime to increase the number of his hits. His amusement at this capacity outlived him, as one of his most famous practical jokes was to predict, on his deathbed, that his body would be exhumed, naming the date. He directed that a metal plate with this date be placed in his coffin, and not surprisingly events resulted in his coffin being opened on that date. Those who knew of this date kept alive the discussion of whether his coffin would be opened, so that the issue did not die.

It is reported that Nostradamus wrote his quatrains in an obscure manner to avoid detection and punishment during his lifetime. In fact, he wrote in this obscure manner to avoid being fingered when he missed the mark. People would interpret his quatrain correctly, as applying to their present day, and when Nostradamus' predictions came true there were smiles all around. However, if the prediction did not come true, Nostradamus would mumble darkly that the interpretation made had been wrong, and let people come to their own conclusions. Thus all manner of conjecture has arisen surrounding Nostradamus, that he has a secret code imbedded in his quatrains which make sense of the garble, for instance. There is no such code, nor were his quatrains intended for any but his day, but since Nostradamus fans are having such a good time dissecting his quatrains and arguing amongst themselves, we suspect our words here will be mostly ignored.

Edgar Cayce

Edgar Cayce (March 18, 1877-January 3, 1945) was an American psychic who claimed to have the ability to channel answers to questions on subjects such as healing or Atlantis while in a hypnotic trance. Though Cayce himself was a devout Christian and lived before the emergence of the New Age Movement, some believe he was the founder of the movement and influenced its teachings.

Prophets bearing impelling messages are invariably inspired. Their message grips those hearing it because it carries a view humans under their own power could not come by. Unlike False Prophets, whose pronouncements fall flat almost as soon as they are made, their words uttered by true prophets have the ring of truth, a thousand facets of reality lining up to support the prophecy as it unfolds. Prophets are remembered or gain notoriety where their track record was astonishing in its accuracy or immense in its impact.

K. R.

Edgar Cayce, due to his accuracy on small personal matters and the resultant widespread notoriety, is living in memory still for his predictions on geological changes. His visions were most certainly inspired by a group of extraterrestrials entities, unknown and unnamed by humans, who operate disincarnate at a high level within the Service-to-Other orientation. Cayce was thus instrumental in alerting many about the coming changes, the tentacles of his prophetic reach spreading into many cultures and lands. He was selected from among the many who give The Call asking for such prophetic assists, not only because of his nature, which was greatly devoted to the general welfare, but also because of his natural gifts. Immensely telepathic for a human, and allowing himself to be in tune with all aspects of the humans he healed and in touch with all disincarnate entities willing to assist with the healing, he wasted not himself or his helpers in any of his endeavors. His gift of healing and his highly accurate intuition spread his fame, which in turn bolstered the widespread belief in his prophecies.

Mother Shipton

Ursula Southeil (c. 1488-1561), better known as Mother Shipton, was an English soothsayer and prophetess. The first publication of her prophecies, which did not appear until 1641, eighty years after her reported death, contained a number of mainly regional predictions, but only two prophetic verses-neither of which foretold the End of the World, despite widespread assumptions to that effect.

One of the most notable editions of her prophecies was published in 1684. It states that she was born in Knaresborough, Yorkshire, in a cave now known as Mother Shipton's Cave, that along with the Petrifying Well and associated parkland is operated as a visitor attraction. She was reputed to be hideously ugly. The book also claims that she married Toby

Shipton, a local carpenter, near York in 1512 and told fortunes and made predictions throughout her life.

Nikola Tesla

Nikola Tesla (July 1856-7 January 1943) was an inventor, mechanical engineer, and electrical engineer. He was an important contributor to the birth of commercial electricity, and is best known for his many revolutionary developments in the field of electromagnetism in the late 19th and early 20th centuries. Tesla's patents and theoretical work formed the basis of modern alternating current (AC) electric power systems, including the polyphase system of electrical distribution and the AC motor. This work helped usher in the Second Industrial Revolution.

Tesla was a genius given to grandiose plans, all of which failed. He did indeed ask for assistance from Service-to-Self aliens, giving The Call, and many of his insights were due to conferences with these aliens, who found him remarkably gullible. Tesla absolutely believed in what he was purporting and became a salesman with remarkably persuasive abilities. The Service-to-Self aliens who toyed with Tesla knew they would not be allowed to give Tesla real technology or knowledge, factors that would trip the balance between the orientations. However, lying to Tesla and setting him off to set the stage for more of such games with humans is within the bounds they are allowed to operate within. So they lied, and Tesla's eyes lit up, and just as expected Tesla ran around gathering disciples and sponsors. To this day there are humans who firmly believe he was onto something and pursue his theories. Tesla postulated that electrical energy could be harnessed to the degree that it could be captured as free energy and likewise redirected as free energy.

He was given enough information from Service-to-Self aliens who answered his call to be able to demonstrate these theories in a preliminary manner, using concepts and devices new to the science field. Therein lay his fame, and therein lies the tenacity of his disciples. However, the Holy Grail they seek is not down the path they have been set upon.

Jack the Ripper

"Jack the Ripper" is the best-known name given to an unidentified serial killer who was active in the largely impoverished areas in and around the Whitechapel district of London in 1888. The name originated in a letter, written by someone claiming to be the murderer, that was disseminated in the media. The letter is widely believed to have been a hoax, and may have been written by a journalist in a deliberate attempt to heighten interest in the story. Other nicknames used for the killer at the time were "The Whitechapel Murderer" and "Leather Apron".

During the era when Jack the Ripper did his deeds there was much interest in the human organs, their function, and the potential for playing God by piecing a human together, with the best of this or that. DNA and the manner in which its influence permeates all parts of the body, or the difficulties doctors face when transplanting organs that soon are rejected by the new host, were unknown to doctors and scientists during that era. That the story of the Frankenstein Monster arose during that era is indicative of the interest in this subject. Where the story of a living monster, pieced together from body parts harvested from the dead or living, is fiction, the story of attempts to create such a monster is not fiction. There were many Dr. Frankensteins, and as doctors came from the upper classes during that era, they were well connected.

The identity of Jack the Ripper is not known to the public, but was known to the authorities, at least those who made the decision on whether to pursue a line of investigation or the path that investigation was to take. The influence the upper classes has on the police and regulatory agencies is not new, and pressure to look the other way or financial inducements have always been a facet of human society. The rumor that the perpetrator was royalty was spread to explain why the authorities had little luck. The common man could comprehend a reluctance to indict royalty, and that royalty would be able to suppress an investigation.

Jack the Ripper was not one man, but a group of scientists and doctors, actively pursuing in real life what Dr. Frankenstein was pursuing in fiction. Fresh corpses were routinely delivered to medical schools for autopsy practice and the training of students, so harvesting fresh organs from the recently deceased was not difficult. However, when those wishing to play God found that dead organs only resulted in a dead body, they sought living organs. Prostitutes were easy prey, as they could be relied upon to follow a client into a dark alley, willingly. Being the weaker sex, they also were anticipated to put up less of a struggle. Each failure to create life from dead or dying body parts was followed by yet another experiment, until the group finally despaired. Were they to have had success, however modest, Jack the Ripper might be with us still today, as at no time did the group feel any compunction to curtail their activities.

Clonaid

Cloning, as with the Sheep Dolly, is not difficult. The difficulty is having a 100% success, such that no one can claim an injury has occurred. Childbirth, conception, and having a healthy baby is not guaranteed even under normal circumstances. However, parents who proceed and have a damaged child normally do not have a right to sue, or complain, unless clear malpractice by the doctor or hospital occurred. If it is a genetic toss of the dice, then no complaints are filed. Cloning should, theoretically, produce an offspring identical to the parents, but what if all the DNA does not transfer, or during early development expresses differently because of a different early environment? A leg not forming, as the nudge to do so is not there, the DNA perfect but the nudge lacking. Thus, cloned human infants are being developed, have been developed, but until the product is certain, no publicity will be forthcoming. Those making the most noise, however, have not, themselves, done this cloning. They are seeking the spotlight, and have secured it, as no court in the land can force them to produce something protected under doctor/patient laws. Before court orders can ensue, an injury must be produced. Was a law broken? No law for human cloning exists that would put the claimants in jail, certainly not without proof of their actions. Thus, their strutting on stage is safe.

•

Fatima Secrets

The Three Secrets of Fátima consist of a series of visions and prophecies allegedly given by an apparition of the Blessed Virgin Mary to three young Portuguese shepherds, Lúcia Santos and her cousins Jacinta and Francisco Marto, starting on 13 May 1917. The three children claimed to have been visited by a Marian apparition six times between May and October 1917. The apparition is now popularly known as Our Lady of Fátima.

According to the official, orthodox interpretation, the three secrets involve; Hell, World War I and World War II, and the shooting of Pope John Paul II.

Of course, everyone anticipates that the remaining Fatima Secret, known to few except the hierarchy of the Catholic Church and Sister Lucia, who received the vision, will encompass the End Times. What else would cause the children to fall, screaming, at what they saw. Few accepted the obvious deflection, announced in recent years, that this involved the assassination of a Pope, which would perhaps stun or sadden a child, but not send them screaming in horror, writhing on the ground. Place yourself, as a human living a life of quiet desperation as most do, trudging through the daily routine, bored, weary, and not really expecting much other than aging and the eventual release of death unless something unexpected occurs to make life more interesting. This on occasion happens, a life suddenly turned to a horror or a quick death because of an accident, a fall from a ladder, the sudden and intense pain from electrocution during a lighting strike, the impulsive act of heroism to save another from brutality or danger with the outcome uncertain. But in the main, sudden and massive Earth changes are simply not expected, and thus screaming in horror is the appropriate response, especially if the one visualizing this, living it during an intense vision, is but a child. Place yourself, then, as the child you were, dependent on others to protect you and under the dictates of others as to where and under what circumstances you as a child might live. How would you react to the following in a vision?

the ground opening up in front of you, a wide chasm that swallows what clings to the edges of the chasm, trees tipping into the chasm and ripping their clinging roots, no path or village square safe from such a surprise;

buildings shattering under cracks that flash across their surface like lightning bolts, falling in dust filled implosions as the infrastructure snaps, and the realization that you are trapped under the debris and your cries are going unheard;

walls of fire forming and falling from the sky, setting you and others running from beneath it on fire so you become a fleeing torch, no hope of putting out the flames by rolling on the ground as all is a holocaust, and your flesh covered with a sticky substance, fuel for the fire;

a quiet tsunami rolling toward you as you stand on the shore, evident at first as water rising over walls and rooftops, silently, relentlessly, until the village is covered in water with nowhere for the floating life to cling until exhaustion takes you down.

Sworn to silence not because there is nothing that can be done to avert the calamity, and not because publication would encourage power grabs by Godless communism, the suppression of the remaining Fatima Secret was done for the convenience of the Catholic Church and those who ally with the Church. Just as with the cover-up, where admitting the presence of Planet X in the inner solar system and the likely outcome is inconvenient to those in political and fiscal control of the world, this suppression was done for convenience. Did not those who gave the children the vision intent it to be known? Would those who denied pedophilia in the Church for so long, while allowing it to continue, put the safety of the innocent children under their care ahead of their fiscal concerns? It is for convenience that the vision is suppressed, Sister Lucia a captive in silence, and a frank lie about the substance of the vision being about the assassination of a Pope put forth. Of course there is a reason to reveal the secret. People can chose to limit the size of their families, can chose where to live, can chose a profession or trade based on anticipated need, and in general can plan to love one another with more intensity if they are aware of what is likely to occur.

This does not jib with the Church's doctrine to increase the size of the flock on pain of excommunication if one uses contraceptives, a doctrine which stands at odds with the apparent acceptance of pedophilia in the Church, as apparently is it failing to increase the size of the flock, not sex, that is the sin. You are told business as usual, stay at your jobs, tithe to your Church, remain on the coastlines and crowded into the cities, and support the comfortable lifestyles of the hierarchy. Those in the halls of power in the Church know otherwise, but comfort themselves that nothing can be done to save mankind anyway. Oh? Are they planning to do nothing for themselves? Nothing to place themselves on solid rock and away from coastlines? Such is the love of those in the halls of power in the Church. Are they following the advice of Jesus to love the least among them? Are they following the Golden Rule? Are they warning those along coastlines and near volcanoes or in crumbling cities? Are they allowing them the human right to make their own decisions about where they wish to be, or where they wish to take those they love? It appears the Church is being run by dictators, looking out for themselves, solely, to the end.

Bon

The ancient Chinese had a tradition of worshipping their dead ancestors that went beyond respect and honorable mention. They ate their dead. This type of cannibalism is not unknown in other cultures, as primitive man has often concluded that one could ingest the qualities of another—courage, potency, or intelligence. However, the ancient Chinese did this not to capture qualities but to protect the souls of their ancestors from what they considered to be preying evil spirits. Their traditions of caring for one another knew no bounds, and failure to partake of the meal was considered gross disrespect. All but the bones were consumed, and these carefully bound and kept in a safe place. Over time this was taken to be, by those who discovered these bundles, an odd burial practice. What has passed forward as Chinese tradition, unaltered, is the sense that the spirit lives on and can inhabit a body other than the birth body—a walk-in. The foreboding sense that one needs protection from evil spirits is still about, reflected in the curved roofs which are to catch and fling back to the skies any evil spirits dropping down to plague mankind, or so they hoped.

Shroud of Turin

The Shroud of Turin or Turin Shroud is a linen cloth bearing the image of a man who appears to have suffered physical trauma in a manner consistent with crucifixion. It is kept in the royal chapel of the Cathedral of Saint John the Baptist in Turin, northern Italy. The image on the shroud is commonly associated with Jesus Christ, his crucifixion and burial. The origins of the shroud and its image are the subject of intense debate among scientists, theologians, historians and researchers. The Catholic Church has neither formally endorsed nor rejected the shroud, but in 1958 Pope Pius XII approved of the image in association with the Roman Catholic devotion to the Holy Face of Jesus.

The current shroud of Turin is a well concocted fake, done by chemists in the late 1950's. These individuals were interested in increased activity in their local area, to increase business in general. They lacked an attraction, so created one. The method used to create the fake left no residuals, as most chemical reactions do not after a time. Thus this fake cannot be proved or disproved, and the controversy only incites interest, so the promoters get the desired outcome, either way.

Déjà vu

The term déjà vu is French and means, literally, "already seen." Those who have experienced the feeling describe it as an overwhelming sense of familiarity with something that shouldn't be familiar at all. The experience of déjà vu is usually accompanied by a compelling sense of familiarity, and also a sense of "eeriness," "strangeness," "weirdness," or what Sigmund Freud calls "the uncanny." The "previous" experience is most frequently attributed to a dream, although in some cases there is a firm sense that the experience has genuinely happened in the past.

In most cases the distinct and haunting feeling of déjà vu is a memory, emerging from a past life. Most of the memories stored from past lives cannot emerge, although the entity is aware of them and never forgets, as unless the current incarnation affords a circumstance where the memory seems appropriate there simply is not an opening. Once such an opening occurs, the human may ponder and dwell on the moment, entranced, and draw out further details. Unless the human is aware of reincarnation, is a believer, they speculate on all manner of causes, such as travel into the future or parallel lives, but déjà vu is simply a memory from the past.

Aliens and UFOs

Extraterrestrial life and terrestris is defined as life that does not originate from Earth. Hypothetical forms of extraterrestrial life range from simple bacteria-like organisms to sapient beings far more advanced than humans. It is currently unknown whether any such forms of life exist or ever existed. The development and testing of theories about extraterrestrial life is known as exobiology or astrobiology; the term astrobiology however also covers the study of life on Earth, viewed in its astronomical context.

An unidentified flying object is any unusual apparent object or phenomenon in the sky whose cause cannot be identified by the observer, or (in a narrower definition) by investigators; though in popular usage it more loosely means alien spacecraft, being one explanation (among several) offered for such sightings. Though UFO sightings have occurred throughout history, modern interest in them dates from World War II, since when governments have investigated UFO reports, often from a military perspective, and UFO researchers have investigated, written about and created organizations devoted to the subject.

Roswell UFO Incident

The Roswell UFO Incident was the alleged recovery of extra-terrestrial spacecraft debris, including aliens, from an object that crashed near Roswell, New Mexico, in June or July 1947.

Roswell is all the rage here in the United States. It is the flag-bearer in the parade of those who march to learn the truth. The facts are well known, and the facts that are known relate almost completely to the truth. This is a true story. What is not well known is that Roswell was not an accident.

At that time, within the United States, many alien groups wanted a dialog with the United States government. We chose the United States because of its leadership in the community of nations. The United States was and is sticking its nose into every activity throughout the globe. We knew we could rely on the United States to be the message bearer for any message the alien groups wished to get out. The United States, as other governments, was not approachable. Individuals who were contacted by the alien groups were treated as though they were infected. They were not listened to. The block in these matters was the human desire to be in control. Therefore, in order to allow the humans in the United States government to be open to our messages, we allowed them to be in control. Several entities within the alien groups trying to contact the United States government volunteered to be of service. They expected to die. The plan was to allow ships to crash, ostensibly at the hands of humans. This maximized the feeling of control the humans would experience, particularly as the front end of any contact was, unfortunately, through the military. Once they felt they could harm us, they were willing to parley.

The rumor that delicate flowers, in shades of white and yellow, were found etched into the impermeable metal on the inside of the crashed ship is true. Were these wall decorations to remind the homesick travelers of flowers in their homeland? Yes. Just as humans decorate their homes with those items that are powerful reminders and trigger emotions, the better to become lost in delicious reverie, just so these travelers carried with them a reminder of their home planet, so far away and, in the case of those setting out to create the Roswell crash, never to be seen again.

They sacrificed themselves at Roswell not because they had nothing to lose, but because of what they hoped the Earth would gain.

The recent Roswell movie adheres closely to the facts, but has added material for dramatic effect and omitted other material at the request of the government. For instance, one is led to believe that all the aliens died, yet EBE lived for a time. Your government is telling you these stories based on your reactions, and the reaction to Roswell, the movie, was favorable. More details to follow. The movie presented true facts in what appeared to be a series of letters or symbols etched into the ship's metal frame. Just as you have key phrases that elicit emotion and are often displayed for this reason, the aliens who sacrificed their lives at Roswell had etched such a phrase on their ship. This phrase, a true likeness of which is above, simply stated that though they were a long way from home, that home awaited their return. You have similar phrases—home is where the heart is, and there is no place like home. Where this fact is true, the symbols shown in the movie were not a replica of the symbols found. The producer was not given access to the actual symbols, and just put together combinations that would have some familiarity to people. The producer reasoned that such symbols would then strike a chord in most viewers, and set them to wondering, which it did.

The Roswell movie used dramatic effect in the degree to which Major Marcel showed material to his family, and the cavalier attitude he took toward announcing all this to the public. He knew full well what he had come upon in that field, and the impact informing the public would have. UFO's were not unknown to those at the Roswell base, and the heavy hand suppressing chatter had already been felt. He agonized, and informed his family furtively. The rancher, Mac Brazel, also is shown as having a virtual tea party when taken into custody by the military regarding his mouth. After some blustering, supposedly, he got bought off with a truck. In fact, he was abused extensively, in the many ways that leave no marks, and finally told frankly that he and his family would be killed unless he complied. The truck was less his desire for a bribe than it was the only avenue by which he could get the word out. Why would the military need to buy him off? People appropriately wondered, and came to the correct conclusions.

Were people silenced via death during the Roswell incident? Yes, and more than the public suspects.

Rumors surrounding the Roswell incident include stories about EBE, the Extraterrestrial Biological Entity, who survived the crash and lived to chat, in a manner of speaking, with the government. These rumors also state that the movie ET was based on this situation, as a small boy, a son of one of the government officials involved, struck up a telepathic relationship with the EBE. Any of this true? Some. EBE was returned to his group, alive, after contact was established over the next few years. Rumors that EBE died were spread so any press to see and talk to him would be eliminated.

EBE, as he was called, was one of seven aliens on board the two craft that crashed at Roswell. One craft was utterly demolished, as it was set to explode close to the ground and did so as planned. The second craft held four aliens, and crashed as planned without becoming utterly demolished. It was expected that the impact would kill all four, who expected to die, but one lived on with injuries. This was a shock to this alien, who was unprepared for the intense interest in his digestive, breathing, and medical needs. He found himself both held at arms length and closely examined by the very nervous humans who recovered him. An officer, called suddenly to the site where EBE was being housed, had his young son in tow, and left him in the car while he conferred inside. When he returned he found that his young son had much to tell him, having been in telepathic communication with EBE. Without having the two ever meet, and without confirming to the young boy that his conversational pal was real, the government subsequently had the two in close proximity and questioned the boy endlessly. To this day he cannot prove that this occurred, other than that questions were put to him.

The impact of Roswell on human culture, and on the government in particular, was that they knew for sure that aliens, intelligent beings from other worlds, existed. The legacy of EBE himself was essentially the quaint story of ET, where aliens are viewed as shy and non-threatening, more vulnerable than humans, and with charming eccentricities. That they bond well with young children is considered by most to be a de facto proof of their acceptability, in line with the adage that a person can be trusted if the dog and the kids take a shine to him. EBE was followed, however, by contacts with the government by a very different sort of alien, those in the Service-to-Self, and this set the stage for the next phase of the government's relationship with aliens.

Brazilian Roswell

The continent of South American is caught in a tug of war between visiting aliens in the Service-to-Self and Service-to-Other. These groups have engaged each other, and in some cases extreme measures are being taken. The psyche of the populace, having been influenced toward fear and self concern by false stories of blood-drained and weakened contactees, required shock treatment. These false stories gave the impression of loss of blood in the contactees, who in fact were only symptomatic of this. These episodes were as a result of visits from the Service-to-Self, where these contactees, having given The Call, allowed themselves to be intimidated into compliance with such treatment. Without this compliance, any physical change in a contactee or even any visit is not possible. The human controls the situation. However, in keeping with the intent of the Service-to-Self aliens, rumors of blood drained and weakened contactees spread.

The shock treatment of choice was similar to the Roswell scenario, where the populace would be given the impression that aliens are vulnerable, can be in pain, and can require the ministration and pity of humans. Where such a situation does not directly counter the blood-drained and weakened contactee story, it has the effect of negating this story as the exact situation with the weakened contactees is not known. Their story could be taken many ways, including human altercations, lovers bites and the weakness that comes from excess, for instance. Thus rumors spread about vulnerable aliens would tend to lean the weight of public opinion into such directions, rather than domination by aliens. Thus, the Service-to-Other win the struggle for public perception, and pity and concern replace fear.

Of course, to create a situation where pity and concern are called for there must be pain and injury and desperation. As in Roswell, several aliens in the Service-to-Other determined to sacrifice themselves and undergo terror and injury, pain and death, in order to achieve this end. As with Roswell, their ship was deliberately crashed, but unlike Roswell where all were supposed to die in the crash, most of the occupants were to live, and live in a pitiable situation. This they did, and their angst was not acting, as they were injured and terrified. Per plan, they met with talkative and impressionable children, who told their story to everyone they could, as expected. Open and innocent, these witnesses have never been doubted, and because UFOlogy nowadays is organized, tidbits of the story were snapped up before they could be drowned in a cover-up. Thus, the cover-up being effected according to tactics well-known in Brazil simply adds to the realism of the situation.

Corso's Roswell

Those intent on getting the truth about what happened at Roswell in 1947 should be resigned to the fact that the full truth will never get out. For this to occur, the secret government would have to:

admit they lied to the public for over 50 years

admit to the alien presence where they have been adamantly denying it

deal with questions about witnesses, both military and civilian, who died due to questionable accidents or sudden illnesses

Consequently, the truth will be told in a manner to allow an element of doubt to exist, always, so that what most would consider criminal behavior cannot ever be prosecuted. In the US, under US law, the defendants must be guilty beyond a shadow of a doubt before they can be adjudged guilty. Given that MJ12 wishes to leak the truth, and have the populace understand what history has wrought, how would they tell the story without incurring prosecution? The answer is to tell the story in a manner that closely lines up with the truth, but with details that can either not be proved or can be questioned. Thus, a former military man, Colonel Corso, was selected to tell a story, which is not his story, to counterbalance the inane Roswell weather balloon and dummy excuses being proffered by the Air Force. Nevertheless, these steps by MJ12 are an improvement over the former rigid cover-up, and should be applauded.

Prior Roswell

Prior to Roswell, visitors were not required to record their visits only in the subconscious of humans. As the book, the Vedas, reports, humans saw their visitors as having all manner of shapes. In trying to relay their experiences, humans often stumbled and struggled. Many described them as odd animals, but beyond the physical appearance of their visitors, how to describe the phenomena that accompanied them? Levitation, space ships suddenly appearing or zooming away, fucking lasers, the ability to disarm humans without touching them, etc. Thus, fire, wind, whatever might relay this experience, became the verbal story. This often confused those who came later, and could not ask for clarification of the story teller. To further cloud the issue are the giant hominoids from Planet X, who lived among mankind until a few millennia ago. They live in the Bible, as the giant Goliath, for instance, and are real visitors in hominoids form. They are the Gods of Mt. Olympus, the Visigoth in Germany, and giants reported elsewhere. Thus, visitors in many shapes and forms are mixed in with myth, and current mankind is left to sort it out. In the main, take your myths and stories in this context, and see what the picture paints! Most folklore is not story telling, but a serious attempt to pass on important information.

Dogon Tribe

In Mali, West Africa, lives a tribe of people called the Dogon. The Dogon are believed to be of Egyptian decent and their astronomical lore goes back thousands of years to 3200 BC. According to their traditions, the star Sirius has a companion star which is invisible to the human eye. This companion star has a 50 year elliptical orbit around the visible Sirius and is extremely heavy. It also rotates on its axis.

Much has been written about the Dogon tribe and their knowledge of the stars. Such a simple people, kept out of the industrial age even today. How did they come by this information? It has been surmised that they were visited by aliens from Sirius, from the constellation of the Dog, due to their descriptions of their visitors, but this is fancy. Their visitors hailed not from Sirius, but from Planet X, who even then had advanced knowledge of the stars as they plotted their travels by them so as to know their place out in space just as ancient mariners held to the stars to know what place they occupied on the vast oceans. The dog heads worn as masks by these visitors were a common ploy, occasionally switched for the heads of birds or snakes. While under the influence of those in the Service-to-Self orientation, they found these masks aided them in terrifying the diminutive humans they encountered, as their expressions could not be read.

Ummo

Ummo or Ummoism describes a series of decades-long claims that aliens from the planet Ummo were communicating with persons on the Earth. Most Ummo information was in the form of many detailed documents and letters sent to various esoteric groups or UFO enthusiasts. The Ummo affair was subject to much mainstream attention in France and Spain during the 1960s through the 1970s, and a degree of interest remains regarding the subject. General consensus is that the Ummoism was an elaborate hoax. The culprit (or culprits) is unknown, but a José Luis Jordán Peña has claimed responsibility for instigating Ummoism. However, there are still a few small groups of devotees, such as "a strange Bolivian cult called the Daughters of Ummo".

Early in the cover-up on the alien presence were a few well orchestrated hoaxes, the Ummo case among them. As with most hoaxes, publicity and the resultant personal attention were the prime motivators, but when a hoax is elaborate and long lasting, other motivators are usually present. There are few opportunities for instant fame in human society—winning the lottery, making a breakthrough scientific discovery, rescuing children from a burning building, etc. The average human, even those with status by virtue of their position among the wealthy or due to being professionally accomplished, live quiet lives. Outside of the family, the circle of friends, and the immediate coworkers, no one is aware of them. For those individuals with a secret longing to be the center of attention, participation in a hoax can be it's own reward. Thus, when those who planned the Ummo hoax were looking for cooperatives, they did not have to look far!

K. R.

When professional individuals participate in a hoax, for personal reasons, they do so because they are given a rational, an excuse for the hoax, that allows them to explain what they are doing in a face-saving manner. It's for the public safety, to help the government learn of scientists who might be contactees and thus traitors to the human race, or perhaps so the government can learn of real technology gifts given to real contactees, and thus share these gifts with the rest of mankind. Of course, the motive on the part of establishment perpetrators is greed and the desire to be in control, to retain their power positions, but this is not the way the rationale for the hoax is put forth.

Thus, the Ummo case was a grand scheme to poll the scientific community and locate those scientists who seem to be genuine contactees. What resulted, to the great disappointment of the perpetrators, was contact with yet more individuals desiring to be the center of attention, not genuine contactees receiving technology from aliens.

Ashtar

Ashtar is the name of a purported extraterrestrial being, who was first claimed to be channeled by early UFO contactee George Van Tassel, on 18 July 1952.

Entities go by many names, and in some cases they falsely represent themselves. One must bear in mind that entities in higher densities are not pure, without self focus or ego, nor are they without failure and the resultant guilt. Service-to-Others is not a purity of service, where the entity thinks only of others. This is not realistic, as the entity must watch out for the self, less the self be destroyed or placed in a position where the incarnation is abortively ended. Service-to-Others is represented by those entities who, in the overall, think of others as often as they concern themselves with the self. There is also some competition between

Service-to-Others groups, as competition is not something that ends in the 3rd Density.

Ashtar is an entity group that at one time made contact with humans with the best of intentions. As they were not particularly forceful by nature, they did not defend themselves well when disinformation schemes were ployed against them, and have since left the Earth in disgust. This left a void, a perfectly good alien entity name, unused. The CIA and other groups associated with them snapped up this name, and built upon the legacy. Of course, the message changed from one of hope to one of deception and control. There are now many religious overtones to the new Ashtar message, including a promise that a Jesus Sananda will return to lift the righteous to safety during the coming cataclysms, but look closely and you will not see a message of love. Nor does the new Ashtar message encourage free thought or independence. The new Ashtar message has all the hallmarks of the Service-to-Self, which is not surprising seeing what lies at its base.

Phoenix Lights

The Phoenix Lights were a series of widely sighted optical phenomena (generally unidentified flying objects) that occurred in the skies over the U.S. states of Arizona and Nevada, and the Mexican state of Sonora on March 13, 1997.

There have been UFO blitzes, that hit the news, in Chicago O'Hare Jan 1, Istanbul Jan 5, Arkansas Jan 15, N Carolina Jan 25, Hawaii Jan 27, London Feb 2, and Phoenix Feb 7 lately. Note the location of these mass sightings, and then note the warnings about what parts of the globe are likely to experience disasters due to the stretch zones pulling apart and related domino quakes as adjustments occur in other areas affected.

The St. Lawrence Seaway is stretching, as the Black Hills have been wobbly on the live seismographs. On days when the rest of the world is quiet, the Black Hills stands alone showing its wobble, occurring in 12 hours intervals in accordance with the tugging on the highly magnetized Atlantic Rift by Planet X, which wants this surface magnet to stay in alignment with itself. The yawing Seaway rumples the land in the Black Hills, which is why this land looks like it was thrown in the air, recently, as it was during the last pole shift and in pole shifts prior. Is Chicago exempt from the stretch? Where cities on either side of the Seaway will find they are merely riding along, it is where the stretch is ripping land anew that violence will occur. Lake Michigan is a clue. Why do you suppose the Wisconsin Peninsula formed? Its land was secured to the West, the weak point ripping the land under Lake Michigan, and this rip ending at the Chicago area.

Africa is turning in place, its base at S Africa firmly nailed and unable to move, the top rolling to the East as the Atlantic yaws open. This action is what is causing the African Rift to spread so rapidly, in the Afar Triangle, where huge crevasses appear before astonished eyes and the land is dropping hundreds of feet. The Mediterranean will be destabilized. The African plate is a straight line across the top, and when it turns it will create a YAW in the Mediterranean, causing volcanoes in the area to become active as lava is exposed to the surface, and certainly destabilizing countries just to the north of the fault line dissecting the Mediterranean from East to West. The Mediterranean, in the past, was a swamp, but now is a sea. What caused the land to drop? The Black Sea participated in this drop, being inundated where formerly land above water. Istanbul lies at the center of the area that will first be affected when a serious roll of Africa occurs.

The great Pacific is not one plate, as assumed, but numerous, uncharted by man who cannot plumb its depths. Hawaii will rise during the coming shift, as the plate it is on is pushed up while others subduct, thus giving Hawaii added protection from volcanic explosions, as their volcanoes will ooze, not explode. But Hawaii will be subject to tsunami, aplenty, devastating its coastlines. Thus, UFO sightings there, among those frolicking in the surf, are a warning.

London also is in the stretch zone, as its many derailing tube trains attest. Any significant adjustment of the yawing Atlantic will result in further land pulls under London, and suddenly so.

The New Madrid is under stress, pulling apart not only from East to West but pulling the N American continent in a diagonal, the New England states moving in a NE direction while Mexico is pulled to the SW. This will do more than rip every fault line from Mexico to Ontario, it will reduce the support under land to the West of the Mississippi, dropping this land in elevation and flooding it. Arkansas, in the Ozarks, will find itself suddenly land that many seek, in their panic.

The Carolinas were affected by the New Madrid quake, buildings needing to be stabilized, even though the rocky Appalachian Mountains were not so affected. Why is this? There is a fault line running from the Gulf up along the Eastern seaboard, and this will certainly participate in any New Madrid adjustment.

And why the anniversary blitz of Phoenix lights? Is not the flat dry desert of Arizona expected to remain relatively undisturbed, during the coming pole shift? When the New Madrid adjusts, Mexico will be too far to the West for the current comfort of the West Coast, which will bow in the Southern California and Arizona region. The fault line that runs along Mexico's West coast runs just under the Arizona border, then on up along the West Coast of California. Before the West Coast of the US starts adjusting to the new position of Mexico, with slip-slide adjustments, there will be a bending of the Arizona desert area that will fracture the dry soil, create a breach in the great Colorado River dam, and allow magma to rise in the calderas in the US—Mammoth Lake in California and Yellowstone. If the Hoover dam breaks, whither the city of Phoenix, which lies on flat land and near farm land irrigated by the waters of the Colorado?

Chicago

FAA blames UFO report on weird weather [Jan 2] Federal officials say it was probably just some weird weather phenomenon, but a group of United Airlines employees swear they saw a mysterious, saucer-shaped craft hovering over O'Hare Airport in November. The workers, some of them pilots, said the object didn't have lights and hovered over an airport terminal before shooting up through the clouds.

Turkey

People claim seeing a UFO in Istanbul [Jan 5] Mysterious lights seen in Istanbul skies have baffled people. Witnesses have claimed that the lights were coming from a UFO. People have called news agencies on Wednesday night and reported unidentified white lights flying in the sky. According to the eye witnesses, the flying object was revolving around itself and blazing.

Hawaii

UFO's seen over South Shore sky [Jan 27] The National Weather Service says nothing showed up on their radar at the time of the sighting and the Federal Aviation Administration didn't report anything unusual. The U.S. military conducted a missile defense test off of Kauai Friday evening but the test didn't begin until 7:20 pm.

London

UFO sighting over Islington [Feb 2] http://www.islingtongazette.co.uk/ Unidentified flying orange objects stopped traffic and left residents staring skyward in disbelief at around 5.30 pm. Islington police informed Contact International UFO Research about the sightings. Between 12 and 15 orange lights travelling across the sky. Then they would stop and then they went upwards.

Arkansas

Air Force colonel reports lights 'not of this world' [Jan 17] http://wnd.com/ Col. Brian Fields, 61, was cooking chicken at his Van Buren, Ark., home Jan. 9 when just before 7 pm he observed two intensely bright lights as he looked to the southeast close to the horizon. The retired colonel spent close to 32 years in the military, flying F-16s as a member of the 188th Fighter Wing of the Arkansas Air National Guard. He says the phenomenon lasted an hour and 15 minutes.

North Carolina

911 callers report lights in sky [Jan 25] Emergency dispatchers around Charlotte handle wacky 911 calls each night. But Wednesday, agencies got the same type of unusual call: A hovering light was in the sky. Others described it as a plane that might be in trouble. A blueish glow. A fire in the sky. A light moving too slow to be a plane.

Moon Landing

A moon landing is the arrival of a spacecraft on the surface of the Moon. This includes both manned and unmanned (robotic) missions. The first human-made object to reach the surface of the Moon was the Soviet Union's Luna 2 mission on 13 September 1959. The United States's Apollo 11 was the first manned mission to land on the Moon on 20 July 1969. There have been six manned landings (between 1969 and 1972) and numerous unmanned landings.

A hot topic on the Internet and among conspiracy buffs is whether man ever indeed landed on the Moon, or all the evidence provided to mankind is faked. As evidence of a fake is apparent wind blowing a flag, dust raised by landing feet blowing about as though air were present to move it, shadows inappropriate for the Moon, and other evidence of atmosphere or staging. Did man go to the Moon? Absolutely. Were dramatizations done in film theaters? Absolutely. Both occurred, and here's why.

As is often reported, the early Moon landings involved startled astronauts making statements on live feed about "we were not the first" and the like. Likewise, live video feed showed trash on the Moon giving evidence that activity had occurred in the past, and perhaps the recent past. Evidence of awareness of the alien presence, or other information not given to the general public, can often be discerned from what is not said as much as what is said. Why the 3 month delay in reporting, by different media organizations, if approval to report was not a part of the process? Likewise, the astronauts were on a need-to-know basis, as they were expected to be mobbed if they succeeded and went on the lecture tour, often interviewed and the like, and slips were to be avoided by telling them as little as possible. Thus, they were genuinely startled by what they found on the Moon, and their handlers in Houston were unaware of the degree of evidence they would in fact find on the Moon. Oops! What to do? Let's just film some new footage, and release that, instead.

NASA was aware that there were alien enclaves on the dark side of the Moon, but unaware of the trash on the visible side. During early genetic engineering projects, the engineers often used the Moon as a lab, fearing and wishing to avoid the large carnivores on Earth. During these genetic engineering episodes, they would scarcely be hiding on the dark side of the Moon! Why hide? The aliens talking to NASA going into the Apollo missions were Service-to-Self—to set up camps off Earth as a survival means during the coming pole shift. They were on the dark side as

Service-to-Self aliens do not do density shifting well, ala the movie The Fly, and their masters do not allow their minions to shift during missions, for this reason. Thus, they are in 3rd Density, highly visible from Earth should they not be on the dark side of the Moon. NASA expected this, but discussion on past genetic engineering projects, which were not done by the Service-to-Self, never came up!

The astronauts were read the riot act when they returned, having blabbered their first impressions on the Moon. It has been obvious to those looking at the pattern that prior to this live feeds were the norm, and after delayed and only partial release of video and audio was allowed. When a heavy job of intimidation is done, with death threats and worse than death threats, it takes a lot to release this. Beat a dog each hour, viciously, for months, and then try to tell it that was all in the past. The dog has lost trust, cowers, growls, avoids, and will likely never trust humans again most certainly if not in the same company. NASA has not changed hands, is still the same agency, infiltrated by CIA, and thus the astronauts, as their beaten dogs, are loath to trust. {C}NASA of late has been dealing with its many failures, its inability to get a space station operational in time to stage escape to Mars, and the months upon months of delays getting any shuttles up at all. Wanting to be a player, perhaps be viewed as important by the elite with money and bunkers and guns, they hope to be influential in the public eye. They have for years denied the public direct Hubble images, been caught endlessly air brushing out UFO's, and are suspected all around the world of a conspiracy regarding the Moon landing itself. Well of course they went to the Moon, and landed, but they also filmed footage on Earth to fill in, as they could not trust their own men to avoid blurting out the truth. Now, covered with the lint of decades of lies and deception, and the increasing pool of specific information on just when and how they have lied, they come forth declaring themselves clean. Why did they announce new information regarding the Moon Landing, and then withdraw? There was a final rehearsal, and all the many glitches that would only inflame the conspiracy theorists were discovered. This pig is too dirty to ever clean up, and the less they say, the better, was the decision.

Norway Spiral

The Norwegian spiral anomaly of 2009 appeared in the night sky over Norway on 9 December 2009. It was visible from, and photographed from, northern Norway and Sweden. The spiral consisted of a blue beam of light with a greyish spiral emanating from one end of it. The light could be seen in all of Trøndelag to the south and all across the three northern counties which compose Northern Norway, as well as from Northern Sweden and it lasted for 2-3 minutes. According to sources, it looked like a blue light coming from behind a mountain, stopping in mid-air, and starting to spiral outwards. A similar, though less spectacular event had also occurred in Norway the month before. Both events supposedly had the expected visual features of failed flights of Russian RSM-56 Bulava missiles, and the Russian Defence Ministry acknowledged shortly after that such an event had taken place on December 9.

The display over the skies of Norway are not noctilucient clouds, which are ice crystals in the clouds catching the light, nor are they earthquake lights. They are also not the smoking and curling light towers caused by methane gas released during Earth movements, suddenly catching fire while aloft in the sky. The Norway display is akin to the neon clouds seen on occasion since Planet X arrived in the inner solar system in 2003 and the grease in the tail of Planet X has polluted the Earth's atmosphere. The neon appearance is caused by a chemical reaction, akin to man's familiar light sticks. Up until recently, such neon displays required a light source in order to be seen, lit in the dawn or dusk by sunlight or the lights from a city. What has occurred over Norway is a neon cloud, a grease cloud, lit by the electrical charge from the tail of Planet X. Why the great swirl in the clouds around the swirling neon display? An electrical charge in the sky is not a static matter, as the path of lightning shows. Lightning is an accumulation between moving air masses that suddenly builds to the point where a torrent of electrons is on the move. But what if the charge does not accumulate in one place, but is constantly present over a broad area? As with all swirls that develop in nature, they start with a small movement in one place that creates a vacuum pulling matter behind it, and thus builds. Galaxies swirl. Water going down a drain swirls. And these large charged atmospheric swirls are chasing after some part of the tail waft that is more or less charged than the surrounding atmosphere. What occurs at the center of such a charged swirl is more electrical charge than the surrounding swirl, thus the center becomes a neon cloud that can be seen even at night, and wants to discharge, ground, in the Earth.

Death

Death is the termination of the biological functions that sustain a living organism. The word refers both to the particular processes of life's cessation as well as to the condition or state of a formerly living body. Phenomena which commonly bring about death include predation, malnutrition, accidents resulting in terminal injury, and disease.

The nature of death has been for millennia a central concern of the world's religious traditions and of philosophical enquiry, and belief in some kind of afterlife or rebirth has been a central aspect of religious belief. In modern scientific enquiry, the origin and nature of consciousness has yet to be fully understood; any such view about the existence or non-existence of consciousness after death therefore remains speculative.

People who have experienced a Near Death Experience report a long tunnel with a bright white light at the end, and those now deceased who were close to them waiting or beckoning. If the moment of death is confusing to doctors, it is no less clear in the spiritual realm. An injured body, such as one sustaining massive brain injury, may cease to be a home for the incarnating entity months before those attending the death watch finally pull the sheets up over the lingering beloved. It is possible, in such a circumstance, that the entity has already been placed in another, thriving, human body—a newborn babe. On the other hand, some entities hang around long after the body has been cremated or burned, as haunting ghosts. Beyond the issue of when the spirit leaves the body is the spiritual issue of how the entity puts the past life to rest, judges progress made on various lessons that were at the fore going into the incarnation, and determines any future course of action they personally might desire as a result—critique time.

If the death was sudden and unexpected, the entity may have many outstanding issues they remain concerned with after the physical body dies. This invariably is the first stop after death, though it varies depending on the general orientation of the entity and their life circumstances. Someone elderly, who had long settled their affairs in preparation for the inevitable, might not do more than cast a backward glance on their way to the future, noting that their death was being handled as they had anticipated. Someone in their prime, with dependent children or oldsters and many outstanding promises, might linger at this stage, visiting those they are concerned about as a ghost, essentially an Out-Of-Body, for days or months until they can see the outcome. This stage differs between orientations, the Service-to-Others lingering longer due to their concern for others and the Service-to-Self wishing only to move on to future opportunities.

At times, those who have been wronged and wish for vindication or revenge may also linger at this stage, haunting in an effort to influence humans affairs. If the spirit is lingering, it is often allowed to do so, else it avoids the current incarnation and is distracted. The spirit, once sparked, does not die, and pain must be dealt with as a resolution on future lives.

Spirits are aware of their past lives, though the human incarnated is clueless, often. Thus, for the spirit, there is no change in this matter after death. The spirit between incarnations is like an Out-Of-Body experience, in that it can communicate more readily, and thus the Guides have no problem getting them to gather. They are talking up a storm, especially if coming from a recent disaster or shared experience. Once reincarnated, the young spirits are intent on learning experiences, pressing agendas forward, and the like. Incarnations are more than discussion groups, they are action oriented!

Ghosts

A ghost has been defined as the bodiless spirit of a dead person that appears before the living. In the past most of the population believed in ghosts. Sometimes they longed to meet the apparition of a friend or a family member, but at the same time were still afraid of their ghosts. Descriptions of the apparition of ghosts vary widely: The mode of manifestation can range from an invisible presence to translucent or wispy shapes, to realistic, life-like visions. The deliberate attempt to contact the spirit of a deceased person is known as necromancy, or in spiritism as a séance.

All humans have visits from those they knew in the past, now dead. These spirits, who are primarily disincarnate but can come from their next incarnation in an Out-Of-Body, are trying to settle things they feel were left outstanding. These matters can be as simple as an apology they wished to express to you, or a bit of information they felt you needed, intended to be told to you when you next met. Death interrupts the plans. Ghosts are such disincarnate entities. Ghosts often show themselves to humans in a form that the human remembers. This is not a willful act on the part of the ghost, it is the way the human's mind perceives the ghost based on the fact that they understand they are communicating with someone they knew. The mind plays tricks where the human see what he expects to see or hopes to see, and fails to see something they do not wish to see.

This is exactly what occurs when humans are being visited by ghosts. The ghost takes the form that the human recalls, the form the ghost took when they were alive. This form is shaped in the mind of the human as it fits with all the circumstances of the conversation between souls that is taking place. The human has formed this image from memory, but because this memory is swarming about, chemically speaking, with all the other circumstances of the encounter, it merges in the mind of the human. Like scenes that the filmmakers in Hollywood make, where a person on top of a wave may in fact be standing in a room, superimposed on a wave, the human encountering a ghost superimposes what the human used to look like. To the human, this has all been received as one impression.

Not all ghosts are from the dead, as a ghost can be a spirit having an Out-Of-Body experience or a normally disincarnate spirit. The majority of time, during 3rd and 4th Density, an entity will find itself incarnated. Upon death, the entity leaves its physical body, and this can also occur slightly before death too. Many humans experience Out-Of-Body experiences, and these are times when what you call the soul separates from the physical body either because it is curious and wants to go somewhere the physical body cannot, or because the physical body is experiencing trauma. Disincarnate entities are in light form. The reason some such entities appear brighter in light form than others is related to their spiritual maturity. The older and wiser, the brighter. They gain in spiritual bulk, one might say.

When an entity is disincarnate, it can wander about just as the soul can in Out-Of-Body experiences. Likewise, as in Out-Of-Body experiences, it is drawn to places it is either curious about or tied to because of emotional trauma. The entity that feels an issue is unresolved will hang about, desiring to influence proceedings. This is much displayed in our media in ghost stories of one kind or another. Just as with visits from entities in 4th Density or higher densities, these disincarnate entities cannot affect humans unless the human gives The Call. It is not because these disincarnate 3rd Density entities are under the same rules as we, the rules from the Council of Worlds, it is because their substance cannot affect the physical world, and they cannot possess another's body unless The Call has been given and permission granted. In this regard, a walk-in or a possession is a reality, and can happen.

The stimulus for an Earth-bound spirit or a lingering ghost is the faculty of the will. If the will of Yellow Ray Mind/Body/Spirit is that which is stronger than the progressive impetus of the physical death towards realization of that which comes, that is, if the will is concentrated enough upon the previous experience, the entity's shell of yellow-ray, though no longer activated, cannot either be completely deactivated and, until the will is released, the Mind/Body/Spirit complex is caught. This often occurs in the case of sudden death as well as in the case of extreme concern for a thing or an other-self.

Mediumship and Channeling

Mediumship is the claimed ability of a person (the medium) to experience contact with spirits of the dead, angels, demons or other immaterial entities. The role of the medium is to facilitate communication with spirits who have messages to share with non-mediums. Mediums claim to be able to listen to, relay messages from, and relate conversations with spirit, to go into a trance (it is not necessary to go into a trance, it all depends on the medium's control and knowledge) and speak without knowledge of what is being said, to allow a spirit to control their body and speak through it, perhaps using a writing instrument (psychography or surreal automatic writing).

Mediumship is also part of the belief system of some New Age groups. In this context, and under the name "channeling", it refers to a medium (the channel) who is said to receive messages from a "teaching-spirit". In some cultures, mediums (or the spirits to whom they are connected) reportedly produce physical paranormal phenomena such as materialisations of spirits, apports of objects, or levitation.

Channeling is an activity that involves the temporary possession of a human body, in order to relay a message. The message can be in many forms—dance, music, prose, or pronouncements. Most channel instruments, the humans allowing their bodies to be temporarily used, know when this has occurred, and so does the intended audience. The channeled message is different from what the human, who in most cases is familiar to the audience in some way, would have produced. Most channeling is done to produce words, the effect of which can be broad reaching as it can be translated into many languages, and shared repeatedly. Channeled dance is brief and fleeting, and prose has impact on a smaller audience in general than written works. Channeled music is also somewhat limited, as the appreciation for music varies by culture. Therefore most forms of channeled information are the written word.

Many channels are imperfectly attuned to the entities they are putting in the driver's seat. Such a simple matter as constipation or a headache can interfere. Most definitely, the human channel's own fixed concepts can interfere, as surely as a locked steering wheel will cause a car to go in a circle. If the channel is blind the entity trying to channel cannot see what is being written, as the entity is in contact with the mind of the channel. If the entity passes a concept to the channel and due to ruts in the mind of the channel this concept loops about and emerges other than what the entity intended, the channeled message has been distorted. The mass of consistencies between true channeled works support each other while inconsistencies fall away, and in this way truth and understanding emerge.

The origin of most channeled work is a mystery to the human channels, who sometimes insist on a name as they otherwise feel uneasy. The channel is asked to explain who relayed the message and has no answer—anonymous, it would seem. In human society the failure to identify oneself is suspect, and the message deemed likely a lie. Channeled works are most often a group endeavor, many voices speaking as one. Names in the higher densities of the Service-to-Others are meaningless and simply not used. These entities, or their fluctuating groups, have no names. Even when one is invented to meet the demands from the audience, as it has no relevance. The group at one moment might be composed of entities from one constellation but migrate over time to be predominantly from another constellation, and then most constellations are simply unknown to humans at this time.

The only valid question is on the source is its orientation, Service-to-Self or Service-to-Other or possibly a mixture of both if the human channel has given The Call to both. This is what influences the message, and it is the message that counts!

Ouija Board

A Ouija board is a flat board marked with the letters of the alphabet, the numbers 0-9, the words 'yes' 'no' and 'goodbye', and other symbols and words are sometimes also added to help personalize the board. Similarly pronounced Hindi word Ojha means the ones who deal with spirits. The Ouija board can supposedly be used to communicate with spirits of the dead. Although nobody knows where the idea for such a device came from, there are records of Ouija-like instruments being used in ancient

China, Greece, Rome and many other countries. It uses a planchette (small heart-shaped piece of wood) or movable indicator to indicate the spirit's message by spelling it out on the board during a séance. The fingers of the séance participants are placed on the planchette, which then moves about the board to spell out words or become physically manifested. It has become a trademark that is often used generically to refer to any talking board.

All intelligent creatures wish to know the future, and humans are no exception. They wish to divine whether the one they have their eye on is likely to return their affections, whether their fortunes will turn for the better or take a loss, whether the path they have set upon will prove to be the right choice, or whether a child that they are flourishing much attention upon will meet their hopes when grown. Humans read horoscopes, tea leaves, and palms, and use any other method they can that promises, however falsely, to give them the answers they seek. It is not surprising, then, that the Ouija Board is held in high regard by humans anxious to know the answer to their burning questions.

The success attributed to the Ouija Board methods, however, are due only to the humans whose hands direct the answers. The Ouija Board is credited with spelling out known names and likely dates, when in truth this is entirely within the control of the humans with their hands on the pointer, eyes closed or not. It takes but a moment to mentally record the pattern of letters and numbers, and the distance between them. Even blindfolded, the human hand can trace what the mind remembers, and sense the tension in the air when this or that target is close.

For those who think that spirits are near on occasion, when the Ouija Board is used, this is entirely possible as the intent of many while using this board is to call these spirits. This is indeed giving The Call, and depending upon the mindset of the caller the result may be a visit from entities in the Service-to-Self or Service-to-Other. Using the Ouija

Board in and of itself is not giving The Call, if the human understands the exercise to be simply a way of divining their subconscious wishes or knowledge, but if the human is convinced that the Ouija Board is a sure link to the spirit world and then proceeds to use the Ouija Board, they are indeed giving The Call.

Tarot

The tarot is a pack of cards (most commonly numbering 78), used from the mid-15th century in various parts of Europe to play a group of card games such as Italian tarocchini and French tarot. From the late 18th century until the present time the tarot has also found use by mystics and occultists in efforts at divination or as a map of mental and spiritual pathways.

The tarot has four suits. Each of these suits has pip cards numbering from ace to ten and four face cards for a total of 14 cards. In addition, the tarot is distinguished by a separate 21-card trump suit and a single card known as the Fool. Depending on the game, the Fool may act as the top trump or may be played to avoid following suit.

Fortune tellers use many vehicles on which to place their psychic perceptions, as the bold faced assertion that the predictions are based on what the questioner is laying before the fortune teller like an open book would tend to diminish the credibility of the fortune teller, and most certainly would ruin the mystique. Whether the fortune teller uses a crystal ball, I Ching, Tarot Cards, or reads tea leaves, the process is the same. The mind and heart of the anguished or eager human sitting across the table are what is being read, and the common sense and compassion of the psychic fortune teller are what determines the result.

K. R.

Numerology

Numerology is any of many systems, traditions or beliefs in a mystical or esoteric relationship between numbers and physical objects or living things. According to numerologists, each number possesses a certain power that exists in the occult connection between the relations of things and the principles in nature which they express. All that humans are capable of experiencing can be reduced to the digits one through nine. These single numbers are derived from the simplification of all combinations of numbers to their basic essence. This essence then vibrates through the single digit.

Humans have a fascination with regularity and rhythm in nature, and find this comforting as their own bodies have such rhythms—in heartbeat, biorhythms, and sleep-wake cycles. The dance, repetitious motions during exercise, rocking the baby, and music all reflect man finding comfort in regularity and rhythm. Nature's patterns are everywhere, from the pedals of flowers evenly spaced in swirls to the intricate and balanced designs that snowflakes form. Thus it is that humans often seek regularity and rhythm in the midst of confusion, for comfort. The overwrought rock themselves, tap a pencil, or rub their chin. If the anxiety involves unknowns in the future, they may look for patterns by which to form predictions. Luck 7, 13 spells doom, he-loves-me-he-loves-me-not, and so forth.

There is no consistent number used in nature, nor is there any spiritual significance to numbers. Nor is there any significance to anything in the Universe!! Numerology seeks to comfort, to put unknowns into familiar categories, but numerology is without basis in fact. There is no magic in it. Those advocates who state otherwise, laying out patterns that fit the prediction, are screening what they see to fit the expectation. However, perhaps they are a bit less anxious and feel more secure.

Astrology

Astrology is a system of divination founded on the notion that the relative positions of celestial bodies are signs of or—more controversially among astrologers—causes of destiny, personality, human affairs, and natural events. The primary astrological bodies are the sun, moon, and planets; although astrology is commonly characterized as "reading the stars", the stars actually play a minor role. The main focus is on the placement of the seven planets relative to each other and to the signs of the zodiac, though the system does allow reference to fixed stars, asteroids, comets, and various mathematical points of interest as well. As a craft, astrology is a combination of basic astronomy, numerology, and mysticism. In its modern form, it is a classic example of pseudoscience.

In an attempt to explain why babes born during different months (in the case of the western horoscope), or during different years (in the case of the Chinese horoscope) have different personalities, humans have looked to the stars. The answer, however, is closer at hand, and is not anymore mysterious than the different personality shadings that siblings develop based on their birth order. The western horoscope describes spring babes as enthusiastic, summer babes as languid, fall babes as guarded, and winter babes as depressive—not unlike the seasons! Babes are highly sensitive to the moods of their caretakers, and adopt more than the mannerisms of those they take to be their role models.

If this explains seasonal horoscopes, what on Earth would affect the twelve year cycles the Chinese have recorded? There are many such cycles, noted even in the western world. New marriages must get past the seven year itch, and youngsters reach the age of reason at the age of seven, and the major phases through adulthood have even been noted to fall into such seven year cycles. Is this a type of biorhythm, a societal rhythm? It is indeed, as societies have a type of life, reflecting as they do the many lives of their members—somber years of marketing retraction followed by adventurous rebellion, years of caution followed by playful extravagance. In the west, such cycles are termed economic boom times or depression, conservative repression or high-flying extravagance such as the roaring twenties. The Chinese cycles were developed when the factors influencing societies moods were limited, and thus had more influence, where the more free wheeling west has more factors influencing its cycles.

Sacred Geometry

Sacred geometry involves "sacred" universal patterns used in the design of everything in our reality, most often seen in sacred architecture and sacred art. The basic belief is that geometry and mathematical ratios, harmonics and proportion are also found in music, light, cosmology. This value system is seen as widespread even in prehistory, a cultural universal of the human condition.

The term "sacred geometry" is used by archaeologists, anthropologists, and geometricians to encompass the religious, philosohical, and spiritual beliefs that have sprung up around geometry in various cultures during the course of human history. It is a catch-all term covering Pythagorean geometry and neo-Platonic gometry, as well as the perceived relationships between organic curves and logarithmic curves. For example, The ancient Greeks assigned various attributes to the Platonic solids and to certain geometrically-derived ratios, investing them with "meaning." For example, the cube symbolized kingship and earthly foundations, while the Golden Section was seen as a dynamic principle embodying philosphy and wisdom. Thus a building dedicated to a god-king might bear traces of cubic geometry, while one dedicated to a heavenly god might have been constructed using Golden Section proportions.

What is called sacred geometry can be derived from logic and symmetry. Modern theoretical physics is based almost entirely around the idea of supersymmetry. Since all the laws of physics are perfectly symmetric and relative. For every action there is an equal and opposite reaction which together sum to zero. This means that nothing really happens unless it is relative to something else.

Majestic 12

Majestic 12 is the alleged code name of a secret committee of scientists, military leaders, and government officials, supposedly formed in 1947 by an executive order of U.S. President Harry S Truman. The alleged purpose of the committee was to investigate UFO activity in the aftermath of the Roswell incident—the supposed crash of the alien spaceship near Roswell, New Mexico, in July 1947. The Majestic 12 is an important part of the UFO conspiracy theory of an ongoing government cover up of UFO information.

Prior to Roswell, the Service-to-Self aliens engaged MJ12. The incident was one that should have resulted in subconscious contact only. This is because Service-to-Self aliens cannot multi-phase well, and get distracted during contacts, so they let go of the control over humans that results in recording only in the subconscious.

Since this breach had been made, the Service-to-Self took advantage of it to press forward, more being recorded in the conscious. Thus, the Service-to-Other aliens likewise made conscious contact during Roswell. It was deemed a fair exchange, and as the military intel was not about to influence the rest of the world, being secretive as they were, this was considered to be a delimited contact.

MJ12 does not operate in a vacuum, as a standalone, off-the-books, agency. It has tentacles whereby it reaches out to gather information and accomplish its goals. MJ12 is the administrative hub, where policy decisions are reached and the center where key contacts with the outside world are maintained. However, it would be short-sighted indeed, in that those in its hierarchy have parallel positions within the federal bureaucracy, to not use those very bureaucracies. In fact, given the structure of MJ12, it is only natural.

The military branches all have intelligence units, which are skilled in various degrees at electronic snooping, interrogation techniques, and undercover activities. Individuals from these units are assigned to a stint of duty to MJ12, just as they are assigned to secret missions, and are no more prone to talk about these assignments than those involving any other.

Both the FBI and CIA have vast pools of information on corporations, individuals, and groups running under the many different charters that can exist in human society. These intelligence agencies have formal arrangements with MJ12, who has but to ask for this information for it to be delivered.

Military installations include many complexes held in abeyance, just in case. Land and buildings are hard enough to come by in times of plenty, and during cut backs are not released, in the main. Idle facilities in remote areas are ideal for temporary use by active MJ12 members, who are almost invariably from the military.

Why are federal employees regularly dealing with MJ12, and yet the public hears at most rumors of this activity? Intelligence groups, and the military in general, operate on a need to know basis. This rule is in place to prevent covert operations from being carelessly exposed, the enemy from learning of plans, and to a small degree to prevent the public from learning what the government is really up to. Also, when services are performed for MJ12, these services are not distinguishable from normal, everyday services. The requests don't have MJ12 stamped in big bright letters on the front, they come wrapped in commonplace covers, and thus raise little suspicion.

What projects does MJ12 now have on its roster?

Facilitating the Awakening is a goal that has a dual agenda. It both gets past the issue of the alien presence, by making it clear that aliens are and have been visiting Earth for some time with no harm done to humans, and holds the potential of helping survivors in the Aftertime. It is Claritin Clear to MJ12 that they or any government arm can do little to alleviate suffering during or after the pole shift. The devastation will be immense, and any actions they take before or after the shift virtually useless. Even should they move all citizens to safety, starvation and in-fighting would soon follow. So opening the door to extraterrestrial help, fact-to-fact conscious contact, perhaps, is something that an expedited Awakening might provide. To the extent that this project does not run amok of the power-hungry agendas of humans on Earth, who view the Earth as their domain and theirs only, this is facilitated by MJ12.

Running interference, preventing disruption of activities they deem positive, is a strong MJ12 program, as it is one with which they feel comfortable and have a long and successful track record. MJ12 is peopled, primarily, with government employees, primarily military, in the intelligence business. Intelligence gathering requires careful planning and many alternative plans to cover every conceivable contingency. Intelligence gathering forays are defended, by nature, as they go into enemy territory under hostile and dangerous conditions. Thus, defense, in secret, is the very nature of intelligence gathering as much as snooping. MJ12 runs interference by taking out, or discouraging, anything they consider a block or a danger to a program they are supporting.

Promoting, to the degree they can influence the media or private wealth, programs they view to be helping with the Awakening or providing some self-help advice to the general populace as a solution to the devastation soon to be upon them because of the rapidly approaching cataclysms. In that being an arm's length away is an understatement, this is easier said than done. MJ12 must be several arm's lengths away, by decree and by their mission statement, and not discovered. Thus a great deal of effort goes into putting distance between their agents and an action the public becomes aware of. It's not as simple as pushing a button.

Illuminati

The Illuminati is a name given to several groups, both historical and modern, and both real and fictitious. Historically, the name refers specifically to the Bavarian Illuminati, an Enlightenment-era secret society founded on May 1, 1776.

In modern times it is also used to refer to a purported conspiratorial organization which acts as a shadowy "power behind the throne", allegedly controlling world affairs through present day governments and corporations, usually as a modern incarnation or continuation of the Bavarian Illuminati. In this context, the Illuminati are believed to be the masterminds behind events that will lead to the establishment of a New World Order.

The Illuminati are European or old world. They are secret societies that wish to be in a power position and are not, and therefore cuddle up to the great wealth of the Puppet Masters almost like groupies around a rock star saying 'how can I serve you'. They have their codes and rituals, as do the Masons, but this is not giving them any power. This is simply the way they interact with each other. Because they will tend to be rigid, following rules, a key factor in the Service-to-Self orientation, and therefore considered reliable. Even Skull and Bones is that kind of a screening mechanism for reliability, where you will do silly things, let them collect blackmail on you, follow the rules to get the perks of membership. They are looking for people who can be manipulated. Therefore, any groups that they would belong to would be more related to that kind of association. But their true bond is that they are both intelligent, completely ruthless, had similar goals, and agreed to work with each other.

The symbol of the Illuminati, the single eye, is discovered so frequently that interest is raised, rather than suppressed. This is to make The Noobs Scream!! This is exactly what the Illuminati want, as they want the populace to feel manipulated, hopeless, left out of the loop, and that others more special and privileged are in control, in the know, and able to manipulate events in their favor. The Illuminate are distorted towards Service-to-Self orientation. STS is the basis of the Illuminati mission and the motive behind everything they do. The eye, a symbol taken from ancient times so as to imply an age-old organization, carries the implication of being all-seeing, never blinking, and thus all-knowing. Peekaboo! We see you! The Illuminati are Clowns and do not have any influence in world's affairs.

The populace reads rumors about Illuminati, reads the names of powerful and well placed persons supposedly in the Illuminati, finds these same persons increasingly in power and concludes, as was intended, that the rumors about the clout the Illuminati holds must be true. This was a well thought out fear campaign, with the moves in the game being played exactly as planned. Bear in mind that those in control of the Illuminati fear campaign are not those whose names appear as members on the lists leaked to the populace. The names on the lists are individuals being guided into power position by those able to manipulate such circumstances, and are individuals of great talent and promise so their planned ascension meets with little resistance. Thus where these names appear as Illuminati members, these individuals are not members of the Illuminati. Look at who is in a position to promote the ascension of these individuals, and who is standing behind those individuals with a gun pointed at their heads, to see who is conducting the Illuminati fear campaign.

The Illuminati worships the Puppet Masters, desires to be associated with this clout and influence, and thus often are used to further the Puppet Masters goals. The Illuminati are an old society, centuries old, and emerging in Europe naturally were composed of royalty, members of court in attendance to royalty, and organized religion which in those days were often so closely allied with royalty, as state religions, to be one and the same. Do the royalty of Europe run the world? Do the heads of organized religions, the Vatican, run the world? On what basis? It is wealth that runs the world from purchasing cooperation from corporations, which they own, to assisting their Puppets into political power via their control of the media and assets to be used for bribery and coercion. The members of the Illuminati seek favors from the Puppet Master, and offer services, and in this regards act as a supplicant, not a master.

Freemasonry

Freemasonry is a fraternal organization that arose from obscure origins in the late 16th to early 17th century. Freemasonry now exists in various forms all over the world, with a membership estimated at around six million, including approximately 150,000 in Scotland and Ireland, over a quarter of a million under the jurisdiction of the United Grand Lodge of England and just under two million in the United States.

Membership in the Masons is often mentioned in association with secret societies holding special knowledge about the alien presence or alien technology. The reason for this association is somewhat natural, given the structure and operation of the Masons—rigid rules, endless hierarchies, and privileges withheld from all but the elite members. As with the structure and operation of the military, this is highly attractive to those in the Service-to-Self—it is their structure and operation, and they feel at home!

The fraternity is administratively organised into independent Grand Lodges or sometimes Orients, each of which governs its own jurisdiction, which consists of subordinate (or constituent) Lodges. The various Grand Lodges recognize each other, or not, based upon adherence to landmarks.

Thus in the early days of MJ12, when fear of what the alien presence meant for mankind held sway, the controlling membership of MJ12 held an inordinate number of Masons. This is no longer the case, but this predominance worked its way into NASA and the Apollo program, as individuals selected for key posts were chosen based on their long standing habit of following nonsensical rules. Those at the top wanted complete control, and only virtual automatons such as the devout Masons often are, were trusted. Thus potential astronauts, faced with the special screening rumored to be in place, often joined the Masons and went through the motions simply to be included in the space program. This surface loyalty often went to the extremes of including Masonic rituals while out in space, a routine that can be best understood if one considers that the astronauts simply wanted to be brought back home alive!

Theosophy

Theosophy is a doctrine of religious philosophy and mysticism. Theosophy holds that all religions are attempts by the Occult Brotherhood to help humanity in evolving to greater perfection, and that each religion therefore has a portion of the truth. The founding members, Helena Petrovna Blavatsky, Henry Steel Olcott, and William Quan Judge, established the Theosophical Society in New York City in 1875. Rudolf Steiner created a successful branch of the Theosophical Society in Germany and eventually in 1913 founded his own successor the Anthroposophical Society.

Theosophists believe that selflessness and traditional virtues, lead people ever closer to their Divine Nature. Planets, solar systems, galaxies, and the cosmos itself are regarded as conscious entities, fulfilling their own evolutionary paths. The spiritual units of consciousness in the universe are the Monads, which may manifest as angels, human beings or in various other forms. According to Blavatsky, the Monad is the reincarnating unit of the human soul, consisting of the two highest of the seven constituent parts of the human soul. All beings, regardless of stature or complexity, are informed by such a Monad.

Theosophiests believe in one absolute, incomprehensible and supreme Deity, or infinite essence, which is the root of all nature, and of all that is, visible and invisible (The Storm). They also believe that man has an eternal immortal nature, because, being a radiation of the Universal Soul, he is of an identical essence with it.

Past Theosophist writings had valid insights, but were not from a channel. Their accuracy came from knowledge the entity brought with it into the incarnation. The early Theosophists were Wanderers of The Storm, whose mission was education of mankind. The Theosophists, being ahead of their time in the concerns they addressed and too intellectual for the masses, were ignored by the establishment, which did not see in them a threat. Thus their message has not been undermined in the same manner as the message of Jesus, for instance, who spoke plainly to the masses and challenged the establishment directly and repeatedly.

The Theosophists, speaking to humans in a language they could understand, inculcated their legends. One uses what is at hand, when trying to communicate and bridge vast communication gaps. The early Theosophists should be read not literally, but as though reading poetry, mythology, thus letting the underlying meaning soak in. This, in its totality, will convey the message intended by the Theosophists, who were telling true history, and relaying the true plans in place for the Earth.

Yin-Yang

In Chinese philosophy, the concept of yin yang is used to describe how polar or seemingly contrary forces are interconnected and interdependent in the natural world, and how they give rise to each other in turn. Opposites thus only exist in relation to each other. Yin and Yang is supposed to represent the balance of polarized opposites, the two primary forces of the Universe. Yang is creative, light and active, while Yin is receptive, dark and passive. Together, they form a complimentary pair which is always seeking balance.

The Chinese put much faith in the influence that Yin and Yang have upon their existence. This concept is an offshoot of the Buddhist philosophy that balance is everything. Problems are looked at as an imbalance, and the solution returning to balance somehow. Thus, Yin and Yang are superimposed on all of life, on social interactions in particular, and even on the seasons and weather. If a group of school children are boisterous and aggressive, their Yin is tempered with more studies in art, inserting Yang. If a wife is sullen and brooding, her Yang is tempered with more outings into the vibrant city, more Yin. If the spring came early and the fields are unprepared for planting, this Yin is handled by the farmers Yang, by meditation in the fields. Does all this help? It can't hurt, and in the main tends to focus humans on the spiritual aspects of life.

Ying and Yang is just one of the many examples of Lost Within the Rhymes of Mystic Splendor. The concept and philosophy is, just as The Secret of Storms, inspired by The Storm but the path of The Storm is a long and complex one. No shame here as it is one of many different ways humans use to focus on the spiritual aspects of life. Meditating or praying does not bring one closer to The Storm, but it can't hurt. If a child is aggressive, that is a symptom, so the issue is complicated; Yin tempered with more art could, potentially, solve the problem (if there is one), but it is not the most optimal way in dealing with issues, obviously.

K. R.

I Ching

The I-Ching is the world's oldest oracle—more than 5,000 years old! Most legends say that the oracle was first devised by Fu Hsi, the godlike first Emperor of China, who is also credited with the invention of writing, and cooking. One day, while bathing in the Yellow River, he noticed the patterns on the shell of a tortoise; this led him to observe the patterns of nature, and thus, understand the very structure of reality itself. Fu Hsi developed a system of trigrams, which he called the Book of Changes.

Two thousand years later, the good King Wen was falsely imprisoned by the last heir to the tyrannical Shang dynasty. While incarcerated, Wen studied The Book of Changes, and by dividing and doubling Fu Hsi's original trigrams, created the hexagrams we see today.

The I-Ching is based on the concept of Yin and Yang—the balance of polarized opposites, the two primary forces of the Universe. Yang is creative, light and active, while Yin is receptive, dark and passive. Together, they form a complimentary pair which is always seeking balance.

The I-Ching is part of a numerological system, with even numbers as Yin, and odd numbers as Yang. In the hexagrams, Yin is represented by a broken line, Yang is represented by a whole line. To use the I-Ching coins one side is designated as Yin, the other as Yang. Tossing the coins, and recording the results, forms the hexagram from the bottom line up. Once you have formed your hexagram, then it is time to turn to the Book of Changes for the supposed meaning of that hexagram. There are sixty-four possibilities.

Does it work??

Fortune tellers and psychics use many vehicles on which to place their psychic perceptions, as the bold faced assertion that the predictions are based on what the questioner is laying before the fortune teller like an open book would tend to diminish the credibility of the fortune teller, and most certainly would ruin the mystique. It does not matter what the psychic uses as their tool. The process is always the same. The mind and heart of the anguished or eager human sitting across the table are what is being read, and the common sense and compassion of the psychic fortune teller are what determines the result. Genuine fortune tellers do not require a crystal ball or tarot cards to place their perceptions, but without such Luls, there is no magic in it! Being of Service-to-Others orientation which indicates wisdom (from hundreds of past lives) orientation is required. That is the only thing which matters here. Thus, be Wary of False Prophets and their Evil Revelations. They are not capable of placing psychic perceptions, and they do not care about you. They care about making money on you, and their services aren't cheap. See The Russians.

Meditation

Meditation refers to any of a family of practices in which the practitioner trains his or her mind or self-induces a mode of consciousness in order to realize some benefit.

Meditation is generally an internal, personal practice and done without any external involvement, except perhaps prayer beads to count prayers, though many practitioners of meditation may rely on external objects such as candle flames as points on which to focus their attention as an aid to the process. Meditation often involves invoking or cultivating a feeling or internal state, such as compassion, or attending to a specific focal point. The term can refer to the state itself, as well as to practices or techniques employed to cultivate the state.

There are dozens or more specific styles of meditation practice. People may mean different things when they use the word, 'meditation'. Meditation has been practiced since antiquity as a component of numerous religious traditions, especially, in Western countries, in monastic settings. In the Eastern spiritual traditions such as Hinduism and Buddhism, meditation is more commonly a practice engaged in by many if not most believers.

The Hindus are a very mystical people, in touch with their spiritual side, and trying all the time to move more in that direction. They study and practice methods to improved communications with the spirit world. Concentration, diet that will improve the ability of the body to concentrate and not be distracted, positions of the body that are helpful, and the right mental attitudes. All this effort brings them little, however, as the ability to communicate with spirits is strictly related to the desire to do so. A human following all the recommended practices religiously may be nowhere, another doing everything wrong, according to the recommended practices, is speaking regularly to the dead or spirits in higher dimensions. However, as would be the case with any group of people, some Hindus who follow the recommendations also have desire, and so connect. There is then a great flurry of enthusiasm for the practices, which had nothing to do with the success.

The Hindu speak of a state, the goal of living, called Nirvana. They attempt to reach this via meditation, and correct living, during many incarnations. They attempt to reach high levels of communication with others, as an adjunct to this state. What they are seeking is termed living in light form, or the spirit only, not requiring incarnations. Incarnations are a learning experience, but spirits grow beyond the need for this, in both the Service-to-Others and Service-to-Self orientations. Incarnations are then used as a learning experience, or a tool, for these spirits.

Yogas

Yogas, who control their bodies to be able to breath with reduced oxygen use, in closed chambers, buried chambers, for hours past the point of death in a normal person, or otherwise resist injury by walking over hot coals, are not operating outside their physiology. If they were, then why are there limits on what is reported, or performed? If one can walk over hot coals, then why not through a firestorm? If breathing less and reducing the metabolism for hours, then why not weeks? If super-human powers were afoot, then limits would not be in place. Yogas learn, through dedicated practice, to control their body's reactions, not unlike a warrior resisting pain during battle in order to survive. Your bodies use of oxygen can take surprising steps, as for instance where a child falls into very cold water and is apparently dead for an hour or more, then revived as normal. This is an indication of the capacity of the body to reduce its normal reactions. Yogas who walk over coals have, in the first place, callused bare feet that have almost an inch of dead skin, thickened, on the soles. They have analyzed and practiced just how long the food must be on a hot coal, how quickly lifted, and where to place the foot. Blistering does not occur, as live flesh has not been burned. Dead thickened skin peels off, rebuilding underneath, and no one but the Yoga is the wiser.

Stigmata

Stigmata are bodily marks, sores, or sensations of pain in locations corresponding to the crucifixion wounds of Jesus, such as the hands and feet. In some cases, rope marks on the wrists have accompanied the wounds on the hands. The term originates from the line at the end of Saint Paul's Letter to the Galatians where he says, "I bear on my body the marks of Jesus." Stigmata is the plural of the Greek word stigma, meaning a mark or brand such as might have been used for identification of an animal or slave. An individual bearing stigmata is referred to as a stigmatic or a stigmatist.

The body can create stigmata through a force of will. This is often suspected. A great deal of illness, almost the majority, is caused by what is termed psychosomatic problems—tension, or a decision by the person to become ill—as astonishing as this may seem. There are a great many auto-immune diseases, infection that just doesn't seem to heal, that antibiotics can't suppress so the infection overwhelms. Cancer itself is a decision by the body to die. If inflammation can be caused by the will, then why can't a person cause an inflammation to the point of burst capillaries in the center of one's palm? This is quite possible. People who walk on hot coals, who are able to hold their breath and be almost buried alive and manage to be dredged up hours later—they have learned to control their bodies as the Yogi's do. This is not all that unusual. It's not common, but not all that unusual. People who have great faith, and wish to join with the aesthetics, with the saints, to merge with them and be dead before their time, will often take on those physical forms that make their life on Earth more similar to where they wish to be, with their admired ones.

Qi

In traditional Chinese culture, qi (also chi or ch'i) is an active principle forming part of any living thing. Qi is frequently translated as "energy flow", and is often compared to Western notions of energeia or élan vital (vitalism), as well as the yogic notion of prana and pranayama. The literal translation of "qi" is air, breath, or gas.

Review the Mind/Body connection, where the mind directs and affects the body, and how exceptional concentration can increase this connection; and the Spirit/Body connection, whereby the incarnated spirit influences the physical body to the degree that the body can respond; and the

Mind/Spirit connection, whereby the spirit likewise influences the mind by affecting the brain chemistry that constitutes thought. In sum, this constitutes the life-force, and there is no force such as chi outside of these parameters. The spirit cannot exhort the mind or body beyond what it is able. All tales to the contrary should take into consideration the suggestibility of the mere mortals who wish it to be otherwise.

Glossolalia

Glossolalia or speaking in tongues is the fluid vocalizing (or, less commonly, the writing) of speech-like syllables, often as part of religious practice. Though some consider these utterances to be meaningless, those that use them consider them to be part of a holy language. Glossolalia is a material phenomenon which has physical and psychological patterns that can be described. Substantial scientific studies have been published that provide an objective description of the linguistics of glossolalic speech and the neural behavior of the speakers.

A long running theme in Christianity is the fainting or babbling hysteria that on occasion overcomes nuns. Where other religious practices such as voodoo have an equivalent, such as the dancing frenzy that ends in a short coma, this is an activity and result that is deliberately encouraged. Christian frenzies are notable for appearing to be visited upon the faithful, as something they neither desired or encouraged, and most certainly not something they incited. The self, and the sexual inhibitions the Christian church often imposes, are precisely the source, however. Even religions as repressive as Islam have sexual outlets unthinkable in Christian doctrine.

Christianity states that sex is wrong, per se, and should only be indulged in when self discipline breaks down.

Masturbation, an utterly harmless and completely natural activity, is postured as a sin against nature.

Those who must indulge are funneled into marriage, their only outlet, and then only a marriage blessed by the church.

For Catholics, this is also a single marriage during a life time.

Then there is the matter of contraception, where those Catholics who allow themselves to indulge in sex, in their proscribed single marriage in a lifetime, must also allow as many children as possible to result.

And those who would side step these restrictions into homosexual alliances are damned to burn in hell!

These strictures mean that very few Christians, and in particular very few Catholics, will have any guilt free sexual outlet. All other outlets than a proper marriage with the single lifetime spouse without benefit of contraception bring with it all manner of baggage. The conflicts are endless, and the specter of burning in hell raised up for the mere thought of getting out of the bind. Thus, good Catholics try not to think about it, try to live a sex free life in spite of their hormones, and some go into the monasteries and nunneries hoping the environment will help them in this regard. It doesn't, and then they are left with even fewer outlets for their sexual frustrations, as now they have the guilt of wanting to leave the priesthood or nun's vows.

What results is silly behavior, the equivalent of the schizophrenic twiddling their fingers, aimless motions and random speech. Speaking in tongues or dancing in circles is nothing more than an outlet, the equivalent of a cold shower or long run but with some added benefits—the practitioner has an orgasm. The church allows this form of masturbation, giving oneself over into antics that incite an orgasm, as it is presented as religious fervor rather than what it is, sexual fervor. Bumping about, falling to the floor, pelvic thrusts, waving arms, extemporaneous cries of joy—take away the church setting and what do you see?

Researchers at the University of Pennsylvania took brain images of five women while they spoke in tongues and found that their frontal lobes—the thinking, willful part of the brain through which people control what they do —were relatively quiet, as were the language centers. The regions involved in maintaining self-consciousness were active. The women were not in blind trances, and it was unclear which region was driving the behavior.

The images, appearing in the current issue of the journal Psychiatry Research: Neuroimaging, pinpoint the most active areas of the brain. The images are the first of their kind taken during this spoken religious practice, which has roots in the Old and New Testaments and in Pentecostal churches established in the early 1900s. The women in the study were healthy, active churchgoers.

"The amazing thing was how the images supported people's interpretation of what was happening," said Dr. Andrew B. Newberg, leader of the study team, which included Donna Morgan, Nancy Wintering and Mark Waldman. "The way they describe it, and what they believe, is that God is talking through them," he said.

Dr. Newberg is also a co-author of "Why We Believe What We Believe."

In the study, the researchers used imaging techniques to track changes in blood flow in each woman's brain in two conditions, once as she sang a gospel song and again while speaking in tongues. By comparing the patterns created by these two emotional, devotional activities, the researchers could pinpoint blood-flow peaks and valleys unique to speaking in tongues.

Ms. Morgan, a co-author of the study, was also a research subject. She is a born-again Christian who says she considers the ability to speak in tongues a gift. "You're aware of your surroundings," she said. "You're not really out of control. But you have no control over what's happening. You're just flowing. You're in a realm of peace and comfort, and it's a fantastic feeling."

Contrary to what may be a common perception, studies suggest that people who speak in tongues rarely suffer from mental problems. A recent study of nearly 1,000 evangelical Christians in England found that those who engaged in the practice were more emotionally stable than those who did not. Researchers have identified at least two forms of the practice, one ecstatic and frenzied, the other subdued and nearly silent.

The new findings contrasted sharply with images taken of other spiritually inspired mental states like meditation, which is often a highly focused mental exercise, activating the frontal lobes.

The scans also showed a dip in the activity of a region called the left caudate. "The findings from the frontal lobes are very clear, and make sense, but the caudate is usually active when you have positive affect, pleasure, positive emotions," said Dr. James A. Coan, a psychologist at the University of Virginia. "So it's not so clear what that finding says" about speaking in tongues.

The caudate area is also involved in motor and emotional control, Dr. Newberg said, so it may be that practitioners, while mindful of their circumstances, nonetheless cede some control over their bodies and emotions.

Voodoo

The power of suggestion is both dismissed and held in awe by humans, who claim it might be able to affect other weak minded individuals, but certainly not themselves. The media presents hypnosis as being able to cause individuals selected at random from an audience to make complete fools of themselves in front of the world, clucking like chickens and attempting to peck at seed, for instance. Likewise, the media shows hypnotized individuals, like human time bombs, walking about in human society in a normal manner, but set to explode into action when a key word is spoken or a visual picture presented.

Hypnosis, of the power of suggestion, does not work in this manner, as in all cases the individual must be in full compliance. One cannot be hypnotized to do what one does not want to do, although the suggestion can certainly be presented during hypnosis. Hypnosis encourages the conscious to relax its hold, allowing the subconscious to communicate. Any suggestions made to an individual are, perforce, being made to the subconscious, which is the solid common sense arena and processes suggestions rather than blindly accepting them. Hypnosis is used to get past the rigidities and denial imposed by the conscious, to place the conscious by the side where it can be an observer and become better integrated as a result of the discussions.

Voodoo relies on the victim's belief systems, as without this no magic exists. Someone who had never heard the myths, subjected to all the incantations and pointing fingers and objects stolen or placed in one's personal quarters, would merely scratch their head. What's with them, they would wonder. On the other hand, humans raised in these cultures are impressed with the belief that voodoo works, palpable fear in the voices of the elders relaying the many tales. Spells cast upon humans thus primed to react set in motion a cycle of fear that can indeed kill. Fear can stop the heart by constricting arteries leading to the heart, or can drive the blood pressure to a point where blow-outs occur. Cast a spell and the ashen victim is found dead in their quarters the next day. Such a cooperative victim!

Acupuncture

Acupuncture is an alternative medicine that treats patients by insertion and manipulation of needles in the body. Its proponents variously claim that it relieves pain, treats infertility, treats disease, prevents disease, promotes general health, or can be used for therapeutic purposes. Acupuncture typically incorporates traditional Chinese medicine as an integral part of its practice and theory. However, many practitioners consider 'Traditional Chinese Medicine' (TCM) to narrowly refer to modern mainland Chinese practice. Acupuncture in Japan and Korea, and to a certain extent Taiwan, diverged from mainland China in theory and practice. In European countries such as the UK almost half the practitioners follow these non-TCM practices. The most notable difference is that these other approaches often are primarily acupuncture, and do not incorporate Chinese herbal medicine. The term "acupuncture" is sometimes used to refer to insertion of needles at points other than traditional ones, or to applying an electric current to needles in acupuncture points. Acupuncture dates back to prehistoric times, with written records from the second century BCE. Different variations of acupuncture are practiced and taught throughout the world.

The Chinese have a long tradition with acupuncture, which speaks to its effectiveness. Surely patients would not submit to a treatment involving needles if it were not so! Yet the success of this treatment has nothing to do with the action of the needles, which are in this but a prop. The success of the treatment is a byproduct, caused in fact by the distraction of pain. So many illnesses are caused by nervous tension, and so many more affected, that nervous tension is perhaps the most prominent cause of physical distress. Headaches, belly aches, aches in the joints or muscles, tight throat, sour stomach, constipation, loose bowel, numbness, blurry eyesight, ringing in the ears—take away nervous tension and most of this goes away.

The suffering one goes to the acupuncturist, in distress, resigned to the prospect of all those needles. Natural anesthesia is used as none else is offered. Put your mind somewhere else, disconnect from reality, float past the stinging pain, think about the relaxing heat coming through the needles, concentrate on the healing process one imagines is in process—and through all of this, like magic, the patient forgets that which was making them tense. They relax, feel better, and credit the acupuncture which, in truth, they should.

Homeopathy

Homeopathy is a form of alternative medicine in which practitioners treat patients using highly diluted preparations that are believed to cause healthy people to exhibit symptoms that are similar to those exhibited by the patient. The collective weight of scientific evidence has found homeopathy to be no more effective than a placebo.

Homeopathy, the concept that physical reactions to disease and the cure have some relationship both has and does not have a valid basis. It has long been known that cancer is sometimes cured by a high fever, such as Chickenpox infection. This is the immune system being spiked, along with a desire on the part of the patient to live, such that the immune system is no longer suppressed due to depression and a silent desire to end the life. Here we have cancer causing weakness and fever, due to secondary infections and lack of appetite, and we have the Chickenpox causing the same symptoms, thus the homeopathy concept applied. Allergy is at times treated by desensitizing the patient, giving them small bits of the allergen until the reaction seems to stop. Is this curing the allergy or managing it, or taking advantage of a natural reaction? In fact, allergy patients will often report that if exposed for long times, years, their allergy reactions reduce. Worse at first, later reducing, as the body sorts out the true onslaught to the immune system over time. So is desensitization, creating more of the same symptoms as the disease, a cure, or a manipulation of the body's natural tendencies? Homeopathy, is primarily a hope, and like voodoo and the placebo effect, where the will or hope effect the cure hoped for, is not factual in the main. Those living in countries where homeopathy is unknown fare as well or as poorly as those in countries where this is a theory respected.

Timewave Zero

Timewave zero is a numerological formula that purports to calculate the ebb and flow of "novelty", defined as increase in the universe's interconnectedness, or organised complexity, over time. According to Terence McKenna, who conceived the idea over several years in the early-to mid-1970s while using psilocybin mushrooms and DMT, the universe has a teleological attractor at the end of time that increases interconnectedness, eventually reaching a singularity of infinite complexity in 2012, at which point anything and everything imaginable will occur simultaneously. Using the "King Wen Sequence" of the I Ching, he developed a 64 number sequence. The 64 hexagrams traditionally appear in a rather random-looking order. There are various systematic ways in which you could order them. Terence McKenna chose the "King Wen Sequence" for no apparent reason (magic?!). Why was this sequence chosen remains unknown. McKenna counted the number of lines which changed from one hexagram to the next in the King Wen sequence, generating a list of 64 numbers between 1 and 6. It was then use to create a line graph. The line graph was then shrunk for some reason and duplicated a few times. Terence McKenna, then, merged all the graph lines together to get a much more in depth graph which takes some mathematical calculations to make it coherent.

The theory is clearly based in numerology and takes shape out of McKenna's belief that the sequence is artificially arranged as such purposefully. Mathematically, the sequence is graphed according to a set of mathematical ratios, and displays a fractal nature as well as resonances, although it was not captured in a true formula until criticism from mathematician Matthew Watkins. McKenna interpreted the fractal nature and resonances of the wave, as well as his theory of the I Ching's artificial arrangement, to show that the events of any given time are recursively related to the events of other times.

"The way he constructed the graph meant that, at some point in history, it would drop to zero, supposedly indicating some kind of "infinitely novel event", beyond which nothing could be said or described. This is where the December 21, 2012 date comes in. A lot of people might be under the impression that he had arrived at that date via some kind of calculation. He certainly gave that impression. I remember being somewhat disappointed to find out that he hadn't calculated it—he'd merely slid his graph back and forth along the timeline of history (as he understood it) until he got the bets possible fit." —Watkins

McKenna chose the atomic bombing of Hiroshima (August 6, 1945) as the basis for calculating his end date in November 2012. When he later discovered this date's proximity to the end of the 13th b'ak'tun of the Maya calendar, he revised his hypothesis so that the two dates matched. There was no particular or mathematical reason to do it. McKenna just slid it over because he assumed it should go there as well. The atomic bombing of Hiroshima was thus put off a month. Instead of it being the highest of novelty, McKenna simply called it the end of World War II . . .

As you see, there is no magic in Timewave Zero. It is silly, at best.

K. R.

Reverse Speech

Reverse speech is a pseudoscience first advocated by David John Oates which gained publicity when it was mentioned on Art Bell's nightly Coast to Coast AM radio talk show. It claims that during spoken language production, human speakers subconsciously produce hidden messages that give insights into their innermost thoughts. Oates claims that it has applications in psychotherapy, criminology and business negotiation. Its claims have been rejected, however, by mainstream science and academia.

Oates' claim is that, on average, once in every 15-20 seconds of casual conversation a person produces two related sentences—a "forward-spoken" message that is heard consciously, and a "backwards" message unconsciously embedded in the person's speech. These two modes of speech, forward and backward, are supposedly dependent upon each other and form an integral part of human communication. In the dynamics of interpersonal communication both modes of speech combine to communicate the total psyche of the person, conscious as well as unconscious. Oates claims that backward speech is always honest and reveals the truth about the speaker's intentions and motivations. The most famous recording that allegedly demonstrates this is the speech given by Neil Armstrong at the time of the first manned lunar landing on 20 July 1969. If played backwards, the words "small step for man" sound somewhat like "Man will space walk."

There is no such phenomena as reverse speech, and all such discoveries are just imagination. The human body is not designed to speak intelligibly in a reverse manner, simultaneous to forward speech spoken at a different speed. The human mind perceives rolling forward and does not replay backwards, and simply is not geared that way because nature does not play things backwards. Humans evolved on Earth to deal with sights and sounds around them, not with an artificial phenomena. Always nervous about being tempted by the Devil, humans as most 3rd Density intelligent species look for signs that this is occurring. Discontent to simply rely on their intuition, they want a truth test that can be applied. It's just so much easier. Of course, if any human is being tempted by visiting entities in the Service-to-Self, is it because they asked for this, by giving The Call, but as it's so much more comfortable to point the finger elsewhere, the pointing finger wants someplace to land. Reverse speech is just the thing.

As an avenue only recently detectable, due to modern electronic playback systems which can play video and audio tapes in either direction, and at any speed, it has recently experienced a rush of attention. In point of fact, any conversation played backwards at various speeds will sound vaguely like a recognizable speech phrase. Don't children lay on their backs on a summer day and call out shapes that the clouds assume? Don't pet owners claim their pets are talking due to the cadence of the meow or whimper? If one expects to find a phrase, and plays speech or music backwards long enough and at different speeds, eventually some sounds will seem to emerge that bear a faint relationship to a word or two. This is particularly true of music or speech that threatens the control of the establishment—parents determined to rein in their teen-agers, or rigidly religious folks determined to eliminate what they term temptation so that their urges cannot run away with them.

Where reverse speech is not truly occurring, there is another phenomena in place in which people are trying to ascribe a physical medium for information that they understand intuitively. Human beings who are barely aware of their incarnated spirit, often have knowledge that they cannot ascribe to any source. Did they hear it on TV, the radio, read it in a book, or hear it from a buddy? No, but they just simply have this information, have no explanation for where it came from. Often people are simply looking for a source. If someone has that information and are trying to relay it, they frequently find they have to package it in some way or people won't even listen. If they simply say they have a thought that popped into their head, who is going to listen? There must be some kind of a logical explanation. Thus, in dealing with reverse speech, one should listen with an open heart and mind to the underlying message, which may have a great deal of truth to it.

Bible Code

The Bible code, also known as the Torah code, is a method described as a "hidden code" of selecting letters from within the Hebrew Bible that form words and phrases supposedly demonstrating foreknowledge and prophecy. The study and results from this cipher have been popularized by Michael Drosnin's book The Bible Code.

Examples have been documented in the past. One cited example is that by taking every 50th letter of the Book of Genesis, the Hebrew word for "bible" is spelled out. The same word is found similarly in each of the other five books of Moses. Modern computers were used to search for similar patterns and more complex variants, and reported in an academic paper in 1994 and later as a book. Drosnin and proponents hold that it is exceedingly unlikely such sequences could arise by chance, while skeptics and opponents hold that such sequences do often arise by chance, as demonstrated on other Hebrew and English texts.

The Bible Code does not exist. This is nonsense. The Bible Code is something that people have pieced together. They have stated that periodically, every third beat or according to some pattern, that something appears in the text. Why would Jesus, who spoke very simply to the common man, who stated his message over and over so it would not get garbled, speak in such codes and then bury them so that only certain individuals could find them? If one took snowflakes landing on the edge of a razor and analyzed them in an attempt to find a pattern, and tried hard enough, one could make them say almost anything. This has been done with Nostradamus. He was quite telepathic and aware of what was going on in his own world and had a great success rate. But he did not predict the future in his quatrains, which can be interpreted in millions of ways. Just because someone interprets it this way or that way does not make it so. The Bible Code does not exist. Anyone who has the capacity to challenge this assertion will find it to be a bunch of nonsense.

Dowsing

The practice of dowsing, using divining rods to locate water, is so common as to not be doubted, but no one, including the practitioner, understands how they work. Some humans can douse, but most cannot, so its recognized to be a talent or ability within the practitioner. Dowsing works best when the dowser is allowed to walk about out in the fields and forest by him or herself, uninterrupted. When crowds follow about, they are less likely to find water, and many dowsers come unannounced at odd hours to assure themselves the privacy they require. Dowsers are called upon when all else fails. Well after well has been dug, following the geologists recommendations on the lay of the land, location of local springs, emergence of underground streams or rivers, stratification of rock layers, and success of other wells in the area. In despair, the dowser is brought in, and against all odds and against all reason they point to an unlikely place and chances are that a well placed there will be productive. What is going on during dowsing, and how does this work?

An oft quoted phrase is that man is 98% water, as is all plant and animal life. Water carries electric current, if fact so effectively that lightning will race through water as well as metal wires on its way to the ground. The human body senses electrical charges in the vicinity, as the movement of electrons in all their many forms is not isolated to where the current is running. An electric current creates an electrical field around it, just as a river of water causes humidity in the air nearby. Humans are sensitive to electric current, as the higher rate of cancer in those who live near high tension wires attests. The dowser listens to what his body is telling him, a very quiet voice but a voice nonetheless.

The electrical current in groundwater is stronger where the water has filled all connected air pockets that might act as insulators. This fact has been noted by geologists monitoring earthquakes, as the electrostatic bursts increase as the ground comes under pressure preceding an earthquake. Geologists recognize that this increase in electrostatic bursts is due to compression of the groundwater. The dowser is locating, with his sensitive body, those places where the groundwater has collected and accumulated, coming under pressure in that it cannot easily leave. The mystery of the divining rods is more easily understood when one understands that the divining rods are in fact the dowser's hands. The rods, extending from the dowser's hands, allow the dowser to note how his hands are reacting. They are a signal flag, helping the dowser note the whispering voice in his body that is saying "here, over here, there is a subtle pull toward an electrical current in the ground".

The pull is within the electrical current in the dowser's own body, which seeks to flow in sync with the electrical current in the ground.

Atlantis and Lemuria

Atlantis is a legendary island first mentioned in Plato's dialogues Timaeus and Critias. In Plato's account, Atlantis was a naval power lying "in front of the Pillars of Hercules" that conquered many parts of Western Europe and Africa 9,000 years before the time of Solon, or approximately 9600 BC. After a failed attempt to invade Athens, Atlantis sank into the ocean "in a single day and night of misfortune".

The legends of Atlantis are based not on actual fact, but a combination of truths which when combined gave birth to the legend of Atlantis. The stories about Atlantis, which has never been found, are supported by myths of great cities destroyed suddenly by rising water. Well, that of course happens extensively all over the world every time there is a pole shift. There were lands that sunk under the sea in the Atlantic, but they were no more developed than the bordering lands at the time of the last cataclysms, stories of Atlantis notwithstanding. The Earth was visited by hominoid extraterrestrials in its past, and these hominoids had access to technology that amazed the primitive humans who stood witness. Many cities in and around the European continent went under the waves during the past few pole shifts. This is because the Atlantic, as a widening ocean, tends to drag down the shore lines and outlying islands during each shift. The floor of the Atlantic drops, pulling its perimeter with it. Beyond what has been told about the visitors from Planet X, there is naught to say about rumors about Atlantis. These visitors did not disappear because they went under the waves. They disappeared because they were put into quarantine.

Rumors of Atlantis aside, mankind did not achieve advances beyond what they hold today, in the past. Atlantis was not a human society, but a society composed, dominated, by the advanced homoinoids from Planet X, the Annunaki. The Annunaki used crystals for communications, had rocket power, but these equated to no more than mankind had today.

Pyramids

A pyramid is a structure where the outer surfaces are triangular and converge at a point. The base of a pyramid can be trilateral, quadrilateral, or any polygon shape, meaning that a pyramid has at least three triangular surfaces (at least four faces including the base). The square pyramid, with square base and four triangular outer surfaces, is a common version.

K. R.

Humans ponder the pyramids of Egypt and some similar structures in South and Central America, and wonder how early man could rise or move such large stones? Of course, they could not. Even today the mechanics would be imposing to the point of being impossible. The answer is, of course, that early man did not build these structures. For majesty, early man went to massive structures such as mountain tops or cliffs or deep ravines. Their gods of force were the wind, as in tornadoes and hurricanes, and earthquakes, who on occasion moved great boulders and rearranged the landscape. So how would visitors act if they wanted to impress these impressionable savages? Move great boulders. The many pyramids they constructed around the world were more than viewing stations, though they afforded a stable point for star gazing, but were more like erecting a flag is to the countries of Earth. A statement. Here I am. Here I have settled. Here I cannot be moved or removed.

This was not an effort for these hominoids, during this time, as they had entered into bargains with Service-to-Self aliens who had levitation abilities, and they moved the stones for them. The rocks used to build the pyramids were transported, and when levitation is used distance is not a factor. They were taken from a mine, in block, and move around the world. The issue was more the quality of the rock, and ease of extraction, than proximity. The aliens who helped erect the pyramids are still influencing the giant homonoids today, which is why their culture is not ready for a Transformation as Earth is, but will be delayed. They have had heavy Service-to-Self influences, and are still recovering, the majority of their reincarnating souls still learning the drawbacks of this existence. They paid a price for these services, and are still working their way out of that. Many of their number developed strong Service-to—Self orientations during this time, and have influenced their culture severely and in a long term manner. For what these Service-to-Self aliens looked like, myths and legends suffice, as do the books from India, the Vedas. A wide range of appearances, and behaviors.

However, the Great Pyramids were built by the Annunaki as Navigational Devices. The Annunaki who in the past visited Earth to the point of taking up limited residence here. Where they are no longer free to visit in this manner, being in quarantine in this regard, in the past they were allowed to do so. Why was it necessary to build such large structures as interstellar navigational guides? Because, in the locale, any astronomical device would be subject to shifting sands. The Great Pyramids, by their great size and weight, ensure stability. All this just to sight an incoming comet, which makes its appearance on a regular basis and can be seen weeks if not months beforehand? The Great Pyramids were not used solely for sighting an incoming object, as their primary purpose was to act as a guidance system for the launches the exiled Planet X residents would make to meet their home planet. This required precision, as their rockets were no more sophisticated than those used to boost man into space today, and once in space they simply coasted until drawn into the gravitational orbit of the water planet they owed their allegiance to.

They did not last on Earth from one appearance of the Planet X to another. Several generations would pass, the knowledge of how to read the stars and what the Planet X kingship expected of them passed from parent to child. Conscientious parents, aging and sure to die before their progeny could return to the home planet where they had royalty status, built a navigational system that was rock solid and sure—the Giant Pyramids. Could the pyramids act as guides for the forthcoming reappearance of Planet X? Many pole shifts have occurred since they were built, each time the crust of the Earth sliding into new positions. One would have to calibrate anew the points, which would in any case not now converge to the point where the giant comet reenters your Solar System. Legend has it that the Giant Pyramids originally pointed near the Orion Star System, and those legends have carried true to their origin. Where this is the original point convergence, the spot where the giant comet first looms into view, the Giant Pyramids no longer act as a guide in this matter.

K. R.

The Sphinx

The Great Sphinx of Giza, commonly referred to as the Sphinx, is a statue of a reclining or couchant sphinx (a mythical creature with a lion's body and a human head) that stands on the Giza Plateau on the west bank of the Nile in Giza, Egypt. It is the largest monolith statue in the world, standing 73.5 metres (241 ft) long, 6 metres (20 ft) wide, and 20.22 m (66.34 ft) high. It is the oldest known monumental sculpture, and is commonly believed to have been built by ancient Egyptians of the Old Kingdom during the reign of the pharaoh Khafra (c. 2558-2532 BC).

The Sphinx is an example of a fancy burial chamber, a mausoleum of sorts, built by visitors from Planet X who were into the sport of lion hunting. The grave was intended for a large and powerful male who stood tall in the circle of hunters, and all felt having his grave guarded by one of his conquests a suitable statement on his abilities and might. As is often the case in the affairs of man, these plans went awry, as he was slaughtered by a rival and went unburied altogether, his body rotting under the sun, eaten by lions, no doubt.

Stonehenge

Stonehenge has influenced many groups over the eons, as it was intended to do. The Druids did not build Stonehenge, but they incorporated it into their rituals. Thus, history tends to credit them with erecting Stonehenge. Religious rituals, or those semi-religious rituals that form in highly structured social groups, are put into place to control the membership and give them outlets for emotions that would otherwise be disruptive. Emotions such as jealousy or fear can scatter a membership, but if given an outlet that tends to support the group's goal, build and support the group rather then tear it apart.

Human sacrifices are one such ritual, as the sacrificed one acts as a scapegoat, becoming a symbol for whatever has caused rage in the membership. The leaders, of course, select someone they wish to get rid of, a troublemaker or an independent thinker. Stonehenge by its very shape implies sacrifice, but it did not cause this behavior in the Druids, as using scapegoats and rituals involving sacrifice occur in all cultures and all parts of the world. The close proximity to such an edifice as Stonehenge to any sacrificial rituals would naturally align into a mental association over time, and this is what occurred—a coincidence, made into cause and effect by historians.

Visigoths

If the giant hominoids from Planet X inspired the myths about the Gods of Mount Olympus, were they also the inspiration for the Viking Gods or tales of the Germanic Visigoths? They were indeed, and left their mark in legend wherever they stationed themselves on Earth. Where their preferred garb looks something like what an ancient Roman Legionnaire might have worn, they adjusted their garb to the climate. Northern Europe, during many eras in the past, was as bitterly cold as it is today, and thus fur robes were standard. Like the Gods of Mount Olympus, the Viking Gods and Visigoths were fierce and did not back away once a conflict had begun. As with their human counterparts, they used all means of transporting themselves, and where mountains abut the sea, ships prove the most effective. What were these giant hominoids doing in northern Europe? Exploring, in the same manner that took them to South American and thence across the Pacific. They were looking for gold, and went prospecting everywhere.

Trojan War

The Greek legends speak of the war at Troy, where a woman was so desired that legions of warriors were sent to free her. Did this occur? It did indeed but with a twist, as Helen of Troy was not the desired object of this battle, a fact her ego did not allow her to accept. A hand maiden of Helen's, one she kept in tight bondage of servitude, was the true cause of this battle, but Helen loudly announced before, during, and after that she was being sought after, and not hearing otherwise the historians wrote it thus.

Legend has it that Troy was successfully invaded when a gift, the Trojan Horse, was left outside the gates and brought into the city. At war, the citizens of Troy were not so naive as to allow in uninspected such an unexplained object. In fact, the Trojan Horse was not simply a statue, a curiosity—it was food, built of food, stacks of wheat bound together, gourds and dried fruit, all tied about a wooden frame. This, they knew, the starving citizens could not resist. To minimize inspection of such a large object, which they knew was being done routinely on any baskets or barrels of food, the camouflage was shaped into a familiar animal. The citizens focused on the food baubles on the hooves, tail, and face of the horse, and so distracted lost themselves in their appetites before they ever got to the belly of the horse where a single infiltrator lay. Thin and agile, he worked his way out in the dead of night and gave access to his fellows at the gate.

El Dorado

El Dorado is the name of a Muisca tribal chief who covered himself with gold dust and, as an initiation rite, dove into a highland lake. Later it became the name of a legendary "Lost City of Gold" that has fascinated—and so far eluded—explorers since the days of the Spanish

Conquistadors. Though many have searched for years on end to find said "City of Gold", no results have proven visible. No one has either seen or touched the gold that could reside in the perhaps mythical city of El Dorado.

The obsession with gold is not natural to man, it is a habit mankind picked up from the Annunaki of Planet X. What about gold makes it so cherished? Platinum is as tarnish free, silver and copper as malleable, and yet gold is accepted as a metal more precious than others, more desirable, a metal to die for. This attitude toward gold, passed as a heritage from generation to generation, was impressed on mankind from those who had to have gold, and did not hesitate to kill for it.

Where mankind uses gold for adornment or as a medium of exchange, the visitors from Planet X were collecting gold for survival. Their home planet, on its long orbit out in space, is subjected to atmospheric abrasion the Earth and the other planets on more sedate orbits around the Sun do not suffer. Consider the rapid path past the Sun made Planet X, when acting like a comet. It moves from one side of the Solar System to the other in 3 months, a fast track indeed. Planet X losses atmosphere here and there, on a regular basis, and where this can be rebuild from its copious oceans, being basically a water planet, certain elements become depleted. Molecules in the atmosphere, containing gold, are necessary to retain the heat and light the planet generates, to keep the heat and light, essentially, bouncing back to the surface, as without these gold based molecules the planet dims and cools.

Thus, the visitors from Planet X came to Earth on a search, a mining mission, and were intent on raping the Earth of its relatively abundant gold and using its primitive hominoids, humans, as slaves to do so. It was impressed upon mankind early that gold was the ruler's due, and death fell to he who hoarded or withheld it. El Dorado, the lost City of Gold, was a staging point where the space ships used as shuttles were loaded and sent aloft at the appropriate time. Since this time only arrived once every 3,657 years, on average, a lot of gold stacked up. Long after the visitors from Planet X left the Earth, having been quarantined, the humans who had heard the stories from those who made deliveries to El Dorado searched for this City of Gold. They search still. However, the ruins, when discovered as they have been repeatedly, are not recognized as there is no gold. Why would these visitors, so desperate for what was essentially a life giving metal, leave any behind?

Tower of Babel

The Tower of Babel was an enormous tower built in the plain of Shinar. According to the biblical account, a united humanity of the generations following the Great Flood, speaking a single language and migrating from the east, came to the land of Shinar, where they resolved to build a city with a tower "with its top in the heavens . . . lest we be scattered abroad upon the face of the Earth." God came down to see what they did and said: "They are one people and have one language, and nothing will be withholden from them which they purpose to do." So God said, "Come, let us go down and confound their speech." And so God scattered them upon the face of the Earth, and confused their languages, and they left off building the city, which was called Babel "because God there confounded the language of all the Earth."(Genesis 11:5-8).

Cooperation among peoples is greatly enhanced by language, though this is not the only vehicle for communication possible. The statement that a picture is worth a thousand words can scarcely be argued. Nevertheless, humans who do not speak the same language essentially do not associate with each other, they avoid each other and segregation results. Nevertheless there are common threads in all languages, based on words that mock natural sounds and developmental associations the child makes. Early races of man, developing in isolation from each other, did not develop common languages, and this situation persists today. In fact, isolation creates different languages that started from the same base. They grow apart.

The legend of the Tower of Babel reflects this common occurrence, but the legend is not altogether fancy. Deliberate separation occurred in mankind's recent past, among groups that were commandeered into forced labor by the hominoid visitors from the 12th Planet. These slave-masters were constantly on the alert to prevent their slaves from gaining their technological advantages. The visitors constructed towers, silos in fact, to surround the missiles they used to shuttle between Earth and their home planet when it made a periodic appearance. When groups of their slave-laborers were found snooping and sharing information with each other, they were separated, forcibly. What remained of the story was the tower, the clustering of man, and the resulting separation due to language barriers. They did not separate because of a language barrier, the barrier developed because of separation.

Crop Circles

A crop circle is a sizable pattern created by the flattening of a crop such as wheat, barley, rye, maize, or rapeseed. Crop circles are also referred to as crop formations, because they are not always circular in shape. While the exact date crop circles began to appear is unknown, the documented cases have substantially increased from the 1970s to current times.

Humans have always stood in awe of crop circles as you can be assured this is not the first era where they have been prevalent. They speak to the subconscious, which sees the patterns and senses their meaning, and the conscious hasn't a clue. What is their meaning? Crop circles are telling you, in a universal language, of coming events, such as the pending pole shift, but spiritual as well. In the past these simple but eloquent messages were left, with increasing frequency and urgency, leading up to the shift. Crops circle creation is managed by a group of aliens that cannot participate in the Earth's Transformation in any other manner, as they are a life form that lives in the water, and thus their ships are filled with the atmosphere that they breath—water. Thus, this is how they serve.

Observers have noted that crop circles seem to appear almost instantaneously. They blink, and then notice that something is different in the vista before them. By what process is this accomplished? If space ships are landing and impressing the ground, then the time seems too short. If rays of energy or a force field are involved, all this passes the notice of the observers. Crop circle creation does not require a landed ship or physical force. The grain lies flat because the structure of the stems has been altered, one side of the stem rapidly growing in a process the reverse of what occurs when growing plants bend toward the light. This growth spurt occurs low to the ground, the particular ray, like laser surgery, focused there. The swirls are created due to the circular motion of the affecting ray, which circles like the hand of a clock, dropping the grain stalks such that they fall almost simultaneously.

Are crop circles more effective than words? Absolutely. They register in many parts of the brain, and tell the story with greater depth. A picture is worth a thousand words. Symbols are used to relay astronomical occurrences, effects of one planetary body on another, motion and direction, pace, change, and for those who have sensed their meaning, they also relay ratios and relative force. Stand before these pictures and let your subconscious speak to you, and see the forest and the sky, rather than the trees. Crop circles began with a simple circle, stating that the Earth is unruffled in her orbit. Then dual circles and rings, relaying the approaching interaction between the Earth and Planet X. The rings, of course, are the influence of gravitational pull, increasing. Long lines connecting circles—does Planet X, acting as a comet, not have an approach? Peripheral circles—the other planets in your solar system, or in the wider system that comprises the Planet X's journey.

And what of the Scorpion Tail, the connected and curving series of dots? Does not the comet travel with an entourage of minor moons? As the giant comet dominates with its gravitational field, the moons are not pulled into conflict regarding their place. They trail after their traveling master, like little ducklings in a row. Would not the Planet X's moons circle, as do moons humans are familiar with? Where the orbiting motion of moons is assumed to be due to a balance between the centrifugal force of the moon and attraction to the home planet, there are other variables. The orbiting moons are in motion because they are reaching for the Sun and other planets, like a twirling dancer forever undecided on a partner.

The helix, misinterpreted by many to be a DNA strand, is a pictorial representation of the Earth's rotation and the manner in which it begins to align with the rotation of the approaching Planet X. The Earth's rotation is caused by the motion of elements in the Earth's core attempting to escape or approach influences in the wider solar system. The Earth's rotation is already slowing, a fact noted by your scientists and various excuses already published in the media. The Earth's normal rotation is a careful balance taking into account all the factors in the solar system and beyond. It takes but a feather to trip the scales when they are perfectly balanced, and the influence of Planet X on the Earth from afar acts in this manner.

The ball of overlapping circles, all touching an inner circle, is meant to convey a new phenomenon occurring on Earth, preparing those who see it for the manifestation of this phenomenon. The Earth's magnetic field currently curves far out in space, so that on the surface of the Earth a compass almost always points north. Increasingly, as the Earth's swirling core is pushed to line up in opposition to the magnetic field of the approaching Planet X, it will send out minor magnetic fields that do not point due north, but wrap back into the Earth in the manner portrayed by the overlapping circles.

Crop circles present an opportunity to understand, at a glance, the decade ahead. As the pole shift approaches, they will present an accurate weather prediction, a guide to family affairs, a time table for settling matters and preparing for the future, the truest touch stone that mankind will be given. Visit them often, if only in picture form, and let the message soak in.

In grappling with crop circle appearances, and in trying to find patterns that would explain their purpose or occurrence, a number of silly theories have emerged.

Crop circles have been analyzed under the theory that they are man made. This theory falls apart when confronted by the clean but unbroken right angles that the grain shafts assume within the bent portion of the grain field, along with the utter lack of foot prints and the lightning speed of production.

Crop circles have been explained as the result of odd plasma energy, the swamp gas that is supposed to explain UFO sightings appearing in open fields in broad daylight. This theory, which had a proponent or two until the complexity of crop circles increased, is no longer even considered.

Crop circles have been analyzed under the theory that they are a communication form from visitors, and represent language in math. This is closer to the truth, but since all language or symbolism represents repetitive patterns, a constant in mathematics, some mathematical patterns would of course be represented. Seeing the trees but not the forest before them, they miss the point.

Crop circles placement has been analyzed, their placement in this or that country, along this or that longitude or latitude. Statistical analysis inevitably did show a pattern as even a mundane occurrence such as the placement of dog poop would show a pattern of sorts. This led to wild speculation that crop circles are caused by some occurrence along grid lines, a manifestation of energy of some sort, or spirits required to stay on the narrow path these lines represent. This silly theory gained credence only due to the lack of other plausible theories. Were this theory to have any merit, all the many crop circles that fall outside of what are termed ley lines would have to be addressed, rather than ignored.

Etheric Grid

The etheric grid system does not exist. There is much ballyhoo about this nebulous and unprovable etheric grid system, however. As with all things that cannot be grasped or pointed to, discussions proceed in various directions. In all fairness, it must be pointed out that many things scientists discuss cannot be grasped or pointed to, yet their existence is firmly believed. Sub-atomic particles is one such instance. But where does information about the etheric grid system come from? Is this a universal belief, such that science can point to the widespread collective awareness, at a minimum? There is little discussion about such a grid system. Is there some measure, however slight, that astronomers can point to? Those putting forth the etheric grid system theory have never attempted to connect with measurable reality, choosing instead to distance themselves from science.

The etheric grid system has been put forth to support a new religion of sorts. This religion looks not to a god in Heaven, as Christians and Jews and Muslims do, nor does it look to animistic gods, such as primitive peoples do when worshipping thunderstorms or voracious predatory animals, nor does it place a select human on a pedestal, as a god, as some cults do. This religion sees the ethereal everywhere, permeating everything, and sees this as the basis of life, the life force. This ethereal substance is the true glue, the true nature, in this belief, and all else an illusion. Where it is true that the human eye and ear do not sense all, the etheric religion discards too much. To replace what has been discarded, it invents the ethereal glue.

Ley Lines

Ley lines are alleged alignments of a number of places of geographical interest, such as ancient monuments and megaliths that are thought by certain adherents to dowsing and New Age beliefs to have spiritual power. Their existence was suggested in 1921 by the amateur archaeologist Alfred Watkins, in his book The Old Straight Track. Some people believe that ley lines and their intersection points resonate a special psychic or mystical energy.

Bermuda Triangle

The Bermuda Triangle, also known as the Devil's Triangle, is a region in the western part of the North Atlantic Ocean where a number of aircraft and surface vessels allegedly disappeared under mysterious circumstances. Popular culture has attributed these disappearances to the paranormal or activity by extraterrestrial beings. Documented evidence indicates that a significant percentage of the incidents were inaccurately reported or embellished by later authors, and numerous official agencies have stated that the number and nature of disappearances in the region is similar to that in any other area of ocean.

The Bermuda Triangle does indeed have unusual qualities, as do other places here and there on Earth. Magnetic anomalies are reported, where compasses swing wildly, clocks stop, and concrete objects fade from sight. What's causing this? These places, fortunately few in number, are an outlet from the center of the Earth for a byproduct of the Earth's compression, a gravity byproduct so to speak. A vent, from where subatomic particles not known to man surge forth periodically, and woe be to the man or fish who finds itself in the way. There are stories of ships and planes disappearing, and it is assumed they were carried off by extraterrestrials, taken off to a far-off zoo, for exhibition. Then why would these only disappear from such sites, and not regularly around the globe?

Here and there around the face of the Earth are similar outlets for this byproduct of the Earth's compression, many of them well known due to the havoc shippers or travelers experience—an area off the coast of Japan, and in one of the Great Lakes, for example. Such outlets also occur where man is unaware of them, as in the depths of the oceans or within inaccessible mountain crevices. What determines the outlet is not only the surface structure of the rock, fractures in fact, but also the structure of the underlying rock, factors man cannot measure.

Area 51

Area is a military base, and a remote detachment of Edwards Air Force Base. It is located in the southern portion of Nevada in the western United States, 83 miles (133 km) north-northwest of downtown Las Vegas. Situated at its center, on the southern shore of Groom Lake, is a large military airfield. The base's primary purpose is to support development and testing of experimental aircraft and weapons systems.

The intense secrecy surrounding the base, the very existence of which the U.S. government barely acknowledges, has made it the frequent subject of conspiracy theories and a central component to UFO folklore.

Are flying saucers being dismantled, assembled, inspected and flown by humans at Area 51? Not any more, though until quite recently this was one of the activities going on at this ultra secret, hush-hush base. Area 51 is all the more in the news because of its desire to be secret. At this point, should they throw open the doors and let the public wander through, everyone would be disappointed. A tomb. Empty, or virtually so, in preparation for just such public exposure. Where did the space ships go, and how did the military come into possession of them? The ships were moved by the alien groups who provided them to the military, and the whole operation has setup elsewhere, not on a military base.

Men In Black

The Men in Black have received a lot of press as their visits are in the consciousness of humans. These entities are allowed to make these visits, as they are in the same density as humans and are not in quarantine. Where do they come from? They are not extraterrestrial at all, but live underground, in tunnels and caverns. Their townships exist in isolation, as they very seldom travel from one township to another, being at risk of exposure to humans in so doing. They fear the Awakening, as humans will then be informed of their presence. Where the eventual outcome of the Transformation, a Service-to—Others world, is not feared by them, they fear the transition. When the Transformation has taken place, this race will continue in 3rd Density, underground. They will then be in quarantine, and will not mix with the eventual inhabitants of the surface world. As they have a steady source of food and reliable shelter that will in the main survive the cataclysms, they fear being inundated after the cataclysms. These fears are not grounded, but nevertheless they have tried to slow the Awakening, in their own way, for these reasons.

The Men in Black have constructed cities underground, structures with multiple stories and tram systems run by electricity, but these are in natural caverns and are not connected to one another unless natural passageways exist. The Men in Black do not generate their electricity from any means that humans are familiar with—rushing water, windmills, steam turbines run by heat generated from controlled nuclear activity or by burning any number of fossil fuels. The electrical energy the Men in Black use is chemically generated, a method learned on their home planet prior to their transplantation to Earth. Their home planet did not have the wealth of fossil fuels that the Earth provides, nor land masses with changes in altitude that allow water to tumble, nor even very much water. Frustration is the mother of invention, as you say, and they worked with what they had. Their electrical energy is not abundant, and would hardly support the average United States homeowner with her many electrical appliances.

If the Men in Black live in natural underground caverns, then how have they escaped the eyes of eager explorers, who pass up no opportunity to discover new underground passageways and caverns? Spelunkers have thoroughly mapped every known crevasse under the surface of the Earth, delighting in every minute of it, as spelunking is an exploration. There are no new lands to discover and explore, as the continents are known and teeming with humanity. Outer space seems out of reach in these days of budget cuts. But spelunking still offers the chance to discover something the eyes of man have never seen. Do spelunkers assume that they have discovered all the caverns and passageways that abound under the crust of the Earth? There are a thousand times more caverns and passageways than they have yet come upon, or even suspect, many far deeper than man has even probed. The Men in Black, being unable to live on the surface, established themselves underground when they first arrived on Earth, in a technologically advanced state. Long, long before humans became proficient at spelunking, the Men in Black were erecting their defenses.

Why have the Men in Black not been found? Look to what clues spelunkers that new passageways exist—air currents, air quality, and sounds such as rushing water. When things are dead still, the assumption is that only solid rock is about. The Men in Black have architect and engineer types who devise ways to test the isolation of their caverns and passageways. Prior to building there, they run a test which essentially pulls the air upward to a vent at the roof. If there are air leaks, connections to other underground passageways, there is air current inward, and this is detectable. Oops, not a good home.

The Men in Black have not been found because of the vulnerability and fearfulness of these hominoids, who do not have the bomb, do not have tanks and bazookas, and in fact do not even have jails and prisons. Why? There is no need. They are not violent, as humans are by nature, but they're scared silly of being discovered by humans. Being no less intelligent than humans, they have spent no small amount of time devising ways to keep from being discovered, like a rat in a hole with no back door. The issue to focus on is not whether the Men in Black have threatened humans, but whether they have acted. When you speak to your dog, whom you wish to impress, what do you do? You act like a top dog! Dogs respond to domination that they cannot overcome by groveling and avoidance. Dogs respond to weakness that they can overcome by either tearing the throat out of a rival that resists or snarling a warning to a rival that turns belly up. The Men in Black have analyzed their co-habitants, and correctly understand what impresses them. Power without the ability to decimate and destroy is ignored. Therefore, threaten.

Mythical and mythological creatures

There are many mythological characters that have lately been ascribed to extraterrestrials. Suddenly everyone sees they have been surrounded by extraterrestrials all along, that the creatures of fairy tales and myths are simply the guys from outer space, in disguise as little people. Nonsense. If they looked like little people, they were little people. One must realize that only recently have little people such as dwarves been socially acceptable. In the past they were killed, more often than not, as representing the wrath of the gods or being an evil omen. Do you suppose their mothers simply handed them over for the knife? They hid them, and nurtured them in secret, taking them clothes and food. On occasion these little people, who would find each other by one means or another, would be seen by others. Surprise! What was that? Mythological creatures.

Dragons

Dragons are legendary creatures, typically with serpentine or otherwise reptilian traits, that feature in the myths of many cultures.

There are two distinct cultural traditions of dragons: the European dragon, derived from European folk traditions and ultimately related to Greek and Middle Eastern mythologies, and the Chinese dragon, with counterparts in Japan, Korea and other Asian countries. The two traditions may have evolved separately, but have influenced each to a certain extent, particularly with the cross-cultural contact of recent centuries.

Mankind has many myths about dragons throughout the world. In the Orient the dragon is featured on pottery and in parades, and European myths are replete with Knights in armor going into battle against firebreathing dragons. The dragons invariable have wings and are shaped suspiciously like dinosaurs. Is there some basis in fact for this common human memory? Indeed there is. Where the dinosaurs died out long before mankind was engineered into being from ape stock, the Earth was not the only planet to give birth to such creatures. Evolution follows similar patterns, and where your Earth brought forth dinosaurs with wings, just so did other planets compatible with the Earth.

Dragons were transplants brought to the Earth by early ambassadors from the Service-to-Self, who anticipated an increased harvest of lackeys from the Earth due to the fear and despair their dragons wrought. Were the dragons intelligent and incarnated with souls? No. On a scale of 1 to 10, where the average dog is a 10, a dragon was barely a 3. This is why, in spite of the massive size and capacity to fly as well as lumber over hill and dale, they were so easily slain. Dumb brutes. Hundreds were brought to Earth, and released on terrified villages. The dragons ate humans, which were neither swift runners or able to barricade themselves in their mud huts, and were a tastier morsel than the deer, which ran fast and had taut, lean muscles. The legends speak of sacrifices, where humans would periodically offer one of their own to placate the dragon. Well, of course this reduced the rampages, as dinner had been brought to the door.

Where some dragons mated, they were scattered to begin with and, dying without progeny, eventually disappeared from the Earth. There were perhaps a few hundred delivered, and their reign, ending only in the last Millennia, lasted for thousands of years. The stories of dragons, all the more impressive as they were true, spread more widely than the dragons themselves. Did they breath fire? No. But when roaring, open mouthed, it felt like that to those within range. Hot breath and a big wind pipe.

Vampires

Vampires are mythological or folkloric beings who subsist by feeding on the life essence (generally in the form of blood) of living creatures, regardless of whether they are undead or a living person. Vampiric entities have been recorded in many cultures and, and may go back to "prehistoric times", the term vampire was not popularized until the early 18th century, after an influx of vampire superstition into Western Europe from areas where vampire legends were frequent, such as the Balkans and Eastern Europe, although local variants were also known by different names, such as vrykolakas in Greece and strigoi in Romania. This increased level of vampire superstition in Europe led to mass hysteria and in some cases resulted in corpses actually being staked and people being accused of vampirism.

Do Vampires exist? Yes, but they are not in human form as legend has it. The Earth has evolved creatures, mammals, that bite and drink blood-the vampire bats that plague certain tropical countries and debilitate range cattle with blood loss. Are Vampire bats the basis of the Vampire legends? In a manner of speaking, as the legend is based on a similar creature that evolved on another world. Just as Dragons were brought to the Earth by aliens in the Service-to-Self orientation, to terrify humans they hoped to later recruit into their ranks, just so were large Vampire bats brought to Earth.

They why the legend of the bat becoming human? The visitations occurred at night, as these bats evolved in a similar manner to the Earth's bats, using squeaking sounds in a type of radar, and using the safety of darkness to escape predatory birds which consider rodents a full course meal. The imported bats were large though slender. When flying they looked like bats, but after they landed their folding wings looked like outstretched arms-the vampire in his black cape. Red eyes? Yes, indeed in any light nearby the eyes, which lacked the protective pigment necessary in harsh daylight, showed only the blood just under the surface of the eye. And just as some hairy monkeys on Earth have hairless, pale faces, just so did these large Vampire bats have hairless faces. They were chosen by the Service-to-Self aliens because they resembled humans, in the dusk. The terrified victims, frozen in fear, gave birth to the Vampire myth of supernatural powers.

Were they found and killed with stakes? They were killed with whatever was at hand, when discovered in their dark lairs, and what was mostly at hand were wooden sticks. Farmers staking fence posts would use the pointed ends to fend off attacks from wild animals, and in most cases this was the only weapon available when fending off an attack from Vampires.

Bigfoot

Bigfoot, also known as Sasquatch, is purportedly an ape-like cryptid that inhabits forests, mainly in the Pacific Northwest region of North America. Bigfoot is usually described as a large, hairy, bipedal humanoid. The term "Sasquatch" is an anglicized derivative of the word "Sésquac" which means "wild man" in a Salish Native American language.

Bigfoot has fascinated mankind for as long as the two races have been in contact with each other, as infrequent and fleeting as that many be. The reason for this has less to do with Bigfoot's size and man-ape like appearance, which would be understandable on this Earth, as with Bigfoot's elusiveness. Gorillas, for instance, are as large. Chimpanzees seem as intelligent. Why is Bigfoot a fascination? The answer lies in his seemingly uncanny ability to elude detection. The reason for this is that Bigfoot was to house a group of entities who are in quarantine. They remain elusive because they are not to intermingle with mankind. In this effort, they do not go unassisted. Bigfoot is there, right under our noses. Why are they in quarantine? These entities have been placed into a primitive condition at their request, so that they can return to a basic understanding of how to get along with each other, with nature, and ponder the wondrous workings of nature. Their quarantine is not an exile. It is a search for peace.

Has Bigfoot something to do with early mankind, perhaps an early model of man? The answer is, not surprisingly, yes! Bigfoot is indeed an interim model of one of the six races of man. How does it happen that only this race retained an intermediate model? How did the others not retain this. During the evolution of man, during periodic genetic engineering efforts, the entire race would be affected. All within a given race were in breeding proximity of each other, and the genetic alterations spread out accordingly. Bigfoot was separated, removed from the others, and moved into remote areas.

Yeti

The Yeti or Abominable Snowman is an ape-like cryptid said to inhabit the Himalayan region of Nepal, India and Tibet. The names Yeti and Meh-Teh are commonly used by the people indigenous to the region, and are part of their history and mythology. Stories of the Yeti first emerged as a facet of Western popular culture in the 19th century.

The Yeti by the locals, is simply a variation of the Bigfoot form. Just as man, migrating, has evolved to fit his environment, so the Yeti adjusted to the climate when it changed after a pole shift. White fur increases the survival in snowy surroundings, and like Snow Bunnies, Yetis born with white fur were more likely to escape predators and grow to adulthood and propagate. There are fewer Yeti than Bigfoot, as having adapted to the snowscape, they cannot safely leave.

Chupacabras

The chupacabras is a legendary cryptid rumored to inhabit parts of the Americas. It is associated more recently with sightings of an allegedly unknown animal in Puerto Rico (where these sightings were first reported), Mexico, and the United States, especially in the latter's Latin American communities. The name comes from the animal's reported habit of attacking and drinking the blood of livestock, especially goats.

During former eras when the battle for men's souls raged hot and heavy, those in the Service-to-Self orientation at times tried to tip the balance by loosing their dogs on humans in an attempt to terrify them. Such was the case when dragons and a large bald faced vampire bat were brought to Earth and unleashed upon the hapless population. Not being native to the Earth and hunted to extinction by angry mobs, these episodes were short lived but live on in the legends about dragons and vampires. Such is now the case with the Chupacabras, an ape of low intelligence which feeds on bodily fluids in preference to meat. A few hundred have been loosed on the Earth, approximately the same number as the number of dragons and vampire bats loosed in the past. Today, other than the Chupacabras, there are no living alien dog packs about, and the Chupacabras are dwindling.

As with other scourges, these creatures cannot attack humans unless the human gives permission, but terrified humans who have concluded they are helpless are giving permission by abandoning the fight. The Earth and her future are in the hands of humans, this is exactly why the Chupacabras have appeared—at the request of not just one, but many humans who are closely allied with aliens in the Service-to-Self. In essence, they hope to win a better place in their future home, to land higher in the pecking order than at the very bottom, but the joke will be on them. They are being used, but given the strength and size of their call to the Service—to-Self aliens in attendance, such a situation as the Chupacabras can occur.

However, as the Chupacabras are of alien origin, restrictions still apply. Unless a human gives permission, in essence acquiescing, an attack against a human cannot occur. This ties up considerable Service-to-Self resources, as where the Chupacabras are residing in 3rd Density, their Service-to-Self alien handlers must likewise linger about to reign them in now and then, albeit with a leash invisible to humans. These handlers, most often the alien life form known as Dino, have also been sighted by humans during tense moments when the normal admonishments to leave alien sightings only in the subconscious has taken second place to attending to the athletic Chupacabras. Were it not for these restrictions such ploys would be endlessly used by the Service-to-Self, who have no sense of fair play.

The Chupacabras, when they die, are retrieved and removed, as a terrifying myth loses it's magic when a dead body can be kicked and dissected. But more importantly, a dead Chupacabras would be identified as not of this Earth, potentially, and this removes the Element of Doubt. Thus, they are not to be left about, for this conclusion to be arrived at, as this would tip the balance of power potentially into the Service-to-Self camps. Like rumors of mass landings, which will not occur nor even be allowed to be staged, by aliens, such dead bodies and the implication of harm coming from alien hands would be greatly used by Service-to-Self aliens. Thus, in keeping the balance of influence equal, between Service-to-Self and Service-to-Other, for humans still making their 3rd Density decision, this rule is enforced.

Elves

There are many mythological characters that have lately been ascribed to extraterrestrials. Suddenly everyone sees they have been surrounded by extraterrestrials all along, that the creatures of fairy tales and myths are simply the guys from outer space, in disguise as little people. Nonsense. If they looked like little people, they were little people. One must realize that only recently have little people such as dwarfs been socially acceptable. In the past they were killed, more often than not, as representing the wrath of the gods or being an evil omen. Do you suppose their mothers simply handed them over for the knife? They hid them, and nurtured them in secret, taking them clothes and food. On occasion these little people, who would find each other by one means or another, would be seen by others. Surprise! What was that? Mythological creatures.

Stonehenge

Stonehenge has influenced many groups over the eons, as it was intended to do. The Druids did not build Stonehenge, but they incorporated it into their rituals. Thus, history tends to credit them with erecting Stonehenge. Religious rituals, or those semi-religious rituals that form in highly structured social groups, are put into place to control the membership and give them outlets for emotions that would otherwise be disruptive. Emotions such as jealousy or fear can scatter a membership, but if given an outlet that tends to support the group's goal, build and support the group rather then tear it apart.

Human sacrifices are one such ritual, as the sacrificed one acts as a scapegoat, becoming a symbol for whatever has caused rage in the membership. The leaders, of course, select someone they wish to get rid of, a troublemaker or an independent thinker. Stonehenge by its very shape implies sacrifice, but it did not cause this behavior in the Druids, as using scapegoats and rituals involving sacrifice occur in all cultures and all parts of the world. The close proximity to such an edifice as Stonehenge to any sacrificial rituals would naturally align into a mental association over time, and this is what occurred—a coincidence, made into cause and effect by historians.

Many situations fraught with injustice take a turn for the better due to reactions, where those injured and those in sympathy are impelled to action where they would otherwise be passive. Such a situation occurred during the era of inquisitions and the political marriage of church and state in Europe centuries ago. Integrity is one of the first casualties when those living by lies come into power, and thus the Knights Templar came under attack. As with most casualties of the inquisitions, they were blameless and set up with all manner of accusations that were totally unfounded. Those offended by this injustice live on today, by proxy, as an organization that has lost all semblance to the original group, becoming, as most groups do over time, simply a group fraught with procedures and rules and hierarchies to be honored.

Coral Obelisk

Many artisans choose their material more for its uniqueness than suitability, the better to gain notoriety. Wrapping an island in colorful plastic or floating colorful balloons is more a media event than art, but if done by one who professes to be an artist, qualifies, it seems. An artisan who fears being overlooked might choose his medium more for its likelihood of attracting attention than any other reason.

Thus it was with a poor immigrant who had more talent than money, being without sponsors in a new land, and in fact being without funds to even buy materials. He turned to what nature provided, in more than one way, as his choice of living coral was both inexpensive, being free, and quite unique. Being at home in the water, this artisan used various techniques to shape the coral, which grows slowly and is alive only on the outer surface. In most cases transplanting was done, skillfully cutting and fitting the pieces which were never removed from the sea water the living coral need in order to live. Scars heal over time, giving the appearance of natural coral growing in these unusual shapes. Where this work of art gained the artisan notoriety, and was certainly an outlet for his talent, it scarcely made him rich. Just as his medium was free to him, likewise viewing his work was free, a legacy left to startle the uninformed swimmer who happened upon them.

Taoism

Among the philosophies from the Orient is one that espouses education through observation, specifically observation of nature. Where other philosophies from the Orient espouse either meditation, removing oneself from the environment and closing off what the sense perceive, or seeking a balance between the attention to self needed for self preservation and cohesiveness and concern for others in the community, Taoism states that nature itself is the teacher and that each man must attend to his lessons alone. Taoism has an obscure beginning, as it was not brought to the attention of man by the normal means, by the hand of a great and popular philosopher. Taoism developed as a result of discussion among men, and was passed through many generations as a spoken work long before being put into print. Thus there is no author, and this was by intent. Without an author, there is less of a target, so the philosophy is less subject to attack by those who would control the minds of men. Thus the Tao philosophy has remained pure, simple statements passed along by so many routes that the message has not become corrupt.

Ganesh Milk

Blind faith does many things for the holder, including settling arguments between what the eyes perceive and what faith dictates. These types of arguments arise where the dictates of the faith are tightly bound to survival or security, or where the faith is perceived to offer the only solution to an intractable problem. Thus a child may refuse to acknowledge the death of a parent until a substitute parent is firmly in place, or the religious, living in poverty, may cling to the notion that their gods are real as thus there is some hope of escaping the grinding poverty. Such a situation arises often in India, where there is both grinding and intractable poverty and a cultural and genetic acceptance of discrepancy. If two ideas, simultaneously held, conflict, then simply don't line them up together and thus avoid the conflict. This type of escape requires coconspirators in the family, the workplace, the media, and the government, and in India this is the case. Thus, if the faithful, looking for distraction and longing for a hopeful sign, see what the heart wishes but the eye belies, then blind faith prevails and blind they must be! Did the deity Ganesh drink milk spooned to it, around the world? Hardly, but milk dries to a clear stain, and thus supports this notion of the faithful.

Divine Nectar

A falsehood promulgated by Yogis is that they nourish themselves not with the same food and water required by mere humans whom they would lead, but by the absorption of light energy, called Divine Nectar. This is a falsehood difficult for the follower to disprove, as to put in place the controls necessary to disprove the proposition, the follower would have to highly insult the master. Do they have a bite to eat in their private quarters, or slip a nibble into their mouths now and then during the day, from under their flowing robes? Who can be certain? There has been no controlled study on this matter, and the reader can be assured that if humans had even a slight inclination in this direction that the massive starvation and malnutrition that occurs all over the Earth, without abatement throughout human history, would have produced at least one human who seemed to thrive without food.

A controlled experiment to disprove the proposition would require that a Yogi master:

be willing to undergo such a test

be placed in an isolated situation where the only input to his system would be the light claimed to nourish be observed continuously by people who are not the Yogi Master's followers and who therefore do not have preconceived opinions on the outcome

No such controlled test has ever been done, and for good reasons—the proposition would be disproved.

Why do Yogi Masters purport that this practice works? What's in it for them? India is a country where starvation and malnutrition are on the rise, and have always been a grim fact of life for all but the privileged classes. The cast systems are rigid, and there is scant hope of escaping. Some Yogis purport that this practice succeeds to give hope to the pitiful, and some have even convinced themselves that they feel refreshed after basking, but most do so simply to raise their status among their followers. How great is their master? He has mastery over Divine Nectar, or so he says.

Scientology

Scientology is not about science, as the name would lead one to believe. This organization is similar to many organized religions in that it wants to control its subjects, extract money and physical services from them, dictate their thoughts, and require absolute loyalty. It purports to be a religion, for tax purposes and other such benefits that accrue to religious organizations around the world. However, unlike other organized religions it does not point to a deity to be worshipped, and thus is considered by most to be simply a cult. Like cults, Scientology demands loyalty based on the followers emotional dependence and the leaders desire for complete control over the followers.

Scientology is a cult, but gets away with having an audience among those who don't know the organization or its reputation due to the inclusion of the word science in its name. Move past the name and all relationship to science disappears. It is an unscientific organization. Science implies a thought process, pondering the evidence and testing theories against the results of experiment. Since Scientology denies its members the right to think, instead dictating to them what they should believe, it not only has no relationship to science, it also blocks its members from attempting to follow scientific principles.

Awakening

Not Alone

The microcosm that is Earth first appeared to humans as the center of everything. The babe, in his mother's arms, proceeds on the same assumption. She is there for his needs, solely. We hesitate to broaden our perceptions because this minimizes the self. Mother does not exist solely for me, therefore I may go unattended. Father chats with the other children, therefore I have not captivated his attentions and may go unnoticed. And in like manner we follow the child into adulthood to discover the human species grappling with the concept of not being alone, the one and only. There are other intelligent species in the Universe, therefore I am not God's crowning achievement. They can levitate and zip about and disappear, therefore I am a technological dummy. All very deflating, especially for the pompous. The reaction is reluctance, active denial, or a pout—non-participation. Look right at the facts and fail to process them. Process them and refuse to accept the conclusion. Develop countervailing theories and attempt to substantiate them. Close all the doors and windows and develop an avid interest in a hobby. Just don't have time for all that nonsense. Well, of course, it won't go away.

Humans, adjusting to the concept that they are not alone, go through stages not unlike the small child adjusting to nursery school. They feel, ordinarily, that they are the masters of their small Universe. A cry of distress brings Mommy or an older sibling running. Throw out a beaming smile and an adult starts chirping. Works every time. Then comes the shock. The babe is not alone. The first reaction to the sight of a room full of competitors and a distracted Mommy substitute is to cling to Mommy.

Humans, reacting to the alien presence, pray fervently. Save me! The babe may strike out at competitors, bonking another playmate, or snatch toys away for a personal horde. The alien presence almost invariably brings a cry from some angry human—leave us alone, the Earth is ours! Unable to mold the nursery to one's liking, the babe may next pout. Sit in the corner, lower lip out, glowering. Want a cookie? No! Perhaps non-participation will make it all go away. Some babes pout forever, and make it a lifelong practice. We find these humans turning their backs on evidence of the alien presence. Non-participants are the least likely to turn and become actively involved—curious and exploratory. In fact, the vocal skeptic is most likely to suddenly stop protesting and let it all sink in. Look to the history of avid believers and one will often find a skeptic. The skeptic gives birth to the advocate.

Alien Presence

Humans adjust to the new and familiar in accordance with its introduction during their lifetime. The babe, in its mother's arms, heard conversation, occasional banging doors, occasional howling wind, and feels no sense of urgency or alarm from the arms it lays in. Thus, banging doors and howling wind do not alarm it to the point of a faint in later life! Extend this to the crowd of children the child later runs with, the workforce peers, the leadership of the clan, or any other substitute for Mother. Where it is a known, or similar, or accepted occurrence, the human being can slot and place the occurrence, and does not react with panic.

Where the alien presence is widely known and talked about, it is presented in various ways. Contactees describe their experiences in terms that seem relatively harmless, but the elite, who do not want humans turning to the alien presence with any but horror and rejection, paint a different picture. Disinformation is presented as though it were from a contactee, an experiencer, and thus the general public is confused. Thus, when a contactee meets, for the first time, the visitors it has been longing to meet and giving The Call to, the contactee is braced for the worst! Panic, and fainting, occur when any unexpected encounter occurs, whether this be the announcement that someone in good health is now dead, or that the lottery has been won and one is now rich. Sudden and unexpected encounters cause one to faint as fainting is a protection, playing possum, which saved many a cave man from being eaten as he was assumed dead and thus rotten by the predators.

Thus, for the general public to become accustomed to the alien presence, and to not react in this manner, the Council of Worlds has determined to introduce actual sightings of aliens lifeforms, on video, for the general public to view. These sightings have already occurred by the year-end of 2001, but are discounted often as fakes. However, the increasing incidence, broadcast mostly as local news, is making the Earth's population comfortable with the alien presence. You've seen an alien? So what. Shut the door and don't slam it please, I'm busy watching the news on TV.

First Impressions

Adjustments to the other are an issue that is present anytime intelligent beings first meet each other. In the past, when humans thought not of creatures from outer space, they had no explanation if they caught sight of us or others from other worlds. Deliberate suppression of conscious awareness was not done in the past, or at least not to the degree done today. This is done today to reduce fear, but in the past curiosity was more often the reaction. What are those strange creatures? They simply gave us names, many different names.

On our part, we too had an adjustment to humans. Such smelly, hairy creatures, always up in arms at the slightest thing! Posturing to defend that not worth defending—the territory. Things we had put aside so long ago, ancient memories, had to be dredged up just to allow us to understand, again. One of the hardest adjustments has been dealing with the lack of understanding from humans, who in the main treat us like invaders. We are ascribed every sort of motive, although in truth those in the Service-to-Self crowd deserve the title, yet we are blamed for their deeds without even a trial. So quick to absolutes, those frightened humans. We have found it best to deal one-on-one. Where the mass rises in the direction the leader points, the single human ponders and lets the truth sink in. Pebble by pebble we build the mountain of truth.

Sings of the Awakening

Biologists in the lab deal in closed systems and open systems. Where the experiment is to be a closed system, every aspect of the biosphere is structured, and as many factors as possible are eliminated. If one wants to document how mice react to more daylight, a longer day, one has a control group of mice where the light is fixed, and another group of mice where the light is varied, steadily increasing. All else is rigidly structured for sameness. Same food, same feeding time, same amount of food, same degree of handling by humans, same amount of cage litter—no variance at all if possible. In an open system experiment few of the factors are tightly controlled, as there are too many variables. How do two different strains of mice get along with each other, and which survives the competition for resources? Put all the mice in one large cage, vary the environment with lots of exploratory debris, vary the feeding schedule, subject the mice to extraneous noise once in awhile, and watch. The Awakening is now in an open system, where formerly closed, and several trends are already apparent.

Decades ago contactees were visited on an individual or at most family basis. Almost always, a contactee vaguely aware of this activity kept it to themselves or at most shared it with a trusted confidant. Closed system. Now contactees are meeting each other, not only in their subconscious during visitations, but in support groups, Internet chat groups, and while browsing at the book store. Government denial has become an indirect education program, religious leaders are formulating their explanations, TV and movie producers want to be on the leading edge of a media opportunity, and politicians are seen gladly accepting alien endorsements. Open system.

Alien Welcome

The story of EBE, at Roswell, plays like a child's bed time story to mankind, eager to embrace the alien presence they sense is present, but denied to them by their governments who have a palpable cover-up in place. The Brazilian Roswell story in recent years shows the eagerness of the populace to embrace the alien presence, children leading the way by caring for the injured aliens they discovered on their path home. Sightings of lights in the sky, UFO's, are cold comfort for those who sense that these visitors mean mankind no harm. Thus, at the slightest excuse, all manner of rumors of sightings are taken as evidence of aliens among the populace. No alien bodies, except those recovered at Roswell and the Brazilian Roswell, which were deliberate, are in the hands of man. However, soon enough live visitors will be at their doors, walking in the mist, and delivering help when life seems grim and hope gone. Thus, the embrace is going two ways, in the heart!

Sightings to Increase

The subconscious is the heart of your awareness, and when the subconscious of the majority of your populace is comfortable with our presence, there will be no need to conceal ourselves from you. Sightings will increase, and will include alien life forms. This will then move to telepathic discussions with these life forms, en-mass with groups of people. An increasing number of photos and videos will develop, and although they will meet with the usual barrage of skeptic-bunkerisms, these photos and videos will speak to the subconscious of many. There will always be those who deny what they see. This occurs today, in your society, in all facets.

Where we and other benevolent groups speak to the subconscious, the subconscious also is cognizant of what the eyes and ears perceive. For those in denial, discord sets in. If discord dominates, then a conscious recognition of an alien ship or personage can induce fear. Should you be filled with resentment at this point over the delays, feeling yourself free of fear, bear in mind that the fear mongers are not wining, nor will they. They have already lost. Their voices have been lost in the din, and the benevolent messages are upwelling at the present time. The battle is over, but some of the stragglers have not yet left the Earth.

Where sightings are on the increase, just where and when they occur depends on many factors, only one of which is the desire of the local inhabitants to experience one. Some sightings such as the dramatic Mexico City sighting seen by thousands and video taped by hundreds, hasten the Awakening by being broadcast and highly authentic. Some sightings in remote locales occur because the majority of the residents are comfortable with the concept of being galactic citizens and ready to experience a sighting without undue anxiety. Some sightings by individuals are like the personalized sign many contactees are given, as encouragement that the path they have set upon is not a foolish one.

But likewise there are areas of the world that receive few sightings, and Muslim countries are included in this list. Where the majority of the humans have been isolated from the gossip that flows freely elsewhere around the world, and have been told that anything outside of the bounds of their tightly controlled world is of the devil, then sightings would do more harm than good. If one cannot see a woman's face, could one be allowed to see a UFO?

Mass Sightings

During the past few decades sightings have almost invariably been a personal experience, and in the main they will remain that—an individual, alone in an isolated area, a family on a camping trip, a couple standing on a balcony enjoying the star lit night. In step with the increased pace of the Awakening, sightings will become mass sightings, affecting the whole populace in crowded or urban areas as occurred recently in Australia and the Netherlands. The media will suppress the news, but they cannot prevent neighbors from chatting with one another or gossip on the Internet. The word gets out.

Glowing Ships

Sightings will become more dramatic as the Awakening progresses, and this is by intent. Initial UFO sightings were of silvery crafts, hovering with apparent mastery of the force of gravity, streaking rapidly, and with the ability to change direction instantly or otherwise maneuver in a manner unlike manmade crafts. These sightings posed enough questions to those with an open mind that no further encouragement was needed. Those with a closed mind refused to believe that what others were talking about, or perhaps what they had seen with their own eyes, was anything but a manmade aircraft, a meteor, or their imagination! To encourage these humans to enter the discussion that is becoming endemic worldwide, we and others involved in the Awakening process have moved to include glowing crafts into the sightings that are increasingly occurring.

Mothership Sightings

There are dozens of motherships hovering around Earth all the time. There are many groups visiting Earth at this time, and they all have their own craft. They are hidden from view, but will show themselves when appropriate. Indeed, mass sightings are increasing, sightings of large craft that cannot be denied because so many people see them from a distance, at angles that correlate. These people talk to each other at the local bars, if the media doesn't carry the news, and in general an area as large as one of the US states can become firm believers simply because they have shared information among extended families and coworkers. This is what happened after the Arizona sightings in 1997.

{C}Motherships are there all the time. You simply don't see them. You can be right under one, and you won't see it. Why? Because we have distorted light rays and we give you a view of what is above the mothership, from below, so you think you're looking right through it where you are actually looking around it. If this seems amazing, think about how light rays change when they go through water. People accept the fact that they see things at an angle when they are under the water. Bending light rays is no big deal, and we do it all the time. The mechanism we use is not a gravity field. It could scarcely be gravity, as the force required would compress us to the size of a pea, and of course we would not live. We use other means, something that doesn't affect us personally. Light is a particle ray, and is influenced by many particles that are similar to it, repulsed or attracted, and we simply utilize those elements, which are unknown to man. Man has scarcely scratched the surface in an understanding of subatomic particles. We don't claim to be experts but we are far more advanced.

UFO's on film

In a rash of sightings, captured on film, UFO's have suddenly moved from ephemeral objects whose film capture is elusive to indisputable objects, regularly captured on film. No less than the Mexican Air Force came forward, having been given permission by their President, to proclaim a capture in infrared. A new phase seems to have begun. Indeed, we have stated that as the populace was ready for more solid proof, ready to accept this without panic and even embracing the notion, that proof would come. The rule always, always, during the Awakening, is not to engender fear and panic as this pushes the populace toward the Service-to-Self orientation. Thus, reading behind the current wave of UFO capture on film and video, one finds increasing eagerness for contact with visitors from other worlds. In step with this eagerness is a resignation by the establishment, preoccupied with Planet X in the vicinity and no way to escape to Mars or elsewhere during the coming cataclysms. Realizing they have been duped by their allies, aliens in the Service-to-Self, they are belatedly trying to make amends. Thus, the almost tepid response to news in the media about all the sightings and film capture. Deflated debunkers, not longer encouraged.

Air Force One

Of course the disappearance of Air Force One from radar screens, a situation which happened several times during 1998, was not just a technical problem. Why does this only happen to Air Force One? Planes do not disappear from radar unless they are removed from the scope's range. And this is what occurred. How better to announce that we are in communication with the US government? This is an awakening ploy, one approved by MJ12 as without their approval we could not approach or affect such person as the President or his Secret Service guard. This does not mean that anyone on board the plane was aware of their temporary removal from the air space, as they were awake only in their subconscious during this time, or otherwise unaware.

Familiar Stranger

Many contactees have the sense that they have met another before, and that there is some activity they are to do together. At times they spontaneously recall a meeting with people they do not recognize, or have a flash of a person's face, figure, or demeanor. Contactees are being introduced to each other by aliens who are coordinating activities. The contactee may meet the others in their conscious life at some point in time, or such a meeting may never occur. If they meet, they have a sense that there is something familiar about the other person, or perhaps think they know them from some place. This, of course, happens all the time in human relationships, so comments about this cause no one to take alarm. However, in the contactee's subconscious all remember the prior meeting and the issues being discussed, and work together toward common goals without needing to mention them openly or to be consciously aware that they are doing so.

Many contactees have become aware, through one means or another, that these types or meetings are occurring and that they have met supposed strangers in their lives that they recognize, absolutely. This is being discussed in contactee support groups, or among contactees who have become friends. This type of awareness will only increase as the need for coordinated activity increases, and as troubled times approach.

Inititation Rite

For many, the Awakening is just so much joking around about aliens and space ships until they are one of many seeing a mass sighting. Suddenly it's up close and personal, and most particularly, no longer a joke. They've been initiated. They're now one of those special people who can speak from experience, and with mass sightings, the supporting statements of others who shared the sighting make this experience one to broadcast, not shutter. Such sightings in the past were denied by the government and suppressed in the media, so that the populace learned to speak only in hushed whispers to others who shared the experience. But this time around the government is if anything adding fuel to the fire by simply denying that the objects were theirs, and the media is granting the mass sightings coverage like never before.

Thus the return of mass sightings is stepping up the Awakening process in many countries, as the reception by those excited by their recent initiation need not be contained. Personal experiences are talked about on the bus, in the lunchroom, and are so commonplace as to no longer raise an eyebrow. This new liberal attitude toward those with personal experiences to relate, the initiated, does more than encourage talk about new experiences, it frees those who have long been experiencers to speak out, often for the first time. Memories suppressed due to fear of the reception are suddenly open for recall, so more than recent experiences are being openly discussed. Thus a single mass sighting can ignite a community, setting up an open forum on the alien presence that can not be repressed once begun. The community itself has become initiated!

Shared

Where most of these sightings do not get into the press, they nevertheless occur and ready the larger pool of humanity that is receptive to an open awareness of man not being alone in the universe, and the presence of alien visitors. Famous, of course, are the Mexico mass sighting during the Eclipse, and the mass sighting that occurred in Arizona, where a large mothership was viewed by most of the state. Recently, in late 2002, some areas are being reported where earlier they were hotbeds of sightings but not reported widely. An example is the mass sighting, by pilots and so numerous and from various areas that no flip explanation could be given for what was seen, was reported in Turkey. Lights moving at right angles, going up and reversing, are not a meteor or another plane, especially when reported by pilots who know how planes behave. The tail reported was to exemplify, for all watching, just what direction the object was moving, as UFO's do not have an exhaust, but did so deliberately this time.

Likewise, there are spots in Norway and Southern California where sightings happen so often as to be local folklore, not at all disturbing to the residents. What is little known is that the red deserts of Australia are frequent spots, as the local farmers as well as Aborigines are accepting. And the vast regions of China, where not news issues forth due to the repressive regime there, have light shows frequently, and missing time those evenings much the talk in the fields the next day among those who take this as a source of pride, their involvement in these mass visits. In South America, Brazil, especially since what we have termed the Brazilian Roswell, is a hotbed in spots of sightings, and missing time. When this occurs together, there is an unmistakable correlation in the human mind, in that the sightings and sleepy mornings the next day, and the sense that they have been a party to a visit, en mass, is strong. Thus, the light shows, in the consciousness of those viewing it, opens the door to discussions about whether one is sleepy, slept well, had an odd dream, or whatever. In the fields, the coffee shops, the local laundry, this is the talk.

Faked

The public is rapt an eager to hear about aliens, and the stage masters rise to the occasion! Following the legitimate mass sightings in Mexico in 1991, during the Eclipse, there were faked sightings reported and produced on video galore. The reason? The locals, having had a tasted of well-heeled visitors to their area, staying at the local motels and restaurants and tipping well, wanted more. So, as we reported years ago when asked about this, the majority of the follow-on sightings were simply faked. The Brazilian Roswell, a legitimate report of live aliens injured and on the ground, seen by school children wandering home along a path through the woods, is being followed by faked Abduction scenes. The fakes are clear, as there are burn marks in the shape of a body on the bed, on the wooden wall, enough such that the human involved would have body wide burns, life threatening in nature. Not at all what contactees experience! Another report, from the Ranch Areas where cattle mutilations formerly keep visitors coming and reports in the local papers, we now hear of similar sightings. The body cannot be produced, the story told by word of mouth only, but those in the US west who hope to keep the interest up will keep it up as long as they do get reporters coming around. This is simply the human wish to keep a good thing going, attention, extra income, and is likely to follow in like manner the increase in legitimate sightings that will be occurring during the Awakening.

Power Outages

In step with increased sightings will be an occasional Power Outage, as where there are those who can deny a sighting no matter how dramatic and well documented it is, there are few who can deny massive power outages. As they affect a broader audience, power outages are timed and placed for maximum impact. There is no point to a power outage that affects only a rural area with a small or isolated populace, or to a power outage that might occur in the middle of the night when few are awake to notice it. But beyond these considerations, power outages during the Transformation will be timed to act as an exclamation point to other messages given.

The establishment movie ID4, scheduled to premiere on July 4th in the US, premiered early as those who would give a false message to the populace, telling them that mass landings could occur and their only hope was a tight alliance with their government and established leaders, were eager to begin their propaganda. Those aliens in the Service-to-Others who deplore such lies for their tendency to create fear and a sense of isolation in humans, thus driving them toward the Service-to-Self orientation, determined to sound a different note. Thus a massive power outage in the middle of the day over the western half of the US was effected to coincide with the ID4 premiere. If aliens could mass land at will, then when they are about in such numbers and with such power, why do they not land? A countering message.

Alien Bodies

A recent trend in the deliberate Awakening of the populace has been the supposed discovery of pictures of dead aliens. Following the Roswell autopsy film a rash of such pictures have emerged. This is not by accident, and is more than just copycat behavior. Such pictures are deliberately being placed before the public to acclimate them to the concept of visitors from other planets and the odd appearance that might be expected. Since rioting in the streets did not occur as a result of the release of the Roswell autopsy footage, a carefully staged fraud which was intended from the start to be discovered as such, those who would have the Awakening proceed post haste have encouraged other such nudges. Accordingly a rash of pictures have come forth, all showing aliens in the most vulnerable of positions—dead, injured, and lying on the autopsy table under the knife of human scientists.

Still pictures of dead bodies are easy to produce, as any film maker will confirm. Most of the dead alien photos are a combination of real human bodies or body parts, augmented by putty or burns, thus the semblance of realism. If living children are sold into prostitution by their parents around the world and the elderly abandoned, how easy would it be to purchase the bodies of dead children and aged? Crematoriums are another source of such bodies, as one urn of ashes looks much like another, and how would the family know otherwise? These dead bodies, all hominoids and none larger than the average human, are to acclimate the populace to the concept of intelligent visitors from other worlds, while reassuring the populace that such visitors can be killed in crashes just as humans are killed on the highway. The intended message is that aliens visitors are not that much different from humans.

The Word

Many humans who gain an understanding of the Transformation and its components feel impelled to get the word out to others. Should others not become aware as quickly as possible of the pending pole shift, the spiritual choices to be made, and the presence of galactic citizens in their midst? They are concerned that failure to act, to broadcast this information, represents a dereliction of duty on their part and fret over how best to proceed in the face of resistance.

Is this necessary? Is this possible? And whose responsibility is this? This is certainly not the responsibility of those humans who personally become aware. Each human who desires this information can and does give The Call and thus receives a personal explanation. But what of those humans who, held in ignorance by a reluctant media, have not had their curiosity stirred? Here also we assume responsibility, by limited sightings or visitations to start the ball rolling. Likewise, issues of spiritual choices are not so much made based on knowledge that such choices exist, but on the steady resolution of issues in one direction or the other. The entity sees the trend, and watching others, realizes the choices that are possible. Should the pending pole shift be loudly announced to warn humans of the many changes their lives will undergo? Any publication would meet with active resistance, such that the volume would mount to meet the challenge. Truth of this matter will not be carried home to humanity by the media, much controlled by the establishment, but by the Earth itself, which will present changes for all to see and none able to explain away.

Therefore, speak to those who will listen, but do not be concerned about numbers.

The White Brotherhood

The White Brotherhood is not from another world, but is a group of psychics supported by various governments of the world, covertly. The White Brotherhood, as it is currently, adopted a name that already had name recognition. This has been a long running fraud, whose purpose is to influence the populace of the world into believing matters that are not true. It is a disinformation campaign, claiming connection with Ashtar though Ashtar had nothing to do with it.

It is a well known fact that telepathy exists between human beings, outside of any influence from aliens from outer space. All life, even plants, share this ability to some degree, as it is related to the flow of communications between living cells. Where there is life, there is the potential to receive a flow of communications from another, and to sympathize with another's flow, and to therefore get inside another, so to speak. When humans are in telepathic communication with each other the communication flow between the brain cells of the one create a pulsing aura of sorts, which expands outward for many hundreds of miles. Getting in tune with this communication aura so as to be in a telepathic conversation involves tuning one's own communication aura to be in sync with the other. Once done, their minds can travel down parallel paths, the listener in parallel with the one listened to. This also has a reverse mechanism, as once this parallel communication is in place, the listener can interject.

It is by this means that the White Brotherhood operates. They are assisted in this with information given to them by the governments they work for. They are even moved physically close to their target human, to maximize the potential for contact. They are given personal information about their target, so as to line their thinking up with what might be in the thoughts of that person. When they have made contact, so to speak, and verified this to their satisfaction by receiving information from the target that confirms they are thinking in parallel with the target, they set to work. First the White Brotherhood interjects a thought, in conversational mode. For maximum effect, the thought is surrounded by visual imagery and emotion, so the thought will impact much of the target's brain and get the target's attention. Then they listen. If the target indicates, by thoughts, that it has received the message and is aware of this, then the White Brotherhood sends another message, and on it goes.

The message the White Brotherhood wishes to extend is that the aliens are not to be trusted. They do not differentiate, but spread suspicion about all aliens. They do this by themselves asserting they are aliens, and making the target human uneasy. What it takes to make the target human uneasy varies, as each person is different. Since they have information on the target, are close physically to the target for easy listening, and can get inside the target's head for endless hours of snooping, they soon figure out what it will take to make the target nervous. They send a very personalized message. The message will be packaged differently for each target, and thus the understanding one target receives may not coincide with what another target receives. If the concepts being relayed are not personally distressing to the target, they will refer to the White Brotherhood as a pleasant experience. If, however, the target resents the concepts being relayed, a battle of wills may result and the experience reported as unpleasant.

What is the goal of all this? It is to keep the world for humans, in the control of mankind, or more specifically in the control of the current establishment. Since the pace of the Awakening is determined to some degree by the fear and anxiety of the populace, they hope to keep the level of fear and anxiety at a very high level. They therefore target authors, journalists, speakers, and others who have the potential of influencing large numbers of others. We are able to tell you of this fraud, as there are not currently any Service-to-Self oriented aliens involved, although this has been the case in the past, particularly at the inception of the concept of the White Brotherhood. Were this otherwise, and were there to be Service-to—Self oriented aliens involved, we would be restrained from divulging this information by the Rules of Engagement.

Drug Induced

Among the myths circulating on how, when, and where visitation occurs is the myth that hallucinogens facilitate. They do not. Many would-be leaders and their hangers-on wish to get on the bandwagon and make a living if not a profit on the increasing curiosity about the alien presence, and are looking for a niche.

Can they compete with genuine contactees who run the gamut of emotions when hypnotized by professionals and exhibit scars that appear overnight or positive pregnancy tests that result in the missing-baby syndrome? They would be discovered as the frauds they are if this were attempted.

Can they compete with genuine channelers, whose work has an internal consistency no matter how voluminous, and connects with other genuine channeled works as though several soloists were suddenly a chorus? This type of fraud requires talent, and is in any case a lot of work, and as these frauds come under increasing pressure to explain contradictions it is not the perfect solution.

Can they claim they saw and learned wondrous things while in a drug induced state, and offer to show the masses how it's done, for a fee? Why not? What basis for rejecting or accepting their statements exist? Its a safe fraud, and more than one such fraud is currently running.

Visitations are not facilitated by recreational drugs, no matter what the users might imagine. In fact, as the contactee would be dysfunctional, it's counter-productive. Any stories claiming otherwise are false, as are stories that alien visitors encourage the use of recreational drugs.

Arizona Coverage

The first mass sighting to get full coverage in the media was the large and undeniably alien object seen by thousands in Arizona in March, 1997. Distinctive for its size, which could not be mistaken for a satellite or shooting star, this slowly moving and hovering gargantuan ship could only be a mass hysteria or an alien ship. Since the observers did not consult with one another, mass hysteria simply would not fly as an explanation. More remarkable than the sighting and the thousands who observed it was the reaction by the media, which reveals the extent to which the media is controlled on matters of the alien presence.

Where windstorms that blow shingles off roofs are reported on the front page, what excuse does the media have for not reporting on a sighting that absolutely proves that the alien presence is real! Lack of witnesses? There were thousands. Lack of credibility? They had videos. A hoax? What could hold a ship the size of several football fields in the air, for over an hour? An illusion? The sighting was visible all across the state, and a projected image, one placed against background stars, can fool only those situated at the right angle. Was the delay due to examination of the evidence and interviewing witnesses? The media traditionally operates by reporting first and issuing corrections later.

What caused the delay in reporting this astonishing sighting was not any issue with the evidence or witnesses, but conflicting orders from MJ12, often itself in conflict over how to proceed. Traditionally the media has been told to clamp shut on all sightings, and proceeded with this approach automatically in Phoenix. Orders to the contrary were questioned, and double checked, and when confusing confirmations were issued by MJ12, double checked again and again. Better to be safe than sorry, especially since a story once aired cannot easily be retracted, as Roswell so amply demonstrated. MJ12 operates like most intelligence organizations operate—on a need to know basis. Thus many in the ranks were slow to hear the new marching orders, and contradicted their leaders.

All in all, a mass sighting that pleased those producing the extravaganza as much as it pleased the majority of the audience, and one providing a second extravaganza, though one must read between the lines to see it. This second extravaganza is the international cover-up, which has been in place since Roswell and affects all major media outlets, bar none. In stark exception to the normal media reaction to truly newsworthy items, the media became catatonic for three months, and then found its voice! Please note, world, the best evidence for the cover-up has just been handed to you on a platter!

Roswell Revisited

Concurrent with the 50 year anniversary of the Roswell episode there have been dramatic sightings world wide. The most notable, due to its media coverage by CNN, was the Phoenix sighting, but this was not the only dramatic sighting. The others suffered the usual media suppression, but the local populace talked among themselves nonetheless. The Roswell coverage was considered safe by the suppression advocates, as various stories countering the truth had been concocted and issued. Thus, the public will have, as usual, a blitz of information to sort through. For those willing to allow themselves to consider the truth about Roswell, there will be a breathtaking array of fresh evidence that the alien presence exists to give the truth a boost. This was, as you say, not an accident.

Demand for Proof

You will find, as the awakening to galactic consciousness proceeds over the next few years, that the demand for proof of our existence will increase rather than decrease. You will also find, in line with what you have already experienced, that there will be no amount of proof that will satisfy these demands. Proof stands before the world today. Crop circles and their residual impact on soil and vegetation, mass sightings, disappearing pregnancies. When one gets into the game of proof, one is speaking to the wrong people. Do you have any doubts about the extent that people in denial will go to? Speak to people accused of horrific crimes against their loved ones. It didn't happen. It most certainly wasn't them. Homo Sapiens, as with most intelligent species, has the capacity to argue against unpleasant facts. As the unpleasant nature of these facts increases, so do the arguments.

Have you heard the argument that the majority of a teacher, or parent, or manager's time is spent on the troublesome? This is certainly true of the efforts of the police, who are a corps only because of the troublesome. The troublesome are few, but receive almost all the attention. We take a different approach in our contacts with humans. We ignore the troublesome, as they make their own bed, spiritually speaking, and must lie in it. In addition, the troublesome don't hinder our efforts. We are beyond their reach. We communicate with those who will make a difference, who are either currently dedicating their lives to worthwhile efforts or will presently do so. We direct our efforts to those who share our goals.

Of course, if we were to give humanity absolute proof, there would be repercussions. It is rather deliberate that the press of information that you are not alone as intelligent creatures in God's universe is very gradual. It is not by accident that toys, TV shows, and everyday conversation in the workplace talk about aliens and have alien figures, and that this is casually accepted without fear. This is because this has been slowly interjected. Were there to be aliens marching down the street or appearing on TV next to the President of the United States, there would be heart attacks, there would be savage attacks most certainly against those individuals who are contactees. They would be torched, shot, or stoned as Pat Robertson has suggested, and it would not be a good scene.

Be advised that the rules in place guiding our contact do not allow us to dance in the skies at your command. They do not allow us to manipulate your reality so that you can claim confirmation of our existence. You need not look far for proof of these statements. It is common knowledge that photos and videos that would be too staunch in their veracity simply do not develop. Likewise, the only physical evidence of alien biological existence or technology is in the hands of your government and other governments in alliance with your government on the alien issue. If this seems to you to be a double standard, it is. How the Transformation and the Awakening is happening on your Earth has been very carefully thought through, and there are definite rules to abide by.

Discord

Human society, like all societies, has microcosms within microcosms—different groups with different viewpoints. Christians may belong to any one of a dozen or more churches, each of which may have liberal or conservative sections, and a liberal group in one such sector may not be the same as another liberal group just across town. During the Transformation, with increasing polarization of groups, these differences will only accentuate. How does the diversity within a society affect its Awakening? Surprisingly, diversity speeds an Awakening along, as there is less possibility of a single viewpoint becoming dominant. However, diversity creates discord, and in this respect differing opinions or stances on becoming a galactic citizen result in just as much discord as differing religious views or differing political affiliation or the gulf know as the generation gap.

Attitudes toward the Awakening, today, range from total denial to joyous embracing. Denial ranges from refusal to admit the possibility to educated skepticism. Those embracing the Awakening range from unquestioning acceptance, come what may, to selective affection and a hesitant handshake. Diversity will only increase, and concurrently discord will increase, as the Awakening proceeds.

As with the Clonaid attention in major media, far outside the usual attention that alien hugging groups get, this is another example of various parts of the establishment hoping to open up the Transformation to get more assistance from aliens. There have been several competing and conflicting forces during the past few decades, since Roswell.

The Hug-Humans thrust

which states that aliens are evil, cannot be trusted, are out to colonize the Earth and eat or enslave mankind, and that only by resisting visitations and hugging your governing bodies, your military, your church, will you be safe.

The Hug-Aliens thrust

which states that the visitors are benign space brothers, here to help us during hard times, and if the Earth gets in a crunch such as a pole shift will lift all away to safety and some magical life on another planet or on a space ship.

The Hug-Reality thrust

which points to past pole shifts or current problems such as starvation and disease that mankind deals with, no rescue there, and the lack of a mass landing to colonize Earth, as evidence that neither Hug-Humans or Hug-Aliens above are correct.

Enter the establishment, which is composed of the wealthy, powerful politicians, and church leaders, not all of whom are logical thinkers. It was known that Reagan, while President, consulted a psychic, and the odd behavior of many notaries would astonish the populace should the truth be known. Pressed to remain on Earth, no escape to Mars, and fearing their underground caverns not to be safe during violent earthquakes, the establishment is looking with horror toward the possibility of a pole shift. Might they have to experience it, like the public they have mislead and used and had no intention of informing? Since the Earth changes have played out as we predicted, and the inbound planet is approaching in the manner and rate we predicted, many in the establishment are reading our words desperately for a way to avoid what they were so happy to allow the general public to experience. In other words, how can they escape! In that we have stated that if 89% of the populace were Service-to-Other, the Transformation to 4th Density physical could occur even before the shift, allowing an escape from the shift, this is one route. However, how to force the some 50% of the populace to accept this philosophy, when guided by those in the establishment who can't even entertain the proper concepts? Not feasible. Another, more likely, scenario, is to have the populace accept the alien presence, embrace it, and thus with aliens walking about on the face of the Earth, ignoring the plight of mankind would be embarrassing and they'd step in and effect a rescue, or so the logic goes.

Thus, you see groups Hug-Humans, and Hug-Aliens above, clashing. Clonaid gets on CNN, on Crossfire, where aliens have never been the focus before. Expect more entertainment as the shift approaches, from an increasingly desperate and shrill establishment. Images of space ships is not new, and NASA has endless images to access. A fight between tight allies, such as Spain and NASA are, is staged, with the intent that both parties, Hug-Humans and Hug-Aliens, would be happy.

Disprove the Proposition

Disproving the proposition can often be impossible, given the parameters. How many angels are their on the head of a pin? How long is a day 12 light years hence? How many life times does the average human repeat? These matters cannot be settled, in human terms, and thus cannot be proved or disproved. Such is the situation where matters on the alien presence cross the human desire for control. This is a multifaceted confusion. There are aliens in the Service-to-Self orientation that can wield deception better than the most practiced human. There are humans in establishment positions who will cloud the issue endlessly, as long as they can stay in control. There are humans who desire to profit from the alien issue, and cook up scenarios and roles for themselves as long as there is an audience. Where does the truth lie, and how can the truth be proven?

Unfortunately, this is not a matter that can be quickly put to rest. The issues at play are many, and involve the free will of man, the engagement rules that govern alien interaction with man, the engagement rules that govern alien interaction between orientations, and the mutability of truth itself. Different people see truth in different ways.

In all of this rises the issue of whether a given alien message, such as ours, is truly from ourselves or Nancy's imagination or government psychics. How can this matter be proved? It cannot. Psychics can insert themselves into others thoughts. Imaginative humans can and do concoct intriguing stories. And the truth can be before you, unrecognized and even rejected. It is for you to judge, listening with your heart and pondering with your mind. And when you have determined what is true, for you, then this you should hold to. It is, at essence, a matter of faith.

False Channels

There is a confusing mixture of channeled information supposedly from various alien groups, and from various human individuals or groups who may not actually be in contact with alien groups,. and this confusion is only going to get worse.

Claims that one is in contact with an intelligence from another world is easier to foist upon the listener than a claim that one is listening to the spirits of dead humans. In seances, for instance, the audience can state that the message being relayed does not sound right, that it doesn't sound like Uncle Joe, or something an old woman would say. But if one is relaying a message that is supposedly coming from another world, almost anything goes, and it does. Fully half, 50%, of all individuals claiming to channel or the like are making this up, and they know it. The majority of those genuinely in contact, another 37% or so, are giving a garbled message so that there is a mixture of truth and uneasy feelings the channel may have. Thus only 12-13% of those making claims are relaying a true message. So the listening audience is completely confused in the main. It's like a kaleidoscope of information and colors. They are hearing about worlds they have not visited, nor are they likely to, so they have no basis of comparison and certainly no way to prove out what is being said. If one is going to tell a fairy tale, one tells it far out rather than with any basis of validation, and in that way validation is never a challenge or a worry.

Each person must sort the plethora of information out for themselves. Balance this information against what you know. What does the Earth itself report to you? What does geological history tell you? What do you, as scientists, know to make sense? What does your knowledge of social science tell you about how people will react? And, last but not least, what have we reported to you. Many times we cannot tell you that you are receiving incorrect information, because of the Rules of Engagement. You must trust your own instincts. The majority of supposedly channeled information is deliberately generated by humans looking to either disinform the populace or generate income.

Those looking to disinform do so for a wide variety of reasons. Some disinformation is to put forth a message they wish the populace to believe. For instance, if some in your government wished the populace to believe that they have cut a deal with aliens, so that immediate conquest by rampaging aliens had been held at bay by negotiating skills, they would create a false channel to this effect. Some disinformation is to counter a message unwanted. For instance, if some humans wanted the populace frightened enough of aliens that they would cling to the establishment for protection, and an alien group, such as ourselves, reported that humans can repel unwanted visits from aliens just by taking a firm stance, these humans would create a false channel reporting otherwise.

In all cases where a fraud is being perpetrated, the false channeler must create a massive amount of details, or a single message as a standalone looks suspicious. Since none of this is provable, and the humans generating the fraud know they won't be challenged unduly, they wax poetic. This situation is not an alien issue. It is a human issue. Look around you at human society. The man who would maintain several wives in a society that allows him only one. What stories does he invent to explain his absences, the wife's inability to contact him at work, his financial shortfalls? Story tellers are in the main not punished by society, which pays good money for stories at the movies. Stories are seen as a way to blunt the painful facts, and an adept storyteller is more often than not rewarded for his talent! What occurs when the various wives discover each other? Most often, they all want the husband to be theirs!

False Claims

As the Awakening progresses, the flurry of increased sightings and communications from alien visitors will encourage false claims, for many reasons. Even in the past, when contactees and those claiming sightings were harassed, false claims outnumbered valid claims. Humans crave attention, in whatever form, as this is a trait that increases the likelihood of survival. The infant that cries the loudest gets rescued from distress and fed so that the parents can get some peace and quiet. The boy willing to step to the center of the group and present his ideas and plans is more likely to be followed on a romp or adventure than one who remains silent and keeps his thoughts to himself, and thus is first to the prize. The human animal demanding attention had the edge in survival, and as the survivor passed these genes along.

How does this human trait affect the Awakening?

Humans who see others receive praise and awards for good grades in school cheat on their exams even at risk of discovery and punishment in order to step into the spotlight. Police files show that copycat crimes occur because the perpetrator desires the spotlight, and those walking into the police station to confess are almost invariably not a criminal but simply an attention getter. The desire to be the center of attention frequently overrides fear of punishment or derision.

The desire to be the center of attention is strong, and where it cannot be satisfied otherwise can drive a human to present false claims. Thus where UFO research groups interview contactees and occasionally publish their stories, it is inevitable, in human society, that false claims of being a contactee would be made. False sightings are another such claim, as are claims of alien identity. How does one sort out the false claims from the valid?

UFO research groups have long held back key data files from their publications, by agreement, so that false contactee stories could be identified. The public, however, doesn't have access to the transcripts, nor are they privy to the patterns the mass of data forms. The public can be fooled. False claimants have enough information at their disposal to put together a credible story, claiming contactee status or a sighting.

Where the false claim includes alien identity, it is easily discredited, as no alien life forms exactly equate to the human shape and DNA composition. All such claims are false.

Those wishing to sort out false contactee or sighting claims from the valid must learn how to do this themselves, as by initial appearance they will both look valid. The false claim, however, will not hold up under intense questioning, as with all lies the truth become entangled in the many embellishments that elaborate lies require, and contradictions emerge. Read the valid literature published in the past by conscientious UFO research groups. Use this extensive data as a basis of comparison. But most of all, learn to discern the traits and profile of the attention getter. They will tend to embellish the story as the attention they get starts to wane, demand attention rather than react to it as it comes their way, contradict themselves increasingly as the story gets more elaborate, fly in the face of logic or known facts and well established trends, and answer questions evasively with a flood of irrelevant details rather than address the crux or gist of the question.

Hoagland

This mishap by NASA, wherein images taken by the Mars Surveyor that could be overlaid to show what NASA has been determined to hide were posted onto the NASA web site, will not be the last such mishap. The nervous peons at NASA, increasingly asked to work miracles during a time of rapid change, unexpected events, and unknown factors they are supposed to take into consideration, are dealing with rage. What causes mishaps? One can be worried, distracted, and this certainly is the case at NASA. They are headquartered at Houston, clearly subject to flooding and likely to be underwater early in the shift time, but at the same time they are expected to remain at their posts, loyal and true! One can be weary, asked to carry too many tasks, asked to keep an eye on too many trends at once, all running in different directions, and simply make a fatigue blunder. Autocratic bosses seldom consider the underling, who is barked at, and asked to do more, and told they are failing and incompetent when the boss is under stress. The boss, of course, can be incompetent, selfish, arrogant, but the underling is supposed to be unaware of that and try harder.

NASA peons are asked to maintain a cover-up of aliens, when their presence is increasing. The bosses, however, expect a miracle, and none can be wrought. So if distraction, worry about getting the self and family to a safer location, and fatigue at being asked to stretch beyond the human ability and capacity is not enough to cause an error, what is? Rage, the seething desire to see the hated bosses fry, get caught, lose it on national TV, themselves get caught in the floods, themselves get caught in a lie they cannot explain, anything but saunter around acting arrogant and untouchable, sneering at the peons like they are less than worms.

So what happened, to allow Hoagland this perfect example of a cover-up, all pieces of the puzzle in place, marked by NASA as authentic, and no explanation other than that some normal steps taken on these images were missed? More than fatigue, more than distraction, but a subconscious leak, allowing these images to get there before a review was done, as is a standard practice at NASA. Ooops, didn't this get reviewed? It was in that pile, in this queue, one assumed, one was sure a comment had been made, what happened to that sticker on the monitor saying go ahead with your days work, etc. This will not be the last such slip, and many will happen because of distraction and fatigue, but more will occur because the peons are enraged. And what does the Summary Image show, of Mars? Indeed, given the mining operations there, avenues for water washing are clear in the images. The standard construction of hominoids, on Earth, of geometric shapes, squares, rectangles, avenues straight away, not what nature designs but what many running vehicles designs. These cities laid out along a bluff, protecting the city from wind, not into or over the bluff, but where the land lies flat. It is quite unmistakable for a human hand design, and none who see it mistake it, despite the pathetic explanations of the NASA peons told to go forth and work miracles amid the public.

MUFON

As one of the first UFO organizations, and one of the most influential, MUFON was early on seen by the secret government as a threat. Thus, they ensured that MUFON would move in sync with the interests of MJ12, by one means or another, and this control exists to this day. Where in early days MUFON was prevented from publicizing some of its more striking discoveries, they are now being pressed to reopen the past and get noisy about it. Expect a number of startling announcements from the scientists who form the core of MUFON, backed up with hard evidence. In that the core of MUFON held fast to the truth through the hard times, it seems only fair that they should now have an opportunity to be the vehicle by which the truth emerges.

Element of Doubt

Indeed it is true that on occasion a video or still photo produces what can arguably be one of our ships, but the point is still hotly contested. In the minds of the populace at large, who cannot discern fraud from fact, the point is still open. In the minds of experts, who on occasion are fooled, even a fraction of a percentage point puts the issue into the category of arguable. We do indeed allow some shots to develop, and others not. Reports from disappointed humans, who took a shot that didn't turn out, tends to strengthen skepticism, and we want some of that for the modulating effect. Were there to be a flood of shots challenging the experts, from humans without the capacity to produce high quality fraud, the level of anxiety would raise too rapidly. An occasional shot, even from a hick incapable of producing a high quality fraud, is arguable. Perhaps the hick had accomplices in a fraud. It's arguable.

The rule is, and will be for the near future, we keep the issue constantly before the populace, with a steadily increasing level of discussion, but always, always, with an element of doubt.

This element of doubt is necessary during the Awakening so your populace does not become unduly alarmed. A faint, a palpitating heart, distractible excitement, arguing with friends and co-workers for a few days, and increased interest in UFO subjects—none of this is considered a show stopper. Were the entire populace to react like this, there would be no problem. The Awakening would occur tomorrow. What we seek to avoid is the nervous breakdown, the fear in friends and co-workers raising to such a level that they take violent steps against the reporter, or the intensity of fear in the observer that would make them susceptible, incline them, toward giving The Call to the Service-to-Self. For this reason visitations are currently recorded only in the subconscious.

Prophet Yahweh

This is a true example of the Element of Doubt in play. I have mentioned that there would be increasing sightings in the sky, mass sightings, and moving to captures on film and video, which has occurred. Police videos, and more and more evidence where as on the early part of 1990, you scarsely found a valid photo of a UFO, they just simply did not develop on film or on video. We have stated that this would occur as readiness in the populace was there. Not anxiety but eagerness, but always with an element of doubt. This is a classic case of this being experienced. Yes, UFO's do appear. No, he will not have 100% success. He will have crashing disappointments just when he expects to have a big success. And we have belabored the element of doubt many times. Where to reduce anxiety, the populace is not given absolute proof. There's always something that those who cannot deal with the idea of the alien presence can cling and say 'it's all a fraud, it's all nonsense, they were all mass hypnosis, a blip on the video' and the like. But he seems well able to handle this, the gentleman does, and it is part of the Awakening process that is out there, getting buffeted about and making these claims and telling people to look to the skies.

ABC Special

Scarcely anything positive could be said about the much publicized ABC special on UFO's, as it presented nothing new and gave equal time to debunking any facts presented, and refused to debunk the debunk. In addition, it gave prime focus on the triangular shape UFO, which we have stated is nothing more than a human stealth plane intended to confuse the issue and claim a human origin for the UFO sightings at some point in the future. Was the Peter Jennings documentary nothing more than an establishment shill? It was certainly sculpted by the establishment, who acted as editors. Thus, the most profound statements on the subject of the alien presence were not included. The repeated statement that there was no proof avoided the evidence, such as:

multiple captures on home videos, simultaneously, in Mexico during the 1991 Eclipse, movements showing, in angle and speed changes, maneuvers not possible by conventional planes;

landing site anomalies, where plants refuse to grow at the site for more than a year in some cases, with no conventional explanation;

crop circle nodes bent 90° and still growing, not crushed, where the crop yield is increased over crop not included in the circle arena, and the geometric precision and almost instantaneous creation of huge circle formations, none of which shows the hand of man but of the alien presence;

implants lately recovered from contactee bodies, simultaneous missing time and visitation reports from complete strangers corroborating each other, and pregnancies confirmed by doctors suddenly disappearing;

the astonishing number of eye witnesses to the Roswell incident, who were intimidated beyond any weather or spy balloon incident would have warranted, who saw alien bodies, which were then taken for autopsy, based against any excuse produced later by the Air Force such as a project Mogul balloon, carefully constructed in the 1990's to line up with the evidence from 1947.

K. R.

Does the Air Force lie? They did during Blue Book, but the Roswell lie was taken at face value and not challenged. Are Harvard professors, debunking away, a credible source? Then why not include the word of John Mack, likewise an esteemed Harvard professor who had actual data to submit, not just opinions. Hypothetical explanations of the abduction phenomena were presented, on equal time with contactee reports which are carefully based on hard data. Why was this ABC special even produced? Why not let sleeping dogs lie? The establishment is aware that mass sightings are on the increase, valid captures of UFO's on video on the increase, and the public's opinions on the matter leaning in the direction of comfort with the alien presence. They are trying to grab the lead, be the force that is leading the public perception, but will not succeed in this. Those who have had contact, or are intrigued enough to be seeking this, know the truth. Those who have or will in the near future have a personal sighting see in such productions as the ABC special a firm determination to turn the public from the truth, and are having their respect for the authorities trashed in the process.

The overall effect of this special is, to disgust those who know the truth, to puzzle those new to the subject so they seek more information, and to ultimately increase the suspicion that the establishment is lying to them. This begs the question, why is the establishment so determined to keep the public in the dark? Tell a child not to peek in a closet, and their determination to do so increases. Watch interest in the alien presence explode, and the truth spread around like water into every crevasse.

Orson Wells

The presentation of the radio drama War of the Worlds some decades ago in the United States was, as many have expected, a test. Given that the alien presence had up until that time been consistently presented as an alien threat, the public reaction was hardly surprising. Radio dramas are often confused with reality by those tuning in, as there are few clues that a fiction, rather than a factual scene, is being portrayed. On TV, the fact that one is watching a movie is quickly apparent. There are clues in the settings, the time gaps and leaps, and the frequent intimate moments which newscasters are not generally privy to. Thus, had War of the Worlds been presented on TV at that time, rather than as a radio drama, the reaction would not have been the same.

This test, which the establishment knew would be taken for a real broadcast by many, was to determine not how the public would react to a threat but rather to determine if they believed in the alien presence. They did, and thus they reacted, and the strength of the reaction told an establishment which had been congratulating themselves on having suppressed belief in aliens that they had not succeeded as they thought.

Subsequently suppression continued but got meaner, with mistreatment of contactees becoming more abusive and physical. Since the establishment at that time was in the main under the impression that aliens were only interested in a takeover, having made contact with Service-to-Self aliens first, and being unaware of the separation of orientations that takes place after 3rd Density, they felt that the panic that ensued after the Orson Wells radio drama was inevitable. They thought of themselves as holding back a flood, putting their fingers in holes in the dike, and looking out for mankind's welfare. The few suicides that the broadcast caused, and the potential heart attacks, were not a concern to the establishment at that time, as they considered themselves to be essentially at war and the nation in essence under martial law. All rules of human conduct go out the window when the leadership is themselves in a panic.

Alien Encounters

During the Awakening, sightings of alien ships will much precede sightings of actual aliens for a number of reasons. Recall that a key concern during the Awakening is to guard against raising the anxiety level of the humans on Earth, which would incline them toward the Service-to-Self orientation due to the self concern that is engendered during threatening situations.

The Outcome: Any sightings of alien life forms must be in a setting where the anxiety is slight, and is balanced overall by a sense of relief that alien encounters have been experienced with a reasonable outcome. The experiencer is not harmed, has not been intimidated, and finds they can communicate with the alien reasonably well.

The Experiencer: Where sightings of alien life forms will be forthcoming during the Awakening, they will occur only where the humans involved are considered strong enough to arrive at logical conclusions rather than panic-driven conclusions. These individuals are few and far between.

The Locale: Beyond the experiencer him or herself, there is the issue of how the humans in the immediate locale will react. The overall result must be a positive view of the alien presence. If an individual here or there will have a fearful reaction, this in and of itself will not prevent the sighting if their reaction is balanced out by receptive reactions in others.

Past

Prior to Roswell, visitors were not required to record their visits only in the subconscious of humans. As the book, the Vedas, reports, humans saw their visitors as having all manner of shapes. In trying to relay their experiences, humans often stumbled and struggled. Many described them as odd animals, but beyond the physical appearance of their visitors, how to describe the phenomena that accompanied them? Levitation, space ships suddenly appearing or zooming away, lasers, the ability to disarm humans without touching them, etc. Thus, fire, wind, whatever might relay this experience, became the verbal story. This often confused those who came later, and could not ask for clarification of the story teller. To further cloud the issue are the giant hominoids from the 12th Planet, who lived among mankind until a few millennia ago. They live in the Bible, as the giant Goliath, for instance, and are real visitors in hominoids form. They are the Gods of Mt. Olympus, the Visigoth in Germany, and giants reported elsewhere. Thus, visitors in many shapes and forms are mixed in with myth, and current mankind is left to sort it out. In the main, take your myths and stories in this context, and see what the picture paints! Most folklore is not story telling, but a serious attempt to pass on important information.

Next Phase

The Awakening is not on a linear climb to some point in the future when it becomes obvious to the vast mass of the populace that the alien presence is real, and among them. It is on a curve, akin to the rapid buildup that a parabola represents. In the past, encounters were few and far between, and reduced to what was taken to be tales and myths. When the Awakening was put upon a path that was to build exponentially until the Transformation was complete, the rules changed to allow few sightings and encounters only recorded in the subconscious. This allowed a reservoir of acceptance to build in the general populace, an acceptance those in authority in human society could not locate or control, though they tried.

Each level of acceptance, within a culture or country, or worldwide, allows another level of exposure in the general populace to ensue.

K. R.

Where are first sightings were deniable, passing quickly and seen by few and most often a single individual, this moved in late 1997 into a phase where sightings are seen by many, are vivid and undeniable, and even recorded on video or film. Still, they are being under reported by the media, and denied by many in authority. Those in authority that realize the inevitable are seeking ways to give in gracefully, while those who are rigid in resisting what they deem a takeover by outsiders are still shrill and becoming increasingly ridiculous in their denials.

The next stage will be glimpses of alien bodies, fleeting at first, and then increasingly solid views. Watch for cries of "demon" from the religious elite, and "insanity" from those clinging to the status quo.

Government

Attack on America

Yes and no, this is what it seems on the surface—an attack by Bin Laden on the corrupt capitalist country that has led so many attacks on Muslim countries. But this attack would not have occurred unless infighting among the financial giants of the world, the major banks, had not occurred. Infighting was the instigator, and the primary culprit, but this culprit will not be the scapegoat. In the infamous attack on America on September 11, 2001, several unlikely bedfellows crawled into bed with each other, each for their own ends. Thus, where on the surface it seems a repeat of the Bin Laden attack on the World Trade Center in New York City, failed in the past and tried before the world in the courts, this was only using as the bullet a Muslim group that would be immediately suspect and placate most inquiring minds. The gun was held, however, by a rival bank of JP Morgan, who was devastated in the attack.

The Stock Markets and worth of so much paper the banks and wealthy rely upon for their status and control are being artificially maintained at this time, the longer to keep these elite on their high perch. We mentioned in November, 1999 that cooperation between the world's banking giants and governments was in place, toward this end. One means of this artificial support is to put forth losers, so that the general public might win and thus maintain their confidence to continue to play the game that the Stock Markets represent. Key players are to enter the field and take a loss, aborting panic, as this is considered a lesser problem than a full scale panic. Where this plan met with general approval, now that tight times and a worldwide recession has become a reality, there is argument among the players. You go first, no you go first, and these arguments have gotten heated. Many felt the time would never come, so agreement was only in principal, not from the heart. Thus those in the financial field with greater clout, threatened to force lesser participants to be the loser, and dark thoughts crossed many minds.

During the day of the attack, there were three things that stood out from the horror and stunned confusion that goes with any unexpected catastrophe.

The first was the absence of the President from a role of confrontation and comfort. He was hiding, on the run, not seen as in command, and took hours to even muster a presence other than a statement or two repeating the obvious. It was clear to all that the Vice President, remaining in the White House, was running things. The lack of leadership was so apparent that this was mentioned repeatedly by the newscasters.

The second was the repeated mention that such a well planned and executed attack had to have more than the usual terrorist support, had to be supported by or in countries unnamed. Muslim pilots were trained in major aircraft operations, undoubtedly in training simulation settings. Were they referring to Afghanistan, primitive and suffering from drought so severe the people are starving? They were referring to a sophisticated country, with the infrastructure capable of training Muslim pilots on the flight deck of these major commercial aircraft.

The third was that the CIA had been clueless, a trend of late but so complete a blackout had occurred that it seemed beyond belief. Had this occurred in prior terrorist attacks? The terrorists were familiar enough with US airport security and the routines and roles of the staff to be able to successfully commandeer four planes, delivering the payload of three of them into the New York skyline and the Pentagon itself. No only was the CIA in the dark, it seems the intel went in the other direction!

The heads of the US government were too frightened, the attack too well planned and executed, for this to be just a terrorist attack. And JP Morgan affiliates resided on several floors of the World Trade Center and were a casualty of the sudden devastation—executives, records, and confidence of the market and public in dealing with them going out in a flash. The target was the banking systems holding the US and their elite and wealthy above those in Europe, in the arrogant manner Bush and his masters have employed of late. To understand the main target, and the support relationships causing a relative collapse among the wealthy and holdings of the US elite versus others, one needs to know the complex and mostly secret relationships between bonding banks, new issue of stock, loans between banks and governments, agreements with the Fed, and who holds what holdings privately or publicly! JP Morgan was the target, as a bank. The stock they were supporting, via their subsidiaries or associates, will suffer.

Insiders

Conspiracy theorists have noted that during the World Trade Center attacks, explosions occurred almost immediately in floors below the strike area, or in the case of the Pentagon, above. The theory is floated that these plane strikes were assisted by insiders, wanting to create the climate that the Bush Administration has been all too happy to take advantage of—civil rights limited, the military beefed up, and no questions asked as it's all National Security.

A plane crashing into the side of a tall building does not just break windows, it creates a minor earthquake in the structure, snapping plumbing, as well as rupturing the fuel tanks. Fuel dropping into a ventilation shaft, mixing with air, is an ideal explosive mix, and would drop down into the shaft to the floors below. This is what occurred in the World Trade Center.

Likewise, where a plane crashes into the lower floor of a building, such as the Pentagon, the fuel will not go down, but spew upward along any avenue it has. Stairwells, for instance, carry not only fuel but fumes, and mixing with the air and having an updraft handy, this is likewise the direction an explosion would take. The Pentagon experienced severe fires, an inferno with no place to go. The World Trade Center fires had all four directions available to them, up, down, and sideways. The Pentagon had the fuel mix going up, creating a heat barrier so the heat of the burning plane itself could not dissipate upward. Like a blast furnace, encased, this creates super high heat, which melts many objects otherwise remaining. It is an untrue statement that there were no plane remains, just not what was expected, and thus rumors abound.

Thus, where those wanting to incite Martial Law in the United States with Oklahoma City and TWA800 and Waco incidents did not succeed, they were handed an unexpected opportunity in the 911 events. In that these New World Order types seem delighted to take advantage of these opportunities, the public is rightfully suspicious, but 911 was not their plan in any manner or degree. Martial Law requires a number of steps outside of what has occurred. The reaction of the United States public to the restrictions that have been attempted have convinced the architects that full blown Martial Law would be a mistake. They will rather use the excuse of Homeland Security to the max, and watch the line so they do not cross it and reveal their true wishes. The constant warning of terrorist acts about to happen are to keep this sense alive, even though most of these warnings are without basis.

The rumor that the Mosad are behind Palestinian terrorist attacks is like the many rumors that spread about the US 911. Where there is some truth to it, 95% of the actions are otherwise. In the main, these attacks are a shock, not wanted. They would like to control these attacks, but cannot. The occasional true rumor gets thus blown out of proportion. We are saying that those in the US wishing Martial Law caused Oklahoma

City and TWA800 and the like, and lost. They did not cause 911, but take advantage of it. In like manner, Mosad is dealing in terror tactics.

Ultra-Right Unease

September 11, 2001 was both a blessing and a curse for the Bush Administration, owned by the elite as anyone following the rulings in favor of corporations and friends of Bush can see. During earlier days, the OKC bombing and Waco affair and shooting down of TWA800 were attempts to trigger Martial Law. This did not happen due to fast action on the part of many in government and the free-lance media who were alerted to the intent, and took steps to counter the planned result. Nevertheless, ultra right Republicans emerged from closed door meetings shortly after OKC, revealing their plan—it was Arab terrorists! Thus, the plan to initiate Martial Law early was thwarted, and went underground into back room grumbling. When September 11, 2001 hit, the Bush Administration and their allies in corporate America were stunned. They had no warning, and a fully loaded plane went into the Pentagon with no resistance whatsoever.

Where the public is told that the fourth plane turned toward Washington DC went down due to a scuffle with passengers determined to prevent the plane's misuse, in fact it was shot down by the military. This and the silly reasons given forth for the plane leaving NYC and crashing into a neighborhood, that the tail took tail winds, are scarcely believed by the uneasy public. Clearly, the safety of the skies is not secure, and bombs can be planted in tails, taking planes down, in NYC, the site of intense security now. Seeing the President by Coup looking frightened and discombobulated during his single TV appearance during the WTC strike, the public sensed something up about the PR campaign to present Bush Jr. as tough. The polls published, showing him popular to high degrees, are utterly false, and who is to know the better. Where the terrorists plan many additional assaults, they are unlikely to have the clout until they have recovered for several months. Bin Laden is indeed alive, and recouping his network, which is hardly devastated. One can note that key men have disappeared from Afghanistan, nowhere to be found, and will emerge later.

The American public is told the economy is about to turn, the Stock Market safe, and the skies safe as well. All of this has a false ring to it, and increasingly the public is speaking privately to friends and confidants that they feel they are being lied to. Enron was not by accident exposed to the world as the cesspool of deceit it was. We, and human allies, made sure the information about accounting irregularities got into the right hands. The New MJ12 at work. Likewise, the facts about the Bunker Government, as the Secret Government plans in operation since September 11, 2001 are called. Part of the Administration is absent, underground, while the other part is operating in Washington DC. And where are the balancing parts of the federal government, so much touted when discussion about the Constitution are before students and the public? Courts and Congress do not count, are not to be saved or salvaged, and this says more about the mindset of the Bush Administration than any Enron or frightened face of a cowardly President could say. They are outside the law, as they have been since they stole the election by shouting, and enforcing, a stop the counting rule, enforced by a Supreme Court never before interfering in elections in this manner. Thus, our prediction that the Bush Presidency would become increasingly irrelevant will be expedited.

MJ12 Mouthpiece

The Awakening and Transformation proceed as quickly as possible, MJ12 has also moved to this stance, having realized that this cannot be stopped and that suppressing the truth only allows the lies spread by those in the Service-to-Self orientation to prevail. Where we fervently wish for humans to understand the control they have over visits from aliens, MJ12 likewise dearly wants this message out, having been duped themselves by aliens in the Service-to-Self. Where we wish to warn humans of the cataclysms which will accompany the pending pole shift, MJ12 likewise cannot bear to think of the million of innocents who will be taken by surprise only because the word did not get out. At a minimum, they wish for the possibility of an approaching pole shift to be much under discussion. Therefore, in a manner of speaking, ZetaTalk is an MJ12 mouthpiece—not because MJ12 controls ZetaTalk, but because it does not suppress it or shut it down. This is also true of many other education vehicles, increasingly, as the Awakening progresses.

MJ12 Documents

A still hotly debated topic is the validity of what are purported to be documents from MJ12, dating back to President Truman's era. These carefully manufactured documents are authentic enough in appearance to convince many that they are real, yet flaws exist that have others convinced they are a fraud. Both situations are true, as the documents are what could be termed a half truth. The release of these documents, the content of which is false, was intended to be a leak by the government that would hasten the Awakening of the populace to the alien presence. Where the documents line up with the facts is in the existence of MJ12, periodic meetings in secret, and in those days the involvement of the President of the United States. Where the documents part from the truth is where they give the impression that MJ12 was a fleeting response, that the matters they addressed were limited in scope, or that they were almost casual about dealing with the alien presence and what this would mean for humanity.

MJ12 has been in the process of unburdening themselves of their tightly kept secrets from some time. This will never, frankly, in our opinion, be a complete bearing of the truth, but increasing mixing in of truth into semi-truths, which are just as effective and in some cases are preferable to the harsh reality of stark truth in that people can gradually become acclimated. They have a revelation. They read it. They sense some truth to this. Then it's debunked a bit. It's all a question. It's much under discussion. And in all of this, people really come to accept the reality. They think about it without having to adjust too harshly. This makes for a faster assimilation of the truth, and this is the route that MJ12 is using because they well understand this mechanism. Therefore, there is some truth mixed in with new documents, and increasingly this will be the case.

In the past, this information was presented in this manner with a small grain of truth and a great deal of brutal discrediting of the messenger. This pattern is increasingly going to be pleasant conversation without the brutality, but no one will actually know how much is true and not.

UN Role

A prior plan to use the United Nations to facilitate survival of the elite in the US and elsewhere has failed. This plan, much the talk of conspiracy buffs, involved placing parklands in the US into United Nations hands, and staffing these with soldiers foreign to the US. The logic was that these soldiers would not hesitate to use guns upon US citizens, or even US solders gone rogue. However, they proved difficult to manage, with many agendas and differing cultures dictating responses, so those who would be their masters became discouraged.

The United Nations today depends upon many factors in order to exist. It is funded by many nations, communications and travel arrangements allow all from around the world to participate, and all this is over and above the desire to have a United Nations force. Now comes the shift, wherein all travel such as air travel, rail travel, travel overland over bridges and roads, will stop. Fuels such as oil and gas will burn and not be pumped or refined, nuclear fuels will be shattered, the equipment not working, and man back to foot and horseback. Phone lines not work, short wave only intermittently between Service-to-Other groups supported, and all people worried about starvation and illness in the extreme. In such a setting, the last thing survivors are going to be worried about is whether folks from around the world are having conferences.

Microwave Towers

Uneasy about the many cover-ups they sense are in place, and the illogical behavior of major powers such as the US, the public sees conspiracy everywhere. The upshot of this unease is that the US public, at the least, suspect reasons behind the cover-ups and tries to make sense of them in this context. Should we list the cover-ups?

Alien Presence

UFOs are being sighted by pilots and masses of the populace at once, such as in Mexico City where these UFOs were caught on film by so many amateurs that it could not be denied. Denying the alien presence makes the most sense in the light of a rumor deliberately spread that the US made an alliance, to gain technology. However, in that the US has yet to emerge with this technology, this is dying out. What then is the reason? Increasingly the public, which has noted that no mass landing or assault by aliens has occurred, thinks perhaps the government does not want the public to learn something that would change their loyalties. Movies such as Signs, or ID4, where aliens capable of arriving wrapped in high tech are easily put down by humans willing to duke it out mano-a-alien, have added to this sense. Clearly, the government is not keeping an evil alien presence away, so ergo the presence must be good, as contactees report. Thus, point one against the elite governments, in this cover-up.

Earth Changes

Global Warming is floated as the cause of melting poles and rising seas and erratic weather, yet the key polluter in the world, the US, is uninterested in reducing emissions. Earth changes are putting companies into bankruptcy, employees out of work, and threatening the insurance industry with default. Nightly news reports that all countries are suffering, and increasingly the truth about starvation and ruin in other countries leaks out. The picture is grim, yet the elite governments chirp on as though the only issue were starting a war with Iraq, a nonsensical emergency in the eye of the common man. If earth changes, the melting poles and wild weather, are being ignored, then the government must know something, so the logic goes. This something, of course, is not being shared with the public, so, point two against the elite governments, in this cover-up.

JFK Assassination

Documented cover-ups such as the JFK assassination, where the ridiculous explanation of a single bullet floats out there today, the truth to remain under wraps for several decades yet to protect the guilty. Point three against the elite governments in this patently obvious cover-up.

Gulf War Sickness

It was clear that US soldiers were sent out unprotected to become sick, inoculated then becoming sick, and there is high alarm in the US Military because of this. The Gulf War sickness was first denied utterly by the US

Military, but due to reporting on this matter and persistence in the horrified Veterans caretakers, the lack of concern by the US Military became obvious. The lack of caring stood out against the principles applied in all other wars or police actions, and thus when the suspicion, the correlation, to inoculations began to spread, a cover-up and unrevealed reason was suspected. What would be the reason that a government would casually send soldiers unprotected into areas suspected of germ warfare poisons, or handling radioactive materials? And why the rush to inoculate, the insistence that all soldiers have this treatment, when the sickness followed so closely those inoculated, whether they had exposure in Iraq or not? What reason would the US Military have for poisoning their own troops? What possible future lies ahead if they are concerned about being able to do this? Thus, assuming a horrific future in which not only the US Military troops, but portions of the populace, would be poisoned to please the elite in control of the US Government, conspiracy theories abound. Point four against the elite governments, in this cover-up.

Chemtrails

Literally millions of the public in major cities, not only in the US but lately in Indonesia and Canada, have noted these clear criss-cross patterns followed by illness. Something of this magnitude, the illness alone, would normally hit the news, but the newscasters seem oblivious, despite being inundated by email and even being filmed with a backdrop of chemtrails behind them. Why the silence? The public suspects, linking this to the inoculation suspicions, that this is yet another means of poisoning the public to aid the elite in mob control at some future horrific event. Thus, point five against the elite governments in this cover-up.

Martial Law

Most evident in the US in the OKC bombing and TWA800 missile cause, are the attempts by the elite in government to create a scenario where martial law could be called forth. The public knows there was an additional leg, in military garb, found in the OKC wreckage, with the other body parts missing, and that almost 300 individuals in New York City interviewed by the FBI before they could talk to each other, saw a missile rise from the ground and hit TWA800. The governments answer? Ignore it. In a scenario where the world will be a good place in future, election or revolution held if elections are denied, the reason for calling martial law forth is missing. However, if a horrific future were around the corner, in line with the need for poisoning by inoculations and chemtrails, then mustering forth martial law now makes sense. Point six against the elite governments, who would have reason to desire martial law being imposed.

Now, with no more evidence that Microwave towers, EMF towers, in place here and there about the landscape, we have yet another conspiracy theory emerging. It has reached the point where the public leaps to the theory before they have a cause. Cell phones, using satellites and booster towers for phone conversations on the air waves, are increasing massively, due to their convenience. Does the public think that these cell phones, which are so sensitive to blockage from the towers that serve them that going under a bridge, behind a building, cuts out a conversation, do not need a strong infrastructure to support this deluge of conversations? In an attempt to service the public, and sell their networks, these towers have proliferated. That this is not a conspiracy theory deserving attention should be based on the rationale of whether crowd control could be done via microwave. Where it is true that babies have been murdered in microwaves, as human flesh can cook as well as potatoes, this is not an easy matter in the great outdoors. One would have to bombard the mob, with intense radiation, from all directions, for this to work. Now, if

EMF towers were placed every half mile, around LA, and every half mile within LA, then perhaps the public would have cause for alarm.

Snooping on Contactees

As a part of our agreement with MJ12, we originally informed them of the contactee status of US citizens. It soon became apparent that this information was being misused by the CIA arm of the secret government, and we ceased this practice, altering our agreement. This was in place during the first two decades of our agreement with MJ12, the fifties and sixties, more or less. Those in the Service-to-Self orientation were also asked to keep the government informed, but as they don't keep their word the list of contactees from these aliens not only lacked their true contacts, it listed citizens who had never been contacted. Thus many were harassed by the CIA during those decades, pointlessly. We do report to MJ12 when we are taking a contactee elsewhere in the Universe, checking the contactee out and back in, in a formal manner similar to US Customs. As this is seldom done, few contactees have been affected by this routine.

As a result of discovering that Service-to-Self aliens were not reporting their true contacts, and our eventual refusal to list contactees at all, the CIA set up their own intelligence operations. In those days contactees were not aware of each other, so locating them was done by scanning for profiles. If a citizen indicated an interest in UFO subjects they were put on the list and subsequently watched through phone tapping or other surveillance. Nowadays this type of snooping and searching for contactees is done primarily in contactee support groups, which are infiltrated by CIA agents pretending to be contactees. As the majority of humans asserting contactee status are making it all up, and as the vast majority of humans interested in UFOlogy don't have contactee status, this is all an exercise in frustration for the CIA, and lately this activity has fallen out of favor. What's the point? They have a list of suspected contactees which is almost entirely incorrect, and the true contactees are unknown to them. Add to that the burgeoning list of contactees as the Awakening progresses and the budget cutbacks the CIA is experiencing, and one can see why the program has little backing any more.

Philadelphia Experiment

The Philadelphia experiment was fictional, a disinformation scheme to divert humans from exploring the real experiment that occurred. The Philadelphia experiment much in the media is a fraud perpetrated to distract people from pursuing the real Philadelphia experiment, which didn't take place anywhere near Philadelphia. Servicemen were indeed injured, and because the risk of questions existed, the cover story was put up to effectively point any questioners to a dead end. The real experiment with moving between dimensions, which can and does occur naturally on your 3rd Density planet, was done in a warehouse in Kansas—rural, remote, virtually uninhabited because of sparse farm houses and farm hands. The area was inhabited only during planting and harvesting times.

Under intense compression, such as occurs in the center of the Earth, 3rd Density matter emits energy rays which approximate those naturally occurring in 4th Density. These rays escape the core of the Earth in bursts on occasion, thus causing the problems reported in the Bermuda Triangle, for instance, where ships or planes seem to disappear, then reappear. Essentially, the 3rd Density matter is temporarily confused as to its proper rate of vibration, and moves into the 4th Density state. This is akin to what we have done to contactees when they report having moved through walls. However, in the hands of humans, who received information on how to produce this effect from Service-to-Self aliens, this ability proved disastrous. Moving into 4th Density requires more than just bombardment of matter to the point of compression tension. It requires a total shift, and if one expects to return, a total shift back.

The humans conducting this experiment were of such an orientation that they did not care about the servicemen being used, or what might become of them. Rather than hesitate, knowing they did not have all the parameters in place, they proceeded. The servicemen, who were encased in a metal box, were left partially in the 4th Density, along with portions of their container. They were, of course, all dead, but the witnesses of this experiment, and the associates whom the servicemen had just recently been mingling with, were many. The government concocted a repeat experiment, which proceeded part way, enough so that the story as to the results was similar. Additional servicemen were subjected, knowing the probably results, but most of these survived to chat among themselves and their families. All secrets escape, leaks occur, and in this way the investigators would be altogether in the wrong vicinity, and talking to altogether the wrong participants!

Montauk Project

Having observed that the Service-to-Self aliens they were in contact with could do marvelous things, the secret government had no doubt that they could also travel through time. That this capacity is strictly regulated by the Council of Worlds and is almost without exception never granted to the Service—to-Self crowd when they request authorization was, of course, not mentioned. In concert with density shifting experiments in the Philadelphia Experiments, time travel was attempted. This was an utter failure, with the human scientists tinkering with their machines under instructions received from the Service-to-Self aliens, and suffering under the wrath of generals who were sure that the project was only failing because of their incompetence. After a time, the project was put on hold, due more to emotional and mental exhaustion than any change in plans.

Eventually, the generals involved realized that those in the Service-to-Self lie freely and without conscience, and abandoned the project altogether. Nonetheless, rumors abound, and due to the sensational nature of the project and the power that would accrue to those who might succeed, the rumors and interest in the Montauk experiment are unlikely to die.

Medical Implants

Imagine a government such as the Bush Administration, pondering the coming pole shift. They are not certain it will happen as we have defined, but note our other predictions have played out and are wary enough to be stockpiling food stuffs and beefing up the military to use as their personal defense force, or so they hope. They are wary enough to be pretending, publicly, that chemtrails do not exist. What might be their plans re the populace at large? Playing God, as they do in their smoke filled rooms, they divide the populace into desirable and undesirables. Those considered desirable are uniformly white, educated, passive in nature, and likely to be dependent upon others and desperate to cooperate. Those considered undesirable are people of color, those whose culture has taught them rebellion, or those prone to disease. In that most undesirables can be sorted out by color, social security number and past work record, or police record, they are not a concern. They will simply be excluded from any government sponsored survivor camp. But what about disease? Medical records are privileged, and few doctors are likely to change this practice over the next year.

Thus, human implants are not to locate those to be saved, but to identify those to be excluded, for medical reasons. Those rushing to be implanted are those who need to be quickly identified in a medical emergency. Ergo, they have a disease, genetic, or needing medication, or some such problem.

Mind Control

The dream of all controlling individuals, a category which includes the military hierarchy, is to create virtual robots out of the population at the flip of a switch. Riot control, preventing resistance, silencing dissent, ensuring complete adherence to orders or edicts—such are the heady goals of those who are control oriented. Humans use drugs, physical restraints, and threats and bribes to gain these ends, but none of these methods are fail-safe. In human-to-human encounters no one is paralyzed unless drugs or physical restraints are used, and likewise leaving a memory only in the subconscious where it can act like a post-hypnotic suggestion is achievable only by battering and splintering the conscious through trauma and drugs. The secret government, which in the early days was heavily influenced by the CIA, longed to master what they considered to be mind control techniques.

In fact, as we have stated, a human cannot be given a hypnotic suggestion they are not in accordance with, and during visitations the human is in control and can terminate contact at any time simply by willing it to be so. Even the paralyzed state, which makes use of an old portion of the human brain that is akin to a possum's brain, can be broken at will by the human. Nevertheless, the CIA did a considerable amount of casting about, trying to discover how aliens were able to paralyze humans and plant what they assumed to be post hypnotic suggestions. Needless to say, they did not succeed, but their fervor and rumors of this activity inspired such stories as the Manchurian Candidate, where humans, while unaware, are time bombs waiting to become absolute robots behaving in a preprogrammed manner. This is all so far from what is possible as to be positively silly.

Remote Viewing

Lest anyone be confused, what is termed remote viewing is simply telepathy, a natural and fairly common occurrence among mankind and the animals who call the Earth their home. Telepathy is intrinsic to life, but only about 10% of the human populace has enough native capacity to take note of it. Those with native capacity soon learn that they can anticipate phone calls from friends, anticipate and guard against personal attacks, and seem to intuitively understand what their loved ones need and want. The government has never failed to use telepathy to accomplish whatever they might consider their ends, but after observing the seamless way aliens could work together, without a word spoken, the issue got hot. As MJ12 was in those days heavily dominated by the CIA, they took up the topic and infected the goals of the operation with their own twists.

Remote viewing under the CIA's auspices was not done to simply garner intelligence on legitimate government security concerns, it was used to invade privacy, secure blackmail material, assist break-ins and thefts, amuse agents who wanted to snoop for personal reasons, and keep tabs on rival government agencies. When the operation failed to curtail enemy actions due to a complete lack of awareness of enemy plans and failure to predict, it ostensibly was shut down. As with all bureaucracy enclaves, it sought to perpetuate itself by reinventing its goals. Remote viewing would become a handy disinformation tool, impressing the public with what might seem to be an ability to read minds, and thereafter spreading disinformation as valid facts garnered through telepathy. To ensure a gullible public will believe, the remote viewing track record is supported by information supplied by the CIA.

Silencing Methods

Individuals in government service who become aware of MJ12 as more than a rumor are of course sworn to silence. In most cases, the motivation to cooperate with the edict is membership in MJ12, which grants MJ12 the right to kill the errant member should they get loose lips. Individuals being initiated into MJ12 membership sign papers granting MJ12 that right, but most think of this as a formality, an indication of the seriousness of the subject, and expect to have endless warnings and discussions long before any such action would be taken. In fact, what occurs when the issue come up is a quick trial and execution, as delays and warnings are what allow leaks to occur and preventing this from occurring is the point of the death sentence clause.

Even during a time when deliberate leaks about the existence and identify of MJ12 are on the increase, uncontrolled and unexpected leaks are still alarming to the leadership of MJ12. These are in the main military men, who joined the military and rose in the ranks precisely because of their need for tight control, so loose lips not intended to be loose are invariably alarming. The MJ12 board is in fact two boards. One is composed primarily of military intel bureaucrats at fairly high levels. Not all of them. Not necessarily the highest. They slip away for meetings and come back, and people think they spent a long time in the bathroom. That's how carefully it is done. The meetings are not held in any kind of a place where cars drive up. They are often times held in cow barns, very out of the way so that they are never seen. They ride to and from by space ship and no one is the wiser. The locations change constantly.

Prior to issuing a death sentence, the guilty party is always brought in for questioning, an almost instant arrangement due to the travel service we provide to MJ12, which comes complete with our ability to cloak the movements of our ships and the activities of the passengers while on an official MJ12 trip. Once guilt or evidence of deliberate intentions is ascertained, often by injecting the subject with truth serum, sentence is rapidly carried out. Because they have many controls and are very strict in their rules, they come to their decisions quickly. There are no appeals. If someone is to be executed, it is carried out very rapidly and the individual has no warning. Assassinations are thus done very conveniently, but if it were not for our travel service, the CIA and the like are very expert at slipping a needle into an arm pit to fake a heart attack, or at using drugs that dissipate and don't show up in the blood stream.

When a prominent individual is silenced, the death is carefully orchestrated to appear as an accident or suicide. If intense public scrutiny is expected, the body in involved in an accident that none would question, such as in the airplane crash that killed Clinton's Secretary of Transportation Ron Brown. The cause of death is obvious, so the body is not examined in detail. Where the individual is living a quiet life, a car accident or perhaps a sporting accident, as in the death of former CIA director William Colby, might be involved. Other options include a simulated heart attack, via a needle inserted through the armpit where puncture wounds would not be discovered, or a simulated stroke—both caused by drugs injected and rapidly disappearing from the blood stream, undetectable upon autopsy.

Cooperation

Most people who cooperate with the government are not doing because they all sat down in a smoke filled room, shared a drink, and nailed down on the board exactly who's going to do what. The process is not at all like that. The private citizen is presented with an opportunity, with a serious person who comes and suggests that perhaps they might do this or that, is flashing credentials, is a most impressive person, intelligent, well groomed, and relays the message that it's necessary to downplay panic, to distract the populace, to counter something else that has gone wrong, and is always dressed in a way that the person feels that they are doing the right thing by cooperating with people who are like parents, looking out for society at large. People can be led to do the most outrageous acts with this kind of approach. They may have a little uneasiness about it, as they have no way of determining whether they are being told the truth., but they usually cooperate because they have a lack of information, and to go with the flow and do what they've been requested to do is the most logical thing, even though their intuition may be telling them otherwise.

Most of the frauds that are being put out to distract the populace have built in self-destruct mechanisms. Build-in discrediting, so that the populace is told a falsehood, but at the same time they're told that it is a falsehood, and discussions go in both ways. The CIA is famous for this, running people forth with a message and then cutting them off at the knees. Most often the people they use understand that this will be done to them, they understand that's it's necessary because the message that's going to be given will be upsetting and that by cutting them off at the knees and humiliating them, the populace will conclude it was just a hoax or a falsehood. Nevertheless, the message has been gotten out.

An example of this is the subliminal message in the false story about a capsule trailing Hale-Bopp. What were they talking about? Some sort of a virus that's going to come in a capsule and drop on Africa and destroy the crops. Are we not going to have crop shortages? Of course we are. People are being told to think about the potential of a crop shortage. Think about the potential of illnesses running rampant with an inability to stop this process. Maybe it's not even terrorism, but common illnesses like sewage that gets into the drinking water. People die from cholera by the thousands after certain earthquakes where this occurs, and this is going to be a rampant situation in your future. The secret government is trying to make the populace think to some degree, and they have allies in this who are willing to put out a message and then be willing to be ridiculed.

Many times these individuals do not know they're going to be ridiculed. They're in fact told they're going to be supported, and when they're trashed it's quiet a bit of a shock. They're also told not to complain and whine too loudly to the public. Then these individuals see the harsh side of the hand that they've been dealing with, now threatening to kill them, to main them, to main their loved ones or destroy their reputation. One only has to look to Bob Lazar to see what can be done. Evidence can be trumped up, manufactured, and prosecutors lined up with a glare pointed toward the individual. It's pretty scary. So most people just take their drumming and walk off and lick their wounds and don't say much.

Black Helicopters

Reports of black helicopters harassing and following UFOlogists and contactees and associated with mutilations are so frequent and numerous as to be considered a fact, even by skeptics. Everyone expects them to be an arm of the government, and would be shocked to learn that their ownership and activities are not under government control. Private members of the establishment have funded and run this enterprise, with the goal of maintaining the status quo. Consider how the activities of the black helicopters and MJ12 differ.

Where MJ12 wants the world to become aware of its past and present, as part of the Awakening process, it has never flagrantly displayed physical evidence of its existence. Why would they have done that over the past years when a prime concern was to deny their existence? Clearly by being noisy, flashy, and lingering about in public view, the black helicopters are not the arm of a government group concerned with secrecy.

Mutilations, not ever an activity of MJ12, have an association with black helicopters, which are frequently seen in the vicinity during and after a mutilation. Again, as mutilations are by design noticeable, leaving large carcasses mangled in ways impossible for anyone to ignore, this would not be something a secret government arm would engage in.

The black helicopters consistently harass contactees who are engaged in communication roles, giving the message that they should fall silent. Where this was the stance that MJ12 assumed in the past, the past few years have found them encouraging awareness of the alien presence. It is an open secret that the movie ET was initiated by MJ12. Why would MJ12 work at cross purposes to itself?

The black helicopters are housed at private facilities, the perfect cover. A barn, a warehouse, or a hollow dirt mound work as well as a vacant hangar at a private landing strip. Helicopters, of course, need only a spot to land upon, and can be draped with camouflage cloth or have collapsible walls of a shack or garage erected around it once landed. In a sheltered and isolated spot, such activity goes unnoticed, with the exit and return of the chopper accomplished in minutes. How does this enterprise learn who the contactees or UFOlogists are, and of their schedules and routes? Consider for a moment the number of ex-government agents, of all flavors, who are expert at tapping phones and at effective surveillance and, in particular, at infiltrating groups such as contactee support groups. Establishment groups who can afford fleets of sleek choppers can certainly lure ex-CIA members into their employ. And the new employer is not asking them to do anything they haven't already been doing—just a new pair of shoes.

Why hasn't a private operation like this been exposed, by either the government, the media, or private individuals? Money buys silence, and where money is not effective, accidents are arranged. Ranchers who have complained about helicopters flying over their land have quickly been silenced, by one means or another. Agents trained in espionage are not sloppy, know not to leave a trail, and can anticipate what steps any law enforcement agency might take. They are not prosecuted by the federal government because they can blackmail the prosecutor, being aware of the existence and operation of MJ12. Squeeze us and secrets you don't want revealed may come out, is the threat, so an uneasy staring contest has ensued, with neither party blinking. In addition, a number of the perpetrators, captains of industry, are members of the larger MJ12, and the good-old-boy system is alive and well.

Autopsy Tapes

The Roswell film is a clever fake, done not by the CIA but by a commercial group hired by those in the government popularly known as MJ12, and done, not surprisingly, on good old USA soil. What was its intent? Of course it was to acclimate the public to the alien presence, the sight of alien bodies, the thought that humans and aliens have contact, the image of their government in contact—but reassuringly with the impression that humans have the upper hand. How could it not be so, when alien bodies are being cut apart by humans in white coats. And for those too frightened by this thought, whose hearts are beating, blood pressure rising, anxieties distracting them from the day's work—there are the doubts about the authenticity of the film, which will soon be strengthened as more and more skeptics come forward with specifics. Ah, one can relax again, as it was just another fraud.

Will someone go to prison for having committed fraud? For what crime? Fraud must have monitory damages, and this has none. Fraud must have some sort of damages, and none will be forthcoming. What would be the claim? I was assured that aliens were real and then found they were not. Laughed right out of court. The perpetrator is expected to raise his decibels along with the skeptics, and is doing so right on call. All part of the plan. Of course the cameraman's story is hokum, and this is because the cameraman is hokum! As with Ray Santilli's story, the cameraman's story has been carefully staged and the search for the cameraman just props on the stage to make the cameraman's story somewhat credible. As we have stated, only one of four aliens survived, whom the government called EBE, and he was unconscious when recovered. Autopsies were performed on the other bodies, piecemeal and over time, and are still in fact being done on the frozen remains from time to time.

The body of the alien in the autopsy film, so human in appearance with few exceptions, was in fact a human. The differences noted were in some cases natural, in some augmented by plastic surgery, and in some cases faked. The base body was of a prepubescent girl who sickened and died in an institution for the retarded, and had long been a ward of the state. Retardation was caused by water on the brain, a condition that creates an enlarged head. The large eye sockets came with the package, but the eyes themselves were replaced by even larger orbs, the reason for the unblinking appearance due to the eyelids being stretched and incapable of closing. This girl was essentially a vegetable toward death, and was unable to consent or refuse treatment. Plastic surgery was performed in her last months to remove her navel and nipples, but the occurrence of six fingers and toes, a common recessive gene, was already present. This unfortunate youngster, abandoned essentially at birth and with multiple birth defects, had a physiological tendency to retain fat disproportionately in her abdomen.

For those who say these are too many peculiarities to occur in unison, we will point out that defects in fact do most often afflict the fetus in multiples. Genetic abnormalities most often result in spontaneous abortions, but where they do not, the surviving infant is ill formed and usually limps through a short life. Visit your institutions and find out, should you doubt. One problem triggers another, with heart, lungs, kidneys, brain, all malformed at once and the endocrine and nutritional systems askew. As for the organs, never seen clearly while being removed, these were substituted while all was a blur and in motion. How would it be that at an autopsy of such importance that a camera man would blur the image?

Does he not understand how to operate his camera? Was he not chosen for his expertise? And if not, if he was inexperienced, why did he seem to have no learning curve in this regard?

All in all, however, we feel the autopsy film served its purpose, which was to set the populace to talking and thinking about the alien presence. The arguments about the authenticity of the film are evenly weighed, pro and con, and this causes the arguments to be all the more long lasting and heated. Just what the film makers wanted.

Information Agents

MJ12 has stepped up the pace of informing the populace. The policy of spreading information is now knocking out the former policy of disinformation, which was hanging about loath to let go. Habits are hard to break, and any established policy always has its advocates, but rules are rules and an order is an order.

Some new trends will become evident. We will still have the same old specialists, but they may be given to moments of honesty about their former role, packaged well in humor so an element of doubt is thrown in, or they may become born-again believers where formerly skeptics. The same old tactics will still be used, which is to assert independence from each other while in actuality supporting each other. They will still attack mutual foes with the old one-two, working in synchronicity with each other, but the foes will begin to change! Where many of the active disinformation specialists were identified or at least suspect, only a fraction were so compromised. These tended to be the witty, well educated, aggressive ones. Others, just as effective in affecting public opinion, were never suspected at all. And then there are the multiple Internet screen names used by most, which allow one to even carry on an argument with oneself.

Overt Agents

Spy and counterspy tales are the delight of many who enjoy a convoluted plot, and in this regard UFOlogy has not disappointed the populace. Everyone is accusing, or at least suspecting, everyone else of being a CIA agent, a disinformation specialist, in the employ of special interests, or at a minimum conning a gullible public out of their loose change. Beyond the heavy handed suppression that occurred in the past and, in truth, lingers today, what is it about UFOlogy that makes it so susceptible to this type of intrigue?

Infiltration of UFO interest groups, contactee support groups, and funded studies does occur, as in the past the government wanted certain discussions suppressed entirely and even in open times spin control is desired.

Competition for center stage is keen, and a time honored method for gutting the competition is to cast aspersions.

The government wants to be seen as promoting, rather than suppressing the Awakening, and thus may deliberately spread rumors about informative individuals, asserting they are government agents, in order to share the spotlight and applause.

How to sort this all out? Don't bother. Concentrate on the information, not trying to discern the source, and judge the worth of what is presented by how it fits into the whole, whether it has the ring of truth, and whether it has contradictions or consistency throughout. Else you will be lost in spy and counterspy forever.

School Surveillance

It comes as no surprise to humans that government agents are posing as college students, given the unrest on campuses that developed during the Vietnam war era, or that government agents are even posing as high school students, given the drug peddling that is done by pushers who wish to addict their customers at a young and tender age. But the possibility of surveillance in the primary grades seems remote. Since no adult could pass as a child, an agent would have to be a teacher or administrator. Such surveillance does occur, a little known and rarely suspected fact, but through indirect rather than direct means. Youngsters are measured in many ways beyond the standard IQ and achievement tests. Report cards, while confidential to the parents and school administrators, are within the reach of government agents, with the parents and child none the wiser.

Given that a child could not conduct a criminal enterprise or be recruited to assist the government until their late teens, what is the point of this scrutiny?

Since the crash at Roswell proved that the alien presence was real, the government has been uneasy about possible infiltration. Could not aliens capable of disguising their ships disguise themselves in human society? Well, of course this can and does occur on many levels, from a contactee given a screen memory to disguise the fact that they have been conversing with an alien to an alien walking in full view through a crowd where all who see him think they have seen another human. Beyond physical infiltration, spiritual infiltration occurs when infants are born as Star Children or walk-ins occur. It was knowledge of the hybrid program, the possibility of very human looking hybrids with alien qualities, that drove surveillance of the young, however, as this was seen as a potential for a super-human race with mixed allegiances, outside of the government's control.

Control oriented members of the secret government determined to find and tag them young, before such youngsters might become sophisticated enough to disguise themselves. Such traits as an exceptionally high IQ or remarkable athletic ability brought the youngster into steady monitoring, as well as any type of precocious abilities that could be termed super-human. A child who could see auras, or hear notes beyond the normal range, or displayed telepathic abilities, or had a remarkable memory for long numbers, or who mastered several languages at an early age—any of these exceptional abilities could bring a child under scrutiny.

This program is little known because it never went beyond peeping. No patterns of exceptional adulthood emerged from these children, nor did the adults differ from the norm in any manner. High IQ youngsters developed as they had in the past; athletic youngsters took advantage of their abilities as they had in the past; and those with precocious musical ability were pressed by their parents into performing, as they had in the past. The surveillance program essentially shriveled and died, though it was never formally closed, as is often the case with bureaucracies.

X-Files

The X-Files premise is that agencies such as the FBI and CIA encounter and investigate the paranormal, the extraterrestrial, and keep files on such encounters. This is quite true, but they are not termed X-Files. This data goes by many names, all designed to avoid drawing attention. The mazes within the intelligence agencies cause even their leadership to get lost. Such files were in existence before the alien presence became a hot topic, as what is termed paranormal, in the form of ghosts and poltergeist activity, has always been present. These files grew by a quantum leap, in pace with the Awakening, about the time of the Roswell incident.

With the X-Files series the secret government hit pay dirt. The series has been wildly popular, in no small part because the producer does not shy away from controversy—he embraces it. Thus, the series has been encouraged to be more and more bold, as MJ12 wishes the public to adapt to the reality of the alien presence and their government's role in this. Where at first the series flirted with abduction and human experimentation and only alluded to the cold hand of the CIA in suppressing information, the series was encouraged to get graphic and to make the CIA the villains they have, in truth, been. The secret government is multifaceted, and many parts did not participate in the brutality that the CIA presumed that secrecy called for. They wish to be disassociated, and where the true story will in all likelihood never be told, the X-Files is coming darn close to it.

Alien Presence

Regarding the issue of the alien presence, and the lack of proof thereof. There is a vast panoply of evidence that far surpasses the evidence required to secure patents at the patent office! There one need not prove the theory upon which the gadget is based, but simply demonstrate that the gadget works. Do not our gadgets work? Do not the traces on radar screens, which those who would debunk hide from the public, demonstrate that our gadgets work?

And what does it matter what humans choose to bunk/debunk, as their actions in these matters, this time around, are as insignificant as the breezes to the tide. The tide is rolling in, and the dams are too flimsy to withstand the steady pressure. The tides in the past ebbed and flowed, without the influence of those who debunk the alien presence. When the tide flowed, they would step up their actions, and when the tide ebbed, congratulate themselves. This was as meaningful as the bird on the back of a water buffalo, who congratulates itself when the buffalo walks in the direction desired. This was and is self delusion, and those of deeper intelligence have always known this.

LSD Trip

During a dark period in US history, the CIA and military performed experiments on hapless and unsuspecting civilians, co-workers, and enlisted men. This is no longer the dark secret it was meant to be, as story after story has been told, and in an age of disclosure, documents have come forth to be waved about as proof to a horrified populace. Where the cover on the nightmare of radiation experiments has been stripped back, the CIA experimentation with LSD still hides behind non-disclosure claims. Did the CIA soak co-workers and inmates of mental wards in LSD, just to see what the effects might be? They did indeed, and the story as told by their victims aligns closely with the facts. The grand excuse in those days was that violating others was justified, and justification could always be found.

The true reason for the dreadful LSD experiments, which ruined many lives and drove many to their death, was an insatiable desire for control—the hallmark signal of those in the Service-to-Self orientation. LSD was rumored to be a truth serum, those dealing with a massive onslaught unable to put up resistance as all the walls were down and realities were running together without boundaries. What they got from their blubbering victims was gibberish, but this didn't stop them from repeating the experiment, just for the fun of it. Violating others is a power trip for those strongly in the Service-to-Self, and the CIA, from its inception, has had more than its share of such individuals calling the shots.

K. R.

Transformation

What is the Transformation? The Earth is undergoing a subtle transformation, as the Transformation is now. This Transformation has been progressing for at least this century, and will go for at least a century more. Transformations occur for many reasons. One reason is that the great majority of the entities native to the planet have reached an orientation decision, and are ready to proceed with other lessons, and 3rd Density planets are checked periodically as to their readiness for harvest in this regard. Another reason is administrative, and that is why the Earth is undergoing its Transformation now. The majority of those on Earth have not yet reached their orientation decision, but will be moved to another planet, as the Earth has been designated as a future home for Service-to-Other oriented entities.

To qualify for Service-to-Other orientation, an entity must consider others as often as the self. To qualify for Service-to-Self, the entity must focus on the self 95% of the time, almost exclusively. Where it may seem that these individuals would stand out, some very diplomatic and cultured people are of this category. They are able to disguise their self interest in condescension to others. They are able to disguise their self interest as the interests of the other. During 3rd Density, entities must decide their spiritual orientations—Service-to-Self or Service-to-Others. Most, the vast majority, decide the latter on almost all 3rd Density worlds. This decision, or the lesson of 3rd Density as it is called, needs to precede almost all other lessons, as mixing the two spiritual orientations together creates chaos and thus other lessons cannot proceed. Many humans on Earth are choosing the Service-to-Other orientation, and mid-incarnation are thus joining the ranks of the Service-to-Others. This occurred in the past as well.

The world involves an increasing separation, by orientation, as the Transformation proceeds. The mix of Service-to-Other and Service-to-Self, and the proportion of undecided, will not change much as the cataclysms near and times get tough. Where some of the undecided will rise to the challenge and move into the Service-to-Others category, there will be others, operating in the Service-to-Other mode when things are comfortable, who will find their self focus increasing as their insecurities increase. Some, a very few, who are operating in the Service-to-Self mode, will find the troubled times pulling at their hearts, and will move back into the undecided category. A greater number will find their selfish nature accentuating during difficult times, and like those on the Titanic, will push all others aside to save themselves. They will move into the Service-to-Self category. So you see that the numbers will move about a bit, but essentially remain unchanged.

Oahspe

The Oahspe is a book read by few but with staunch devotees, as it speaks to truths mostly unspoken by man. Written at a time and in a place where Christianity was the only dogma allowed, the Oahspe could only have come from the mind of the man and by the hand of the man who wrote it. Thus it is clear to those who encounter it that it is channeled work. The battle between what mankind calls good and evil, the existence of many types of spirits with different motivations such as ghosts or demons or angels, and reincarnation are not new topics to mankind, as they are addressed in one form or another by the major religions. But the Oahspe addresses such subjects as

immature spirits,

spirits so poorly formed that they fail to prosper

the fluidity that incarnations can experience when there are more disincarnate spirits than bodies to accommodate them, the rapture that some spirits find in corporeal pleasures.

reincarnation with a mission to right wrongs done during previous incarnations

administrative oversight of developing worlds by spirits in higher planes

the approaching transformation of the Earth and the interest in this among gathering spirits from many other worlds

the use of the periodic passages of what the Oahspe calls the Red Star to create change on Earth

the mentoring of democracy in the world in keeping with its approaching transformation

Those who would delve into the rich wealth of insight the Oahspe provides should bear in mind that it was written at a time when all books intended to be serious works spoke in the Biblical style. The reader should not be put off by the use of new terms for spirits in different stages of maturity or with different orientations or allegiances. Many of these new terms have a parallel term, and these parallels are useful in helping the new reader relate. Read with an open mind, letting what is being relayed sink in. As the reading progresses the reader will get a sense of what those who were speaking through the author, a simple man who practiced dentistry in the last century, hoped to relay. As with the Book of Ra, it can be difficult to understand, and is subject to many interpretations. The best advice we can give no this matter is to read with your heart as well as your mind. Follow the flow, let the nuances lie unanswered and unchallenged in your mind. Treat this as a garden you are walking through for the first time, and experience it fully without trying to categorize it! Much of what you will learn will be processed in your subconscious, and influence your conscious mind later. If you must dissect each phrase, and correlate it with each piece of information taken from another source, you will trash much of what you could otherwise gain. Live in the gray, not always insisting on black and white and strict compartmentalizations.

Harvest

The Transformation is sometimes referred to as the Harvest. On your Planet Earth, because of the geological changes that periodically happen, the Transformation to 4th Density has been planned to coincide with these geological changes. The reason is simple, though some may view it in horror. During the coming geological changes the vast majority of your Earth's populace will perish, suddenly. Those who survive will find a world without food or shelter from the elements. Medical treatment will be scarce, and hygiene the least of anyone's thoughts. Consequently, even after the cataclysms, the die-off will be huge.

Reincarnation will not be affected by the pole shift any more than normal life cycles. Humans died young in the past. In the days of the cave man life was far shorter, so this is common to your species. There will be much death, and this has horrified many people, but at the present time the majority of humans on Earth, in fact four-fifths or more, do not have reincarnated souls but can spark new souls. This has happened because of the population explosion. Reincarnation on new worlds does not happen because of every intelligent life that harbors the possibility of this. We call these aborted souls. This is not any decision on the part of an administrative force, it just simply happens. Nothing sparked a soul. Nothing sparks a soul in a parakeet or a dog. If there is an indolent life, or one without challenge, frequently the soul dissipates upon death rather than remaining to reincarnate and grow and increase in mass.

Therefore the pole shift will result in quite a number of souls suddenly looking for reincarnation, but because this is a Transformation time they will be gathered, if they have not made their orientation decision to be Service-to-Self or Service-to-Other, and whisked off to a water world to be reincarnated into a type of octopus and carry on their lessons. Those who are Service-to-Other will reincarnate into more intelligent hominoids on Earth, and those who are Service-to-Self and have firmly decided this will be sent off to various worlds, at times in human form, for what we would term a very unpleasant life among others of their own kind.

Hindu Yugas

Where the current Earth Transformation will encompass the entire population and even the physical density of the majority of the Earth and its Sun, there have been partial harvests in the past. These harvests involved parsing out mature entities to either the Service-to-Self or Service-to-Other orientation, while leaving the vast majority behind to continue their orientation deliberations in their 3rd Density setting. These harvests occur in what could be termed cyclical periods, predetermined time frames, due to the work load involved in doing the evaluation and arranging the transfer. Individual harvests also occur, if the individual has given The Call on this matter and is ready for harvest. The Hindus, in touch with matters spiritual, are aware of these periodic harvests just as they are cognizant of reincarnation and lessons that span lifetimes.

As the majority of transfers in any harvest are entities who have determined to be in Service-to-Others, those remaining behind are the worse off for their transfer. Thus, the Hindus see the Yugas as cycles leading to increasing degradation. The balance is maintained, however, as the disruptive influence of those strongly in the Service-to-Self has also been removed. After a harvest, things seem more placid all around, the clashes between entities attempting domination and entities fighting for freedom leaving the scene temporarily. The Hindus are also confused about the significance of events, mixing in the start of certain preparations for the Transformation, for instance, with the regular activity of harvests. The Hindus had scant knowledge of the harvest dates, and scant understanding of the harvest cycle outcome, ascribing an eventual destruction to those entities not having made their orientation determination at a certain point in time. No such destruction of 3rd Density entities occurs, no matter how long they delay.

Foreknowledge

Many people, when encountering information about the coming geological changes due to occur just after the millennium, feel that the information strikes a resonance with them, is something they somehow knew about all along, and due to this connection with their own internal knowledge these individuals begin to seriously prepare for the changes. Such foreknowledge is due to one of three information pathways being in place.

The individual may be a contactee, and due to the frequent visitations that serious contactees receive, the subject invariably comes up. Not all contactees have foreknowledge of the coming cataclysms, as this information is not imparted due to our wishes, but because it fits into the context of The Call given. Say, for instance, that the contactee is concerned about a child and the changing world this child will have to live in. This is a natural context to discuss the coming cataclysms. If the contactee is concerned about an aging parent who will shortly die, or the ethics of receiving a reward for something they were inclined to do anyway, the subject may not come up. Thus a contactee may or may not have foreknowledge.

K. R.

The individual may be perceptive regarding geology, inherently logical, and find the towering mountains and separating continents not explained at all by conventional explanations. If they encounter information about wandering poles and coal seams in the Antarctic and flash frozen mastodons with green grass in their stomachs in the Arctic Circle, their unease increases. Thus the subconscious begins to put things together, and they have arrived at a logical conclusion at odds with the explanation prated by scientists at Universities and published in the news. They know something has been left out, and when they hear about the periodicy of the geological changes, and the theories about the 12th Planet, it all falls into place. Thus inherently logical, independent thinkers may arrive at foreknowledge on their own accord.

They have foreknowledge from birth, actually prior to birth, as due to discussions with the birthing envoys prior to selection of their next incarnation the subject came up and they pressed for an incarnation wherein they would have a significant role. Such incarnations allow alien visitor answering The Call to cut to the chase, as you say, and discuss the issues right off. Such pre-birth knowledge going into an incarnation finds the human vaguely aware that there is a role they have chosen that is out of sync with the routine flow they see about them. They have had a sense of preparing, all their life, for something, but are not consciously aware of what the something is. When they encounter others aware of the coming cataclysms, the overwhelming earth changes and concurrent societal changes, they suddenly understand the mission.

Understated

The Transformation proceeds apace, but is understated for several reasons.

If the choices are made based upon orientation, then the focus is not on action, and true change, but on posturing. How often have you heard someone say they are Service-to-Other, or have decided to become Service-to-Other. This is not a conscious choice, but the characteristics are clear enough in write-ups, so posturing can occur. It is deemed better to have the actions of the Transformation out of sight, below the horizon, so that humans can act according to their true orientation.

Bait and switch is in plan to a great degree, among those who would foil the Service-to-Self in their gambits. If they think they have won, a country, a city, a political group, then they relax and gloat. Behind the scenes, it is otherwise. And likewise, there may be a false scuffle where no such battle reigns. This draws the Service-to-Self in that direction, away from where the true battle is waged. Thus, what is on the surface, in the open for humans to observe, is not indicative of the true state of affairs. Suffice it to say that the Transformation not only proceeds apace, but is doing better than expected, here on planet Earth!

Growth Rates

Entities grow in different directions. Some move toward Service-to-Others, and quickly learn this is their orientation. Others move steadily toward Service-to-Self, and desire the greater power that a higher density will grant them. They beg to move forward. The entity being incarnated has little say in the matter, however. Were this otherwise the lessons to be learned would be avoided.

Entities do not grow, spiritually, at the same rate. Some even grow backwards, losing ground. Some take full advantage of the learning experiences offered to them by an incarnation, and others coast, avoiding unpleasant lessons and simply enjoying the pleasant experiences the incarnation offers. Thus during any season of harvest, the harvesters discover that there are entities who have not grown at all, entities who are not ready to emerge from the current density, and entities who are ready to move forward. Many of the entities who are ready to move forward have, for some time, been ready. They are ahead of their time.

There are paths by which entities who are ready to move forward can hasten their emergence from the density. This is, essentially, a call to the administrative powers for a type of hearing. Those who are ready to emerge from their density know, instinctively, how to call. Were they not to know how to call, they would, by definition, not be ready. However, most in the Service-to-Others orientation do not desire to leave the density prematurely, as they are bound, in their hearts, to help their density mates. They wish to help others to arrive at their conclusion. They wish to help others with the struggle. They are self-sacrificing and devoted, and concentrate on the problems of others to the same extent they concentrate on their own struggle.

Therefore, where the Service-to-Self emergents clamor to move forward, wanting the greater powers that await them in a higher density, the Service-to-Others emergents most often remain. Thus at any harvest season we find these entities, laboring among their benighted kindred, without complaint.

Gradual Change

The word Transformation brings to mind in many sudden change, but as the Transformation is now it is obviously happening gradually. What changes have already taken place, and what are the signs of change? Throughout history there have been places and times noted for cruelty and repression—Inquisitions, the Dark Ages, Nazi death camps, and recently Bosnia. Likewise there have been other places and times noted for the opposite—ancient Athens, the Bill of Rights, socialized medicine, and Civil Rights. In this matters have been not black and white, but gray, for if a theme was then dominant proponents of an alternate way of thinking were also hard at work. During the Dark Ages great discoveries were made, and ancient Athens had its close-minded bullies.

During the Transformation to 4th Density, however, polarization occurs so that alternatives are not so much present as elsewhere. Here we have open-minded exploration of ideas and democratic ideals, and there we have repression. At first, this polarization and separation takes place family by family, then township by township, then spreading to larger areas. Bosnia is an example. Those of kind heart wishing to live harmoniously with their neighbors were not only not heard, they were driven out. Some areas of Argentina have never recovered from the Dirty Wars, and are not about to. If one looks to Scandinavia, one finds legislated consideration, support of others, and public access to information of all kinds. Those who do not find this climate to their liking leave to settle elsewhere. These trends toward separation will continue, and acerbate, during the Transformation.

In step with spiritual change, physical change has taken place. The concepts espoused by the Green Movement, begun in the Netherlands, are now espoused worldwide, and words and thoughts have been followed by action. Pollution control and abatement, once the purview of minuscule government agencies, now hits the front pages regularly and occupies the hearts and minds of researchers world wide. The results, evident only within the past few years, include microbes that eat pollution, plants that cleanse the soil, and alternative natural products that don't pollute. Likewise, some religious movements such as Islamic dictates have become more harsh and repressive, resulting in increased restrictions on women. In racial relations advocates of separation have grown bolder and even managed to reverse progress of late. If one takes note of the physical signs and follows them to their source, one can almost delineate the boundaries of spiritual separation. Signs of transformative change!

Polarization in the main goes on undetected, with humans migrating to areas they sense will be more compatible with their thinking. Humans join groups, decide what shops to shop in, take walks in this or that park, all based on orientation, increasingly. Political groups, religious affiliations, all are affected by orientation leanings. Decisions as to what groups to belong to, what locales to live in, what employer to work for, are made daily based on the sense the human has that their chosen orientation fits in.

If a group plays ball, hard, with ridicule of those losing, and another plays ball for exercise, and ensures that all attending get a fair physical workout, these are attended by humans with different leanings.

If a political party is elitist, cruel to those in need and giving increasing power to the strong and ruthless, this is not a Service-to-Other oriented group.

If a church is so rule oriented that the elders cannot be challenged even when they rape children, and refuse to be called to account, this is not a Service-to-Other oriented leadership.

At a certain point, during a polarization period, these trends are noticed, as they become extreme. This is the point reached today, thus noticed. In the past, where the vast majority were undecided, only the occasional fully developed Service-to-Self or Service-to-Other would be about to influence matters. Jesus, or Genghis Khan, so their influence was obvious. During the Tranformation, where an influx of Service-to-Other Star Children, including Walk-ins that increase their numbers dramatically without the birth or maturation of children being required for influence, those in the Service-to-Self are threatened. The percentage of Service-to-Other on the Earth is tipping, and the Service-to-Self among humans feel uncomfortable. They group more tightly, to be with their like kind. They seek more control, get more shrill, dictate more rules, and restrict access to themselves. This is all to increase their comfort level, to return to the comfort level they remember in prior times. This desire for control, to return to the good-ol-days, is what in fact drives the polarization, as the Service-to-Self willingly separate!

Mixed Groups

In a mixed orientation society there are several barriers to the complete polarization that is the end result of the Transformation process. As might be expected, these barriers are all to the favor of those in the Service-to-Self, who prefer to have those in the Service-to-Others around, as prey. Beyond the obvious fact that the two orientations can physically intermingle in a mixed orientation setting, there is the tendency of those in the Service-to-Others to feel responsible for others, and to linger. Ultimately, through death and the sorting out that goes on prior to the next incarnation, the orientations do separate, if only because all those not in the Service-to-Others have been removed. Is there nothing a responsible human in the Service-to-Others can do during this time to avoid the traps being continually laid for them?

As life on Earth will get increasingly desperate, with food shortages and injuries and a continual high level of panic, those in the Service-to-Others will feel strongly drawn to remain with those in need. In truth, there is not much that can be done to change the circumstances, as life will be rough at best and subsistence about the best that can be hoped for among humans not living in hybrid communities. But what can be adjusted are attitudes and expectations, which can be adjusted to reality and in anticipation of future circumstances.

Separation of the orientations is inevitable, and any guilt trips those in the Service-to-Self try to lay on conscientious humans should be put firmly into this context. Humans are not in charge of this separation process, and cannot influence its outcome or pace. Those in the Service-to-Self should be thrown onto their own resources, to fend for themselves, which in any event is the setting they can anticipate in the future. To placate and wait on those in the Service-to-Self only creates, ultimately, a ruder shock in the future. Thus, it is in fact a kindness to refuse to be their servant class.

The standard of living will drastically drop, titles and positions attained will lose their meaning, and any false sense of security from savings accounts or possessions will shatter. Thus all those who survive the pole shift will need to adjust to the new reality. Where this will be difficult for all, it will be most difficult for those who are used to demanding service. Their demands will increase in proportion to their sense of deprivation, which will be acute. Exhausted and half starved themselves, stoic humans in the Service-to-Others orientation will find themselves surrounded by a chorus of wailing and angry demands. Do something about this situation, will be the demand, when there is nothing to be done. Thus, those in the Service-to-Others orientation, anticipating this, should learn to tune a deaf ear to all demands on them, as they will have their hands full simply doing what they know needs to be done.

Self help, wherever possible, should be the rule, as the burden on responsible individuals in the Service-to-Others orientation, attending to the needs of all around them, will be overwhelming. These individuals will be the ones keeping the mechanisms of food and energy production and shelter construction in motion, who will do the planning and organizing and rallying the distraught to address the steps that need to be taken. These individuals need to keep themselves strong, else if they drop from exhaustion there will be no leadership. Thus whimpering and ploys for assistance should be met with the counter demand that such assistance only be requested when self help has been tried, and tried repeatedly, and given only when it is obvious to all that assistance from others is needed.

Separate

In that the 3rd Density world that man currently lives in is such that they cannot easily group by orientation, into Service-to-Other or Service-to-Self groups, this is a point of confusion during this Transformation time. A group of Service-to-Other individuals, seeking to separate, will soon find themselves being visited by those wanting to take advantage of them. A group of Service-to-Self individuals are the first to arrive in such a setting, as this is ideal to their way of thinking. Most Service-to-Other individuals have family and friends they are intertwined with, who have mixed orientations, are undecided. Then enter the rule of law, societal laws, which require these relationships to continue. Governments do not want groups to isolate themselves, and consider this a great threat. Look to the rage with which the FBI invaded isolated groups a decade or so ago, to see how this is viewed. They consider all citizens to be their property, and insist on the entanglements that are wrapped around the individual from childhood on, remaining. One must have schooling, be papered, get a job, be taxed, produce offspring that are likewise controlled. The rage over abortion is an example of how far this sense of control and the importance to those power mad can go. There must be no escape.

So how does this change, after the shift, during the Transformation? First, isolation and separation from government control is automatic. Governments will lose control utterly, and isolation be the norm, not something sought. Thus, it comes down to how a small group, or a community, might separate and polarize. Think of your family, how family members or workforce members find compatible associates and tend to migrate toward them in their free time. If the controls over family support or showing up for work were gone, this would occur increasingly, and become full time. You have the Service-to-Self minded, who go off to loot and look for the weak. They thus are removed from strongly Service-to-Other groups, as these groups tend to cooperate well with each other, and defend themselves. Now you have the undecided, remaining with the Service-to-Other or straggling along on the periphery of the Service-to-Self. In a Service-to-Other environment, there is much serious discussion, and expectation that all will work hard for the general welfare. Undecided find this grim, no fun, and at the first opportunity peel away and set off on their own. Thus, if doing well, they establish their own communities, and if not doing well, die off.

To a great extent, the every-day life that man has today, in civilized countries, will not exist. Disease, infections, and accidents will strike quickly and decimate survivors. Thus, Service-to-Other communities will increasingly find themselves the survivors among survivors. When this occurs, they will find themselves in contact with high tech communities of humans and hybrids, living together. At this point, if not earlier by being assisted unannounced, they will find their lives improved. Thus, to imagine this polarization, this separation by orientation, remove the rule of law, the demands of society, and carry forward the natural trends you see among people today.

Catholic Church

The Catholic Church, long in the know about the possibility of the passage, has also been making their plans. The Fatima warnings, which they have withheld from their flocks, combined with confessions by high level Catholics which were relayed to the Pope, have convinced the inner circle around the Pope that this is a likely scenario. They have two choices, to:

inform their flocks and go through the distress with their flocks, and

to save their own skins and emerge as leaders of those left living.

They have clearly chosen the latter, in that they announced the Fatima warning as a planned assassination of the Pope, and are willing to risk the loss of membership in the scandals surrounding the priesthood lately, in preference to closing the inner circle. Cleansing the church, at this time, would remove too many of the inner circle needed for a tight cover-up into the end times. Thus, pedophiles are protected, and victims paid off, as the higher priority is saving the skins of the inner circle. They will not do this in Rome, likely to be a mess of volcanic ash, but will move to a site as yet undecided. Likely sites are Africa, in places where the church has dominated the local folk, or South America, in countries where they feel an allegiance with the government. Their expectations that they will be leaders in the future is of course absurd, but arrogance seldom is realistic. They will be on the streets, with those of their flock they have abandoned, no better off, and not at all able to deal with the situation. Thus, an ignominious end, to an ignominious life.

The Catholic Church is unique in knowledge due to the grip of fear they place around those born into the religion. Confession, without which the poor souls are told they will burn in hell, is mandatory. Those who state that confessions are confidential are lying, as information deemed important to the Pope, to the inner circle, to maintaining the wealth of the Catholic church, is passed on. Corporate heads, government heads, in confession, are deemed thus, and get confession by special priests in many cases. Other religions do not have such information inroads. Given the information the Catholic Church gained, who said what when, they then had blackmail to learn more, and did gain the information they sought. Those giving them the information had their confidence, as they had mutual goals:

maintain the wealth,

maintain control and leadership,

save their own sorry skins before those they are responsible for, such as the flock or the public in the case of governments.

Repressive Control

Lately the FBI has been in the news in the US by being freed from many restrictions, by the Bush Administration, re domestic spying. This has caused an uproar, but is scarcely unique in the US or elsewhere. Look to Arabian, which runs all internet access through one portal, so as to restrict access to web sites elsewhere not to their liking. Look to China, which thought to lie to the world on Tianaman Square, until they found Fax machines had done them in. Look to North Korea, which punishes any citizen, even children, crawling across their borders to seek food, at the point of death from starvation. Look to the Catholic Church, which tells the sheep to fear the shepherd, their priests, even when the priests are committing the worse crimes against the children in the flock. To what extent will those in power resort to maintain their control, as it slips?

It is not so much what they will do, as what they have done. This may be increasingly revealed, causing the public to think that this is new, but it is the old, now exposed, not new. Thus, spying by the FBI is not new, has been done even without permission, for decades. Do you think Congress, in hearings, is being told the truth, or even presented with those in the know? Those reporting to Congress are purposefully kept in the dark, so as not to slip or have a conscience problem. Those in control, behind the scenes, do as they wish, in the smoky need-to-know rules that the CIA and NSA and similar agencies in Russia and Europe have. In countries where it is no secret that spying and repression exist, this is hardly new.

China has jailed political dissent for decades, mistreating these humans in the worst manner, as did Russia in the past, in the Gulag.

Organs harvested from still live inmates, starved and brutalized for the enjoyment of sadistic guards.

Indonesia treatment of East Timor is an example of raw power, exposed to the world only because of brave reporters who risked their lives, repeatedly. Kill the populace, with Indonesian military, and lie to the world! This is not news, and where meeting with objection, just goes underground.

In Africa, the oil interests sent in brutes to spray the natives objecting to pollution practices, birth defects, and the like, with bullets. This is defended by the oil interests in the US, the offenders excused from the world court, as it were.

In the US, the worse polluter in the world, the US, is excused from restrictions, while the rest of the world goes to Kyoto. Such is the supposed leadership of the free world!

Spying on citizens has gone on, is going on, to the extent the forces doing this chose to do so. In future, as this year plays out, this will diminish, those forces far too busy defending themselves to keep track or even care. Thus, those bugs, those wire taps, can be disconnected, placed elsewhere to fool those who might check on them, and the truth increasingly flow, those wanting free communication increasingly free to talk to others. Such is the progress of the Transformation!

Breakaway Consternation

During the Transformation, gradual polarization of the two spiritual orientations occurs, so that Service-to-Other groups emerge and grow in numbers while Service-to-Self groups harden and become more intense in their power trips. The Service-to-Others groups are increasingly operating in the 4th Density spiritual mode, working together in a highly cooperative mode that requires few rules, and when isolated from those in the Service-to-Self enjoy increased productivity and freedom from slavish obedience to often irrelevant policies and procedures. However, when the polarizing groups encounter each other the freewheeling activity in the Service-to-Others groups causes consternation in those firmly in the Service-to-Self orientation—breakaway consternation.

Those strongly in the Service-to-Self have often learned to use the rules of society to their advantage, from robbing others through the stock and bond markets to riding on the backs of hard working individuals whose ideas and work products are taken by the Service-to-Self with as little credit or financial return to the workers as possible. Their maneuvers are clothed in laws and religious strictures, and without all these rules that the state and church enforce, their power trips would be curtailed. Thus, when they see Service-to-Others groups operating without these rules, they become nervous. Might this trend continue? What kind of a life does this foretell for the Service-to-Self individual who has no intention of doing their fair share or letting those they think of as their virtual slaves escape?

Those in the Service-to-Self will attempt to bring the emerging Service-to-Others groups under their control, and failing to do so will tighten their grip on those already under their control. Their breakaway consternation manifests in intrusive checking on the plans of those under their thumb and vicious attacks when they find simple cooperation replacing slavish obedience to rules. They feel the grip they have loosening and slipping, and this makes them frantic. How dare the Service-to-Others breakaway!

Change Agent

Raised to follow the rules or face the consequences, most humans in all cultures worldwide do so in adulthood without stepping outside the bounds. For Islamic cultures, woman adjust to being draped head to toe when outside the home, the horrific example of rebels stoned and raped ever on their minds. Stop at the red light or be fined, regardless of whether cross traffic exists at the time or not. Pay your bills or lose your possessions and credit rating. Mind the corporate policies and nod approvingly at the dictates of the boss or lose your job. Go through the motions with the spouse even though love has long gone, as this is the only approved sexual outlet and divorce makes one an outcast, socially. Rules, regulations, confining expectations, so much a part of life that other than a quiet seething anger adults are not aware of these invisible ties that bind them to walk in prescribed ruts.

What happens, then, to create a rebel, one who openly rebels against the rules and antagonizes those enforcing them? Anger that has boiled over and cannot be contained, once expressed often puts the rebel into a mode where he cannot go back, and thus in an almost suicidal plunge, he moves forward, free at last to express his resentment. For every rebel that flashes defiance, there are thousands in a quiet revolt, a personal revolution building and waiting for an opportunity. There is the building process, then the opportunity where the threshold drops temporarily, and another rebel is born.

The Muslim woman, long resentful but feeling her situation hopeless, finds during warfare and upheaval in her country that she can dress as a man, take up a weapon, and move about the streets freely, her bravery part of her disguise—the warfare spilling into her village the opportunity. Once having stepped out of her bonds, she plots another course for her life, freed of her invisible bonds. When the women in the village find themselves trapped in their robes, but needing to flee, she suggest another mode, the rebel now a leader.

The dutiful citizen, paying his bills and minding the traffic signs and wearing the appropriate dress and prating the corporate agenda at work, is presented with earthquake upheaval that has reduced his home and workplace to rubble—the earthquake, the trapped and injured neighbors, the opportunity. Thinking survival, solely, he breathes more deeply and finds his head clear for the first time in years, the focus not on the rules but the emergency at hand. Is it looting to take rope from a store, without paying, to rescue those trapped under fallen trees? Once having cast the net of expectations aside, the adult thinks about these matters, and no longer reacts in a programmed manner.

The spouse who finds love gone but the ties that bind still in place deals with the cold shoulder in bed, the hostile comments at the dinner table, by distractions and sadness, but one day a flat tire on the road provides a socially acceptable meeting between two lonely people, and by the time the tire is changed and a cup of coffee in thanks has passed, the rules about fidelity are being ignored—a simple flat tire, the opportunity. The life long gone is suddenly a possibility again, and plans are laid on how to complete the process, divorce, arrangements, and being bold.

Given the upheaval to come during the increasing earthquakes and volcanic activity leading up to rotation stoppage, breaking roads and twisting rails, shattering cities and exploding pipelines, what can be expected of those living today under the rules they were raised to abide by, without question? For every individual harboring seething resentment, anger over senseless and inhumane rules, there will be an opportunity to step into a different mode of action. The soldier, told to point his gun at a child and shoot, not only refusing but turning his gun to protect, not main, the child, rebelling. The housewife, told by her husband to stay in the house, no longer safe, with the children, taking the car keys and leaving home and husband for good, rebelling. Police and firefighters, told by officials to let the buildings burn and to blockade escape from the city as their presence in a Martial Law directive is required blocking roads so looters cannot move to more affluent areas, turning a deaf ear to the orders and doing what their hearts tell them is the right thing to do, rebels all. Thus, in those counties where it seems freedom is dying, democracy stolen, dictatorship on the rise, take comfort. Help is on the way, the Earth changes will allow an opportunity for all to live lives more real, more caring, than was imagined.

NESCARA

NESCARA [National Economic Stabilization And Recovery Act] is a concept only, being floated out to determine interest in such a concept by the establishment who is aware that the common man will increasingly experience personal loss, and become increasingly desperate.

Taking the US as an example, the Fed has cut interest rates to a low not experienced since WWII, and is practically giving away money.

Bush and the GOP, against their usual inclinations to support only the rich and powerful, have decided to allow federal funds to be paid to the unemployed, who have recently run through their compensation and are now without weekly checks of any kind.

The economic indicators are all down down down, though the "experts" pronounce otherwise, with one company after another going belly up or laying off workers.

Workers from private to government jobs are taking pay cuts or declining wage increases, even when warranted by cost of living increases, in order to retain their jobs at all.

The Stock Market, maintained under tight control by money managers given firm orders not to sell but to buy, is floating where it is only because of a monumental control efforts, and would crash if neglected for a day.

K. R.

The public did not buy for Christmas, in spite of promises in the media that this would be a big spending year, and as soon as 4Q results are in, the stocks will start plunging again.

Bankruptcies are at a record high, and will soon overwhelm the courts.

What can the establishment do to forestall panic, riots, placards waved in the air over angry heads in front of the White House, a story that would surely get in the news somewhere, in spite of media control, and the cat out of the bag. Would the public buy that some general amnesty was about to be issued? Would they even consider such a concept? If rumors were to circulate, on the Internet, would this get around, get mentioned at coffee houses, at bars, at the workplace? If so, then such rumors are worth floating, if not, then another tack needs to be taken.

NESCARA was such a test ground, and determined that where this was highly attractive to the man on the streets, none of whom are without debts, it was deemed impractical by any but the most childish. Who would buy that banks would forgive all debts? This is how they make their living. Who would buy that politicians would resign? They fight tooth and nail to get into politics, where they are in the power structures, on the stage, and must be pried away from this life, in the main. And how to adjust the inequities? If one man owes another a debt, is this not absolved, while debts to the banks are? Where is the line drawn? Rent past due? Home ownership recently arranged forgiven the same as home ownership one payment from completion? The concept is ludicrous, when examined as to workability, and after an initial perk of interest, soon falls into this type of discussion on how it would be implemented. Thus, the establishment has determined that other means, such as frank payment of unemployment benefits, an extended coverage, needs to be done.

Science Fiction

The media—movies, books, and TV shows—often portray transformative aspects, but this is taken to be fiction by the audience. One such aspect is the definitive battles between good and evil, as portrayed in the Star Wars series, which quite accurately mirrors the determinations on spiritual orientation to be made during 3rd Density. In Star Wars the fictional portrayal shows this to be a physical battle, rather than a spiritual decision, but the battle is won at key points because of spiritual decisions—young Skywalker facing his fears and standing up to all manner of intimidation; Darth Vadar saving his soul at the last minute by following suit, concern for his son overpowering all concern for self; Hans Solo, uninvolved and self protective, joining a cause in a heart-beat to save his friends, risking all; the moral slavery those serving the Empire live under and the terror tactics used by the Master to enforce subservience. Do these not exemplify the spiritual crossroads faced by humans in 3rd Density?

Other such transformative aspects portrayed in the media are the variety of life forms in the Universe, the degree of habitability throughout the Universe, interdimensional or what we term differing density shifts, rapid space travel, and time travel. These aspects are skewed to show primarily hominoid life forms, primarily dry land planets, and free movement during time travel—all of which are incorrect assumptions. However, presentation of the concepts in general is transformative to the audience. How do the writers and the cinematographers come by concepts that mirror the world to come? Have they been inspired? Without a doubt. Select creative writers and artists, who give The Call and are sufficiently motivated and talented, are taken on tours of the Universe, presented directly with life forms, conditions on other planets and engagements between those in the Service-to-Self and Service-to-Other. They are portraying, in human terms, what they have seen.

New Age Trends

Where the ideas expressed by New Agers are not all that new, having been present in many oriental philosophies and a cornerstone of the Hindu beliefs, their upsurgence and universal application is new. Those espousing what is termed New Age philosophies come in for a lot of abuse because many fear the trend. New Age philosophies are quite the opposite of those espoused by the New World Order crowd, but both will sharpen and escalate in their attempts to influence mankind as the Transformation progresses. Where the New World Order crowd wishes mankind to see itself allied only with humans, and in particular only with those in control of human society, New Age viewpoints stress a universal alliance. Concern for the ecology and recycling efforts are also characteristic of New Age groups, who stress living in harmony with nature rather than brutalizing it. The New World Order crowd has disdain for such concerns, treating ecological concerns as an imposition. It is no coincidence that then President George Bush, a strong advocate of the New World Order, held back committing the US during the most important ecological conference of the century. The battle has commenced, and during the Transformation it is a fight to the finish!

Culture Differences

Human cultures have much in common with other 3rd Density hominoid cultures, but have less in common, as one would expect, with 3rd Density cultures where the intelligent life form is amphibious, lays eggs, has no limbs, or flies. Culture is a factor of the concerns of the life form, and of the environment the life form finds itself in. For instance, on a planet with little water and searing sun at midday, it would be an unthinkable crime to bar one's door to a stranger needing shelter. An open door philosophy would become part of the culture, else the struggling members find themselves decimated due to being fried, literally, due to lack of civility.

Because humans have evolved on a world with large carnivores, human cultures are notable, through not unique, for violent tendencies. You kill, maim, and brutalize each other to a degree which would never even be imagined on other 3rd Density worlds, and think not much of it. This violence, and it's acceptance, creeps through your culture, so that teachers punishing small children with a slap, or fist fights among small boys, are considered normal. During future galactic encounters, this will be put into a different perspective.

Meaning of Life

Humans, unsure of an afterlife and without proof that reincarnation exists, often wonder what the point of it all is. Why struggle to be good when good guys seem to finish last. Why work to build an empire when disaster can strike and bring it to ruin. They look around and ask, is this all there is? They wonder if there is a God, or if there is why atrocities are allowed to occur. It all boils down to the question—what is the Meaning of Life?

Confusion is deliberate during 3rd Density, a relatively short density, as the single lesson to be learned comes to a focus fastest when the eye cannot see past the horizon. Service-to-Self or Service-to-Other is the decision to be made, but as this is an emotional and moral decision, rather than an intellectual decision, not knowing the outcome of this decision keeps the action going in the proper arena. Imagine if youngsters in school were given no descriptions on the outcome of their curricular decisions. This is a trendy idea which is scarcely followed, as parents and teachers and family and the media all influence youngsters by pointed references and applause or punishment if not by outright demands. The youngsters might be entranced by building things with blocks but be told that will only lead to a dirty job working with one's hands, or be gifted at music and be enthralled in composing music to the exclusion of all other activities but be reminded just as constantly that performers don't have the lifestyle that white collar professionals can look to. The youngster's choices, in short, are not made based on their inclinations in the main.

During 3rd Density the spiritual choices to be made crystallize quickest when no influences are allowed to interfere. Being aware of the outcome during the learning incarnations slows the process because intellectual decisions are made that are contrary to the emotional and moral leaning, so backsliding and vacillation set in. In situations where 3rd Density entities are told the outcome of their decisions they almost invariably announce they are Service-to-Other, when in fact they are dithering between the orientations and haven't decided. Then hypocrisy sets in as self-centered motives are masked, and when the entity cannot deny to themselves that they are acting with self-centered motives they may abandon the effort altogether in self-defeating rebellion. When unaware, they are more honest with themselves, ponder the results of actions and how they feel about this more openly, try various alternatives more playfully, and in general proceed with the business at hand in a more genuine manner.

During the Transformation few entities complete their 3rd Density lesson under the duress of the rapid pace of change. Some entities leaning toward the Service-to-Other rise to the opportunities presented to do greater acts of service. Many entities leaning strongly toward the Service-to-Self act out their orientation choice without hesitation, practicing for the life they are sensing awaits them, where the spoils go to the strongest and boldest. Those entities who are incarnated undecided into the Transformation, which is now, almost invariably remain in that state, as the increasing polarization in the world around them detracts from, rather than adds to, their own introspective search.

Thus, the Meaning of Life during 3rd Density is to determine your spiritual orientation, which we can tell you now as we are well within the Transformation.

Who to Believe

We have explained that many channels are false, claiming to channel either for personal glory and attention or to deliberately disinform, and that true channels often speak poetically in metaphors and analogies or become so fascinated with a concept that they give it undue emphasis. We have also explained that many prophecies become misinterpreted messages due to the ear of the listener wishing to hear what they want to believe. Thus, the brief rescue that those firmly in the Service-to-Other orientation have been offered during the worst moments of the pole shift has been interpreted as the Ascension by Christians. We have also explained that the exact year of the pole shift is erroneously reported by many true channels, either because the human channel wants to deny what is in their future or because the aliens themselves are reluctant to give humans such terrifying news when there is little that most can do about it, and where dates have been reported in antiquity the measures by which the prophecy can be determined as a present date are not accurate.

Thus, humans receive many conflicting messages. Who to believe?

This situation of mixed or conflicting messages is certainly not new to humans, who deal with such elements in every aspect of their lives. Lovers say the three little words—I love you—but may be speaking of sexual desire or the need for affiliation or protection. Political promises are rife with conflicting statements, to say nothing of false intent. Both employer and employee misstate their qualifications and ability to deliver, the employer promising an exciting and educational environment and the prospective employee claiming competence to do the job. Product advertisement is so overstated that whole sections of the government are tasked with being watchdogs of such behavior. Criminal and civil prosecution find both sides giving conflicting claims of guilt or innocence and following up these claims with elaborate explanations and evidence. So why is it that humans expect to find absolute precision and truthfulness regarding the millennium prophecies and channeled claims?

As with all of life, you must think for yourself and make your own determinations.

Belief Systems

During the Transformation some things line up nicely and undergo change smoothly and other things are on a collision course. Where people hold belief systems that stand at odds to information increasingly accepted by the populace as fact—a crisis is in the making. As with the crisis a round Earth presented to those convinced the Earth was flat, or the crisis the bones of Early Man presented to those convinced man was formed in a day—the alien presence presents a crisis to those convinced that man is the only intelligent species in the Universe or was brought forth by God in his likeness. This crisis is not peculiar to the highly religious, but as the precepts of many religions align with such concepts, the devout are prone to find themselves in this position.

On the first point, that man is the only intelligent species, the belief system is assaulted on all sides. Space ships indicating interstellar travel, feats such as rapid travel or disappearance, reports from contactees of medical miracles or genetic engineering feats, the ability to levitate objects—all point to a higher intelligence than Homo Sapiens possesses. Those resisting this fact must either capitulate and admit what their senses and logic are telling them or turn the other way and refuse to even contemplate the onslaught of information. These people are not hard to identify. They turn red in the face and start shouting their beliefs when presented with facts that challenge those beliefs, as though the argument were to be settled by volume.

On the second point, that man was made in God's image, the belief system places the individual in the position of having to choose. Either the belief can be broadened to include all life as being in God's image, placing Homo Sapiens in a peer relationship with other intelligent life forms, or the belief system holds and the alien visitors are held to be ungodly—demons. Here too the individual rigidly clinging to a belief system at odds with the facts can be recognized. As more and more information on the variety of intelligent life forms is made available, this individual turns away from the discussion with a dark face, muttering warnings.

How should those eager for the Transformation and comfortable with the new concepts being presented deal with those so rigidly caught in inappropriate belief systems? Pressing the facts on them does little good, as resistance only increases under pressure. In fact, the opposite approach works best. Make a casual comment now and then, but back off the subject. Do not confront. Let the facts work their magic, as they often do.

Judgement Day

The millennium, with its transformative aspects, has been colored in many ways by many religions. The Christian religion paints this as the day of judgment, which in some respects it is! During the Transformation, those souls who have been practicing a true Service-to-Others orientation, where they care for others as much as the self, will get their reward, in a manner of speaking, by being allowed to incarnate again on Earth for what they would consider better times—life with others of the same orientation, or a Heaven on Earth. Likewise, those souls who have been practicing a determined Service—to-Self orientation, where they care for themselves 95% of the time and scarcely ever think of others, will find they are destined to what most would call a Hell—life with others like themselves!

Will the graves open and the dead walk again? In that all spirits who have been incarnating on Earth will be sorted out during the same general time period, this story has a relationship to the facts. Jesus did not mean that he himself, personally, would be returning to act as judge and jury, but that he and his group, along with others, would be involved with the Earth at this time.

Blue Star

The coming Transformation propagates so many expectations that it is no surprise that stories abound. Some of the favorites involve being transformed by light, a take-off from the notion that entities evolve toward existing only in light form and the awareness that contactees have that highly evolved entities visit them in light form. Along those lines is a fanciful story that a Blue Star will arrive during the Transformation to bathe the Earth in healing rays. There is no such Blue Star nor is the Transformation to occur in this manner. The Transformation looks inward, to the hearts and minds of Earthlings. It is here where the healing light, so to speak, comes from, not some magical saving ray from outer space. Humans looking for salvation must look to themselves, and this is one of the lessons to be learned. Only spiritual infants look to others for salvation, as the infant looks to its parents.